Ian Thorpe

The biography

GREG HUNTER

MACMILLAN
Pan Macmillan Australia

To my parents, Bob and Barbara, whose encouragement has been worth much more than they know;

To my wife Gina, who kept everything afloat while I was in the bunker;

And to my good friend Graem Sims, without whom this book would never have been written.

First published 2004 in Macmillan by Pan Macmillan Australia Pty Ltd
St Martins Tower, 31 Market Street, Sydney

National Library of Australia cataloguing-in-publication data:

Hunter, Greg, 1956– .
Ian Thorpe: the biography.

ISBN 1 4050 3632 X.

1. Thorpe, Ian, 1982– . 2. Swimmers – Australia – Biography. I. Title.

797.21092

Typeset in 13/15 pt Adobe Garamond by Midland Typesetters
Printed in Australia by McPherson's Printing Group

Papers used by Pan Macmillan Australia Pty Ltd are natural, recyclable products made from wood grown in sustainable forests. The manufacturing processes conform to the environmental regulations of the country of origin.

Every endeavor has been made to source the photographs and to contact copyright holders to obtain the necessary permission for the use of photographic material in this book. Any person who may have been inadvertantly overlooked should contact the publisher.

CONTENTS

PROLOGUE

The first time I met Ian Thorpe, in a suite at the luxurious Rydges Hotel at Cronulla Beach in Sydney, I was interviewing him for the now defunct *ABC Sport Monthly* magazine. As usual, he'd put aside a whole day between training sessions for a series of media appointments, and when my allotted time was over I was to be followed by none other than Dame Edna Everage. The then 20-year-old Thorpe was not daunted by the prospect of matching wits with the comic genius of Barry Humphries; he gave no thought to how he would deal with the abrasive Aussie battleaxe. Instead, he was intrigued by the logistics of the situation: would Humphries come swanning into Rydges in full Everage regalia, enquiring at reception as to where he might find Mr Thorpe . . . or would he knock on the door, bolt straight into the bathroom and then, some time later, emerge as Edna, the housewife's friend and interviewee's nemesis?

It was an indication of two things. Firstly, Ian Thorpe was living a very interesting life. (As it turned out, the Everage interview was cancelled at the last minute, but the point was that sort of thing was the norm rather than the exception for Ian.) By the time this book is on the shelves he'll have just turned 22 – still a baby in terms of biographical subjects – and many people would question how one so young could possibly have experienced enough to justify such close examination. But the Thorpean time-frame is different to everyone else's. He was a household name at 14, Australia's most prominent athlete at 15, and since then the most recognised, most lauded, most decorated and most scrutinised young person in this country's history. Overlay that with his highly individualistic personality, and the result has been that in eight years of living in the spotlight he's had a great many experiences unique to himself. It seems fair to suggest that no high-profile Australian Ian's age has led a more unusual, more colourful, more *intense* existence.

It was also an indication of the type of mind Ian has. He's an analytical person. He wants to understand the how, the why, the wherefore of everything – and, having once gathered all the data, he has a remarkable ability to produce a simple, clear take on the subject. That's as good an indication as you can get of pure intelligence. Ian's analytical approach, combined with the opportunity he has for endless hours of cogitation as he grinds up and down a swimming pool, have produced a tremendous consistency of thought. It's almost never necessary to go back over interviews and ask him for clarification. Not only does he know exactly what he thinks about things, but also exactly what he's prepared to say about them. And that has turned out to be a great deal more than I dared hope. In spite of all the scrutiny he's received, Ian has somehow managed to maintain an aura of mystery, so his candour during these exhaustive interviews was a real surprise. Only once in the course of many hours of talk between us did he preface a statement with the infuriating phrase 'off the record'.

In conversation he is relaxed, pleasant, animated, refreshingly inclusive. He's as natural a man as you might expect to find in the lofty sporting environs he inhabits. But he is not entirely without armour. He doesn't cultivate the knockabout mateyness of, say, a Grant Hackett. He has a presence which is somehow aristocratic, and seems initially at odds with his image of exceptional humility. In fact he *is* quite humble, but his humility is never of the tiresome, cloying type. He's quite capable of statements that are blindingly self-confident – the prerogative of the ultra-elite athlete – and he's surprisingly honest when it comes to self-appraisal. It ain't what you say, but the way that you say it.

When you consider the fact that Thorpe is by far the richest swimmer in the history of the sport internationally, and makes more than twice as much annually as Australia's next biggest earner (Hackett), it seems amazing that there's so little resentment of him within swimming circles. It's even more amazing when you take into account that outside the top half dozen or so, the 40-odd members of the Australian team live below the poverty line, while Thorpe's earnings are often vastly exaggerated. (An English tabloid in 2002 somehow estimated his annual income at 12 to 17 million *pounds* – about ten times the true figure.) Human nature would suggest a level of jealousy, but it's scarcely in evidence. No one can be all things to all people, and a few anonymous barbs have been launched in recent years, but they've amounted to nothing much in the scheme of things. The Thorpedo enjoys his status as 'one of the boys' on the Dolphins team, and that's not about to change.

Likewise, in the wider sphere, Ian's ignominious fall from the blocks at the Olympic Trials back in March 2004 led him to make a decision (to accept a swim in the 400 freestyle in Athens) that was not by any means universally embraced by the public – but nonetheless, when the annual *Sweeney Sports Report*'s survey of athlete sponsorability was delivered only six weeks afterwards, Ian remained in his customary position: at the top of the pops, with daylight second. Australia's love affair with Ian Thorpe continues unabated. It's some sort of phenomenon.

Thorpe has been for several years the most widely approved of person in the country. Even in a book of this size it would have been tedious to list all the evidence to that effect: all the surveys and polls he's headed up, all the popular voting awards he's garnered. It's enough to record the fact that one of the more recent of these public inquisitions, in late 2003, placed him above Sir Donald Bradman as 'Sydney's Greatest Ever Male Sports Star'. Bradman never actually hailed from Sydney, but anyway, that *Daily Telegraph* survey turned upside down the most fundamental axiom in Australian sport: *nobody beats The Don.*

Ian was somewhat embarrassed by the award, and said as much in his acceptance speech. He was well aware that no-one in the international history of sport, himself included, has been more superior to his contemporaries than Bradman was – and it's likely no-one ever will be. Thorpe has been anointed as the world's best male swimmer four times by the sport's unofficial Bible, *US Swimming World*. He has won the most prestigious award in sport – the American International Athlete Trophy, formerly the Jesse Owens Award – which recognises the world's greatest athlete. He's been runner-up in that award as well. He has never been beaten in a long course 400-metre freestyle race since late 1997. In serious competition he has lost only twice over 200 metres since then. These two are his signature events, and over the past half dozen years he has surely been the most dominant competitor in any major international sport, setting 13 individual long-course world records and gathering five Olympic gold medals, three silvers and one bronze in the process. Statistically, that makes him Australia's greatest ever Olympian, with the most gold medals and the most medals in total – and he's recently announced that he'll be swimming again in Beijing in 2008. However, even if Ian had been able to pull off an historic freestyle treble over 100, 200 and 400 metres in Athens – a feat which would arguably have made him the greatest swimmer in history, and one which he may yet achieve at Olympic or World level – most people would still place him somewhere short of Bradmanesque in sporting stature.

But clearly that's not the point. Ian's popular appeal isn't just about what he achieves in the pool. He's long held the view that if all he did with his prodigious talent was collect monuments to himself in the form of gold medals and world records, that wouldn't amount to much in the end. People scramble to support Ian Thorpe because he's young, idealistic, committed to making a difference to the world because he knows he can, keen to inspire others to do likewise in whatever way *they* can, transparently prepared to put his money where his mouth is, and even willing to sacrifice some of his dignity in the process as long as it helps to swell the coffers of Ian Thorpe's Fountain for youth Trust, which is currently working to help ease the health crisis in remote Aboriginal communities. In that youthful flowering of unabashed social conscience, he gives hope for a bright future. People believe in him, and so they ought.

My personal view is that they also see in him a kind of instinctive understanding of what it is we're all supposed to be doing in this life.

PROLOGUE

There is in the collective unconscious the idea that some among us are 'old souls' – people who seem to have been here before, people who have such an understanding of things that they can see the big picture before the rest of us, and act accordingly. It's not just a matter of intelligence. Plenty of smart people lose their way completely in the world. It's more about *wisdom*, as opposed to mere intelligence, aligned with moral courage. Its distilled essence is what the term 'leadership' means. It's that precise quality that they've seen so much evidence of in Ian Thorpe as they've watched him grow, before their eyes, from a boy into a man.

They've seen it in his refusal to get involved in a slanging match when he was accused in the lead-up to the Sydney Olympics of the most heinous transgression – doping – by a German coach and then a German swimmer who in both cases seemed motivated by a combination of jealousy and abject stupidity. They've seen it in his staunch refusal to make any kind of excuse for his rare failures – even when subsequent evidence has shown that an excuse was virtually begging to be made. They've seen it in his tremendous tenacity and spirit in the face of adversity, his magnanimous sportsmanship, his generosity toward those less fortunate, his reluctance to place himself above others in the scheme of things as he tries to inspire everyone to be the best they're capable of being. They've seen it above all, I believe, in the quiet dignity he's been able to maintain in the face of the most unrelenting campaign of rumour-mongering that any Australian athlete has ever had to endure.

For years it's been nigh impossible for anyone in the scene – swimmers, coaches, journalists, officials, parents, friends and hangers-on – to talk to the general public about Ian Thorpe without the question of his personal life arising. That question remains an obsession in the collective Australian sporting psyche. It's something Ian faces up to every day he goes out in public, and that's been the case since he turned 17. Depending on your perspective on such things, it might be hard to imagine how any athlete could have the strength of character to completely dismiss the omnipresent backdrop of speculation while continuing the relentless and single-minded pursuit of excellence that is the *raison d'etre* of Thorpe's sporting life. There's some sort of irony here, in that Ian's immense popularity suggests that people are capable of seeing past their own prurient interest to understand what sort of courage and resilience it takes to be Ian Thorpe.

Dave Flaskas, Ian's mild-mannered manager, had little experience in athlete management when he took up with the 14-year-old Thorpe. He now reflects on the story that's unfolded before him with a kind of awe: 'It's been a real eye-opener for me to see the highs and lows that go with his level of fame. I feel very protective because I've seen what he has to deal with. He's such a gentle, honest kid – but the courage and the toughness he's shown in races, especially in the big events . . . it staggers me sometimes. And so does the way he's kept so level-headed in light of everything he has to deal with as a human being. It's been an amazing journey for all of us.'

And it's been an enjoyable one too, because Ian Thorpe hasn't just *survived* the ordeal of his own mega-celebrity; he's turned it into the celebration it ought to be. He has consorted with the cream of the world's entertainment industry, strutted with supermodels and given himself some fantastic platforms to express his individuality. Even in the day-to-day business of life outside the swimming pool, he and Flaskas have assembled a team of people to help them, then set out to conquer new worlds – but always with the aim of keeping it as much fun as possible. Whether he's launching a new range of underwear or pulling off lucrative new business deals in Japan or meeting Chinese political and sporting heavyweights, Thorpe has the capacity to fire up everyone around him. Other sporting champions hoard up their greatness and then, at career's end, search for ways to purloin the sheen of medals or trophies into something – *anything* – useful to themselves. Ian started testing his talents in other areas even before his swimming career had peaked, all the while suggesting to his companions: 'We *can* do this. And we're going to have a really good time doing it.'

Lurking always around that breezy attitude, however, is the spectre of Thorpe's perfectionism. Not all swimmers share this characteristic

– but it's almost a prerequisite for success at the highest level. And it can be a killer, as athletes wedded to the hegemony of the stopwatch can so often fall into a morass of despair if they fail to meet their own expectations. The American writer P.H. Mullen, in his book on the culture of elite swimming, *Gold in the Water*, observes: 'When a person cradles the soft head of a newborn, is it possible to divine whether the child will grow into a perfectionist, one who sets great expectations and lives by higher standards than the rest of us? And if that kind of existence could be intuited just as the infant is starting life, is the trait something to encourage or discourage? It is great to be a perfectionist. But it is often a hard way to live.'

Ian knows the truth of that better than anyone, because as a swimmer he is the ultimate perfectionist. But luckily he also possesses the *wisdom* – that notion again – to know when the time has come to leave the training pool, just for a while, and indulge some other interest. That's what's kept him sane, together, and happy. He's a very fine example, in fact, of a happy man, and that alone makes him a subject worthy of attention. If ever a person has revelled in the demands of perfectionism, Thorpe is the one – even if it *is* a hard way to live.

Hard but rewarding, and all the more meritorious because his path has been strewn with so many difficulties – and therein lies the beauty of the story so far. It's a story that is far from over yet. But so much that's extraordinary has been crammed into such a short period, it's high time to begin the telling of it.

1

A GIFT FROM GOD

AS A YOUNGSTER IAN THORPE NEVER knew how good a batsman his dad had once been. Ken Thorpe would sooner slit his own throat than brag about his ability at anything. Besides, the story of his cricketing life was hardly a happy one. It wasn't until long after he'd begun to set world records in the pool that Ian came to realise, via snippets of chat with his father's contemporaries, that Ken had been a real prodigy with the willow: good enough, everyone reckoned, to have played for Australia. And when he eventually learned the tragic details of his dad's career, Ian understood that this was a story that underpinned a great deal of his own life.

Ken Thorpe inherited an obsession with sport from his father Cec, whose own aspirations to wear the famous baggy green cap of Australian Test cricketers had been snuffed out, at the age of 22, by an attack of rheumatic fever. The illness had left his body painfully contorted, and meant he could no longer toil on the struggling farm he owned in Armidale, in northern New South Wales. So when Cec met and married Gwen McLeod, a dairy farmer's daughter, they headed straight for the Big Smoke. It was late in 1946.

Postwar jobs in Sydney were plentiful, but Cec took one position – doing shiftwork as a crane operator in St Peters – and stayed there for the rest of his working life. Ken was born in November 1949, the eldest of six surviving children: three boys and three girls. His earliest years were spent in a rented apartment in Kings Cross, then in a disused army hospital. When he was seven the family moved into a Housing Commission place in Padstow, which was then an outer south-western suburb of Sydney. Gwen – Nanna Thorpe – still lives in that house today.

Cec and Gwen's sizeable brood was nothing unusual in those days. And there was no social stigma attached to Housing Commission people. It was just a convenient way for honest, hard-working folk to snaffle a piece of land in the rapidly expanding city. The family lived without luxuries, but got by well enough.

The Thorpe clan was steeped in Christian faith. Back home Cec's parents attended the Baptist church three times every Sunday, and several times during the week as well. Although Cecil Thorpe had worried the life out of them by being a bit wild in his youth – boozing and brawling around the backblocks of Armidale – some godliness eventually seeped into his soul, and he became a pretty fair model of a clean-living and devoted suburban family man. Meanwhile, Gwen was involved with the Baptist church at nearby Bankstown.

Cec had other priorities as well, though, so he'd normally drop the kids off at Sunday school and church while he joined his mates for some fun and games. Sport was his real religion, and so it was too with the strapping but quietly spoken young Ken, who felt at liberty to drift away from the church when he was 15 and concentrate every ounce of his spiritual energy around his cricket bat.

Cec was constantly urging his eldest son to *practise, practise, practise* if he wanted to even dream of taking his place in the Australian batting order. No doubt his frustration with his bent-over body had caused him to live the sporting life through his offspring, but there was never a hint of coercion, because from the beginning young Ken absolutely *loved* the discipline of parrying a thousand deliveries pounded into the black soil of their backyard pitch by the old man. Every day he practised for up to three hours after school. He'd have done more if he could. By the time he was 16 and gainfully employed, he was paying his brothers to bowl to him when Cec wasn't around. The pitch had absorbed so much punishment by then it sat about 15 centimetres below ground level.

It was a red-hot local under-16 side Ken played for, given the opening bowlers were Jeff Thomson and Len Pascoe, who would later terrorise batsmen around the world – but Ken beat both of them into the Bankstown first-grade team. He was just 17, an inch shy of six feet tall, lean and muscular, when he played the last two games of the 1966–67 season in the firsts. He top-scored with 66 in the second innings of his first game, facing an attack that contained a current Test fast bowler, Graeme Corling.

Ken's natural caution limited his strokeplay – apparently he never once hit a six – but he could accumulate his runs quickly enough, and as he entered season 1967–68, still a first-grader and still just shy of his 18th birthday, the world was full of promise for a boy who lived for the game.

But it wasn't that simple. Ken didn't always succeed, and every time he faced the sickening sight of an umpire's raised finger, his guts wrenched. Cec would be waiting at the end of his slow walk back, and at some stage – maybe not straight away, but soon enough – the inquisition would begin: '*Why* did you play that shot? *What* were you thinking?' And Ken never felt that he could just reply: 'I don't know.' It was not an answer that made any sense to Cecil Thorpe. Ken sometimes thought he'd need to write an entire essay to explain himself, and even that would be insufficient. The pressure became acute. At the end of that season, he made the most momentous decision of his life. He decided, at the age of 18, to quit playing cricket.

It would have been a reasonable outcome if Ken had just renounced his sporting obsession and filled the void with some other interest. But he didn't. He remained a total sports nut. He continued to live with his parents for the next ten years and had no social life to speak of, apart from spending every Friday night at the trots with a few like-minded mates. Being a non-drinker – he just never liked the taste of beer – he didn't frequent pubs or clubs and had no involvement with girls because, by and large, they didn't speak the language of sport.

Ken kept on playing soccer with Bankstown's top-level team in the winter – even got paid a few quid for it – but it had only ever been a way to fill in time during the cricketing off-season. He could have taken any number of jobs, but stuck with a small outfit in St Peters that manufactured canvas tarpaulins only because the other employees were all as sports-crazed as he was. At every opportunity they'd knock off work and get up a game of handball, cricket, soccer . . . whatever.

The worst thing was that Ken found the withdrawal from cricket too punishing, so he ended up playing for the next seven seasons in the far inferior local afternoon A-grade comp, where he racked up prodigious records that still stand today, even though he abhorred the lack of a competitive challenge and got little enjoyment from the game.

Then, just as he was about to turn 26, Ken decided to take another crack at the big time. He never told Cec his intentions – just went down to the nets, showed the selectors what he could do, and was immediately picked in Bankstown's first-grade team again. The old man was delighted.

Incredibly, after such a long lay-off from serious competition, Ken got five consecutive 50s and managed to top the 1975–76 Sydney first-grade averages with 57, just ahead of the great Bob Simpson. Neil Harvey, then a selector for the New South Wales Shield side, came to see him compile a neat 50, and he ended up being invited to play for City against Country in a Doug Walters testimonial match at the SCG. He top-scored in that game too.

But you don't compromise seven formative years as a batsman without paying a heavy price. As it was, Ken's strokeplay against these superior bowlers was adjudged not quite potent enough. He couldn't take the next step. Realistically, he'd known all along that this would be the case; he'd given too much away. But at least he felt he'd proved a point: that if things had gone differently, he could indeed have played cricket for Australia. He padded up for one more first-grade season, again averaged better than 50, then gave it away for good, resigning himself to a lifetime of melancholy reflection: 'What if . . . ?'

Ken Thorpe's experience left him with a set of principles that would forever guide him in the parenting of his own children. Firstly, he would never seek to live his sporting life vicariously through them. He would encourage them to succeed, and help in every way he possibly could; he would certainly impress upon them the need for dedication and commitment if they wanted to achieve anything significant; *but he would never, ever push.* So long as they'd done their best – and more importantly, as long as they *knew in their hearts* that they'd done their best – he would never, ever criticise their performances. The paramount thing was that they should enjoy themselves. If they weren't enjoying themselves in their sport, they ought to be doing something else. These were the foundations of Ian Thorpe's life as a swimmer, and although he may once have regarded his philosophical outlook as being all his own work, maturity has shown him otherwise.

Ken is obviously still a fitness fanatic. His powerful physical presence is a constant reminder of the sporting soul that lives in him. When you ask him now how he could possibly have penalised himself so heavily, he sighs and offers, quietly: 'It's a hard question to answer.' Obviously he was not a mentally tough person, and will readily admit to that. In recent years, though, Ken has become a deeply religious man, and is now convinced that even if it is a hard question, it does have an answer: *It was God's purpose that he should have to learn these lessons in order to open his eyes and prepare him for the arrival of his son, Ian, who was himself a gift from God.*

≈

Margaret Hathaway knew all about Ken Thorpe the cricketer when she was at Sir Joseph Banks High School in Revesby, a suburb next door to Padstow. Ken was always cropping up in the local papers, and besides, Margaret was a girl with a rare interest in sport and a fair bit of ability herself. Dark-haired and tall at five feet ten (178 centimetres), big-boned and solid, she was playing A-grade netball for

Bankstown at 17 and would, she reckoned, have been a rep player if she'd had more time for training.

As with the Thorpes, it was the availability of land that brought Margaret's family to the working-class suburb of Padstow. Her mother, Gertrude Watt, had been born in Belfast, but arrived in Australia aged two, and via a circuitous route landed in Padstow in time to meet Jim Hathaway, a Sunbeam executive originally from Young, in central New South Wales. Jim's main claim to fame was that he was a descendant of the clan that had produced Anne Hathaway, wife of William Shakespeare. If that is a fact, then of course Ian Thorpe has The Bard himself on a far distant twig of his family tree.

Gertrude and Jim were married early in 1951, and Margaret arrived in March 1952. Her parents, who eventually opened a shoe shop in nearby East Hills, were strict Congregational Christians who never swore, smoked or drank, and believed in the literal word of God as recorded in the Bible. Accordingly, so too did Margaret.

She'd never lived anywhere but Padstow when, in September 1971, the family of four (Margaret had a younger brother) moved into a newly built house in another neighbouring suburb, Milperra. Just a few months later 19-year-old Margaret, having finished her training as a primary school teacher, was anxiously awaiting the letter that would notify her of her posting. It could have been anywhere in Sydney – even an impossibly exotic location such as, say, Narrabeen or Darlinghurst or Vaucluse – although most graduates were being assigned to schools in the newly developing western suburbs around Mt Druitt. Didn't matter: at least she would be going *somewhere*. She opened the letter and looked at her destination: *Milperra Primary School*. Margaret was disgusted.

There wasn't much choice but to stick around at home in Milperra with Mum and Dad, waiting for something to happen. And there was plenty of waiting to be done. It wasn't till May 1977, when Margaret was 25, that Ken Thorpe's youngest sister Cheryl, who was a good friend and netball team-mate, approached her at church and asked if she was going out with anyone. Margaret wasn't. Cheryl said cryptically: 'Oh – all right.' And then, on the following Thursday night, Ken rang to ask if Margaret would like to go on a blind date with himself, and Cheryl, and Cheryl's husband. Margaret would.

Ken's cricketing career had finished just a couple of months previously, and he was looking for someone to join him as he got on with the rest of his life. Margaret's thinking was along similar lines. But until that fateful evening, Ken reckoned he'd only once gone out with a girl at night, and his natural humility was exceeded only by his shyness. He jumped into his own car with Margaret, planning to follow his little sister and her young spouse all the way across the southern suburbs of Sydney to a restaurant on the shores of Botany Bay. It would have been *at least* an hour's drive. Whose idea was it to put such a yawning gap between themselves and the safety of mixed company? What on earth would they talk about, if anything at all?

Well, why don't we try, for starters, the subject of . . . *sport*? It got them through the journey with relative ease, and Ken was much relieved, for some reason, to find that Margaret was not a supporter of the St George Dragons Rugby League Club. Over dinner, Margaret and Cheryl dominated the conversation – completely – but Margaret liked the cut of Ken, and knew that even if he was not at that time a committed Christian, he shared with her a fundamental set of values that revolved around decency, sobriety, discipline and hard work. It was a whirlwind romance. They were engaged by the end of July.

Both of them had generally put away whatever money they could. Now, with a solid cash injection from Margaret's folks as a wedding present, they were able to buy a standard block of land in – where else? – Milperra. They were married on 14 January 1978, and the foundations for the house were dug two days later. Ken didn't see any need for an architect. They simply constructed a near-exact replica of Margaret's parental home, using the very same builder. (The new Mrs Thorpe could probably have waltzed through the entire place blindfolded.) Ken reckoned Jim Hathaway was a perfectionist, so if he thought this bloke was a quality tradesman, that was recommendation enough.

Even so, unlike all the project homes in their street, the Thorpe residence was a split-level job, complete with three bedrooms, kitchen, dining room, family room and double garage. Stylistically it was what you'd call Aussie suburban minimalist – with a dead square backyard devoid of any plants, and a Hills Hoist smack bang in the centre – but it was an impressive brick structure, and very expensive by local standards.

Ken, an inveterate worrier, was determined they should have the house paid off before taking on the responsibility of children. He'd previously bought an old place at Revesby, which his brother was renting, as an investment. With the sale of that property there was plenty of cash for furniture, carpet, appliances and such. Both working two jobs – they each put in as many extra hours as possible at the Hathaways' shoe shop – Ken and Margaret managed to wipe out the mortgage within two years . . . just prior to the arrival of their first child, Christina, on 16 February 1980. It was all going *exactly* according to plan.

2

THE MILPERRA MAFIA AT WORK

CHRISTINA THORPE HAD WEIGHED IN JUST a bit above average as a baby, but Margaret's second child looked to be a different proposition. Since he was such a big boy, the obstetrician recommended an induction on Wednesday, 13 October 1982. 'You're not superstitious, are you?' he enquired. Since the father himself had been born on the 13th of November, Margaret said it would be all right.

Ian James Thorpe weighed 4.1 kilos and was exceptionally long at 57.5 centimetres. He was dark-haired like his parents, and 'looked about three months old when he was born', Margaret recalls. They'd originally planned on three children, but Margaret's blood pressure soared after Ian's birth and the doctor advised her to leave it at that. (The condition is called eclampsia; it's quite common, and even at that time this doctor's recommendation was old-fashioned.) But not to worry: they had two healthy children, and most importantly from Ken's point of view, *one of them was a boy.*

Not that he didn't dote on his pretty little daughter. In fact, Ken's bond with blonde-haired, blue-eyed Christina was to become a very powerful one. It was just that, in Ken's world-view at the time, females and sporting prowess didn't seem to belong in the same sentence. And apart from that – notwithstanding all that he'd learned about parenting and sport and the proper way of doing things – he really *did* want a son who'd end up playing cricket, or at a pinch maybe soccer, at the highest possible level: just so the boy could experience the exquisite joy of doing one thing really, really well. To that end, Ken had actually engineered it so that Ian would be born as soon as possible after 1 October, which was the cut-off date for registrations for the cricket season. It would mean his son would have the advantage of being that much older than the rest of the players.

Obsessive? Ken? Well, he just wanted to provide *every* opportunity. Some years later the irony became apparent: it's a massive disadvantage for a young swimmer to be born late in the year, since their age grouping at school starts in January, and swimmers develop at a far greater rate than junior cricketers. Ken can laugh about it now.

With the Thorpe clan it was always about proximity and family ties. After Margaret had taken a year of long service leave to take care of Ian, he was then doted upon by a combination of his Pop, Jim Hathaway, and the so-called 'maiden aunts' – unmarried Hathaway kin – who lived only half a dozen doors or so down from Ian's place. What with Ken's parents still holed up in neighbouring Padstow, and Margaret still teaching at the local school, and everybody as keen as mustard to help out with child-minding and such, things could not have been any cosier. It was the Milperra Mafia at work: both Christina and Ian spent hardly a moment of their formative years without being stimulated, mentally or physically, by one or other member of the Mob.

Ken, of course, took particular responsibility for hand-eye coordination work, which in Ian's case started when he was a baby. No doubt Dad figured that with his son's rich genetic inheritance, it was only a matter of patience and practice. He wasted no time introducing a bat and ball, and would spend countless hours tossing the simplest lobs to his heavyweight son, who would almost invariably swing and miss. By the time Ian was six, Ken Thorpe knew he had not produced a batsman. It just seemed to take too long for the synapses in Ian's brain to send their messages to his powerful limbs. And Ian's bowling was unlikely to redeem him, given that his action resembled that of Max 'Tangles' Walker.

Ken may have been disappointed with that outcome but he certainly never mentioned it. Not ever. Close friends – those who knew him for his competitiveness – were amazed at how stoically he accepted the situation. But Ken Thorpe was determined not to waste his own bitter experience, nor was he a man to compromise his principles. Sport was primarily for enjoyment, after all. If Ian was not going to be a top cricketer, what point was there in flogging a dead horse and making both their lives a misery?

As it turned out there were greater ironies in store, because it was Christina who was endowed with excellent hand-eye coordination and athleticism, whereas Ian's relative shortcomings in those areas were matched by a general disinterest in sport. Ken never stopped encouraging outdoor play for both his kids, but most of the time Ian preferred to be inside with Mum, either helping with the cooking (he was always chucking whole spuds and onions into pots and making 'soup') or playing endlessly with his Lego pieces, while his big sister would be out in the backyard, urging her dad to join in some more running, throwing, catching, kicking . . . whatever. Ken always obliged.

Fast forward a few years, and Ian would be preoccupied with Scrabble, or Boggle, or some other cerebral challenge, while his sister was psyching herself up to shoot 100 consecutive goals through their backyard netball hoop as Ken looked on approvingly. Ultimately, Christina was to become a female mirror image of her father: intense, driven, very talented, but prone to an excess of worrying. Ian cleaved far more toward his mother's nature: quiet, placid, compliant, but confident and self-contained. It was a personality schism that would strongly influence the outcomes of their respective sporting careers.

Apart from his mental acuity, Ian the youngster had another great talent: the ability to be unobtrusive – which is not easy when you're much, much bigger than most kids your age – and a consequent knack for staying out of trouble. Whenever he and his sister fought (which, as they got older, was just about all the time), it was always Christina who'd end up being sent away to do 'time out', while Ian played merrily on. She was, admittedly, a bossy piece of work, and enjoyed calling him 'Fatty', which was about the only way to fire him up. Christina could never figure out why she was always the one in the doghouse.

Ken had grown up close to his siblings, always been strongly imbued with a sense of family, and since his five brothers and sisters had all started reproducing at roughly the same time, it just seemed natural they'd stick together as much as possible. Every week, after Sunday school or church, the family descended on Nanna Thorpe's Padstow house for the traditional roast dinner, a routine that would continue, practically week in, week out, till Ian was 14 years old.

The closest of Ian and Christina's cousins were Michelle and Paul, Cheryl's offspring, and then Ben and Melissa, children of Ken's younger brother Keith. When this crew all turned up together, which was often – and not just at Nanna's, but at every birthday party or other ceremonial gathering – it was a case of survival of the fittest around the kids' dinner table. Ian, the youngest of the lot, was determined not to miss out. He'd just shovel the food in with his hands. Heaps of it. Ben, several years older than the others, was awestruck by his capacity.

Ian Thorpe had one other talent – the most important one of all, especially for children. He got on easily with other kids. His compliant nature attracted company, and he had an innate self-assurance, so he never hungered for approval, and could never see the need to try and impress anyone. He just *belonged.* There were plenty of children in the neighbourhood to play with – almost all of them boys, which annoyed Christina no end – and when they weren't running or cycling or skating around in the local parks or, later on, exploring the bushland surrounding the nearby Georges River, the Thorpe household was something of a magnet for their entertainment. That suited Margaret, who liked to keep an eye on them.

When the Thorpes were the first in the street to get a modest-sized above-ground pool – Ian was three or four at the time – the kids would come around and dive off the high decking, or spend all day belly-sliding across the soap-covered pool cover, or jumping on the trampoline, which doubled as a frame for making cubbyhouses. Sometimes the neighbouring kids would congregate to play cricket down the Thorpes' driveway during the long summer evenings. Sometimes they'd play soccer on the expansive lawn on winter weekends. But when there was no-one about, Ian was perfectly content to stay inside, watch TV or play with his toys. Especially the Lego. He was a self-contained entity: happy in his own little environment, and just as happy to share it, on an equal footing, with whoever came along.

Christina was much louder and more assertive than Ian among people she knew, but very shy and timid in unfamiliar situations. When the time came for her to be packed off to Milperra Primary School, she howled. Ian, almost three years her junior, howled because he wasn't allowed to go with her.

He couldn't wait to get started. Margaret had gotten herself transferred from Milperra Primary to another local school the year after Christina arrived, not wanting to be at the same school as her children, so on the day of Ian's enrolment, she dropped him off at the appointed hour and Pop Hathaway picked him up that afternoon. Next day, Jim went to escort Ian inside, but his grandson objected: 'I know where my classroom is. Don't come with me.' Pop said maybe it would be a good idea, just this once, if he came along to see where the room was – in case Ian ever got sick, or something. Reluctantly, the youngster agreed. But his grandfather knew, next morning, not to bother getting out of the car.

Ian might not have been a perfect angel as a child, but he wasn't far from it. Partly it was because he was very sensitive to criticism. 'If you called him a bad, naughty boy,' recalls Margaret, 'he'd burst into tears.' That hardly ever happened. He had the great advantage of having a mother who, naturally, understood children – especially their need for routine and certainty.

Multiplication tables were recited in the car on the way to school. Spelling was tested every night of the week while Margaret peeled the potatoes. She would read to them each night before prayers. Everything was structured; the Thorpe kids got their all-important grounding in time management very early. As well, Margaret was always inclined to talk up to her children rather than down. Having spent all day addressing Year 5 students, it just seemed natural to use the same pitch to her much younger son. Ian would have a biscuit, not a 'bikkie'. Before long he was packing his own lunch box, then writing his own lunch orders. That was lesson two: personal responsibility.

It was, in Margaret's words, 'a proper Christian upbringing', but there was nothing Calvinistic about the Thorpe household. Far from it. The toughest corporal punishment Ian ever received was a slight hint of a slap on the behind. (Margaret once waved a wooden spoon at him in a threatening manner, and that seemed to hold him for several years.) On Saturday mornings both kids would jump into bed with Mum and Dad for a whole hour, just having cuddles and tickling games and pretend battles. Ken and Margaret had the occasional disagreement, but they never fought in front of their children. Neither Ian nor Christina can remember a single parental argument. There might have been the odd raised voice, but they can't seem to remember that either.

Ian became ever more independent, more confident, more self-reliant. Milperra Primary was a school that was big on handing out awards. Ian, a top-five student in every subject, was always a recipient of something, and there was generally a family member on hand to witness the occasion. Nan and Pop Hathaway were both there when Ian's Year 2 teacher, handing over a prize of some sort, asked indulgently: 'What can I say about Ian Thorpe? He's turning eight, going on twenty-eight.' The grandparents beamed.

The Thorpe horizons did actually stretch further than Milperra-Padstow, at least once a year, when they towed the Hathaways' little van up to Forster-Tuncurry Caravan Park, on the coast a few hours north of Sydney. Ian was only ten weeks old on his first trip. They managed to squeeze Nan and Pop and Ken and Margaret and Margaret's brothers and their girlfriends and Christina and baby Ian into this 16-foot Jayco van with its pop-up top and modest annex. The more the merrier, as always, and the kids had a ball. They went back every year, sometimes with cousins Michelle and Paul, usually not, until Ian was nine. The park had a wading pool and a deeper one, and Ian traversed them with his first dog paddles.

They could even afford a couple of family camping trips to the Gold Coast in 1987 and '88, with Dreamworld and Seaworld high on the agenda. Ian couldn't wait to grow tall enough to be allowed on the roller coaster, but backed right away from the water slides. He was actually a bit scared of water.

≈

There is no insult more damaging to an Aussie kid than the label 'unco'. It's short for uncoordinated, and if you're a deadset unco, you're hopeless on a sporting field of any description. Ian Thorpe as a kid was never described as an unco – that is, not until he became a famous swimmer and journalists looking for simplistic points of reference would write about his pre-swimming days with clever catchphrases like 'Fish out of Water'. It became such a media cliché that you got the impression young Ian was barely capable of supporting his outsized frame on dry land.

Not true. He had nothing like his father's extraordinary ability, and could never compete with Christina at any of the physical games they played, but he was not a disaster either. Ian's gross motor skills were below par, his fine motor skills quite good; the combined package made him around about average at most sports.

He took up Little Athletics at age five – admittedly, he was the biggest boy by far – and was about the third-fastest runner in a group of five. He started soccer a year early in the under-6s and, playing in goals, was prone to punting the ball back over his own head – but fortunately, never into the net. It was difficult for him at first, but he stuck with it till he was 11, and held his place in a Milperra Lions team that won the comp every year and was maybe the best in its age group in Sydney.

Being somewhere in the middle rank of players, Ian substituted in all positions as they rotated around to give everyone a go. But he was able to kick with both feet – and when he did manage to connect with the ball, it stayed kicked. The coach of that team, for five years out of seven, was Ken Thorpe, who had the arduous task of convincing opposition parents that his son really was playing in the right age group. People often demanded to see his player ID card. No-one could believe it.

Milperra Primary had only two rugby league teams, junior and senior, and when Ian first played, in Year 3, he'd have been almost two years younger than some of the other boys, but was still amongst the biggest, if not *the* biggest, on the paddock each week. With all the padding Margaret insisted on him wearing, he resembled Frankenstein's monster as he lumbered around the field – but was far less frightening to the opposition. Even with the tree-trunk legs he'd inherited from his father, he struggled to make any impression in attack or defence. He got better in Years 4 and 5, but the fact was he didn't get a real thrill out of smashing another kid in a tackle, and was no keener on being smashed himself. In rugby league, more than any other sport, Ian's talent for unobtrusiveness came to the fore.

As much as raw ability, what Ian really didn't have in those days was fire in the belly. When Christina thrashed him at every game, he'd sometimes get a bit annoyed, but never angry. In his second-last year of soccer for the Milperra Lions, and the last with his dad as coach, Ian was playing in yet another grand final when, with the score at 1-1 in the dying stages, he was presented with the ball on a platter: nothing in front of him but fresh air and an open goal. He blew it.

Did he cry? Did he rant and rave? Did he sulk for hours? Did he even *care*? Not really. He was over it in a matter of seconds. As it happened, in the grand final replay against Padstow RSL the following week, he came on at nil-all after sitting out the first half and somehow lobbed a half-volley over the goalie's head and into the net – 'half luck, half skill', he reckons it was – and the Lions went on to be victorious once again.

That was good fun but the thing was, it didn't really matter. Ian always wanted to put in his best performance, and so would try his hardest whatever the sport, but if he or his team didn't win, he just couldn't see the point in getting upset about it: 'From the time I was little, I could never understand that mentality. As long as I felt I'd done the best I could, I'd be happy with the result . . . and not just in sport. That was the way I approached everything in life.'

Actually it went even further than that. Perceptive people who knew him well – such as Paul Butler, his favourite primary teacher, who had him in Years 3 and 6 – noticed that even at such a tender age, young Thorpe was developing the quality of magnanimity. He could revel in the joy of others, could experience a vicarious pleasure in the thrill they'd got from victory. He seemed to understand intuitively that everyone needed to have their time in the sun; and *that* was why, in the end, it didn't really matter whether you won or lost.

Naturally, Ian's outlook was just a refinement of the principles his dad had quietly instilled in him. While Ken and Margaret spent half their lives ferrying their kids from one sporting fixture to another – the Thorpes had only one car, a Toyota Camry, so it was never logistically simple – they encouraged, but they never criticised, and they never pushed. The only thing Ken would insist on was *commitment*: if you saddled up for a season – whether it was Ian with soccer or league, or Christina with netball, tennis or gymnastics – you had to see it through.

In the nonstop round of training and competing – *pick-up-drop-off-come-back-pick-up-drop-off-come-back, etc. etc.* – one sport that was never considered was swimming. Both kids had to *learn* to swim before doing anything else, in order to be safe from drowning, but swimming as a sport would have been the last thing to enter Ken's mind. It came about literally by accident that the Thorpe kids got involved in competitive swimming. And the supreme irony of all was that Ken Thorpe – a man who would do just about anything to help his children succeed at sport, and would have spent countless hours donating his own expertise in the process – could not swim a stroke.

3

A CHALLENGING INITIATION

WHEN KEN WAS NINE YEARS OLD he was taken by his teacher to Bankstown Pool for his first swimming class and thrown immediately into the deep end. He panicked, started flailing around like a harpooned seal, and prepared himself to die. Someone yelled out: 'Put your feet down', so he did, and found himself standing up. It wasn't that deep after all. But he was so traumatised by the incident, he couldn't bring himself to get back in the water. Much later, standing on a sandbar in the surf, he felt it collapse beneath him and was *certain* he was going to drown. There was no way Ken was going to allow his own kids to experience such horrors. Like just about every other Australian child, they'd have to learn to swim.

So when Christina was five, Margaret took her to learn-to-swim classes. She did fine. It was assumed that Ian, in about three years' time, would do the same, and that would be it. Then came the accident that changed everything. Christina was at Ian's pre-school Christmas party in 1987. She was running around with some older kids when she tripped over and broke her wrist. She had to go straight to hospital; Ian refused to come along because he wanted to see Santa. As it turned out, Christina's fall was to lead eventually to a greater gift for her little brother than anything a jolly old man in a red suit could come up with.

The surgeon told Margaret that Christina had to quit gymnastics for at least six months. She should be strengthening her wrist, and the best exercise for that would be swimming. So she did a bit of swimming – not actual training, just some paddling around in the local pool at Revesby under Margaret's watchful eye – and it was enough for her to win her freestyle race at the school carnival, and again at the zone carnival. She was a definite talent.

How much of a talent, Margaret didn't know, but she figured that if Christina could win at regional level as well, then she'd better let her start training properly straight away if she wanted to. Christina did win. Winter was coming on by then, so Margaret told her that if she was really keen to pursue it, come springtime she could join a squad at the Doug Frost Swim School at Padstow. Christina didn't need to be reminded: 'It's September, Mum. You said I could go swimming now.' And that was the beginning.

Obviously Ken was way down at the shallow end of the gene pool when they handed out the swimming ability. Margaret wasn't. She was never a squad swimmer – that is, she didn't compete for a club – but trained only for the school carnivals in summertime. She held records at primary and high school, won at zone carnivals, and made it to the Combined High Schools carnival, but never won at that level. She wasn't highly competitive by nature and didn't want to be bothered travelling to a heated pool to train through winter. She was mainly doing it for the love of swimming. Margaret might have been among the three percent of swimmers who are regarded as 'natural' talents, and she might not have been. She never put in enough time to find out.

Since Christina was already training a couple of sessions a week at the five-lane heated indoor pool at Padstow, that was where Margaret took Ian for his first learn-to-swim class. He was almost six years old.

As soon as he put his head underwater the pain in his nose started; by the end of the half-hour session he was really suffering. His mother knew something was amiss – but in any case, after three weeks he got seriously sick and ended up at the local GP, who diagnosed bronchial pneumonia. He had to stay out of the water for 12 months.

But this doctor also noticed that Ian's nose was in bad shape. He was obviously allergic to something. A second doctor performed a battery of allergy tests, and came up with nothing major – only slight reactions to seafood, tomato and eggs – and so suggested a visit to an ear, nose and throat specialist. As soon as this guy clapped eyes on the X-ray of Ian's hugely swollen adenoids – masses of lymph-filled tissue blocking up the nasal passages – he wanted to know what Ian had been up to lately. *Learning to swim.* Whereabouts? *At the indoor pool at Padstow.* The specialist was on the money: 'This has to be an allergy to chlorine. I suggest you give the whole thing away – unless you're wanting to produce an Olympic swimmer . . .'

Margaret laughed – *of course not* – but she did want him to learn, so the doctor suggested an outdoor pool because he wouldn't be so badly affected. The likelihood was that his adenoids would shrink as he eventually outgrew the allergy. Ian served out his 12-month suspension, then went for one lesson at the outdoor pool at Revesby – and even there, it was useless. He just couldn't keep his noggin underwater. But anyway, Margaret noticed that Ian seemed to be able to do a sort of advanced dog paddle, holding his head out of the water, and she reckoned that was going to have to be good enough. They gave up on the lessons.

Meanwhile, with a couple of years of training under her belt, Christina had become a very good swimmer. Her little brother had to follow her around from carnival to carnival as she raced for the Padstow club while Ken and Margaret looked on. Without Christina's involvement, Ian wouldn't have been found anywhere near a swimming pool. But after months of spectating, boredom finally forced him into the water, and he'd paddle around in his odd fashion.

Then, at the start of Year 2 in 1990, aged seven, Ian decided to enter the 50-metre freestyle race at the school carnival. Fifty metres is a long way when you can't actually swim, but somehow he won anyway. This might not have been too remarkable, even when you throw in the fact that he bellyflopped into the water because he couldn't dive off the block. But when he did it again at the zone carnival a few weeks later – again using his standard bellyflop entry – *that* was something. How could a kid who couldn't put his head underwater beat others who could not only swim properly but were already training every week?

He was of course much bigger than they were, and stronger, and must have had good control of his stomach and back muscles. Even with his head upright, his rotund body sat high in the water and he could hold it straight with his legs behind him; like his sister, he had natural buoyancy. Christina's coach Jenni Ashpole (now Jenni McAdam), who watched that race, remarked to Ian's very surprised mother: 'He's such a natural. Why isn't he in squad training at Padstow?' Margaret told her about the chlorine thing. 'Well then, let's get him a nose clip so he can get his head down.' They hadn't thought of that.

Ian, who had up till now been a mere participant in sport rather than any sort of star, was pretty chuffed at this turn of events – but not elated. He didn't suddenly start envisioning a panorama of heroic possibilities. That wasn't in his nature. But he was pleased that he'd found something he had a real talent for, and he took it comfortably on board. It looked as though he was going to be a swimmer.

However, it wasn't that simple. Even with the nose clip in place and the allergy slowly abating, he was still constantly suffering from sinus trouble. The previous bout with bronchial pneumonia was another complication – if the pain went to his chest, he'd have to be out of the water for a while. Ian also suffered from migraine headaches, so he had to learn to distinguish between them and sinus headaches. If it was the sinus, he'd be straight to the doctor and on antibiotics. He was only doing one half-hour training session a week to start with, and being aware of the problem, Margaret felt she could keep it under control. But in Friday night club races Ian would refuse to wear the nose clip, not wanting to look different from the others, and that didn't help.

All in all, it was a challenging initiation into the sport. The Padstow indoor swim centre was just large enough to house five 25-metre lanes, a tiny learn-to-swim pool and a metre or two of floor space on either side. When you opened the door into this claustrophobic environment, the wall of atmospheric chlorine literally stopped you in your tracks. Ian, with his particular susceptibility, would be suffering before he even got into the water.

Why would any kid want to put himself through all that? Ian's answer: 'I used to enjoy swimming because I felt good when I was in the water, and I was good at it. I liked the fact that when I trained hard, I felt good about myself. I'd be coughing at the end of a race, my nose running, but I'd be satisfied. I was happy to go to training for two weeks and then be sick for a week, then train for two weeks and be sick again. I was on so many antibiotics it was just a joke. I actually made myself seriously sick sometimes. But it was what I wanted to do.'

It begged the question: was sibling rivalry a factor? Margaret seemed to think so when she said of that first school carnival race: 'He showed he could swim as well as his big sister when he won the 50 metres with his head out of the water.' Ian wasn't so sure: 'I guess I would have liked to be swimming at the level my sister was at – but that was never the driving force.'

In any case, it was only a few months after Ian's unconventional debut that Christina made the state team in the 10 years and under division for the Australian Primary Schools titles in Canberra. Ian went along with his parents, and stayed at Margaret's brother Bruce's house. Christina, still timid and threatened in unknown territory, had to be billeted with a host family. Those were the rules. Of course, she hated it – even tried to make herself sick so she could go and stay at her uncle's place with Mum and Dad – and spent a lot of time crying when Ian wasn't around. But she talked up the experience whenever he was, just so he'd know how much fun she was having.

Naturally he watched her race, and saw her efforts rewarded with three shiny medals: a silver in the 50 freestyle, and two relay golds. Christina now thinks that might have fired him up a bit, but Ian insists it was not pivotal. Still, whenever his big sister returned from any of her early swimming adventures, talking a big story of fun and excitement, Ian would listen intently. Christina admits her brother knew her well enough by then to realise it was mostly just bluff and bravado. 'But he was also thinking to himself: "I'm going to handle it all much better. I'll be right".'

≈

Jenni Ashpole, who had herself been coached by Doug Frost, was the glue that held both Christina and Ian at Padstow. She was a compassionate coach, great with children, and had already formed a very close bond with Christina by the time Ian arrived. Christina always insisted that Jenni put her goggles on for her; Jenni would often say reassuringly that she'd still be putting them on for her before an audience of thousands in Atlanta in 1996.

The Padstow swim school was a small-scale version of the typical Australian coaching establishment. Children were classified according to ability into groups with cute aquatic names, and allocated to separate (always crowded) lanes with assistant coaches as they worked their way up the hierarchy . . . until, if they were both serious and talented, they'd come into the state squad, and finally into close contact with the guru himself – in this case, Doug Frost – who'd be in charge of the national squad. These state and national squad swimmers were the ones who trained 'doubles' – that is, in the chill early morns and again in the late afternoons – racking up endless kilometres of interval training as they chased Olympian dreams founded not only on technique but also on stupendous levels of fitness.

For the younger kids, though, fitness training wasn't a factor. It was all about using a range of drills, or techniques, to learn and then perfect the various strokes. Ian immediately leapfrogged the lesser classes of 'halfway rowboats' and 'rowboats' into an outfit called 'tugboats', where he'd learn breast-stroke and butterfly. It was no surprise he'd already shown an aptitude for backstroke, since it allowed him to keep his troublesome nose out of the water.

Jenni knew Ian was different from the other tugboats straight away; he had the ability to immediately translate an instruction into action.

One of his first freestyle drills required him to visualise his hand being picked up by a crane, carried forward, and placed back in the water when it got as far away from him as it could possibly go. She watched him do it perfectly, all the way up and down the pool.

Jenni left after a year and was replaced as Ian's coach by another former Frost protégé, Chris Myers, master of the so-called 'jetboats' and an equally gentle soul. Ian was the most coachable pupil he'd ever seen: 'He was such a good listener, a perfectionist in training even at that stage, so if you told him to keep his elbows high or work a bit harder off the turn, he'd do it for the whole session and you'd never have to tell him again.'

And so for the next few years, as his schedule was increased from two to three to four afternoons a week, Ian perfected his drills. The general idea was to isolate one part of the process, focus on that part exclusively until it became automatic, then go on to another, and finally put them all together in a robotic jigsaw that formed the stroke. For instance, you might be doing 'one arm freestyle', where you'd hold a kickboard out in front with one arm and stroke with the other, so as to practise the right head position for breathing and the right (high) elbow position. That could be followed by kick drills using the kick-board to stabilise the body while generating maximum power through the ankles and legs. And so on. All the strokes naturally had their specialised drills, and these could be augmented with equipment like hand paddles and flippers to create more speed while working the muscles a bit harder.

This was, and remains, the stuff of junior coaching throughout the land. But naturally, it wasn't going to do any good unless it was based on endless repetition. A kid with a mind as active as Ian's just had to come up with a diversion. In the beginning he used to envisage himself as a machine – a gigantic ocean liner – with his heart the engine, his brain the battery, and masses of tiny people inside his body, operating various levers to help the ship go forward. If he had to go faster, the invisible people would work harder. The whole structure was guided by his eyeballs, through his goggles. When he took a drink, he pretended to be refuelling. It made things seem more fun, anyway.

Chris Myers could see that Ian had an innate feel for the water – it was obvious he was a 'natural' swimmer – and his exceptional buoyancy, aided by a generous coat of puppy fat, meant he could swim long distances effortlessly. Ian's tremendously powerful legs obviously gave him great kicking strength, which allowed him to forget about stability and concentrate entirely on his stroke. As well, he had extraordinary flexibility: essential because fast swimming is all about gaining maximum traction in the water, and that means being able to put your limbs in positions where they don't naturally, or ordinarily, want to go. All children lose flexibility as they get older, but even now, as an adult, Ian has a range of party tricks which includes swinging his arms behind his shoulders and clapping his hands at head height (*give that a try*); and very slowly arching his back so that his hands touch the floor behind him with his feet still on the ground, forming an inverted 'U', before snapping back to an upright position (*don't give that a try*).

What was (and still is) most rare about Ian Thorpe was his combination of extreme flexibility *and* exceptional strength. Swimmers normally base their techniques around one or other of these attributes, because muscle bulk just about always shortens the range of movement in a limb. You're either a Daniel Kowalksi type – all sinew and bones and bendability, *snaking* through the water – or a Matt Biondi – all pedal-to-the-metal power, *ploughing* your way through it.

Obviously every swimmer lies somewhere between the two extremes, mixing and matching and finding their own way; but Ian was simply endowed with more than his fair share of both. Backstroke was always a forte, breast-stroke a weakness (even with all his leg power, he couldn't seem to get that frog kick happening). But with all the things Ian had going for him in those early days – *plus* the fact that he stood a full head taller than any of the other boys – he was a truly formidable swimming package.

Yet he was beaten in competition all the time. The reason was that the overall program devised by Doug Frost, and strictly followed by all the students at his school, was extremely light on for junior swimmers. Ian really got stuck into it when he did train, but that was hardly at all compared to a lot of his opponents, who'd started early-morning sessions long before he did.

The reality is that for kids aged around eight through to 11 or 12, the results of races don't mean much at all, because everyone is training at different levels. A lot of coaches flog youngsters in the pool, leaving them mentally and physically jaded and finally lost to the sport. Some of it's just glory seeking, fuelled by the dreams of ambitious parents. Some of it relates to economics. Coaches don't make any money out of their elite athletes, who pay on average about $2 an hour each for the highest level of coaching expertise. The real dough is in learn-to-swim classes, and the best way to advertise is to breed youngsters who clean up at school carnivals. Doug Frost has been accused of over-training his senior athletes – more of which later – but that could never be said of the juniors in his program.

The upshot of all this was that as Ian got older and trained longer, he naturally became more and more successful. In the NSW State Age Championships in February 1992, when he was just nine, Ian managed a fourth in the 100 freestyle, second in the 100 backstroke, second in the 100 butterfly, and 23rd in the 100 breast-stroke. Pretty good results, but hardly headline news, and no real inkling of the total dominance that was to come.

The other consequence was that, with Christina a few years further down the track in her training progression, she was definitely the star of the Thorpe family show. Ian lived (quite happily) in her shadow, and it was a long time before he came to realise that he was actually more talented than his sister. By the time the Pacific Schools Championships were held in May 1992, 12-year-old Christina was training in the state squad and doing eight 90-minute sessions a week – three in the morning and five afternoons – while Ian was doing only four one-hour sessions.

These Pacific Championships, substituting that year for the Australian Primary Schools titles, were a relatively new concept and a very big deal. They involved high schools as well – Christina was in Year 7 by then – and attracted swimmers from 36 countries, most notably Australia, New Zealand and Japan. Held at four-year intervals, they loomed as a sort of Kiddie Olympics – and most enticingly, in 1992 they were to be held in exotic Darwin. Ian was excited enough to give it everything he had at the state titles, held at the Warringah Aquatic Centre in April, qualifying with a first in the 50 back and a second in the 50 free. He was off on his first big trip away with a swim team.

Christina, on the other hand, was freaking out. Even though Mum and Dad would be there in the grandstand as usual, the rules remained the same: swimmers travelled as a team and had to be billeted. They could, however, state a preference, and instead of Christina being paired with one of her friends, Margaret requested that both her children be billeted together. The unspoken agenda was: 'Don't worry, Christina – Ian will look after you.'

So Margaret and Ken flew out to Darwin the day before the kids, who stayed overnight at Nanna's. Next day, in the car on the way to the airport, Christina was bawling while Ian tried as best he could to comfort her. 'When we got there,' Christina recalls, 'Ian just took over straight away because he knew how scared I was. The first thing they did was ask if I wanted a sandwich, and Ian stepped in and said: "Yes please – my sister will have Vegemite on hers".' The perfect gentleman.

Ian also took the opportunity, around this time, to inform Christina that she was no longer to regard herself as his boss. (The concept, she happily admits, didn't really take hold for a long, long time.) Definitely she still reigned in the pool, winning eight medals in all – five of them gold, three silver. Being born in February was a huge advantage for her in the school system, based as it was on the age you turned that year. Ian, racing in the 10 years and under division, weighed in with three medals – gold in the 50 backstroke and silvers in the freestyle and medley relays.

The Thorpes had borrowed a chunky hand-held video camera and Margaret shot footage of Ian trying really hard to do his warm-up seriously – flailing his arms all around like they do on TV – before splashing in with his crowd-pleasing bellyflop. He was keen to do well, of course, but his main interest was swapping pins. In the end he had one from all 36 countries stuck in his special New South Wales cap. It was an impressive sight.

Shortly after the Darwin trip, the Thorpe family took their last annual holiday at the Forster-Tuncurry Caravan Park. It was a great one, too, because cousins Paul and Michelle, who hadn't been along for a couple of years, joined them. They'd spend all day at the beach, and each night would walk over the bridge to the ice-cream shop, where the proprietor had expressed the view that Christina had to be a ring-in. She couldn't possibly be part of this family, because she was so fair while the others, especially Ian, were deeply tanned. Ian would rib her about it, but they were so close, the four of them, and about as happy in each other's company as any bunch of youngsters could be.

But it was in a sense the end of an era. Swimming was taking over. Ken and Margaret, who'd sacrifice anything to watch their children swim at any meet, especially the major ones, couldn't afford to follow them all over the country *and* have a separate holiday of their own choosing as well. Ken worked out that the Darwin episode cost the family, in airfares and accommodation for himself and Margaret and an $1800 levy for the two children, about $7000 all up. It was money they didn't really have.

Christina was soon to enter swimming's version of the major leagues – the Age Nationals as they're known – where the best of the best swimmers aged from 13 upwards from around Australia would congregate every April in one or other of the capitals to sort out their positions in the aquatic pantheon. It was a given that her parents would need to be there for her, just as they would be for Ian wherever the Australian Primary Schools titles might be held.

It wasn't just about cost, though. Swimming at the level Christina was at, she simply couldn't afford to lose any training time. Fitness lost in any lay-off is very hard to recover, so really the only window available each year for holidays was the swimmers' month off at the end of the Age Nationals carnival. The Thorpes would henceforth tack their holidays on to the Age Nationals trip, wherever it happened to be – and if they couldn't afford that, then the carnival itself would become the holiday.

The swimming calendar is virtually a nonstop round of racing at squad and school level. It begins with weekly Friday night club races, and then district meets, where the Padstow club would be up against other local clubs for a total of eight times a year. Then there's the club's own local carnival, and because Doug Frost was keen on his swimmers getting all the racing experience they could, they were always trooping off to other club carnivals. Then came Metropolitan Age Championships each December and State Age Championships, usually in January, just before school resumed. Then the whole school program: school, zone, regional, state . . . and finally Australian Championships at primary level; same thing at high school, but without the shoot-out between big guns at national level, because at that point squad swimming becomes much more important – State Age Championships in January, Australian Age Championships in April (the Age Nationals). And then there's the winter short course meets: Metropolitan Age in July, State Age in September – and within all this framework, open championships at state and Australian level, which older swimmers would enter along with their age-group events. Even that list doesn't cover everything.

Most of these meets were held in Sydney – at Blacktown and Warringah, and eventually Homebush when the Olympic venue opened – but the Thorpes' petrol costs still mounted up, plus there was generally an entry fee of $10 per race. (Some years down the track from here, Ian's full program alone would cost $130.) Parents of swimmers had to pay $20 each per weekend to watch their children.

But these expenses paled in comparison to the burden of keeping fuel levels up for the kids' training regimes, especially after Ian joined his sister in the early morning sessions. It all had to be good quality food, as recommended by their dietician – and huge quantities of it. The Thorpes' grocery bill alone was $400 a week (we're talking ten years ago here) and on top of that the kids were always guzzling an expensive energy drink called Exceed. Christina's lycra costumes used to rot in the mix of heat and pool chemicals and would have to be replaced at least once a month, while Margaret was forever rinsing them in fresh water to try and get some more wear out of them. And then, finally, the coaching bill: just on $200 a month for the pair of them.

Obviously it was a massive commitment. The Thorpe family could divide their financial history into two parts: Before Swimming and After Swimming. Before, having paid off the mortgage, Ken was banking the whole of his wage (he'd long since quit the tarpaulin factory and become a gardener with the local council), and they were living entirely on Margaret's. After Swimming, they were just getting by on both incomes. The annual cost, then, was equivalent to one gardener's entire earnings.

It was fortunate they were both able to work, and equally fortunate that in doing so, they could still organise themselves to fit in with the rapacious demands of the sport. Their lives, like those of every other swimming family in the land, were about to become finely calibrated and calendarised, marching along in lockstep with the workings of the Doug Frost Swim School and the scheduling of the annual swimming program.

When a swimmer goes into the state squad, it means there's going to be no time for much of anything else. Sporting-wise, it's definitely the end of any other involvement, apart from whatever might be fitted in at school. It's at this pivotal point that parents of swimmers have to face down an unavoidable question: did they really want to be hauling themselves out of bed long before dawn to get their kids down to the pool for the morning training session? For Ken and Margaret, of course, there was no hesitation; if their children wanted to make that commitment – and in Christina's case it had been a big decision to give up netball, considering she was a star player in the best team in the state – then so be it. It was just natural that, when the time came, Ian would follow.

To his credit, head coach Frost would always aim to hold back boys from Chris Myers' state squad till they were at least twelve. But Ian was just too far advanced in his swimming; he had to take the next step. Aged 11, in the Christmas holidays prior to his last year of primary school, he started Saturday morning sessions, then backed off when he returned to school, but some months later resumed, and later still he began training Tuesday and Thursday mornings for a total of seven 90-minute sessions each week. (Even so, Frost remained conservative; he didn't have Ian doing the full program of ten two-hour swim sessions and three gym sessions until he was 14.)

So now the routine was set in stone. Ken would take the kids to training at 4.30 in the morning. Christina, in Frost's national squad, would start no later than 4.45 am, Ian at 5.30. Ken would come home and Margaret would take him to work at 6.50 am. She'd pick up the kids at 7.00 from training, bring them home, serve their breakfast, make their lunches, drop them off at school and head on to her own work at Picnic Point Primary. She'd finish at 3 pm, pick up Christina at 3.10 from East Hills Girls High, then Ian from Nanna's, where he'd been minded after school, then Ken at 3.30 from work. They'd race home; the children would shovel down some food, get changed and be back at the pool by 4 pm.

Margaret would come home and start preparing the evening meal, Ken would pick the kids up at 7 pm, and dinner would be on the table at 7.20. (It became a bit simpler when Ian went to high school and could catch the bus home.) If a little bit of help was needed from Mum to get their homework done, or the odd school project, that was okay . . . as long as they were in bed, *asleep*, at 8.30 pm. Ian and Christina would usually be unconscious before you could even say 'Goodnight'. Mentally and physically it was a challenging routine for children, but the Thorpe kids thrived on it – Ian even more so when he realised he'd finally overcome his chlorine allergy.

There's a popular misconception that swimmers in serious training just stick their heads in the water and swim, kilometre after mind-numbing kilometre, their only company being that familiar black line at the bottom of the pool. That *was* pretty much the case as far back as the mid-1960s, but interval training, which is the basis of all swim training today, isn't quite like that. It's hard work, for sure, and nowhere near as convivial as, say, footy training. But there's still some time for a chat and a laugh during the rest period between exercise sets.

It definitely helps, though, if you have the capacity to enjoy the process of passive thought – to just let your mind tick over, or let your imagination run wild if it wants to. Most athletes block out the world when they train; Ian, at least when he wasn't concentrating on his stroke, preferred to actually think about the world and his place in it. Sometimes, though, his mind was a blank, and sometimes it was just full of useless junk – but whatever was happening up there, he could go with it.

Ian and Christina enjoyed the discipline; they appreciated the sense of achievement; they liked maintaining friendships formed at the pool; they generally loved the fun of it all. A lot of swimmers in the state and national squads had to be dragged out of bed by their parents. With the Thorpes, it was the other way around.

But nonetheless Ken, in keeping with the most important element of his philosophy, would always wait until just after the climax of the yearly cycle – in primary school, the Australian schools titles; in high school, the Age Nationals – and then put the question in the simplest terms to his children: *Are you absolutely sure you want to continue? It'll be another tough year, another endless round of sacrifices, and once you commit, you have to see it through . . . so think about it HARD. Are there any second thoughts about it?*

There were none at all.

4

'I'M GONNA KICK YOUR BOY'S ARSE'

IAN'S LAST YEAR OF PRIMARY SCHOOL, 1994, was full of events that turned out to be somehow pivotal in his life.

At one of the early squad meets that year he was interviewed for the first time by a young reporter named Catriona Dixon, who'd been assigned by the *Telegraph* to write a weekly column, 'Tomorrow's Champions Today', in the run-up to the Sydney Olympics. (The optimistic idea was to try to engender the athletes' loyalty to the tabloid paper.) Among the half-dozen swimmers she was to pursue for the next six years, Catriona picked Ian as the standout candidate for Olympic glory. She chronicled his every move diligently, interviewed him dozens of times before anyone else was interested, introduced Ian and his family to the sometimes devious ways of the media and helped them to cope with the demands of journalists, becoming a family friend in the process.

'At first he'd be sheepish and embarrassed when you walked over to him for an interview, and would always cross his arms to cover his body,' she remembers. 'But I always thought there was something special about him. He had this aura of serious determination even then – something like a young Lleyton Hewitt. He was a person you could bank on. And he was so eloquent, so articulate, even in that first interview.'

Ian reckons it was also early that year when he suffered the only injury of his overly cautious life as a youngster: a broken little finger, sustained during an altercation with his sister at home. (Christina, by contrast, managed a broken wrist and four broken arms by the time she finished high school.) In fact, Ian felt quite constricted by his natural conservatism. He was unconsciously looking for some kind of breakout experience, and it arrived one midsummer day when his 19-year-old cousin Ben came around to pick up Ian and Ken and take them to Wanda Beach, at Cronulla, for a bodysurf.

The swell was HUGE. Ken was obviously a mere onlooker, Ben was *really* scared, but Ian was insistent on getting out there, and much to his amazement, Ken was prepared to let him. So Ben figured he'd better accompany his brave young cousin. Of course, once they'd made it almost out the back, a monster wave broke on the sandbank directly in front of them, and even though it was high tide and they dived right to the bottom and tried to hang on to the sand, they were *still* sucked up and pounded by the wash; and then, short of breath, they had to do it again; and then again, even shorter on air, as the third massive wave in the set smashed over them. They were exhausted.

Ian – scared, but not quite terrified – knew they'd made a mistake: it was actually bigger than he'd first thought. Once out the back, it was then a matter of figuring out how to get back in. They rested, waited for a lull, collected themselves, and swam conservatively for shore, figuring they were going to cop another three-wave deluge about halfway in. They were right about that.

Ian and Ben ended up literally dragging themselves onto the beach and safety. 'What have we just done? That was *ridiculous*,' Ian panted. But having encountered, for the first time, a life-or-death situation, and having survived it, Ian felt he'd somehow symbolically freed himself from the yoke of being his mummy's boy. He was ready to take more risks and get more fun, on his own terms, out of life.

It was more than a simple coming-of-age experience. Ian now thinks it was actually pivotal to his whole approach to swimming: 'I think people have a primal fear of water. When we get into the water we have nothing to stabilise us except those walls at either end – so what happens is people swim to keep themselves "up". If someone pushes you over on land, your reaction is to extend your arms and legs and put your head back to protect it. When most people swim they do the same thing – they use their limbs to stabilise themselves, keep their head back and look forward. I've always been more comfortable in the water since that day at Wanda, because I'm not subconsciously afraid of what could happen. I've only recently realised that a lot of swimmers – even *good* swimmers – have that primal fear of water.'

By now the pattern of Ian's race performances had become very predictable. His backstroke was superb, his freestyle and butterfly very strong, breast-stroke still a weakness, but his overall strength so good that he'd be an even more unbackable favourite in the individual medley (IM) than the backstroke at any given meet.

So to the 1994 primary schools state titles, held at Warringah in late March. Ian won the 12 years and under 50 freestyle by half a second; won the 50 back by a full second; scraped in to win the 50 breast by three-hundredths of a second; came fifth (a bit of an aberration here) in the 50 fly, a long way behind a butterfly hotshot named Scott Perry; won the Open 100 free by three-quarters of a second; and then came his signature event – the 200 IM – where he blew the opposition out of the pool, winning by almost four seconds. None of these five gold medal swims, though, broke state records. Those were generally held by swimmers who were trained into the ground as youngsters and never heard of again.

It was at this meet that coach Chris Myers learned something about the Thorpe family mentality that he'd never forget. Ian approached Chris before a race to get his instructions. Chris was sitting next to a coaching mate of his whose protégé happened to be Ian's rival in that race. There were plenty of people around; Chris thought he'd chance his arm with a bit of a joke, so he told Ian to say to the other coach: 'I'm gonna kick your boy's arse today.'

Dutifully, Ian said exactly that: *I'm gonna kick your boy's arse today.* Ken Thorpe, seated nearby, absolutely flew into Chris: 'He told me in no uncertain terms that that wasn't what we were here for – that it didn't matter at all whether Ian won or lost, as long as he gave it his best shot. I realised Ken was right, of course, and I never, ever said a thing like that to a swimming pupil again.'

Ian's efforts at that state carnival led to him being named 'Swimmer of the Meet' and captain of the New South Wales team for the Australian Primary Schools titles, to be held in Melbourne in early May. Catriona Dixon rang him at home for an interview. Ken and Margaret worried about how he'd handle it, but they need not have: he was already performing like a veteran. Then, just prior to heading south for the most important event of his life thus far, Ian did a real kid thing. Without consulting anyone, he tried to reinvent his freestyle stroke.

He happened to be doing sprint 25s with just two other swimmers – the tiny Padstow pool was nearly empty, which was an unbelievable luxury – so there was room for a bit of experimentation. Ian's legs were tired, so he decided to try lengthening his stroke as far as possible while virtually forgetting about the kick. The pace clock told him he'd swum just as fast as usual. He thought: 'This is all right – I'll extend my stroke even further if I can – and then if I kick hard with it as well, I'm going to go heaps faster. And if I make my arms go faster, with this new stroke, then I'll go faster still . . .'

These were the thoughts he took with him to Melbourne, having told Chris Myers, who got to come along on that trip, nothing about it. Generally he swam very well, winning the 50 back by a whisker, the 100 back by almost two and a half seconds (setting his first state long course record), and the 200 IM by the sumptuous margin of three and a half seconds. In those events it was business as usual, even at the highest level.

But his 50 free swim was a disappointing fifth, and he didn't even make the final of the 100 free, swimming his heat in 1:08.97 compared to his winning time of 1:05.35 at the state titles. Something was clearly amiss. Chris immediately saw it: Ian was revolving his arms at a frantic pace while scarcely moving his legs, which had been his great strength. (Obviously, with all his concentration on the experimental stroke, Ian had forgotten about the lower half of his body.) In swimming parlance, he was 'spinning his wheels'. So when they returned from Melbourne, Chris and Jenni Ashpole (who had since returned from overseas) set about pulling Ian's stroke apart.

It involved a lot of drills designed to slow down the stroke and re-emphasise the kick, but the most important change was something that evolved naturally out of those drills. This innovation – which was mainly Chris's input, with a lot of encouragement and help from Doug Frost, who later refined it further – involved what's called the 45 degree stroke. For the majority of swimmers, when one arm enters the water, the other one pulling back is at about 90 degrees to it. With this new stroke, the second arm follows the first much more directly, so they're forming an angle closer to 45 degrees.

But hang on – aren't we trying to *slow down* the stroke, rather than speed it up? Yes, and in order to make this new-fangled pattern happen, Ian has *got* to slow down his stroke – that is, make the recovery part, where he brings the arm overhead, much 'lazier'. As a result he's reaching further forward for the 'catch' and further back at the end of the stroke, thus maximising his efficiency in just the way Ian had envisaged when he started the experiment in the first place. This is not by any means a Padstow Swim School invention; there's mention of it in all the textbooks. But the crucial thing is that you need a *really* strong kick to be able to do this – and you *have to use it*, or else you don't have enough propulsion and end up bobbing up and down – so the corollary was that it forced Ian to utilise his greatest attribute to the fullest.

The catch is central to the Thorpe freestyle stroke. Normally when a swimmer's hand enters the water, it goes straight in and starts to pull back immediately, but because of water slippage, the catch won't actually begin to take hold for another 15 to 20 centimetres. But with Ian's more languid stroke (and great flexibility), he's able to keep on extending the hand and arm *after* it enters the water – so, putting it simply, he gets hold of a lot more water a lot further forward than the average swimmer, so he's able to shove more of it around. And that's the main reason (but not the only one) why he can swim faster than guys who are flailing their arms much more quickly than he is. To comprehend the importance of all this, consider that when Ian Thorpe met Grant Hackett on neutral territory – the 800 metres – in 2001, he was two centimetres shorter than Hackett, but his average stroke length was a full 37 centimetres longer. He averaged only 33.7 strokes per minute to Hackett's 38.2.

Chris Myers had actually issued all these decrees to Jenni Ashpole, gone on a two-week holiday, and returned to find the transformation complete. No doubt the process was aided by the fact that Ian felt he owned a fair bit of the intellectual property himself – although, typically, he never said anything about his own initial experiments prior to Melbourne. But even so, there had to be a lot of trust involved. As Ian puts it now: 'Chris and Jenni were both exceptional coaches, and they haven't received enough credit for my career. Jenni was a family friend as well, and I'm sure that trust helped me to go about totally changing my stroke. If it was someone else, maybe I wouldn't have done it.' Anyway, the upshot was that Ian started to swim freestyle a whole lot faster – immediately. 'I could feel,' he recalls, 'that this was me finally swimming at my best.'

So, if this method was clearly superior, shouldn't Chris be teaching the 45 degree stroke to all his swimmers, since logic would suggest they're all 'spinning their wheels' to a greater or lesser extent? The answer is yes – but the problem is that hardly anyone has the kicking strength to do it: 'I've only got one boy now who can actually do it, and he's sixteen. I've tried with all the others, but they can only swim the way they're able to swim, and whatever I say isn't going to make much difference.'

So the Thorpe freestyle stroke, although not a radical concept, was really in a sense a prototype, and knowing that gives you an even greater appreciation of its beauty. When you watch him swim from above – an angle too rarely afforded by the TV cameras, but one you can arrange for yourself at just about any swim meet – that's when you notice his very deliberate, almost exaggerated catch of the water.

Rather than slapping the surface with his hands, it's as if he's gently, almost tenderly cradling the water back with that unhurried arm movement. The precision of it, even by comparison with other world-class swimmers, is quite breathtaking.

≈

The swimming calendar turns into short course meets in the winter, and because these come under the squad rather than school system, the age you are at the start of the meet is the criterion, which was a huge advantage to Ian. (He'd actually been breaking state short course records since he was nine.) At the NSW State Age Short Course Championships, held at Warringah in early September that year, Ian got to swim as an 11-year-old, just a month or so shy of his 12th birthday. Even though short course swimming doesn't matter anywhere near as much as long course – it's a bit like one-day cricket was before anyone cared about it – all the big guns would still turn up, and Ian's dominance was almost total: he won the 50 free, 100 free, 50 back, 100 back, 50 breast, 100 breast, the 100 fly and the 200 IM.

Only Scott Perry, the butterfly specialist who'd beaten him by a full three seconds over 50 metres at the state schools titles in March, prevented a clean sweep by taking out the 50 fly. But Ian turned the tables on him in the 100 metres fly, by precisely implementing a race plan, conceived by Chris Myers, that was designed to frighten the life out of young Scott. Ian won by over half a second, with Myers suitably impressed with his protégé's ability to carry out race instructions to the letter.

This was fine as far as it went, but again, as with his freestyle stroke, Ian was starting to think outside the square. How, he reasoned, could anyone swim faster from point A to point B than they were physically capable of, just by taking into account what other people were doing in the race? Swimming fast is all about smooth consistency of stroke; therefore, worrying about the relative positions of other swimmers – and chopping and changing your own stroke as a result – would always have the opposite effect. (Of course, this was what had happened to the unfortunate Perry.)

The more he thought about it, the more ridiculous it seemed to Ian when a swimmer would say something like: 'I went out really hard because everyone else was going out hard – and then I tried to bring it back, but I was really struggling . . .' *WHY*, Ian would think, exasperated, *don't you swim the race the way you've TRAINED yourself to swim it?*

So Ian decided to apply that inexorable logic to his own swimming, and stick with it no matter what. He would draw a curtain over himself in a race and concern himself only with what *he* was doing. Later on, opponents might try all sorts of tactics on him – say, burning him off early in the hope of scaring him out of his rhythm, or swimming extra close to his lane, eyeball-to-eyeball, to try and psych him out – but they might as well have been telling jokes underwater for all it mattered. Ian's tactic was to have no tactic: he swam point-to-point, as fast as he knew how, as fast as he had trained himself to do, so that at the end of each race he would be completely spent. Since winning or losing wasn't the point anyway – he was only interested in doing his best, which meant trying to put up a personal best every time he swam – he was mentally impregnable.

What *didn't* he have in his armoury by now? He already exhibited a natural feel for the water, natural buoyancy, great power in both legs and upper body, amazing flexibility, superb stroke efficiency, very high intelligence, a perfectionistic attitude combined with dedication, determination and mental toughness – and, not least of all, sheer physical size. Ian towered over his Year 6 teacher and would top the six foot mark before the end of Year 7. He'd also inherited from his mother exceptionally large hands and, famously, a whopping big pair of feet. There was nothing to add to the package except a few years of hard interval training – a process already begun with his ascension to the state squad, and building steadily as he worked toward the national squad and the full-time attentions of Doug Frost.

Because of the hierarchical structure of the swim school, Frost had had little to do with Ian in his formative years, and would not become his full-time coach until just before Ian turned thirteen. But he'd always kept an eye on proceedings, and he knew, like Chris Myers, that

Ian Thorpe was winning multiple gold medals at the highest level on very limited training compared to his opposition; and that when he finally shed the last of his puppy fat – which happened soon after his 12th birthday – and got further into the full-time training program to build up his aerobic fitness, there weren't going to be a whole lot of swimmers capable of stopping him.

Chris had a few extra clues about Ian's capabilities. On Wednesday nights, a while after the 11-year-old Ian had begun work in the state squad, Chris had him doing sets of 6 × 300 metres freestyle at increasing speeds – each repetition faster than the previous one – on intervals of six minutes. 'One day – I'll never forget this – I watched him swim 3.30 for the last 300 in that set of six – and I nearly jumped out of my skin. To be swimming 1.10 pace at that point . . . it was just phenomenal.'

It wouldn't be long before Frost himself would be double-checking his stopwatch and babbling incoherently over Ian's training times. But for the moment, he was content to add the youngster to an elite squad of half a dozen, including Christina, which he took three times a week to the Aquatic Centre at Homebush, site of the Sydney Olympics, very shortly after it opened in October 1994.

Doug had bought a clapped-out old minibus for the purpose and hired a single lane for his squad. The main reason was to lighten the load on Padstow and get his top swimmers into long course water, where they'd no longer have the luxury of a tumble-turn every 25 metres. But no doubt, as he glanced up at the grandstand in what was one of the finest natatoriums ever built, he'd have envisaged himself somewhere at the centre of this impressive stage in the year 2000. Ian was undoubtedly thinking along similar lines.

≈

Paul Butler, Ian's teacher in Years 3 and 6, remembers a student who was remarkably mature, capable of totally focusing on the task at hand, reliable, good-natured and uniformly friendly toward everyone. He had only one pet hate: being asked to talk about his feats in the swimming pool. Returning to school from any swim meet, he would avoid the subject as far as possible, but would knuckle down to the task of catching up with the two or three days of missed work. He had a quiet confidence, but as word of his outstanding abilities seeped into the general consciousness of the school, he simply craved normality.

Socially he was inclined to mix with the quieter kids, those who didn't seem to attract a lot of trouble. But although he was quiet, he was also somewhat individualistic, so he would always strive to do things differently. His favourite part of the school week was when he got to do his report on a segment of *BTN*, a kids' current affairs show, because he could present it in any way he chose. It gave him a sense of being his own person. Academically he wasn't quite the sharpest tool in the shed, but he wasn't far off it – still in the top five in all his subjects, but not really threatening to unseat the Dux of Year 6, who happened to be his best friend, Ryan Barclay.

Toward the end of that final year at Milperra Primary, Paul Butler took Ian and his Year 6 classmates to a five-day sport and recreation camp at the beachside suburb of Narrabeen. For Ian it was a memorable time – a chance to bust out of his demanding routine and just hang out with his friends, sailing, canoeing, orienteering, cooking, camping and such. Paul still has an hour-long video he shot that week: '. . . and here's Ian in the picture . . . *almost*'. Somehow he manages to stay just on the edge of the action, avoiding the spotlight, never quite in the frame.

There's an exception, though: in one shot, a particularly boisterous kid is standing next to a campfire and rabbiting on about making damper, while another figure towers over him, taking up two-thirds of the screen, cramming huge quantities of the food into his mouth while smiling down in an indulgent sort of way at the chattering one, but saying nothing. You can look at this piece of video for ages before realising that the towering figure is Ian Thorpe.

Paul still has the *1994 Yearbook* as well. In it are two contributions from Ian. The first is the Senior Cricket Report (Ian, who was still a very ordinary exponent with bat and ball, played for the school team in Years 5 and 6): 'Milperra Seniors didn't play all that well this year, only winning one game all year . . . on the odd occasion we lacked in enthusiasm . . . we weren't tight enough in the field. WE MUST TRY HARDER. But it was a fun year.' The second, stuck in amongst an assortment of poems, jokes and other trivia from his classmates, is a concerned diatribe about wildlife smuggling out of Australia: 'These animals are taken out of their proper environment and they often die.' The young Thorpe was already developing a social conscience.

Paul's most vivid memory of Ian Thorpe was the time he privately asked Ian where he wanted to go with the whole business of swimming. 'Without blinking, he looked me straight in the eye and said: "I want to swim at the Sydney Olympics". Nothing was said about him winning medals – that would have been too presumptuous. But he was already focused, six years before the event. You could see he definitely meant what he said.'

5

IAN SWIMS, IAN WINS

IAN HAD BEEN BEST MATES WITH Ryan Barclay since pre-school, when Ryan lived just around the corner and could see Ian's bedroom from his front yard. Both academically and athletically, the pair were always pushing each other. Ryan had a proper backyard pool, and when they were eight and nine and ten, they'd challenge each other to various kinds of triathlons. Ryan, who was the second-best swimmer in the school without ever doing any training, would normally win because he always gave Ian the dud bike. Ian never minded about that: everybody needs to have their time in the sun.

Throughout primary school there was a third member of this elite group, Nathan Page, who was academically right up there with Ryan and Ian, as well as being an outstanding golfer. Ryan ended up being a competitive Malibu board rider.

When they started Year 7 at East Hills Boys High, these three hung out together most of the time. They kept on pushing each other to do well. High achievement was a big factor in their friendship – but at the same time, being of much the same temperament, they kept each other grounded. 'We were always trying to be more mature than the other kids,' Nathan remembers. 'We'd try to have conversations about important things, instead of just talking crap.'

They definitely weren't known for being mischievous, this crew, but they weren't real pain-in-the-butt, goody-two-shoes types either. Ryan reckons it was Ian's idea to superglue a 50-cent piece to the road outside his house and get a laugh out of watching people try to pick it up. (An old guy actually came back with a chisel and removed it.) Another time they got into trouble for belting a pile of explosive caps with a hammer as cars went by, trying to convince the drivers they'd had a blowout. All good harmless fun. But they were boys who saw themselves as being of a certain calibre: they were into being healthy, fit, smart, and staunch in their beliefs; and there was an incident in the very first week of high school that typified what they were about.

Ryan and Ian were in the school bus on the way home. A group of kids sitting right up the back were smoking and otherwise playing up, when the driver, a woman, slammed on the brakes and screamed: 'Right – everyone off the bus NOW.' But the miscreants up the back weren't going anywhere. Instead, they just started hurling abuse at this woman. It was looking pretty ugly when Ian turned to Ryan and said: 'Let's get off and walk home.' Ryan was happy to join him, even though they had several kilometres of walking to do. They just didn't want to be associated with that type of student.

That type of student was plentiful at East Hills Boys. It wasn't exactly the mean streets of Sydney, but this was a school that had more than its share of violence, much of it race-related, and it wasn't the sort of place you'd want to stick your head up too high in case someone decided to pummel it back into place. However, there was an ever-present sporting elitism at the school, engendered by the famous alumni who'd passed down those corridors – among them celebrity Test cricketers Steve and Mark Waugh, Test bowler Wayne Holdsworth and New South Wales batsman Steve Small, Wallaby giant Laurie Monaghan and Olympic swimmer Graham Windeatt, along with a host of other sportsmen who'd gone on to make their marks in one way or another. East Hills High was a real sports hotspot – something like the New South Wales country town of Wagga Wagga, which just seemed to produce one top sporting gun after another, for no reason that anyone could ever discern. This was a good thing for Ian. It inspired him to think that people from his little neck of the woods could take on the world, and it helped to protect him from the jealousy of other students.

The school swimming carnival is always the very first thing on the annual calendar of events – and of course, every year there's bound to be some Year 7 hotshot who rolls up and makes a big impression because he's a serious squad swimmer. But with Ian, it was a different order of magnitude. He was just about the fastest swimmer in the school in every stroke, and nudging the Open records in most, even though he wasn't actually trying too hard because he had to train again that afternoon.

Teachers and students alike were just dumbfounded by what he could do in the pool. And among a few of the older swimming legends, noses were pushed out of joint and some harsh words spoken. But it never came from classmates, only from kids who didn't know him, and the flame of envy was quickly extinguished because Ian wouldn't give it a breath of oxygen. He just kept on unassuming his way through the business of life, in his typical manner, until it was just a given: *Ian swims, Ian wins* . . . It wasn't even a subject of conversation after a while.

Water polo, which Ian played as summer sport in Year 7, was plain ridiculous. How was anyone going to stop a kid who could just give the ball to a team-mate, swim twice as fast as anyone else toward open water, collect the lobbed pass in either of his outsized hands, and simply flip it into an open goal? He could literally score at will – and sometimes, when the mood took him, he did. Witnessing such a game might have been something like watching a mature Bradman bat against primary school bowling – except that wasn't the way Ian usually played it. Where Bradman was ruthless, Ian got real joy from watching other guys of lesser ability shine. Most of the time – unless the team really needed to crank it up – he'd take a back seat and allow his team-mates to score the goals.

Olga Sovo, the teacher who coached the undefeated team (and again, with Ian the lynchpin, in Years 8 and 9), observed a boy who was ordinarily 'very quiet and reserved, who kept to himself and his friends – but when he came to the pool for water polo he was transformed. He was full of character, playful, but very much part of the team and very good with the other players. He just blossomed.'

But 1995 was not the year of Ian Thorpe. The spotlight fell directly on Christina, because that was the year she set out to make the Australian swimming team. Just a week before the Australian Championships, which doubled as the selection trials for the Pan Pacific Games in Atlanta, *ABC School Sport* ran a TV special on the Thorpe siblings. Ian confidently informed the audience that he was now training a maximum of eight times per week, and that his short-term goal was 'just to do my best – but long-term it would have to be the Olympics'. Doug Frost opined that Christina would be 'an outside shot' to make the Atlanta Olympic team in the distance freestyle events, and added: 'I'd like to see her on the Pan Pacs team this year – that'll give her just a taste of it.'

By now it was obvious that Christina's talent was eclipsed by Ian's. She had the intelligence, the work ethic and the determination – she'd train harder than *anyone* at Padstow – but she wasn't tall for a swimmer. Her maximum height was only 169 centimetres, or less than five feet seven in the old numbers. She was good enough, though, to win five gold medals at Combined High Schools level every year – for freestyle, backstroke and butterfly – and was always up there somewhere in the finals at Age Nationals in freestyle events, with a leaning towards greater distance as time went on. But she was not the preeminent swimmer of her age group. That was Emma Johnson, a private school girl who was just eight days younger than Christina and almost as dominant at age level across the board as Ian Thorpe would soon become.

But anyway, Christina travelled to Perth for the Australian Open at the end of March, swam in the 400, 800 and 1500 metres freestyle, and scraped into the Australian team with a third placing in the 800, 20 seconds behind Hayley Lewis and eight seconds behind Stacey Gartrell. Selection was automatic: top three go to Pan Pacs provided they make the qualifying time. Christina had only just turned 15, and she was IN – the second-youngest member of the Dolphins team after Emma Johnson.

There was rejoicing in the Thorpe household. This was, after all, what the whole adventure was about: there was no greater honour than to represent your country, as Ken had said so many times. Sure, it was not as big a deal as making the Olympic team. But Christina was just a kid, years younger than Lewis and Gartrell, the Olympics were looming the following year . . . *and* she'd swum her best-ever times in the 800 and 1500, so she believed she could handle the pressure. Just a couple of weeks later she beat Emma Johnson to win the 15 years 400 free at the Age Nationals in Adelaide, and won the 800 free as well. She was on fire.

So too was Ian at his first ever Age Nationals, but it was a smouldering kind of fire, and you needed to know a bit about swimming to recognise its significance. Back in late January Ian had taken an eight-medal haul from the State Age Championships in the 12 years division – five of them gold, including, ominously, the 200-400 freestyle double. (Obviously that modified freestyle stroke was working nicely in combination with his increased aerobic fitness.) He'd also swum a handful of qualifying times for the Age Nationals. Ordinarily only a couple of 12-year-olds would qualify for any given event at the 13 years-and-over Age Nationals, because boys around that age undergo such massive growth spurts. Doug Frost always insisted that if you'd qualified for an event you should swim it just for the experience, even if there was no expectation of success. So Ian duly went along to Adelaide with his sister.

When he took bronze medals in both the 200 and 400 free – lopping four and five seconds respectively off his times at the state titles a few months earlier – that was when Doug Frost got *really* excited. He knew then that he was about to take charge of a phenomenon.

As far as Ian was concerned, he was just a kid – but one whose big sister was doing altitude training in the US in the build-up to Pan Pacs and fraternising with some of the superstars of the sport: household names like Lewis, Housman, Kowalski and Perkins. She'd call from the States and tell him stories – *true* stories, now, because she'd actually grown up – about how much fun it all was.

And there were these little tidbits of insider knowledge, such as how Kieren Perkins, the great KP, would actually cheat on his kicking drills – Ian was *shocked* – and when she came back from the first altitude camp with ten different flavours of chewing gum that nobody had ever heard of, and which Ian could take to school and share with his friends, the whole thing just seemed too unreal for words. This was when the thought first occurred to Ian that his life was turning into something special. From now on, when he went to a major swim meet, famous athletes would know of him because he was Christina Thorpe's little brother. How cool was that?

Christina's second trip to the States lasted two solid months, with Pan Pacs following on from another round of hard altitude training. Before leaving for the airport she stood outside the house in her new Australian tracksuit, posing for photos. 'It was just a keepsake,' she recalls, 'because at that stage you didn't know if it would ever happen again – it could just be a one-off.'

In early August, only a few days before her big debut, Ian swam in the NSW State Open Championships at Homebush – a confusing title, since they were actually age-based events – and took away ten gold medals: a clean sweep. He won the 12 years 200 IM by a staggering 15 seconds, and was the only 12-year-old in the 13-and-under 400 freestyle, yet he beat the field home by a lazy four and a half seconds. Still, though, the focus remained on Christina. Ken and Margaret couldn't spring for two airfares all the way to Atlanta – a huge expense – so Margaret travelled alone to the Georgia Tech pool, bearing a card from Ian with the same reminder the kids always gave each other: 'You've done the hard work, now have fun – and KICK THOSE LEGS!'

Mrs Thorpe watched her daughter compete in the 400, 800 and 1500 free. Christina didn't make any finals, but after swimming the 'B' finals was ranked seventh on times in the 800 and fourth in the 1500.

She wasn't disappointed with that. She'd produced her fastest-ever swims in all three events; she knew, now that she was training with the big names, that she was doing all the right things herself, and so it was just a matter of getting older and stronger.

Christina reckons she returned from Pan Pacs 'a different person'. Having had a taste of the big time, there was only one place she wanted to be, and that was in the Australian team – specifically, the Australian Olympic team. She came home with a head full of dietary dictums that she would follow to the letter, plus a grab-bag of motivational quotes handed down by revered sages like Laurie Lawrence. She typed them up in big bold letters and stuck one copy on her bedroom cupboard door, one on Ian's, and one on the back of the toilet door, where it would have a captive audience.

Ian looked at that piece of paper so many times it was photographically imprinted on his brain:

Only the pain of a hard workout can save the agony of defeat
The difference between ordinary and extra*ordinary is that little* extra *effort*
The greatest thing in life is doing what people say can't be done

Ian was always a dedicated trainer, but when Christina came back from America with the fire in her eyes, her little brother fired up too. It was always an encouragement having her with him on those cold early mornings as they headed off for the pool; but the biggest bonus was that Ian was starting to beat her in their training sets, so their rivalry became intense as they pushed each other to the limit. Christina trained with the boys from that point on, and she'd be damned if she was going to let Ian out-perform her: 'I look back now at some of the sets I did – it was amazing. Ian and I were so competitive. And we were closer than we'd ever been.'

≈

Ian was yet to experience his biggest growth spurt – that would come around the time he turned 14 – but it was close to his 13th birthday, in October 1995, that he finally measured up to a pencil mark he had etched on his bedroom wall. The mark was set at a height of six feet; you couldn't be an Olympic swimmer, Ian reckoned, unless you were at least six feet tall. So that was one hurdle cleared.

But this whole size thing was the main area of contention among those who followed the sport at junior level. There was a definite buzz about Ian Thorpe, and many were in awe of him. Others delighted in pronouncing that he wasn't going to last the distance: he was only dominant at age-group swimming because he was so *big*. There had been so many kids who were pre-eminent in their age group across the gamut of strokes, then disappeared in their early teens as if they'd been mere apparitions. Catriona Dixon, the *Telegraph* reporter, suffered ridicule from some of the hardened cognoscenti for showing such faith in an oversized brute of a boy, even though it was plain to see his technique was superb. Nothing really counted, they reckoned, until Open swimming and the finally level playing field.

No doubt about it: the attrition rate in swimming *is* heavy. Most of it is from overtraining too early, which often leads to mental and physical exhaustion: not a problem for Ian. A lot comes from kids realising belatedly that they were never really given a choice, their own enjoyment never considered in the scheme of things: not a problem for Ian. Sometimes a swimming prodigy is simply much bigger than his early opponents and never gets to develop his stroke efficiency, so as time goes by he comes back to the field: not a problem for Ian.

And sometimes it's a case where a kid has everything going for him, then comes face to face with a coach he just can't get on with. When he came into the national squad just before turning 13, this could have been a very big problem for Ian, because he would be leaving behind what was familiar – the level-headed, gentle, nurturing approaches of Chris Myers and, before him, Jenni Ashpole – and linking up full-time with a coach whose personal style could hardly have been more different.

6

A FORMIDABLE CAPACITY TO INTIMIDATE

THERE HAS ALWAYS BEEN A FEELING around swimming circles that because of Ian's personal attributes, mental and physical, *anyone* could have coached him to great success. The consensus was that when Ian Thorpe walked into the Doug Frost Swim School in 1990, it was the crusty old coach rather than the raw youngster who got lucky. Apart from Frost's loyal mates within the old-school coaching fraternity, you'd be hard-pressed to find anyone who doesn't hold that view today.

Don Talbot, legendary head coach of the Australian team from 1989 to 2001, would surely have more authority on this subject than anyone. In his autobiography, *Talbot – Nothing But The Best*, he concludes: 'Ian was the making of Doug Frost. That's the way it is in sport. I think all athletes make their coaches, rather than the other way around. I think also that coaches who think it *is* the other way around are kidding themselves.'

Talbot never pulled a punch in his life. But in any case, coaches in individual sports have always had to face down an army of doubters.

After all, it's obvious to anyone that a mob of extravagantly gifted individuals still has to be given plenty of direction to become a champion football team. But when someone like Ian Thorpe turns up – a *natural* in every sense of the word – shouldn't a battling suburban swimming coach just sink politely to his knees and thank the Lord for his providence?

Doug Frost doesn't think so. He'd be the last person to downplay his own role in Ian's success, and he finds the whole idea deeply offensive. (When Michael Klim observed in 2002 that his mum could probably coach Ian Thorpe, Frost was furious with Klim, and still hasn't forgiven him.) Reflecting on his contribution today, Doug can point to Ian's supremely efficient style and contrast it with, say, that of Grant Hackett – and as he proudly observes, 'There is no comparison.' He can also point out that all the knowledge about swimming technique that Ian gleaned from Chris Myers and Jenni Ashpole had been derived, ultimately, from Doug Frost himself, since he'd originally coached both of them to national level. Frost had in fact hired them for his swim school because they were his protégés, they understood exactly his views on stroke development, and they could be relied upon to impart them without any argument.

It's much more difficult to put a value on Frost's contribution to Ian's later development as a swimmer: the direction it took, and whether the training he subjected Ian to was ideal for that direction. There is *nothing* simple about this question: it involves a vast amount of sports science. Frost had some familiarity with most of that science. He would spend countless hours on the laptop fine-tuning programs for his elite swimmers. But as someone who'd spent several decades watching people make their way up and down a swimming pool, he felt he'd earned the right to rely a fair bit on basic observation, a stopwatch and a heart-rate reading – and he would defy anyone to argue with that. In fact, he would defy anyone to argue with him about anything.

Born in the central-western New South Wales town of Orange in 1943, Doug had to follow his father, who was a county council engineer, through seven different country towns as he tried to finish high school. By the time he reached Lithgow, west of Sydney, at the age of 15, he decided to give up and go to work in a small arms factory. As always, he'd joined the local swim club there, found himself taking on a squad in 1963, and realised he was good at it and enjoyed it. So he got into coaching boots and all, absorbing every morsel of information he could from prominent coaches including Forbes Carlile and Don Talbot. The shortish, nuggety, blond-haired former rugby league player who'd missed out on a tertiary education was determined to make a success of himself.

It was a strange time to be a professional swimming coach. Feared and despised by the stuffed-shirted amateurs who ran the sport, they were treated like vermin. No coach was even accredited by the Australian Swimming Union until the Perth Commonwealth Games of 1962, and it would be many years before Australian coaches were accorded the sort of status and respect they got as a matter of course in other countries. Simply, if you weren't a scrapper, if you weren't prepared to stand your ground, you had no business being a swimming coach. No doubt that history had a lot to do with the development of the old-school Aussie coaching archetype: a formidably tough, defensive, autocratic, barking dog of a bloke who'd take no prisoners and show no mercy.

By all accounts Doug Frost fitted the mould well enough. Don Talbot's assessment of him: 'Doug's strength is that he's very passionate and he wants to win. He just doesn't like losing . . . His temper is the main problem that he has to wrestle with. His anger gets in the way sometimes. He says things that are destructive and hurtful to people. He's fiery and he's hungry and he's passionate about swimmers and going fast. Those sorts of people tend to trample on others and a lot of people don't like that. But he's a winner, and Australia needs winners.'

Frost was well known for attacking pool staff for any perceived transgression, and in situations where you could either take a diplomatic or aggressive approach, he invariably chose the latter. He was highly argumentative, and on occasions when he realised he was wrong, he'd refuse to apologise. That wasn't his style. He liked to keep people on the wrong foot, always guessing as to where they stood with him. He had a formidable capacity to intimidate people, and wouldn't hesitate to unleash it.

However, nearly everyone who got to know him intimately would speak of a softer side, a warm-heartedness that was all too rarely put on display. He had a genuine concern for all his swimmers – as evidenced by his refusal to overtrain youngsters – but his lack of people skills mostly concealed it. He was also reputed to have mellowed a little over the years . . . but not very much.

And he did have to fight tooth and nail throughout those early days, from the time he left Lithgow late in 1965 in search of heated water, through an odyssey of appointments around Sydney's west, until he finally landed at Padstow in 1978 and was offered the lease on the little tiddler of a pool 12 months later. It might have been claustrophobic, but it was heated water – a scarce commodity in those days – and Frost would be running his own show. Close to ideal, he figured.

Doug immediately installed a program that would allow him to develop kids right through from learn-to-swim to elite national level. And he must have had a clue what he was doing, because the little Padstow establishment always punched way above its weight in the club pointscore at the Australian Open titles. But although he kept producing classy swimmers, such as Lisa Burnes (1978 Commonwealth Games swim team) and Wendy Bowie (1982 Comm Games team), he couldn't get a guernsey as an accredited coach on the Australian team. It became one of his driving passions, and in 1992, with 400 IM swimmer Phil Bryant, he was looking for a booked passage to the Barcelona Olympics. 'I should have been on that team, I can tell you – but I wasn't selected,' he reckons. 'They played favourites, and I wasn't in the inner circle. I had to pay my own way.'

Bryant was the best-performed swimming athlete in New South Wales in 1992, just missing the Olympic final, so Frost was automatically named NSW Coach of the Year. But the current system of automatic selection of a coach to the Australian team based on his swimmer's world ranking didn't come into force until the following year. Anyway, when Frost had both Bryant and Christina Thorpe in the 1995 Pan Pacs team, he should have been a certainty, he reckoned, under the rankings system. But there were dark and mysterious forces at work, according to Doug, and somehow the letter of the law was overlooked. 'After my non-selection that year, I just went in and tore strips off them. There were political selections, and they knew it. Some of the people that went weren't even coaching.'

The blast had an effect, and Doug was somewhat mollified when he was allowed to join Christina at her two altitude camps in the US that year – but he wanted the kudos of being on the Australian swimming team. And why not? It was the ultimate level of professional recognition. As it turned out, he'd have to wait until he could showcase an athlete whose performances and potential would brook no opposition.

In terms of both technique and conditioning, Frost was not a radical coach. But there are lots of things swim coaches disagree on, and one of the most important is body position. Frost would teach all his swimmers to try to tilt their bodies upward, rather than keeping horizontal to the water, by pushing their chins forward, allowing the water level to just cover their goggles, and sinking their hips a little, so as to maximise the efficiency of the kick. But it's a familiar story: as with the 45 degree stroke angle, most swimmers don't have enough power in their legs to be able to do this properly. They might well be better off in a horizontal position. Crucially, Frost believes that because Ian *can* incorporate that kicking power into his stroke, 'he can get into a position where he can *plane* a little – like a surfboard – riding the bow wave produced by his body'.

For the past three decades, swimmers have been encouraged to employ an inverted 'S' pattern on the downward pull stroke, sculling their hands in an outward, then inward, then outward sweep. The idea is to be always pulling against still rather than moving water, which naturally helps forward propulsion. It's an extension of Bernoulli's Principle, which explains how lift forces cause aeroplanes to rise off the ground. (Stick your hand out the window of a moving car, adjust the pitch of the hand so it rides up and down on the currents, and you've grasped Bernoulli's Principle.) But the more exaggerated the inverted S, the less efficient the stroke, because it takes longer.

What Ian does is minimise his S-stroke by using his great flexibility to exaggerate his body rotation, so that when he pulls his arm almost straight down the centreline of his body, he's actually pulling against still water and effectively carving an S pattern without wasting time or energy. At least two studies in the 1990s have shown that true 'naturals' all share a propensity for downplaying the S-stroke and using tremendous hip rotation. It seems to be part of what's now meant by 'an innate feel for the water'.

(There's more to being a natural than that. Ian doesn't necessarily subscribe to the view that he belongs in that category. But when you listen to him talk about the sensations he strives for when he swims – and then you *watch* him do it – it's impossible to doubt it. P.H. Mullen described the true natural most eloquently in his superb book *Gold in the Water*: 'Natural swimmers . . . work intuitively with the medium instead of against it. They form a relationship with the water and instinctively adjust every part of their bodies – hips, elbows, shoulders, head – to reduce drag and move forward more efficiently. The changes are minute and often indiscernible: a subtly altered hand pitch, a few extra degrees of hip rotation, an invisible tempo change to the kicking. It takes years of refinement and practice, but on a cellular level, a natural swimmer seems to know how to manage this, just as a natural musician can adapt to a new instrument.')

On top of that, there's Ian's extraordinary kick. Only Alex Popov, the great Russian freestyle sprinter, has comparable kicking strength. If you listen to race commentators, you'd swear Ian was doing something entirely different from the rest of the swimmers when 'he's bringing in that big outboard motor now . . . Look out! . . . HERE HE COMES!' But that's not right.

Competitors in Ian's events will generally employ a six-beat kick – that is, six beats per two arm strokes – for most of the race. They might also have some sort of 'overdrive kick' – still referred to as a six-beat kick – and in Ian's case he can crank it up to eight beats, or even ten; and he's kicking deeper and harder by fully employing his powerful quads and hamstrings, hyperextending his knees and using the great flexibility in his ankles, as well as getting more thrust by virtue of the size of his feet. In other words, he's just doing it better than the other guys – and always has done. When he entered Frost's national squad, Ian was asked to grab a kickboard and make his way at full throttle down two laps of the 25-metre pool. He did it in just under 30 seconds. Doug, who was monitoring the performance on his stop-watch, raced over to Chris Myers and screamed: 'LOOK AT THIS, WILL YOU?' It was hard to believe.

All of this is pretty straightforward, although admittedly it's a vast oversimplification of the subject of swimming technique. But what's really difficult to come to grips with is the complex process of conditioning and preparing swimmers for their program of events. That's the real core business of coaching at elite level, and absolutely integral to the direction of Ian Thorpe's career. For the layman, anyway, it goes something like this . . .

Coaches know that the body produces energy in three ways:

1. The ATP (adenosine triphosphate) system, which is explosive energy existing in the body, good for only a few muscle contractions – only really relevant in swimming 50-metre sprints;
2. The anaerobic system (or lactic acid energy system), where glycogen in the muscle is the fuel, no oxygen is burned, and lactic acid is produced, which is what causes pain – mostly relevant in swimming through the shorter and middle-distance events; and
3. The aerobic system, where carbohydrate and fat are burned in the presence of oxygen – the main energy source for long-distance racing.

Coaches know that the body has limited stores of carbs, so the useful training limit is about two and a half hours. But because a swimmer's weight is supported by water, they can get away with doing it at least twice in one day, given sufficient rest – and so they do.

They know they have to train their athletes for power, using the anaerobic system, and endurance, using the aerobic system. Obviously depending on the event, they'll change their training emphasis. Science will tell them exactly how much each system contributes, simultaneously, during a given event. For instance, the 100 metres is 15 percent ATP, 50 percent anaerobic, and 35 percent aerobic; the 200 metres is a ratio of 10 to 30 to 60; and the 400 metres is 5 to 25 to 70.

Suppose they have the simplistic task of training their athlete for a single event. They will still recognise that if they have them swimming up and down the pool at one 'ideal' pace, they'll end up with the same effect you get in the gym if you never change your workout: stagnation. The body adapts and refuses to improve, so they have to continually challenge it by varying the workouts as much as possible. They do this by creating a whole lot of different levels of exertion, and giving them names – for instance 'A1', or aerobic 1, which is 50 to 70 beats below maximum heart rate; then A2 and A3, up to AT (anaerobic threshold) where, as the swimmer increases speed, the body switches into the anaerobic system, the lactic acid level (lactate) starts to soar, and the pain sets in; and then on to MVO_2, or maximum oxygen uptake, which is 20 beats below max right up to maximum heart-rate level: absolutely flat out.

Then they figure out what all these levels correspond to for their individual athlete. (For a superfit Ian Thorpe, max heart rate is 213 – and you don't hear of anything higher than that.) Then they work out what exercise set will produce the level they're looking for. For instance, if they're doing an A2 set, they're working at 40 to 50 beats below that athlete's max heart rate, which for a swimmer of Ian Thorpe's calibre might be maintained by a set of 10 × 200 metres freestyle at intervals of 2 minutes 30 seconds, holding a time of 2:10 for each 200 – in other words, 20 seconds of rest between repeats. That's what interval training is all about.

Throughout the process, they have three tools on hand to assess the athlete's performance: a stopwatch, a heart-rate reading taken from a monitor, and a lactate reading taken from a spot of blood (that is, when the boffins from the Institute of Sport turn up at the pool with their equipment). The heart rate tells them how hard the athlete worked to produce that time, and the lactate tells them how much it hurt to do it. Put them together and they've got an objective measure of the swimmer's fitness.

And then – this is the fun part – they collate all that information into a program, and that program will depend on what part of the yearly cycle they're in. For instance, leading into a big meet, Doug would put his middle-distance freestylers into a 'quality endurance cycle': a three-week 'aerobic' phase, followed by an 'adaptation week', followed by a three-week 'endurance' phase, followed by another adaptation week, followed by a three-week 'quality phase', and then into a three-week taper, where the workload is drastically reduced so as to produce a 'springboard' effect, catapulting the superfresh, superfit athlete into a glorious realm where they can produce their fastest times.

So now we get to the wheels within wheels. Just to take one example: the aerobic phase, which runs for 60 kilometres in the first week, then 70 in the second, then 80 by the third, is broken into all these different levels of exertion: an A2 session Monday morning, an MVO_2 in the afternoon, an A1 Tuesday morning, followed by an AT in the afternoon . . . and so on. Most, but not all, of the work in each session will be within the set heart-rate parameters.

And now, at last, we're ready for the fundamental question, the absolute bottom line of the whole thing: how the hell do you know how to mix and match all these different levels of work in order to get the best performance from your athlete? Even if you had only one event to train for, there's no computer program in the world that could tell you. Obviously every athlete is different. And when you're trying to prepare an elite athlete to swim across a broad spectrum of events – say, with Ian Thorpe, the 100, 200 and 400 freestyle – how would you even know where to begin to evaluate the overall effectiveness of what you're doing?

And that, of course, is the art of it – because it is *definitely* an art, not merely a science, especially in the 100-400 metre range, where all the energy systems are crossing over simultaneously. Doug Frost mightn't know much about art, but he knows what he likes in a swimmer: 'The whole point, in the end, of heart rate and lactate readings is to know what an athlete's maximum capabilities are. If you can kick the shit out of them one day, and then again the next, and then again the next . . . then you'll do that. But how long can they sustain that effort – for how many weeks or months? You've got to be very good at observation. It's all about the constant reproduction of training sets and structures, and it takes a long, long time – years of accumulated knowledge – to get to a point where you know what's the ideal mix for your individual athlete.' That's the kind of talk that'll always get you a seat at the bar at the crusty old bastards' coaching club, where it's probably not the done thing to admit that a lot of this stuff has got to be a mix of intelligent guesswork and an instinctive desire to cover all bases. In the final analysis, though, who can gainsay results? They always speak loudest.

Every coach has his forte, his area of greatest expertise, and Doug Frost's was middle-distance events. So too was Chris Myers', so Ian Thorpe's training was naturally tilted in that direction – and it so happened, fortuitously, that among young Ian's greatest attributes was the ability to withstand pain. Frost believed that 'the whole secret of middle-distance training is getting the athlete to maintain maximum tolerance of lactate throughout the race'. Lactate tolerance training is the most stressful type there is. You can only do it a maximum of three times a week, if you're careful, and it's the first thing any wavering athlete will try to avoid. These are the sessions that often end with the swimmer's body retching so violently in its desperate attempt to clear the built-up lactic acid that the veins in his neck will pop out like telephone cables. Ian has done this many times, and he can handle it. It's what coaches have traditionally referred to as 'a marvellous capacity for hard work'.

So, how was the 13-year-old Ian Thorpe going to handle Doug Frost? Obviously he'd had enough advance warning from Christina, who'd often been reduced to tears after being subjected to a humiliating public outburst from the coach – to the point where she'd actually wanted to quit. Frost never took swimmers aside for a private word. He did his bollocking of them in front of the whole squad, and Ian had witnessed plenty of this from the sidelines. So, naturally, he started carefully. He was, after all, still a kid.

It helped that Frost was not a 'motivator' in the mould of, say, Laurie Lawrence. Ranting and raving in a pre-race psych-up would have offended Ian's sense of logic, and directly contradicted his philosophy, which was to swim his own race regardless of what anyone else was doing. Frost didn't fully subscribe to Ian's approach but, at this point at least, there was no direct conflict, because the coach's objective was to train Ian in such a way that his swimmer would always be certain he was optimally prepared. Knowing that he could not possibly have done any more, Ian would then be in a perfect psychological state to reproduce what he'd done in training. Much of that training involved simulating the entire race program, so there was nothing left to chance. 'With a lot of athletes,' Frost observes, 'you get all this emotion coming into it, which clouds everything. Not with Ian.'

So the foundations of the relationship were fairly solid. And most of the time, with Doug dictating terms, Ian agreed with the direction anyway and so was happy enough to comply. On the occasions when he had an issue – such as Frost's insistence on getting racing experience at minor meets when Ian reckoned he was just too tired – he'd bow to the coach's experience. There was no point, he realised, in making a stand unless you were certain of your ground.

But in spite of his innate humility, Ian was also a very self-assured person; and as time went on, he became more and more prepared to take the boss on – especially if it was a training issue he felt strongly about, or if something was said that he found offensive. For instance, one of Doug's methods of keeping people on their toes was to make everyone start a whole set again if one swimmer had made a mistake. Ian thought it ridiculous, and said so numerous times. Older swimmers in the national squad never felt they could express their views to Doug in the way Ian did.

No doubt this was partly because of Ian's ever-increasing stature as a swimmer: it was natural that Frost wouldn't want to deliberately get him offside. As well, he had a great deal of respect for his young charge, because Ian was the most dedicated trainer he'd ever seen. He was always first in the pool, *never* missed a session, never gave less than 100 percent effort – so he was rarely in Frost's line of fire. And if Ian did want to put up an argument, you could be sure it wouldn't be some snivelling adolescent whine, but a well-reasoned position on a subject he felt passionate about. Its objective would always be to improve himself as a swimmer rather than to somehow avoid hard work.

Doug could respect that. But he sure as hell didn't *like* it – and he had to deal with it, because Ian was quite determined about what he believed was best for him. So there was plenty of confrontation in training, and on rare occasions even stand-up blues in front of the squad. It seemed to Ian that Doug was more concerned with the fact his authority was being questioned, rather than the actual content of the argument. Would he try to keep his cool? 'No – he'd always yell at me.' Was that hard for a young man to cop? 'Well, it was just what I'd always known of him – it was the way he coached.'

Although two people could hardly have been more opposite in temperament, for the most part, at least in the early years, they shared a kind of mateship. On pool deck, though, it was all business, and far from convivial. Ian was mature enough to derive a lot of enjoyment, primarily in the form of satisfaction, from a situation that was not about having fun. And Frost was at least capable of sensing when to pull in his horns.

An example was the issue of hypoxic training – 'lungbusters' as they're known – where the swimmer deliberately takes fewer breaths than normal to try to force his body to better utilise the oxygen it's getting. It sounds horrible, although it isn't actually that unpleasant, according to Ian, but he struggled to see any benefit in it. Rather than a useful training regimen, it seemed more like a party trick, a skill for showing off. 'I'd tell him to do it,' says Frost, 'and he dug in his toes a few times. He wouldn't do it properly. I did think it would help him, especially in his shorter events . . . but after a while, I decided to let it drop.'

You have to wonder whether he'd have been so compliant with anyone other than Ian Thorpe.

7

TEARS CAN DO NO JUSTICE

IT MIGHT NOT HAVE BEEN A PERFECT paradise at Padstow pool, but something about his very regimented lifestyle was agreeing with Ian, because he leapfrogged from a top-five primary student to numero uno in high school: Dux of Year 7. Ryan Barclay had this theory: 'I'd say it was because he was so disciplined and organised from his swimming training, and because high school is a much more independent scene, it gave him an edge. He just seemed to know how to handle things better.'

It didn't help him to organise his study, though, because he didn't actually study. Not as such. He found that if he absorbed things the right way in the classroom, he didn't have to go over them. For Ian, the right way was to use the fact that he was a highly visual person: 'If I read something, or saw it, then I could remember it. If you told me something, such as a phone number, I wouldn't remember it – but if I saw it written down, it would stick in my brain. The same with, say, a maths formula – and if I applied it a few times, I wouldn't have to force myself to retain it.'

People have likened this facility to a photographic memory. That's probably going way too far, but Ian was constantly surprised at how he seemed to be able to pull information out of nowhere. Very handy. It got him to the top of Year 8 as well.

Ian had the usual adolescent obsessions. He fell in and out of love with a swimmer called Jana. 'For weeks and weeks,' Ryan reckons, 'all I heard was Jana . . . Jana . . . Jana.' He had his entire bedroom – every inch of it, even inside the cupboards – festooned with posters of Jennie Garth, an actress in *Beverley Hills 90210*. He was a computer buff, but you'd have to climb over a mountain of dirty clothes and assorted junk to get to it. His room was a disaster. Even at this age, though, he had a particular interest in fashion, and was always asking Christina for advice on the subject.

His level of dominance in swimming meets just kept increasing as the benefits of hard training kicked in. Just before the start of Year 8, at the NSW State Age titles in January 1996, he won nine gold medals, broke state records in the 200 free, 400 free, 200 back, and 200 IM, and became the first swimmer in history to win a medal in every event at that level. Catriona Dixon told her readers Ian Thorpe had already achieved all his goals for the year; he was now going to set new ones – the main one being to break the Australian 13-year-old 200 freestyle record.

Just a fortnight later he was jetting across the Tasman Sea in an invitational team to compete in the New Zealand Age Championships. He found himself up against much older swimmers – the age-group categories were all different – but he still swam PBs and won medals. The buzz, though, was in getting his first passport, and staying in an actual hotel rather than being billeted, with team-mates who were up to 17 years old. He felt the heady onrush of maturity. Then the biggest thrill – being upgraded to business class on the way home. It was just a little taste – albeit an exquisite one – of where a boy from Milperra might find himself if he continued to work very hard and eat all his greens.

And then in early April came the Age Nationals at the Chandler pool in Brisbane – the most important meet of Ian's life thus far, because this time he'd be 13, not 12, and properly matched in age against the cream of Australia's young swimmers. He came second in the 50 free, won the 100-200-400 treble, got second in the 100 back and won the 200, placed fifth in the 100 breast and third in the 200, came third in the 100 fly, and won the 200 IM. (Doug Frost's tiny swim school finished fourth in the national pointscore, with Danielle Woods and Brooke Townsend also winning multiple medals.)

Ian's performance was an extraordinary feat by anyone's reckoning, but it was the margins of his victories that had people rocking in their seats. He swam the 200 free in 1:58.80. The second-placed time was 2:03.01. He swam the 400 in 4:10.74; second place was 4:18.43. The 200 IM he covered in 2:14.93; runner-up touched in 2:21.80. Both the 200 free and 200 IM were national and Australian All-comers records.

But it was the 400 freestyle and 200 backstroke swims that got him qualifying times for the Australian Championships at Homebush a couple of weeks later – that is, the Olympic Trials. In accordance with the Frost philosophy, Ian had to go along and swim, in theory at least, for a spot at the Atlanta Games. Of course, he was never any sort of chance – it was purely for the experience, although Ian regarded it more as a novelty and a bit of fun. His time of 4:11.96 in the 400 free put him in 23rd place. (A 15-year-old named Grant Hackett, from the Miami club in Queensland, swam in the final and placed seventh, almost 15 seconds quicker than Ian.) Three days later, Ian managed a 36th place in the 200 back.

For the young Thorpe it was weird watching everything happen in reverse. Instead of gaining an immediate advantage on the dive, and increasing his lead on each turn, as he'd always done at age level, it was exactly the opposite against the big guys. But he knew that his skills would progress in due course, and because nothing was expected of him, it was no big deal. Better than just sitting up in the stands watching his sister.

For Christina Thorpe, however, it was a very big deal: she had real prospects of making the Olympic team. It's impossible to overstate how important that was to her; it was her entire aspiration.

The swimming lifestyle was not some sort of investment made by parents in a gilt-edged future. There was no expected financial return on all those early morning rises, all those gruelling training kilometres, all those crippling costs. Even today, with the sport attracting big dollars from the corporate world, hardly anyone makes serious money out of swimming – perhaps only the top half-dozen in Australia, the most swimming-mad country on earth. In 1996, there would have been only one, possibly two – Kieren Perkins and to a much lesser extent Susie O'Neill – with a handful of others picking up some pocket-money. For the parents of swimming families it was simply a monumental and selfless investment in their children's happiness: a chance for them to experience the incomparable satisfaction of making the Olympic team.

And that's the whole crux of it: *making the team*. People outside swimming think of the Olympic Games as the ultimate pressure cooker – and maybe that's the case for the biggest stars of the sport, those who might expect to carry off a swag of medals. But for the majority of swimmers the real pressure comes at Trials, because to fail at Trials means you don't even get to dance on the big stage; you're not even in the picture. All that effort, all that sacrifice, becomes instantaneously null and void.

There are no second chances. First and second place-getters are bound for the Olympics, provided they meet the qualifying time. Third place stays home. And in swimming, it is axiomatic in the Australian and American teams that the biggest nightmare in the sport – the most soul-destroying prospect of all – is not, as you might expect, a fourth place at the Olympics, but a third place at Trials. As P.H. Mullen observes in *Gold in the Water*, competitors at these national championships experience joys so great they cannot be articulated, disappointments so profound that tears can do no justice.

Christina went into her first event, the 200 metres free, thinking that if she could swim really well she'd make the 4 × 200 relay team, and that would take all the pressure off her main events – the 400 free in a couple of days and her biggest chance, the 800 free, at the end of the program. It was a swim at the state age titles in January, where she'd come second in the 200 to Emma Johnson by just one-hundredth of a second, that gave her the firm belief there was a spot up for grabs on that relay team. But she'd have to perform at her very best to make it . . . and she did just the opposite. She was a full three seconds slower than she'd been in her January race. 'I put so much pressure on myself – because I knew it was going to be close. I forgot that I was going to swim for fun . . . I can't explain it . . . It's just that once you make that Australian Olympic team, your name's up there. *People know who you are . . .*'

Christina was distraught. She cried for the entire day. Margaret and Ken had to convince her to go back and swim the 'B' final that night; she wanted to give it away right then. For any swimmer, it's awfully hard to come back from a bad first-up performance. Ian was full of sympathy for his sister, but figured the best course was to steer clear of her while she came to terms with her disappointment. The pressure of Trials, he understood, could do terrible things.

Mum and Dad took her to McDonald's for dinner that night to try and introduce some cheer into proceedings, to try and remind her that it was all about enjoyment. She felt physically sick before the 400 two days later, but somehow got herself up to finish second, four and a half seconds behind Hayley Lewis. In the circumstances it was a great swim. However, Lewis had just missed the Olympic 'A' qualifying time, which meant she would still go to Atlanta, but the second place-getter would only go at the discretion of the selectors. More trauma.

Two more days passed, and by the time Christina got to the 800 heats, she had somehow pulled herself together, and swam easily, almost effortlessly, to qualify third-fastest behind Lewis and Stacey Gartrell. She wasn't even puffing when she emerged from the water. Kieren Perkins' coach, the venerable John Carew, advised her to swim the final with a smile on her face. But she froze on the blocks. Her nerves were shot; she felt she was swimming as hard as she could, but getting nowhere. Christina finished sixth, exhausted, in a time only a couple of seconds faster than her heat. It was a disaster. The howling in Doug Frost's old minibus on the way home, Chris Myers recalls, was 'absolutely gut-wrenching'.

Her last hope was a reprieve from the selectors in the 400 freestyle. Of the six borderline cases, three made the Olympic team, and three did not. Christina was among those who were told they wouldn't be going to Atlanta. She hadn't swum anywhere near her best times in any of her events. Even now, it's hard for her to talk about this: 'I can tell you – at the Olympic Trials, I cracked. I just couldn't handle the pressure – and that's the difference between Ian and me. I possibly had a very similar talent, but he had the mental ability and I didn't. I didn't acknowledge it was a mental thing at the time . . . but now, looking back, I can.'

Physically, Christina Thorpe was as tough as anybody. Attitudinally, she was even tougher. She trained harder than a lot of male distance swimmers who were in the national team. But emotionally, she was vulnerable. She was *still* her daddy's girl. Like her father, she worried too much; like his mother, Ian did not. 'I get up on the blocks,' Ian says, 'with the intention of swimming as hard as I can. But I just don't see any point in worrying about the outcome . . .'

It was that same Thorpe family schism that could be traced all the way back to Ken and his cricket bat and the infernally dispiriting *pressure* to succeed. Typically, though, Ken takes a wider perspective. Reflecting on the trauma of those Olympic Trials, he now says: 'People think it's all fun and games, but we've seen the disappointments as well as the highs with this whole thing . . . In hindsight, I think there's a bigger picture, and what happened with Christina has helped Ian to progress to where he is.'

≈

A piece of Ian Thorpe folklore says that he once asked his mother: 'If I break all nine records at the state titles, can I have the Monday off school?' This actually did happen. It was at the State Age Short Course meet at Homebush in early September, which meant Ian again had the age advantage of being able to swim as a 13-year-old, and those short course records were ripe for the plucking: 50 and 100 free, 50 and 100 back, 50 and 100 breast, 50 and 100 fly, and the 200 IM. (Ian tried the holiday trick a couple more times, successfully, until Margaret woke up and stopped gambling against her son's ability.) By this stage, at age level, it was just one clean-up after another. Ian wasn't going to lose any race other than breast-stroke (sometimes), and records were tumbling whenever he got wet.

But, as always, he'd just take things in his stride. There was never any fist-pumping jubilation, nor even anything like it. With each victory he would slip unobtrusively out of the pool, go quietly back to wherever he was sitting, and contemplate what he had to do in the next event. Obviously Ian recognised that these were significant accomplishments, but as he now reflects on it: 'If I was going to walk away from the sport, then I'd have been happy with those achievements. But since I had no intention of doing that, it wasn't the be-all and end-all. I felt I hadn't yet achieved what I was capable of.'

Even though Christina had missed the Big Show in Atlanta, she was still only 16, and the local papers started comparing the Thorpes to the famous Konrads kids, John and Ilsa, who'd rewritten the record books way back in the late 50s and early 60s. When the TV crews came calling for Ian, as they inevitably did around this time, everyone else was more amped up than the young champion himself.

Wide World of Sports reported that 'at six feet one, or 185 centimetres, and wearing size 15 shoes, Ian is an imposing 13-year-old . . . Doctors say he'll probably grow another 10 to 12 centimetres. [It turned out he grew by 11.] He's considered the fastest swimmer for his age in the world.' When the journalist canvassed the possibility of the Sydney Olympics, Ian replied carefully: 'I think about it a lot. I will be very young for a male to swim at Sydney – but if I'm good enough, I'd *love* to go.' He allowed himself a slight grin.

Doug Frost told the *Nightline* program: 'Some of his times are just amazing. *Freakish*. Someone said to me: "They're *scary*". I don't find them scary – I just think it's exciting.' Ian quietly stated: 'I'm still enjoying the sport, which is probably the most important thing. Like, I won't be doing it if I'm not enjoying it.' If he said it once, he said it a thousand times over the ensuing years. But he wasn't just reading from the Ken Thorpe songbook; you could see he meant every word. It was exactly as Margaret and Ken would have wanted.

8

IT ALL HAPPENED SO QUICKLY

IT'S A STRANGE PIECE OF HISTORY that New South Wales, the premier Australian state, was the last to get its own Institute of Sport. The Institute (NSWIS) finally opened late in 1996, and Ian was offered a scholarship in January 1997. It meant that Doug Frost could now take his elite squad to the Homebush pool, book a session with the NSWIS boffins, and tap into a whole lot of scientific backup that had long been available to athletes in other states: underwater cameras analysing stroke technique, lactate testing, physiotherapists, massage therapists and so on. All these specialised services were otherwise only accessible at the Australian Institute of Sport in Canberra (which you could only attend full-time at 17 after finishing high school), or at the various state and national training camps that were held from time to time throughout the year.

Actually, Frost found much of the testing needlessly repetitive, and never put a lot of emphasis on it – he generally thought it was disruptive, and preferred the eyeball approach. Lactate monitoring was somewhat useful, though, and the other support was there if he wanted it.

Doug may have been ambivalent about the science, but he was never in two minds about the $30 000 a year coughed up by Australian Swimming's high performance fund. It was a Don Talbot innovation, very helpful to Doug in defraying the costs of computers and travel to camps and such, and a real accolade for the veteran coach because only about a dozen of these grants were handed out each year, and only one would have gone to a minuscule set-up like the Doug Frost Swim School. It helped Ian get through what would otherwise have been difficult times.

≈

Shortly after he turned 14, Ian had his biggest growth spurt. He shot up from 185 to around 190 centimetres in a matter of a few months, and weighed in at 90 kilos. If he'd been merely 'imposing' as a 13-year-old, at 14 he was something like an adolescent version of the Incredible Hulk. And now that he was usually doing the full program of ten swim and three weights sessions each week, he was readying himself to be competitive with the sport's top guns.

It all happened so quickly, it was quite weird. One minute he was a (relatively) unknown kid, happily thrashing away on his PlayStation and getting all excited about every new toy, featuring once in a while in the local papers and on TV segments in which the odd squeak emanated from his breaking voice . . . and then, a few days before Christmas, at the Australian Short Course Championships in Melbourne (which were trials for the World Short Course titles in Gothenberg, Sweden), Ian amazed himself by qualifying second-fastest behind Australia's gun medley swimmer, Matt Dunn, in the 400 IM. He hadn't even pushed himself in the final freestyle leg because he knew he was going to qualify. It seemed anything was possible in the final – until he dived in and his goggles filled with water.

Ian can't swim with water in his goggles. It's something that harks back to the days when he had to swim with his head out of the water. He bombed out, finishing the final in a much slower time than his heat – but the worst thing was that everyone was consoling him afterwards because they thought he'd succumbed to the pressure. 'It's okay,' they were all saying. 'It was your first big final.' The hell it was okay.

He swallowed a bitter pill. Then, in January, he found himself hard on the heels of Atlanta Olympian Malcolm Allen in the NSW Open 400 free, in the process smashing the Australian All-comers 14-year-old record set by New Zealand's dual Olympic champ Danyon Loader back in 1990. Loader's time of 4:03.51 was annihilated by Thorpe's effort of 3:59.43. More importantly, though, Ian slashed eight seconds – *incredible!* – off his own PB in that race. All of a sudden he was somewhere in the frame when eyes were cast toward the selection trials for Australia's Pan Pacs team to compete in Fukuoka, Japan, in August. That's long course racing. The big time.

One headline-seeking tabloid journo turned up at the Thorpe home for an interview and, according to Ken, who was acting as a sort of chaperone, asked Ian no less than ten times whether he thought he was going to be better than Kieren Perkins. Ian played a straighter bat than he'd ever done on the cricket field, repeatedly informing the pressman that he always just tried to do the best he could, and didn't compare himself with other swimmers. Ken marvelled at his son's aplomb, while the scribe left without his headline.

And then came the Pan Pacific Trials, held in Adelaide in the middle of March. What happened here was to dramatically affect the course of Ian's swimming career. Because of the solid aerobic base he'd been given by Chris Myers and Doug Frost, Ian had always been stronger the greater the distance involved. (Typically, for example, he'd win a backstroke event over 100 metres by one second, and over 200 metres by three or four seconds.) The result was that his best two events now were the 400 IM (ranked number two in Australia, but this was a false ranking because a few of the top swimmers weren't included), and the 400 free, where his sensational NSW Open swim had him ranked number four in Australia.

Up until this time, it had been pretty much assumed that when it came to the crunch, Ian Thorpe would be a medley swimmer. That's what the bulk of his training was based around, that's where his greatest dominance had been throughout his competitive life, and it just seemed natural to take advantage of his tremendous versatility. Anyway, Ian swam in the heats of the 400 IM, qualifying fourth-fastest for the final, and the 400 free, qualifying third-fastest. He needed a top-three placing and a qualifying time to make the Pan Pacs team.

He looked at his times and studied the opposition. Fatefully, both Daniel Kowalski and Kieren Perkins were injured and out of the picture in the 400 free. Thorpe felt good about his freestyle stroke; even though he hadn't concentrated on it in training, it just seemed to be getting stronger. A couple of days earlier, he'd swum a fantastic PB in the 200 free final – by 2.5 seconds – to finish seventh and set another Australian age record. So he figured the 400 free was his best chance. 'If I'm going to make this team, it'll be in that event,' he told Frost. They took a gamble by pulling out of the 400 IM, the most gruelling event in all of swimming, the night before the freestyle final.

Fox Sports TV was covering the Pan Pacs Trials. John Konrads, the youngest man ever to make an Australian swimming team, commented: 'It'd be great to see Ian come down to 3:56, maybe even 3:55. I think it'd be great to have some new blood on the team.' Laurie Lawrence opined: 'That'd be a sensational race, but I don't think he can swim 3:55, John . . .'

Malcolm Allen was the fastest qualifier and strong favourite, but the young Grant Hackett led him by a body-length at the 350-metre turn. Ian had been quietly sitting in third place, some distance behind Allen, until the last lap – then suddenly seemed to come from nowhere to challenge for second place. Hackett was an easy winner in 'a boilover', as the race caller put it, with Thorpe closing so hard at the finish that Allen just held him out by a margin of 0.05 seconds. But it didn't matter. Ian had swum 3:53.44 – slashing another six seconds off his PB. He was *in the team*.

Twenty-three-year-old Malcolm Allen, who was famous mainly for keeping Kieren Perkins out of the 1996 Atlanta 400 metres race, swam faster in that final than he had at the Olympics, yet was well beaten by a 16-year-old and within a whisker of being overhauled by a 14-year-old. Hackett had bettered his own PB by a full five seconds. As far as swimming officials could tell, Ian's time was a new world age record. 'I am just astonished,' was the official quote from young Thorpe. But in a way, he knew it was coming. And when you analyse the massive resurgence of Australian men's swimming over the next few years, you could argue that the starting point of it all was that 400 metres freestyle final. Kieren Perkins' trail-blazing was critical, and Michael Klim's sprinting pivotal, but these young guns would form the backbone of successful Australian teams year after year. Duncan Armstrong, the great middle-distance swimmer who'd won gold and silver at the Seoul Olympics, summed up the race that heralded the arrival of a new era: 'I just can't get over it.'

Doug Frost couldn't get over it either. He was in shock. Ian's new world ranking of ninth in the 400 was enough to put his coach on the plane to Japan. After all those years of frustration and perceived injustice, Doug had been catapulted onto the Australian swimming team by a 14-year-old. And Ian was now the youngest-ever male member of an Australian team – Konrads had been 14 years and six months old when he made the squad for the 1956 Olympics, while Ian was one month younger than that. But before he could get the official stamp of approval, he had to submit to his first drug test. The novelty wore off long before he became the most tested athlete in world swimming.

Between that event and the Age Nationals, which followed just a fortnight later at Homebush, the nickname 'Thorpedo' got an airing a few times in the media, and after a while it caught on. It meant that Ian had definitely arrived in Australian sporting circles – you're nobody until you've got a recognised sobriquet, something much sexier than just plain 'Thorpey' – and although he despised it at the time, he eventually warmed to it.

Spectators at those Age Nationals would have been hard-pressed to come up with a more appropriate name, because the 'Thorpedo' blew the opposition completely out of the water, winning an unprecedented ten gold medals and two bronze, and setting six new Australian records. (Luckily, Pop Hathaway was right then in the process of building a massive trophy cabinet to house Ian and

Christina's collective booty. It took pride of place, and a lot of space, in the lounge-room at Milperra.)

Predictably, the minor medals were for the 100 and 200 breast-stroke, while the new records were for the 100 free, 100 back (twice), 200 back, 200 fly and 200 IM. Ian already held the 200 free, 400 free, and 400 IM marks, so outside of breast-stroke swimming, he'd just about rewritten the record book. And although he'd actually planned to peak with his taper at the Pan Pac Trials, he was *still* carving massive chunks out of his personal best times: over four seconds in the 200 fly, and almost a second in the 100 free. As an age-group swimmer, this meet was Ian's pièce de résistance. From time to time he'd return to age-group racing to tune up for the odd event, but he would never swim the program at Age Nationals again. Those who witnessed that meet in 1997 saw a remarkable piece of history.

Among them was a diminutive 45-year-old man of Greek extraction named David Flaskas, who ran a very small management company called Grand Slam International (GSI) at Milsons Point, next door to North Sydney. It was more of an event management outfit at the time, heavily involved in iron-man racing through an association with Uncle Tobys. But Flaskas, formerly a talented soccer player, had been on the fringes of athlete management, and was looking to expand his involvement in the lead-up to the Sydney Olympics. And he was a good mate of the affable and influential Australian Swimming media director, Ian Hanson. Hanson's family was closely linked with the Thorpe family via the friendship that had developed between Christina Thorpe and Brooke Hanson, Ian's daughter, when they'd been to Pan Pacs in 1995 and roomed together on the Mare Nostrum European grand prix tour after both missed out on the Atlanta Olympics.

By early 1997 Margaret and Ken were getting numerous letters from would-be managers of Ian Thorpe. Initially they asked Hanson if he'd be able to take charge of Ian's affairs, but that would have been impossible. Obviously they trusted his judgement, and so they put the question to him directly: 'Who do you think should manage our son?' Hanson was well aware the Thorpes would be horrified by any smarmy spruiker who fast-talked a big story and promised to treat Ian as a commodity. They didn't need to watch Tom Cruise playing Jerry Maguire at the movies to know there were plenty of those guys around.

David Flaskas was just about at the opposite end of the spectrum: a quietly spoken, unpretentious character who, Hanson believed, had a particular affinity with young people. Obviously the Thorpes needed someone who was canny enough to manage Ian's financial interests, but more importantly, someone who could deftly manoeuvre him through the matrix of problems his outsized talent would inevitably lead to. Given that Ian was very much an individual, it needed to be someone with considerable empathy and understanding. The media director had a strong hunch that, given the chance to not only manage but nurture a young athlete, his friend Dave would really shine. So on the last day of the Age Nationals, he introduced Flaskas to Ken and Margaret up in the grandstand at Homebush, and threw in a strong recommendation.

Margaret, Ian and Christina all made the trip over the Harbour Bridge the very next day, and spoke further with Flaskas at his office. A couple of other athlete managers based in the glitz-and-glam advertising heartland of North Sydney were also given the once-over. The first of these, according to Margaret, did a very fine impersonation of the original Jerry Maguire himself, while the second left her cold. The Thorpes had already decided in their own minds that Flaskas and GSI would be getting the nod. It was a radical sort of move, given that GSI wasn't actually managing any major athletes at the time, but the Thorpes would always go with their gut feeling and Dave Flaskas was their kind of guy.

However, there was no hurry on either side. Flaskas wasn't pushing, because that wasn't his style, while Ken and Margaret and Ian were content to let things bowl along. They didn't need an actual manager at that stage – there'd be plenty of time down the track to stitch together sponsorship deals, a consideration that was far from their minds. They just needed a worldly person to advise them on how to deal with the overwhelming media interest, which was already threatening to make their lives unbearable. It was driving them nuts trying to figure out whether or not to answer the phone. David put forward some strategies and generally lent a hand when asked.

For his part, Ian did as he'd always done: kept things close to home, trusted those he knew, and treated everyone else with caution. All these people ringing for interviews – were they swimming writers? Or gossip writers? Or what? Ian didn't want to talk to journalists when he had no idea how they were going to approach their stories. If they didn't know anything about swimming, and they didn't know him personally, he figured there wasn't much of an advantage in presenting them with his thoughts. He decided that wherever possible he'd express them through Catriona Dixon, 'because she'd been there, we'd formed a relationship, she knew what I was about and I trusted her'. That was very much the Thorpe way.

Catriona had several times been invited over to Ian's house, and on those occasions he'd always gone to the trouble of baking a cake or some biscuits. It was his way of showing appreciation for her faith in him, which had of course been vindicated in triplicate by now. One day she turned up at East Hills Boys High and sat next to Ian through all his classes. Apparently the then headmaster was keen on a bit of positive publicity, and this was a unique opportunity arising from her column in the *Telegraph*. Catriona, young and attractive, caused enough of a stir to have boys elbowing each other out of the way to sit near their friend Ian, who found it all very amusing.

Although the lads were all hot to lay some lines on her, she noticed there was never any attempt to peg Thorpe down. He had a particular air about him when dealing with people, she remembers, which was exceptionally mature without being at all arrogant – a difficult thing to pull off – and it seemed to protect him from the petty jealousies of classmates. 'Also, he had incredible support from all the teachers. And he'd become so big so fast, I believe it sort of took everyone by surprise.'

≈

There is, in a sense, something wrong with this picture. Ian *did* have the ability to present as a highly articulate and almost spookily mature 14-year-old, and he would consistently do just that in front of the cameras and in press interviews, so that was how he was always publicly portrayed. Any story on his personality would always lead with the 'M' word – oh so *mature* was he. And yes, he *was* generally reserved and respectful, carrying himself with a quiet dignity and doing everything to the best of his ability. But he was also *fun*. He did a hell of a lot of mucking around; and like any other adolescent boy, he enjoyed being, as he put it, 'a complete tool'.

He was a joker. He loved doing impersonations of movie characters – the more ridiculous, the better. And he was always playing the type of childish games that end in some sort of violent ritual. For instance, there's the one where he'd casually form a ring with his thumb and finger while involved in a conversation – and if you happened to look into the ring, as everyone does out of curiosity, he'd get to punch you, hard, on the arm. There were numerous variations which culminated in the same punishment. He'd been playing these sorts of games since early primary school – and he *still* does it, and other banal and idiotic stuff like it. Constantly. 'I've always got to be doing something silly,' he admits.

The biggest victim has been Christina. 'He doesn't know his own strength – one punch and you've got a dead arm,' she reckons. He's also got a running gag with her that involves a hideous gorilla mask that she's been petrified of since she was little. Margaret had kept it hidden away, but Ian found it when Christina was about 14, and every six months or so, he'd set the scene for maximum freak-out factor, sneak up with the mask on, and *frighten the living daylights out of her*. Sometimes she'd get to do it to him – it all depended on who got to hide the horrible thing last.

Just after Christina started dating her husband-to-be, David Williams, in late 1996, Ian arranged for David to stand in the bathroom with his camera while he dimmed the lights right down, put on the mask, and waited for her to emerge from the toilet. The resulting shot is a picture of sheer terror. 'It's my favourite photo,' Ian observes smugly.

Christina: 'I've got that mask hidden at my house now and he's *never* getting it back.'

Ian: 'The best thing is I know *exactly* where it is now – only she doesn't know that.'

So there's another side to Ian Thorpe, as you might have expected. He's rarely shown any of it to the public, partly because he seldom gets a decent platform for it, but primarily because he doesn't really mind having a serious, thoughtful image. (What did it matter, really, if people didn't know *everything* there was to know about him? Ian thought they already knew enough.) In those early teenage years he wasn't giving journos any real sniff of the alternative Thorpe. But in Year 9, he was at least prepared to divulge an obsession he and his best mates, Ryan Barclay and Nathan Page, were developing with the cultish movies of Adam Sandler, in particular *Billy Madison*.

Billy Madison is a classic piece of teen schlock about an indolent rich kid who's forced as an adult to return to school and pass through every grade from kindergarten to graduation – he gets only two weeks per school year – in order to inherit his father's business. There were no particular parallels in Ian's life. He just enjoyed a brand of humour so idiotic, you had to be amused by it. Ian was definitely no intellectual snob when it came to entertainment. He watched *Billy Madison* something like a hundred times, talked about it incessantly – and *still* laughs at it. 'A stupid movie like that, where you don't have to think, you only have to laugh – it makes you walk out feeling good.'

The Thorpedo's notoriety was not yet at a stage where he felt the need to hit the cinemas regularly, just to experience some personal space and be transported to another world for a few hours. That would come a little way down the track. But the *Billy Madison* thing, with all its attendant silliness – Catriona called him 'Billy' and his email address even started with 'billym' – was definitely a sort of release for him. It took him outside himself for a while, a skill that was to become really useful to Ian when, within a fairly short timeframe, the pressures in his life became a great deal more intense.

9

IN THE TEAM

MEMORIES ARE, OF COURSE, OFTEN clouded by the passage of time. Doug Frost's version of events at the Pan Pac Trials had him specifically targeting the 400 free as Thorpe's best chance of making the team, on account of the absence of Perkins and Kowalski. He'd identified it as a weak event. 'Credit is due to me,' he now says, 'for having the foresight to see that.'

Whether that's the case or not, fate had twice intervened – first with the goggles incident at the short course titles, then with the unexpected opportunity at the Pan Pac Trials. The result was that Ian was now concentrating the bulk of his training on middle-distance freestyle, purely because he'd claimed his spot on the Australian team in the 400 free. 'The IM and backstroke were probably the way we were initially going to go,' according to Frost. (And the training was to continue to move in the same direction, so that by early 1998 it was 95 percent freestyle and he was only doing the other strokes for a bit of cross-training.)

Of course, the ramifications for Ian's career were huge. His program at, say, the 2000 Olympics might have been entirely different. At the time he was 'more than happy' to go along with Doug's direction, because he was *in the team*. Psychologically, it wasn't difficult for him to progressively kiss the form strokes (back, fly and breast) goodbye, even though he'd had such great success with them: 'It was different to what I'd expected – but still, I was achieving what I'd always hoped for.'

Hindsight presents, for Ian, a slightly different picture. What if he'd not made it at Pan Pacs Trials, but had another crack at the Australian Championships in October 1997, which doubled as the trials for the 1998 World Championships? Possibly, with that bit of extra development, he'd have qualified in both the IM and freestyle events – and continued with the 200-400 freestyle double and the medley double to this day. Maybe it would've taken a little longer, but it was surely inevitable, given the scope of his abilities, and it would have opened up a vast range of mix-and-match possibilities which would have definitely included the 200 back and the 200 fly.

As it turned out, to expand on his 200 and 400 freestyle program at the Olympics, Ian had to add the 100 metres – a very difficult proposition, as we'll see, when the essence of your training is middle distance. No swimmer had ever won the 100-200-400 treble at world level. 'In retrospect,' Ian muses, 'maybe a program of 30 percent medley training at that stage would have been ideal . . .'

Doug Frost's view: 'You can't swim the program. To win at world level, you've got to be a specialist. Otherwise there'll always be someone better.' Of course, from a coach's viewpoint it's all about the extent of an athlete's talent: how thinly can you spread it and still be the best? Ultimately you've got to make a judgement, and you've got to stick with it. One thing Doug Frost didn't lack was the ability to make up his mind. And stick with it.

≈

Early in June, the *Australian* reported that 'the two youngest swimmers in the national team have struck serious snags in their preparation for the Pan Pacific Championships in Japan in August'. Apart from Ian

Thorpe, the other swimmer was Natasha Bowron, a tiny 15-year-old whose talent was almost as remarkable as Ian's. She'd appeared in newspaper features alongside him, shared awards with him, done all that – but she had an abdominal complaint that carried on interminably, and she was lost to the sport before she could even put an adult stamp on it. That was tragic.

Ian had been suffering appendicitis attacks for about 12 months, and they were getting worse. He didn't want to make any noise about it and jeopardise his spot in the team, and he didn't want to have the surgery and miss a whole slab of training. *Fitness lost is so hard to recover*. But it was just too dangerous not to in the end; his appendix could have burst. It turned out there was a method of performing the operation that would take a lot longer, but would allow a quicker recovery period: the surgeon cut along the lines of the muscle instead of directly across it. Ian was only out of the water for two weeks.

And when he got back in, he was determined to regain lost ground. Doug suggested they train three times a day through the school holidays. Ian jumped at the idea. The sessions were a bit shorter than on a normal 'double' day, but overall he covered a lot of extra kilometres. In a matter of a few weeks, he was back to full fitness. 'A lot of people,' Doug observed, 'would consider that extraordinary.' Ian never stopped surprising him.

Then, just before the Australian team was due to go into camp to begin its Pan Pacs campaign, Omega, the watchmakers, roped Thorpe into a one-off promotion of its products at the Homebush Aquatic Centre alongside the man who'd been his biggest hero for years – Alex Popov. One of NSW Swimming's heavies, Glenn Tasker, had been asked by Omega to nominate a young male swimmer, preferably Sydney-based, who'd be most likely to make a big noise at the Sydney Olympics. The promotional idea was a passing-of-the-baton concept from the established champion to the hot up-and-comer. (Surely it couldn't have been too difficult a choice for Tasker.) Anyway, Popov fronted the cameras to present Ian with Omega's latest-model sports watch with the inscription: *Every success for the Sydney 2000 Olympics – Alex Popov*.

It was a huge thrill for Ian – not only was he fraternising with the great man for the first time, but it was his first real sponsorship. Omega 'pledged its support over the next three years' at the press conference. What exactly this entailed was not made clear at the time, but there was a small financial component, and Omega, without ever really exploiting the Thorpe association, turned out to be as good as their word.

Of course, Catriona Dixon was attending this mediafest, and was struck by the contrast between the young man's behaviour and that of Popov, who'd long been sponsored by Omega but spent the whole press conference up the back ignoring proceedings and chatting with his wife. Ian was a model of corporate decorum, charming the assembled throng with his usual articulate performance. Popov obviously had a powerful distaste for the commercial aspects of the game.

After Ian's return from the team's orientation camp in Brisbane, where the chosen swimmers had gathered with the chosen coaches and administrators to meet and greet and fill out lots of forms and get their precious Australian team gear, there was the obligatory photographic session on the Thorpes' front lawn. The sight of Ian smiling in his brand new Australian Dolphins tracksuit brought back memories for Christina. She was going through a particularly hard time in the pool, having suffered two broken arms in quick succession at the end of 1996, and then a dislocated shoulder. It was a down year for her.

She was struggling at school, too, trying to do a special Year 12 program for athletes called 'Pathways', where the HSC subjects are split over two years to allow time for training. The timetables just weren't working out, and in the end she gave school away, never sitting for the final exams. She could always come back as a mature-age student, but her swimming career couldn't be put on hold – and she was absolutely determined to wear an Australian tracksuit again. She waved her brother goodbye with the traditional reminder: 'Have fun – and KICK THOSE LEGS!'

The next phase in an Australian team's campaign is the staging camp, which is held somewhere in the vicinity of the competition so the swimmers can adjust to the time zone and climate. Singapore was the choice, and the most notable happening was the traditional Rookie Night, where new members of the team were ordinarily subjected to some form of ritual humiliation for the amusement of the elders.

Half the team consisted of rookies – in a rebuilding period after the Atlanta Olympics, it was the youngest Dolphins outfit ever assembled – so they were divided into three groups of half a dozen each. Ian wasn't too keen on the idea of being a target, and neither were some of the others in his group, so they came up with the idea of turning the whole thing on its head. The elders would become the targets. They announced that they'd do a *Sale of the Century* quiz show. They already had a few bits of juicy gossip about various people, and they used them as currency to expand their knowledge: 'Tell us something about someone else, and we won't use this embarrassing little item we have on you.' Before long, they had the lowdown on *everyone* – swimmers, coaches, ancillary staff. They presented it all in the form of multiple choice questions, where two of the answers were somehow funny, and one was the awful truth.

'We didn't necessarily keep any of our promises,' Ian recalls, 'but we paid out equally on everyone.' And they skated pretty close to the line as well. 'Some of the things that got aired . . . I'd be a bit hesitant about them now.' But collectively they chanced their arm, and got away with it . . . just. Although Thorpe reckons it wasn't his idea alone, you can bet he was at the centre of it. It was in a sense his formal introduction to the team: what he was like, how he did things. And how he did things was, quite obviously, different.

The evening actually came to a bizarre end when the 'winner' of the quiz, backstroker Dyana Calub, was made to scull a glass full of used toothpaste that had been spat into by the other rookies as they passed it down the line. Someone had seen this stunt done at school and they wanted to work it into the act because they thought it would be worth a laugh. They dared Dyana to do it beforehand, and for some reason she agreed. Ian reckoned it was the most disgusting thing he'd ever seen. Rookie Calub was obviously a bit different, too.

The flight from Singapore to Japan included a Japanese menu, and Ian was keen to experiment – a habit that he's stuck with despite some dire experiences. When his meal arrived it seemed obvious that he had to open the sachet and mix whatever was in it with the seaweed pasta, so he bunged in all the green paste, stirred it up and took a mouthful. Until that moment, he knew nothing about wasabi. His mouth went into shock. He couldn't get out of his seat to grab some water because the trolley was in the way, so he threw down the nearest drink, an orange juice, which contained a preservative he's allergic to . . . then, realising what he was doing, sprayed it everywhere. All in all, not a successful meal. Ian couldn't at this stage view himself as an international sophisticate.

Even without that sort of trauma, swimmers don't get to have a lot of fun on economy flights. It's a comedy watching them try to get comfortable. Even if they're lucky enough to get an exit row with no seats in front to drive their knees into, they still have to sit one forward, one back, one forward across the row to fit their shoulders in. Sardines look to be more spaciously accommodated in a tin can. And under Don Talbot's strictly egalitarian team policy, *all* swimmers travelled economy, no matter what they might have been able to afford. On arrival at their destination, they could spend days getting treatment to iron out their crumpled bodies.

There was something about Japan that just grabbed Ian immediately: a sense of intrigue and fascination that has never waned. It was like another planet. Swimmers at major meets spend almost all their time either at the pool or cooped up in their hotel rooms recovering – heats were always in the morning, finals at night – but it was a one-hour bus trip from the hotel to the pool. Although Ian was largely preoccupied on the drive with a major English assignment he had to get done, he saw enough Japanese sights and sounds in Fukuoka, a port city on the southernmost island of Kyushu, to know that he wanted to come back and have a much closer look.

With money as tight as ever, Margaret was again the sole member of the family to witness Thorpe's debut swim for Australia. At Pan Pacs there were no qualification rules, so he chose to swim in the 200 free (as well as the 200 fly and the 400 IM), although of course his main mission was the race that got him there, the 400 free.

First up, in the 200 free, Ian was introduced by the Japanese announcer as 'Iron' Thorpe, a boost he probably didn't need to inspire him to yet again better his PB in the heat, this time by almost a second and a half, as he touched in 1:51.46 to take fourth place. Whatever the event, it seemed he couldn't get wet without hacking a big slice off his best time. Still, it wasn't quite enough to get him into the final, but did earn him a spot on the 4 × 200 freestyle relay team at the expense of Matt Dunn. He dashed off into the stands to give his mum a hug.

Only the eternally optimistic Don Talbot was a bit disappointed the following night when the team of Michael Klim, Grant Hackett, Ian van der Wal and Ian Thorpe just failed to pull off a shock win in the relay. They settled for silver behind the Americans, making Ian the youngest ever Pan Pac medallist. He'd matched strokes all the way with his American counterpart on the second leg, Tom Malchow, not realising Malchow was an Atlanta Olympic butterfly silver medallist. 'I had no idea who he was,' Ian said, innocently.

In the 400 freestyle Malcolm Allen was laid low with a virus, so the 17-year-old Hackett and the American Chad Carvin, who'd survived a suicide attempt to return to elite swimming, were the main opposition. Prior to the race Nicole Stevenson, the poolside commentator, asked Ian: 'I guess your plan is to try and take it out with Hackett and the American, then power home in the Thorpe tradition?'

'*The Thorpe tradition*?' Ian didn't really know he *had* a tradition – but he did have the approach he'd been sticking with for years, which was to draw a curtain over himself and swim as fast as possible from point to point, regardless of where anyone else happened to be. Logic decreed that this would mean always swimming the same way. Training analysis told him exactly how long he was capable of sustaining that final scorching sprint where he'd bring in the overdrive kick. Naturally, this was not a variable but a finite amount of time. Therefore he'd begin the sprint at precisely the point where he was *able* to begin it: no sooner, no later. 'That's the only way I go about it,' he mumbled to Nicole. Simple . . . primary school stuff, really.

That was exactly how it went. Hackett had a big lead at the 300 turn. Ian had dropped back to fifth at one stage, then powered over the final 100: '*Look at Thorpe – he's coming home like a scalded cat – let's see what he can do . . .*' What he did was improve his PB by *another* four seconds, down to 3:49.64, but Hackett had done exactly the same. His effort of 3:47.27 would have won gold at Atlanta. Carvin was out of the picture, somewhat shocked, as Ian Thorpe picked up another silver medal.

He had reduced his 400 time by an astonishing 20 seconds in a little over a year. Among opposition coaches who'd never before seen the young Australian phenom, minds were blown. No 14-year-old in history had gone anywhere near where Thorpe was at now. The two teenaged Australians were now ranked one and three in the world, with only the Italian Emiliano Brembilla separating them. The future of Australian swimming was suddenly looking even rosier, especially with the 20-year-old Michael Klim finally fulfilling his potential by winning the 100-200 freestyle double.

Back home two old stagers, Kieren Perkins (who'd sat out this meet to concentrate on getting fit for the World Championships) and the injured Daniel Kowalski, were hastily reassessing their positions. Hackett seemed to be closing on Perkins' cherished world record in the 400 metres, albeit with a good four seconds still to go, and was obviously going to be the man to beat in the 1500. Thorpe looked as though he could do anything.

There was never any doubt who was the greater prodigy. As far back as April, Hackett's own coach, Denis Cotterell, had rather dolefully observed: 'I'm not getting carried away because most of Grant's times will be obliterated by Ian Thorpe, and yet I don't have any doubts that Grant can create a good career for himself.' Hackett himself was even more direct: 'He makes me feel like an old man. This guy is a freak. Words can't explain what I think of him.'

Grant would certainly have meant no offence, but Ian had already developed a powerful aversion to the word 'freak'. It seemed to diminish all the work he'd done in training, especially when the f-word was linked to his now size 16 feet, which one TV commentator gauchely referred to as 'flippers'. He especially hated that.

In the week following Pan Pacs there were appearances on the *Today*

Show, *The 7.30 Report* and *A Current Affair*, with Ian taking his standard low-key approach while the reporters tried to wind him up. Oddly, *The 7.30 Report* stated: 'Ian's managers say sponsors have been told his swimming must come first.' He had no manager as such, outside the informal GSI association, and only the one minor sponsor, Omega – two if you count a tiny deal with the swim costume outfit TYR. Still, Doug Frost decided he might as well get on the front foot, telling the reporter: 'I just make it very clear that training is how he's going to be successful, and he's got to not forget that, and his sponsors should realise that.' To *Sydney Morning Herald* reporter Jacquelin Magnay he was even more direct: 'There is no way a manager will have control over Ian like some of the managers do with other swimmers . . . With Ian, *I* will keep control.'

It was time to sort out the management issue. Ian obviously had no qualms about it, because he'd told Nicole Stevenson in a poolside interview at Pan Pacs: 'I'm with Grand Slam.' Immediately after Ian and Margaret returned from Fukuoka, the association was crystallised over a baked dinner at the Thorpe home. While the two Ians, Hanson and Thorpe, continued to demolish the leg of lamb, Dave Flaskas and Ken had a quiet chat outside. They'd not really spoken since that first meeting at the pool. The two men spent some time working out whether they'd played soccer against each other, being of similar vintage. Both low-key personalities who shared simple tastes, they clicked from the beginning.

Naturally, Ken didn't go blathering on about the tragic twists and turns of his cricket career, but he made a few allusions – enough for David to understand clearly what he was about when he said: 'You know, Ian can walk away from this at any time, either if there's too much pressure or he's not enjoying it.'

For his own part, Flaskas openly questioned his small company's ability to deal with the phenomenon of Ian Thorpe, whom he knew had been approached by the legendary hypemaster and doyen of all celebrity agents, Harry M. Miller, before he'd even left for Japan. 'I didn't really promise anything, other than that I'd try to protect Ian as much as I could, and commercially do the very best I could, while guaranteeing to Ken that what I did wouldn't affect Ian's training or preparation.' Flaskas added that he understood swimmers had finite careers, he had great admiration for Ian and the family and what they'd achieved so far, and if at any time the Thorpes felt they could do better elsewhere, he wouldn't have a problem with that.

The two men agreed that the nature of their relationship would not be the same if they were to formalise things with a contract, so they called it an agreement and shook hands on it. Ken actually made the statement: 'My word is my bond.' But David already knew that.

A couple of weeks later Ian's first major sponsorship, with Qantas, was delivered. That was an auspicious start for GSI. So too was Flaskas' first meeting with Doug Frost, who pronounced: 'You and I are going to get along just fine as long as Ian doesn't ever miss a training session or turn up tired.'

David had no argument with that. In fact, he was so keen to ensure Ian's continued progress, he and Doug expanded on 'The Rules'. Ian would not fly anywhere interstate six weeks out from a major meet; between six and three weeks out, he might do a limited media or sponsor appearance if it wasn't too tiring; and from three weeks out, when he started into his taper, he would do nothing at all. Every potential sponsor would be made to understand The Rules, which were non-negotiable. In theory, it sounded tremendous.

10

THE HEALING POWER OF JOY

IT WAS A MEASURE OF IAN'S NEW-FOUND stature in the sport that he didn't get overexcited about sinking his opposition, including a less than fit Kieren Perkins, in the Qantas Skins event on the last day of August. He swam well, pocketed $3500 in prize money, and moved on – eyes cast toward the Australian Open meet in Brisbane in early October, which was hopefully to be the springboard into his first World Championships in Perth in January.

It was an odd year, 1997, with effectively two Australian Championships – the Pan Pac Trials in March, then these 'Worlds' Trials, as they're known, seven months later. Even though they lack a little in tradition, with the first of them held as recently as 1973, the Worlds are second only to the Olympics in importance among swimmers, with the Pan Pacs and then the Commonwealth Games a long way behind. So the month ahead was critical.

Ian put in a great preparation for the Worlds Trials – perhaps the best he's ever trained before or since. Frost had to restrain himself from shouting it out from the rooftops when reporters came to enquire about Ian's form. Then he got to the pool in Brisbane, and something odd happened. He didn't swim all that fast . . . not nearly as fast as he'd expected.

The first of his events, the 200 free, wasn't too bad. He actually lowered his PB by a little in the heat, and again, by over a second, in the final. He was down to a very respectable 1:50.07. But instead of carving a swathe through the field, he scraped in fourth behind Klim, Matt Dunn and Dan Kowalski. He hadn't nailed an individual swim in the 200, but at least he'd landed a possible slot in the promising 4x200 relay team.

Ian also swam in the 200 fly as a 'surprise' entrant, and again reduced his best time by a fraction. But in what he'd come to regard as his signature event, the 400 free, he couldn't reproduce his Pan Pacs swim and trailed Grant Hackett by three and a half seconds at the finish. He'd anticipated closing in on his rival, only to find the gap had suddenly widened by more than a second. And he just barely held out Kowalski by 0.29 seconds to take the second of the two positions available for the World Championships.

On one hand it was great to secure that spot, because it meant that the Thorpe-Hackett combination had clearly dethroned the old regime of Perkins-Kowalski. But at the same time it was baffling, because up until now, the equation had been so simple: *train hard, swim fast, train hard, swim faster*. Was it possible that he'd peaked *already*?

During the race Laurie Lawrence, the 'sideline eye' commentator, had meant to describe Hackett as the heir apparent to Perkins – only he pronounced it 'the hare apparent'. Oddly enough, that description fitted perfectly. Hackett had taken it out so hard in the first half of the race, he was on world record pace at the 250-metre mark, and it was difficult to imagine the tortoises finishing in the picture, regardless of how strongly they might sprint home. Grant told Lawrence in the post-race interview: 'I *love* racing and I *love* winning. It's the BEST.'

Just two days after those championships ended, on Ian's 15th birthday, Doug Frost took up a new post as head of the elite squad at the Sutherland Leisure Centre (SLC), on the southern outskirts of Sydney. It ought to have been a real boost for Ian's spirits – he'd be joining Doug at a first-class training facility with heated long course water, adjacent gym, and access any time to the scientific squadron from NSWIS. Christina, Danielle Woods and Brooke Townsend would also be coming across from the Padstow pool as part of the elite group, and teaming up with Thorpe's friend and room-mate at Pan Pacs, the fast-rising breast-stroker Simon Cowley, 1500 metres up-and-comer Craig Stevens and young sprinter Kirsten Thomson, who were already training at Sutherland. After three years of shuffling between Padstow and Homebush, the set-up seemed ideal.

But it was a longish drive from Milperra to Sutherland, with Christina now at the wheel – long enough for Ian to nurture a cloud of despondency. It wasn't just about one disappointing swim. He was really struggling: trying harder, getting tighter, going slower. Each morning as he heard the alarm kick in just after 4 am, there was no likelihood of him bouncing out of bed and wolfing down his breakfast; instead he'd have to force down a slice of toast and slouch towards the waiting car as Christina stewed in the driveway. He'd suddenly become irritated by the fact that it was *hard* to get out of bed at that ungodly hour, day after day, and swim somewhere between 75 and 100 kilometres every week. Slowly, inexorably, he felt his passion for the sport diminishing. He didn't know why.

Then, in mid-November, came the sudden, shocking news that Ian's close friend, Michael Williams, the younger brother of Christina's boyfriend David, had developed a disease that could kill him – very likely *would* kill him – in a matter of days. It was beyond belief. One day Michael was a stocky, round-faced but athletic young cyclist and bundle of raucous humour; the next he was learning that he had an incredibly aggressive cancerous disease called non-Hodgkin's lymphoma. The day after that, on 13 November, he was rushed to Sydney Children's Hospital at Randwick with his kidneys failing, a 3.6 kilogram tumour inside him, the cancer attacking his bone marrow, spine and brain. Nine days later, on his 12th birthday, he was wheeled out of intensive care.

When Ian saw him from the doorway of his hospital room, he was unconscious, just hanging on to life with the aid of a ventilator and a dialysis machine, a blood-filled tube dangling from his neck and another jammed down his throat, his mother Sylvia in attendance, sobbing. Ian couldn't go all the way to the bed. Gripped by nausea and revulsion, he clung to the wall.

They'd become friends late the previous year. The 11-year-old Michael and 14-year-old Ian sometimes tagged along with Christina and David when they went out together. It was an unusual arrangement, but David Williams was fond of his younger brother and didn't like leaving him at home. Ian, whose life seemed to be getting more serious by the week, just enjoyed the company of a kid he could muck around and be silly with. They'd hit the PlayStation in Ian's room for hours on end, or sit around babbling dialogue from *Billy Madison* at each other without missing a beat. In the scheme of the relationship, Michael was beyond being a friend and a fan; he lived and breathed Thorpe's performances in the pool.

Now, living and breathing were all he could do, and only with the help of high technology. Ian knew he should be going back to visit his friend, but it was just so hard to envisage getting through that door to confront the horror of it all. Virtually none of Michael's friends could face it either. Conscious, but with his mind clouded by morphine and nauseated by chemotherapy, Michael's spirit was slipping away.

One day, when he was in the city doing a sponsor promotion, Ian vanished from view, turned up at the hospital, and managed to cross the floor and look into Michael's dark, hollow eyes sunk deep into his steroid-swollen face. He had no hair, no eyebrows, no eyelashes, no voice. Ian swapped horror for humour, as he knew Michael would have done, and called his mate 'Uncle Fester'. The kid managed, somehow, to smile. Ian resolved to do all he could to help Michael back to life.

Not that this would be easy. Michael was riddled with lumbar punctures delivering the chemotherapy to his spine; his arms were bruised up and down by needles, his mouth was ulcerated, his hair falling out in clumps, his appetite nonexistent. The only evidence of his being alive was the constant pain. In his loneliness and despair, he told his mother that he wanted to die.

But then Ian started turning up from time to time – with a new video they could watch together, or a PlayStation game, or an autographed poster or T-shirt from someone famous whose path Ian had crossed. Slowly, falteringly, young Michael found his will to live returning. Ian had touched a switch inside him that no-one else could find. One day he got out of bed, stood upright, and for the umpteenth time compared the size of his foot with Ian's. It was the one time Thorpe wouldn't have minded being called a freak.

Shortly afterwards, Ian began to enter other rooms in the cancer ward and talk to other children. He got to know many by their first names, but tried not to form such strong attachments that he'd be gutted if he were to walk in and find an empty bed. The whole experience of what he saw was transforming for him. He'd been living in what's known as a 'liminal period' – the transitional state of uncertainty and doubt that accompanies any major change. It's a state recognised across all cultures, usually culminating in some sort of rite of passage. For Ian it was a passage to a place where he was strangely relaxed, yet suffused with energy, as he entered the pool in the predawn light. Somehow the exchange of wills – the will to live, the will to swim – between himself and Michael was complete.

The insight needed to describe these changes accurately will often come much later. It was just prior to the 2000 Olympics that Ian reflected with maturity on the subject in a profoundly moving article by American *Sports Illustrated* writer Gary Smith, who quoted him saying: 'I came to realise what was wrong – that my talent was a gift, and that I'd started questioning it, expecting too much of it. I'd almost gotten greedy, instead of being grateful for it. What I saw because of Michael was how precious life is, how important it is to love what you do, every day. It changed my life. It opened my eyes to the world. When I started feeling pain in workouts, I'd start thinking, "This is *nothing*. Michael's feeling much more. There are plenty of people feeling much more".'

Now Ian was the one trying to gee his sister up for training. He'd get her to play games with him on the way to the pool – spotting BMWs and Hondas and adding up the points for each one – to take her mind off the situation. Christina had really suffered through Michael's crisis, which was far from over. She'd never been so close to the prospect of death before, and of course, neither had Ian. His new-found strength was passed on to her, and their friendship became ever closer. As for Michael, he actually found himself looking forward to something, for the first time in his drug-addled memory. His mate, his special buddy, Ian Thorpe, was going to swim for Australia at the World Championships. And Ian could not have been more ready for it.

≈

Michael Klim won the 200 freestyle final to become Australia's first world champion in 1998, holding off Massi Rosolino of Italy and a Dutchman who'd imported more vowels into the country than any other athlete – Pieter van den Hoogenband. Klim was clearly the man to head up Australia's 4 × 200 team; the Aussie tactic in relays was now for the fastest man to lead off, rather than swim the anchor leg, in order to get his team into clean water.

But the other spots were up for grabs. With Kowalski, Dunn, Hackett and Thorpe looking for the final three places, it came down to times swum in the heat. Ian was definitely the outsider, but his split time of 1:48.85 in the morning was very quick, and even allowing a 0.7 second advantage for the flying start, it placed him in front of Dunn's career-best swim in the 200-metre event. He was IN – and with the team ranked number two behind the Americans, he had a great chance for a medal at World level.

It had at one stage been mooted that Ian should just be given a swim in the heat to 'blood' him for the big time – as if he needed to be shielded from the pressure of holding up his leg of a World Championship relay. For any other kid who'd just turned 15, fair enough, perhaps – but they didn't understand the Thorpe mentality. Of course he would be in a high state of arousal, and equally aware that he had a huge responsibility to perform for his team-mates. But he was not, and never had been, a worrier. In fact, he couldn't have been any more relaxed. He'd had a great time at the team's ten-day staging camp at a

Perth naval base. Then he was assigned to a four-man room in the Dolphins' beachside hotel with his mate Simon Cowley, Grant Hackett, whom he knew quite well already, and Michael Klim. The four of them had been to Fukuoka together, and now they were all bunking in the same space, they found themselves having so much fun it was ridiculous.

Hackett, son of a Gold Coast policeman and younger brother of an iron man, was the quintessential knockabout Aussie bloke. He was so laid back, according to swimming writer Nicole Jeffrey, that she once saw him fall asleep on a mat between interviews – something she reckoned Ian Thorpe would never have done. 'Hacky doesn't give a shit how he's seen,' says Catriona Dixon. 'That's what makes him so special.' But like Ian, he could reel off information, especially numbers, with amazing accuracy. He was smart.

So too was Michael Klim, but he was much more intense, more driven, the son of a Polish immigrant, Wojtek, who was very keen on instilling discipline. Simon Cowley was a fine all-round sportsman, somewhat quiet but, again, very intelligent. Along with Ian, they shared an enormous appetite and talent for having a good time. While everyone else in the place was stressing out, Room 8 was jumping. When they weren't focused on destroying each other on the Nintendo, they were constantly mucking around, playing idiotic pranks and laughing their heads off. It was a hoot.

Michael was the most surprised about it. Acknowledged as the world's best male swimmer in 1997 by the recognised bible of the sport, *US Swimming World*, he'd come into these championships hoping to win no less than seven medals, in butterfly, freestyle and relay events. He figured he was in for some serious psyching sessions, as well as taking on the responsibility of leading the younger swimmers in the team by example. Instead he was confronted by a pack of hyenas in his room. He slipped straight into the vibe, and loved it. 'The amazing thing was that we hardly ever talked about the swimming,' he remembers. And it worked very nicely for him too, because in the end he took away seven medals, and four of them were gold.

≈

Head coach Don Talbot made a habit of delivering a speech every afternoon during major meets, just before the athletes boarded the bus to confront their various destinies in the finals. He'd get everyone together – swimmers, coaches, managers, masseurs, publicists – because he regarded everyone as a significant team member. Talbot could turn on a wellspring of passion and aggression that would inspire anyone who was relatively new on the scene. It wasn't stock standard footy coach fare – 'We're gonna kill these bastards' or whatever. It was a much more reasoned brand of motivational spiel. If you'd been around for three years or more you'd have exhausted the head coach's repertoire, but in those early days Ian found himself tapping into the energy and enthusiasm of the man.

Ken Thorpe couldn't help worrying. Seated up in one of the temporary grandstands at the 12 000-capacity outdoor Challenge Stadium – the biggest crowd ever assembled for a swim meet – he whispered to Margaret as the men's 4 × 200 relay team marched onto the pool deck: 'I hope he doesn't embarrass himself.' After all, he *was* just a boy, and this was by far the most important race of his life.

Klim got the Aussies off to a good lead. Hackett took over and looked to be cruising, until a surge by the American Josh Davis pulled him marginally in front at the 350-metre mark. Crucially, Grant grabbed back the lead with a great final turn and handed Ian a narrow advantage of half a body-length over the man he'd matched up against in Japan, Tom Malchow.

Ian made a perfect changeover and charged away from the American. By the time he was done, the Australians were three seconds in front, and two seconds under world record pace. Ian had swum a sensational 1:47.67 – precisely the same as the world champion Klim's time, although of course Ian had the flying start. Daniel Kowalski only had to swim in the low 1:49s to break the record.

Channel Seven expert caller Neil Brooks, a member of the once-lauded relay 'Mean Machine', was screaming into his mike: 'Remember, if they break the world record, there's a 15-year-old in this team – how special is *that*?' But with the massive lead Ian had secured, Daniel opted for a conservative changeover; it would have been stupid for him to break. They ended up missing the world mark by half a second. Still, they'd swum the second-fastest 4 × 200 in history, annihilated the field, and humiliated the Americans, who could only manage fifth place. It was the first time Australia had won the event at this level – Worlds or Olympics – since 1956.

As the swimmers huddled and cuddled, the Perth crowd went berserk. Ian panted a bit of self-deprecating nonsense into Linley Frame's mike at poolside, smiled gawkily, and headed for the warm-down pool, where he'd do some slow laps for 20 minutes to help his body burn off the accumulated lactic acid – standard practice for all swimmers. Later, when the foursome returned for the medal presentation, commentator Dennis Cometti observed: 'It's important when young people in any sport really feel as though they belong – it really is a turning point in their careers. I think Thorpe feels that he belongs tonight.'

Not *quite* true, because from a social point of view, Ian had felt a comfortable sense of belonging in the team from the beginning; but from a purely sporting perspective, Cometti's comment was on the money. The future of Australian freestyle swimming – Klim, Hackett and Thorpe – had joined forces in the 4 × 200 the previous year in Fukuoka, but they formed a far more potent partnership on this night, one that was to become, for the next few years, about as bankable as anything in world sport.

The athletes received a standing ovation as they got up onto the dais. The medal ceremony was a jingoistic riot of gold, silver and bronze-coloured Akubra-style hats and Australian flags and native wildflowers. Unselfconsciously, Ian mouthed the words of the national anthem as the flag flew at full mast. He may have felt on the verge of tears, as he often would at such times in the future, but he did not cry. He was not an unemotional person, but his personality tended to be more cerebral than most.

Up in the stands, though, Ken and Margaret were both teary-eyed. Ken was always vulnerable to a lump in the throat during any medal ceremony, but this was something else: his own son, representing his country as part of a team and beating the best in the world . . . suddenly it made everything they'd been through as a family seem infinitely worthwhile. And then, as the victorious Australians filed out of the stadium, the crowd noise became overwhelming. They were into that deafening slow-handclap-and-stomp thing, European-style – and they weren't going to stop anytime soon.

Catriona Dixon got an interview with Ken and Margaret, who'd pulled some strings via Ian Hanson to get through three or four heavy layers of security and embrace their son as he displayed his gold medal for the cameras. 'I can't describe the feeling,' Ken told Catriona, 'but I've never had anything like it before – it just cuts you up . . . We're just so happy for Ian and all the other boys in the team, including Matt.' Typical of Ken to mention, in amongst all the emotional talk of Ian's proud sister and grandparents and aunts and uncles and friends, the one guy who was not there because Ian had taken his spot on the team. Matt Dunn would no doubt have appreciated it.

Two evenings later, going into the 400 metres freestyle final, Ian appeared so calm as he sat behind the blocks that Neil Brooks was moved to exclaim, mock-seriously: 'Someone wake him up – he's got to swim the final!' At precisely that moment, on the other side of the continent, Michael Williams was glued to his television set, a massed bundle of nervous energy, babbling repeatedly: 'Hope he's gonna win, Mum. Hope he's gonna win.'

Thorpe went into the race ranked number four in the world. Number one was the Italian Emiliano Brembilla, then Hackett, then Massi Rosolino. Brembilla had gone as low as 3:45.96, while Ian's best was still the 3:49.64 he'd done at Pan Pacs. But Brembilla's coach had been putting about a story that he'd been ill recently; Hackett was swimming well, but his 200 relay time had been slower than Ian's; Rosolino had taken silver in the 200 – but the 15-year-old Australian was obviously on fire. Was there a chance for an individual gold?

Doug Frost wasn't having any of it, and actually snapped at some reporters who suggested the possibility. He reckoned, publicly, that Ian would do well at this level to get anywhere near the medals. Privately, he was looking at maybe a silver behind Hackett, and told Ian: 'Don't give him any water.' However, Ian wasn't going to chase after Grant under any circumstances. That would have contradicted his whole racing philosophy. As it was, Hackett, who knew exactly where the threat was coming from, took off at a murderous pace. He was so far ahead of the field by the start of the fourth lap, in an eight-lap event, Neil Brooks pronounced: 'I can't see anyone getting near him.'

Two laps later, the gap had widened. Brooks: 'Hackett's going to blow this away. It's a question of the time – it's going to be a ripper.' By the 300-metre mark the margin between Grant and Ian was 2.29 seconds, or more than two body-lengths – an impossible chase, it seemed. The others weren't even in the picture. But that was when Ian put the pedal down – at precisely the point he was able to. No sooner, no later. By the last turn it was down to 1.53 seconds – still, apparently, a forlorn hope. But Ian just kept on coming, and coming, relentless with the overdrive kick, his sprint stroke at full throttle, and Hackett was no longer swimming his own race, but thinking: '*Oh my God . . . here he comes.*'

There was nothing he could do about it. Grant Hackett led for every single stroke except the last. Ian touched him out by 0.15 of a second. Neil Brooks was confounded. Others among the commentary crew were gasping in disbelief. Only the greatest of performers can make genuine experts look like they know nothing. 'That,' said Brooks, somewhat ruefully, 'is one of the best tactical races I have ever seen.' In that respect, of course, he was entirely wrong. Ian was simply doing his thing, just as he'd always done, just as he'd trained himself to do. *His tactic was to have no tactic*. He had no idea where Hackett was at any time during the race, and only realised he'd won when he looked up at the scoreboard.

Ian's time was 3:46.29 – the fourth-fastest of all time, and well over three seconds better than he'd ever done. Naturally, in the excitement of it all, he explained to the media that he was amazed, astounded, shocked that he could swim so fast. At the post-race poolside interview with former world champion Linley Frame, Ian lost his composure for once. He just couldn't stop laughing. 'I really can't get over this,' he said. 'I don't think I'll believe it for a while.'

For athletes in the rush of euphoria these statements seem true at the time but, on reflection, Ian *did* know he was capable of swimming that fast. He knew it from his previous preparation, where he'd done everything right but disappointed himself at the Australian Open, and he also knew how much mental and spiritual strength he'd gained since then. 'I guess I was *surprised* by it,' he now muses. 'But I wasn't shocked.'

Grant Hackett was. But he swallowed his disappointment, handsomely praised his friend and rival, and began to get used to being the second-fastest middle-distance swimmer in the world.

Ken Thorpe was. Interviewed on the evening news, he said: 'Ian's astounded us again. That's all I can say, really.'

David Flaskas was. He'd watched the race on television back in Sydney, picked up his phone and dialled Ian Hanson's mobile. Hanson threw the phone to Ian in the warm-down pool as the TV cameras captured the moment. Flaskas knew he had his managerial work cut out from that day on.

Michael Williams wasn't. Even when Ian was four body-lengths behind Grant Hackett, literally out of the picture on his TV screen, his mother watched him pump his fist and bellow: 'GO, IAN! YOU CAN DO IT!' He might have been the only person on the planet who'd have believed it. When the nurses came running into the ward after hearing his screams, he could only croak: 'Ian won the World Championship! Mum, you gotta tell everybody on the ward!' Then he lapsed back into the healing power of joy, knowing that he was the special friend of the youngest male world swimming champion in history.

'That was when it all started,' Ken Thorpe observes. His son was no longer a prodigy, no longer a potential champion; he was now, on the back of a couple of days' swimming, an international star. No-one knew for sure – some questions will stump the most pedantic of stats men – but Ian might actually have been the youngest male world champion ever in a seriously contested adult sport.

Neither Ian Hanson nor Dave Flaskas could turn on their mobiles without looking at a message bank longer than their arms. Michael Klim's seven-medal haul may have been the story of the meet, along with the Chinese doping scandal (one Chinese swimmer had been arrested at the airport with 13 vials of muscle-building human growth hormone or hGH, and four others had tested positive for steroid masking agents), but there was no equivocation over Ian's 400-metre swim. Expert commentator and Olympic veteran Nicole Stevenson called it 'arguably the most significant achievement in Australian swimming's history'.

So it was appropriate that *Telegraph* journalist Wayne Smith sought comments from the only other Australians to win individual World Championship gold medals at the tender age of 15 – Steven Holland (1973, 1500 metres, Belgrade) and Tracey Wickham (1978, 400 and 800 freestyle, East Berlin). Holland, who'd been just six days older than Ian in Belgrade, was blunt: 'Welcome to adulthood. Your teenage days are gone for good. History. And there is nothing you can do about it.' If there was more than a trace of bitterness there, it would have been understandable. Australia's last hope for a single Olympic gold medal at Montreal in 1976, Holland was made to feel a failure when he could deliver only a bronze in the 1500 metres. He departed the sport a dejected figure.

There was nothing in Tracey Wickham's story to brighten Holland's prognosis. 'I wish I'd been a hell of a lot older when it happened,' she told Smith. 'There was so much pressure on me. The media and public were hanging gold medals around my neck long before Moscow.' In fact, she never even made it to those 1980 Olympics. Ostensibly she'd withdrawn from the team in protest against the Soviet invasion of Afghanistan; in reality, she was an emotional wreck, unable to sleep, and too scared to go out and be recognised by the starers and sneerers and sniggerers. One of the greatest female middle-distance swimming talents of all time, Wickham simply couldn't cope with the whole deal. She became, for some time, a sad recluse, and finally retired before she turned twenty.

There were plenty of other examples. Shane Gould: retired soon after winning five medals, three of them gold, at the 1972 Munich Olympics at 15, got married at 18, completely disappeared from view, and has only resurfaced in recent years, having finally come to terms with the maelstrom her life had been. Hayley Lewis: a superstar at 15 after the Commonwealth Games of 1990, struggled with fame, fought constantly with her coach, achieved nothing like what she was capable of at the Barcelona Olympics in 1992, then retired and came back repeatedly. She had no idea, in her mid-teen years, whether she wanted to be the best female swimmer in the world.

It's very difficult, obviously, to handle the full glare of the international spotlight when you really don't yet know who you are. Australia's former Olympic swim coach, Bill Sweetenham, advanced the theory that any swimmer who'd achieved phenomenal success a few years ahead of schedule would inevitably crash and burn into an early retirement. Ian was asked whether the Sweetenham theory would apply to him. 'It depends on how you handle it,' he replied.

Of course it does. Ian reckoned he had a very good idea of who he was. And he had every reason to think that his level-headed personality, combined with the sophisticated education programs conducted at the Australian Institute of Sport (AIS) for potential stars, the tremendous support of his family and friends, the experience of his coach and the protective attitude of his management would see him clear any of the hurdles he'd have to confront. At that stage, though, he had no idea how high some of them would be.

11

THE THORPE TRADITION

THE TWO WEEKS IMMEDIATELY FOLLOWING the Worlds in Perth were a baptism of fire for the new 400-metre freestyle champion. Initially he was overwhelmed by public support – thousands and thousands of faxes, letters and cards. As well, media commitments reduced his sleep time to 30 hours in the first five days – swimmers need much more than that – and at the same time he was competing at the Sydney World Cup meet just a couple of days after returning from Perth, then the NSW Open titles immediately after that. It was a ridiculous schedule, and unnecessary, because World Cup events weren't compulsory, and he only needed to post a qualifying time to swim in the Australian Championships. However, Doug insisted on it for race practice, and Ian didn't quite feel ready, at that point, to take him on. But he was mentally and physically exhausted.

At the World Cup meet, he tried to deal with his new celebrity status by giving autograph hunters signed photocopies of himself. The tactic was a total failure – everyone wanted something personal signed as well. At the same time, David Flaskas was trying to work out some sort of strategy for handling the queue of potential sponsors, all of whom were looking way beyond the upcoming Commonwealth Games and wanting to leverage themselves with Team Thorpe for Sydney 2000. As Flaskas accurately observed at the time: 'Ian is in the right sport at the right time and in the right country.' Of course the interest was welcome, but David didn't want to sign his client up for long-term arrangements on the spot. The Thorpes had never been money-grabbers; other things had to be considered. Events were spinning a bit too fast in all directions.

As well, Ian was copping unexpected criticism for his decision not to return to school. He'd announced straight after his gold medal swim that he would instead do Year 10 by a modified form of correspondence. The performance at the Worlds hadn't influenced him; he'd already made up his mind at the start of the year. He was frustrated by the fact that he couldn't be a top-level swimmer, training mostly twice a day for at least five hours as well as competing in minor and major events around the world, and still do the best he possibly could at school. In Year 9 he'd slipped from the top of the form to about five places down in most subjects, and much lower in maths. The perfectionist in him found that unacceptable.

Even at this stage he'd begun to percolate the idea that he wasn't going to finish high school. It wasn't firmly in place just yet – but he could never picture himself preparing for the HSC and training for the Sydney Olympics in the same year. How could anyone do both those things to the best of their ability? Ultimately he figured that if he could just get through Year 10 by correspondence, even though it was hardly ideal, then at least he'd have marks on the board and a School Certificate. He could then come back later, pick out exactly what he wanted to do, and achieve the results he wanted without having to compromise. He *hated* compromising. If he couldn't do something perfectly, he didn't want to do it at all.

Had Ken and Margaret opposed him, he'd have dug in his heels. But they didn't. They'd already faced down this question before with Christina: should they insist on the full education safety net, or allow their children free rein to pursue the dream? They'd consulted dozens of people from all walks of life, and always got the same answer: *go with the dream*. Education could always be revisited, but youth and athleticism could not. That was why Christina started 1998 working in a health food store and training like mad to make the Commonwealth Games team. If it was good enough for her, it would be likewise for her brother.

Ian was risking a lot, though. If everything somehow went off the rails, the boy who envisaged one day, post-swimming, becoming a diplomat, a doctor, a real estate entrepreneur, an economist, an anthropologist, and just about everything else would have had very little to fall back on. But he had faith in his ability, and he was utterly committed to the goal of being the best swimmer he could possibly be.

Doug Frost wasn't happy, but wisely decided to steer clear of the issue. Catriona Dixon was dismayed. She believed all the stability and normalcy in Ian's life would be gone. He already lived in an increasingly surreal atmosphere; surely losing the companionship of his friends at school could only make it more so.

Thorpe was often a procrastinator, but once he'd finally made up his mind about something, he was immovable. And of course, the thing about Ian was that he was *different*. Ever since primary school he'd always wanted to do things differently, and Catriona was reminded of that one day, shortly after the school year started, when she was invited out to the garage at Ian's place to check out his little experiment. He'd been given a long assignment to write on nutrition, but instead of doing that he decided to turn it into a practical experiment. He built two separate mazes out of Lego pieces, with several options for changing the maze patterns, then went down to the pet store and bought 20 mice. One diet consisted of Twisties and green cordial; the other was the recommended mouse food plus water. He timed all the animals' runs along the two mazes and kept meticulous records of their adaptability to the changing maze patterns. For the record, the mice on the Twisties and cordial diet outperformed the others by a street, which left Ian to make a complicated speech about blood sugar and insulin levels – but this was the kind of thing that gave him satisfaction.

Although he was good at it, the conventional approach to learning bored him.

Moving into the Thorpes' orbit at the time of the mice experiment was the Brisbane-based athlete management company International Quarterback (IQ). Dave Flaskas had been invited to the Milperra household for yet another baked dinner so that he could explain his decision to merge GSI with IQ. The idea was to combine the strengths of GSI on the corporate side and IQ on the athlete management side. Ian would still be personally managed by David, but his day-to-day schedule would be handled by IQ from Brisbane, with David staying in Sydney to concentrate on event management and corporate leveraging while still being kept in the loop on everything to do with Ian.

No doubt the Thorpes were scratching their heads at this turn of events. Flaskas had only been in charge of Ian's affairs for a few months, and now with his new client's star in spectacular ascendancy, he seemed to be passing the ball. Triangular management? Management by proxy? It must have seemed like a good idea at the time.

At the end of February 1998, the Thorpe family (with enthusiastic support from Doug Frost) put a bar on any further media attention for their son. One journalist later referred to it as 'Thorpe's Greta Garbo routine'. Ian had to get stuck into preparing for the Australian Championships in late April, which doubled as the Commonwealth Games Trials, and he had to get settled into the correspondence groove, which was mainly co-ordinated by his former water polo coach, Olga Sovo, with a bit of help from Doug Frost's assistant coach, Tracey Menzies.

But apart from all the novel pressures of stardom, Ian also had to deal with the ever-present and oppressive threat to the life of his friend Michael Williams. 'It was a strange time,' he told the *Sports Illustrated* writer Gary Smith. 'All the sponsors coming into my life, all the interviews and the limelight. It's wonderful – don't get me wrong – but I realised how little it meant. It gave me no power to help Michael. At the end of the day, fame counts for nothing.'

Or so he initially thought. But there had to be a way of making it count for something. Applying himself to that question, Ian came up with an answer. Michael's chemotherapy and radiation treatment dragged on for another six months, and every time there was a regression, Ian would be on hand to lift the kid's morale with something only he could deliver. He parlayed his fame into experiences Michael could never have dreamed of: the chance to meet people like the Waugh brothers, Ian Chappell, Dawn Fraser, David Campese, the Sydney Kings, the whole Australian swim team . . . and even Belinda Emmett, the soap star Michael had a crush on. Michael was presented with so much precious memorabilia by all these people, he could have opened a second-hand shop.

Ian even got the youngster into the locker room of the Sydney Swans Australian Rules football team. This adventure was almost catastrophic because Michael was so excited he couldn't bring himself to go home, even though his feet had turned completely black. He ended up being rushed back to the hospital, where a doctor told him that with his blood platelet count near zero, he'd almost died. But still, it was a memorable outing. And later, when the Williams family was snowed under with medical bills, Ian grabbed every piece of swimming memorabilia he could find and sold the lot at a fundraiser, collecting around $30 000.

This was all very personal, of course, because of Ian's relationship with Michael. But in the wider sense, Ian had always wanted to help other people, because he realised early on in his life that 'it's about feeling good because you make someone else feel good, rather than just satisfying your own desires'. And he was idealistic enough to believe everyone could be influenced to do the same: that everyone had an opportunity to change the world in a small way – 'and it should be because they *want* to do it'.

Swimming gave Thorpe the profile, he quickly realised, to make all kinds of contributions, financial and otherwise, to the world at large. And over the next few years he'd do that, in a lot of different ways. It began at this point with his support of the Children's Cancer Institute, which became the beneficiary of any unexpected financial windfall or bonus that came Ian's way outside his normal sponsorships. This was just an extension of the quality of magnanimity that he'd displayed as a youngster.

Michael's struggle against cancer was, Ian said, his primary source of inspiration. But it was more than just that. It was really the seed that eventually grew into a much greater principle than the simple notion that by doing good, you could make yourself feel good. Some years down the track, at the full flowering of his maturity, Ian could see this principle with absolute clarity: that even if he were to achieve his goal of becoming the best swimmer he could possibly be, and even if that were to make him one of the greatest swimmers in history, if he didn't *do something* with all the consequent fame and fortune – something constructive, something beneficial for others apart from himself – then he would really not have accomplished anything much.

≈

After all the dramatic events at the Worlds in Perth, followed by a succession of rinky-dink meets and very little rest, a lot of swimmers struggled to get themselves up for the Commonwealth Games Trials in Melbourne. Ian had been through an especially tough time – but the Comm Games, as they're known, didn't seem like such an anti-climax to him, since he'd never been to them before. He managed, in spite of everything, to put in a good preparation.

In fact, there was a lot of talk leading up to these Trials about what Ian might do in the 200 metres. He was training so well for the event that Frost even tabled the possibility of him breaking the Italian Giorgio Lamberti's world record of 1:46.69, which had stood, sometimes precariously, since 1989 – the oldest men's record in the book. Thorpe was actually faster through the water than Lamberti, but he still had a bit of work to do on his starts and turns. As soon as that was achieved, Frost reckoned, his swimmer would erase a record that was widely suspected of being drug-fuelled. Everyone in swimming wanted to see it go down.

Michael Klim had gone off the boil, apparently suffering an emotional let-down after his heroic efforts in Perth. Ian went into the final a warm favourite, with Klim way over in lane 7. But the clean-shaven Victorian almost stole the race from out there in the boonies. He was under world record pace at the 100-metre mark, still more than a body-length in front at the 150, and Ian had some serious work to do. 'Michael Klim dictating the terms . . .' observed race caller Ray Warren. 'But *look at Thorpe . . . effortlessly, you would think . . .* rounds up the world champion.'

By now the 'Thorpe tradition' – that final, withering burst of power with the full-throttle kick – had started to take on official status in sporting lore. It all seemed to happen in the final 20 metres this time, and Ian won by the easy margin of half a second, clocking in at 1:47.24. That beat his former PB by almost three seconds – about what he expected. This was no world record, but the time eclipsed Duncan Armstrong's ten-year-old Commonwealth record by a hundredth of a second, and would have taken Klim's World Championship gold medal away from him in Perth.

Knowing he didn't have Ian Thorpe's extraordinary back-end speed, Michael would try the same tactic again and again, every time they raced over 200 metres. 'I thought perhaps if I could put enough pressure on initially, it could put him off his pace and rhythm, and maybe take away from that final burst of his – but it never really worked.' How could it, when his opponent was swimming, as always, inside his curtain?

For Ian it wasn't just a matter of knowing that he could only sustain his sprint for a finite period. It was also a fact that, whether the distance was 200 or 400 metres, if he covered the pre-sprint part of the race any faster than the *exact* optimal speed, then he'd be too fatigued to produce the sprint properly. The whole objective was to be swimming with maximum efficiency, with perfect technique, in the dying stages of the race, while everyone else's form was deteriorating. To do that, Ian would increase the intensity of his work in the second half of the swim, counteracting the effects of lactic acid, so that the ideal would be a dead-even split – that is, covering the second half in exactly the same time as the first. The perfect swim came down, in a way, to a mathematical formula. (Some people would actually count strokes in a race, but Ian could see no value in that. It should be totally automatic. Ideally, during a race he would think of nothing at all.)

For Ian Thorpe, a dead-even split would logically mean that he'd covered the distance as fast as he possibly could. Obviously, anyone can produce an even or a negative split (that is, a faster second half than the first) if they go out slowly enough. But only the absolute cream of swimmers can even or negative-split a race when they've already gone out at a relatively high speed. Kieren Perkins didn't have Thorpe's back-end speed, so he'd have to go out at a heartbreaking pace; but then he had the ability to hold it up pretty well. Ian took the principle a step further, and then swam it that way consistently.

To be able to do that, you don't just have to be in superb physical condition. You have to have tremendous lactate tolerance. In the 200, Ian would start hurting at the 100-metre mark; in the 400, the pain would kick in at 300 metres. In either case, he would reliably charge over the top of world-class swimmers in the last 100 metres because he was very, very gritty in the face of pain.

The effect of what he was doing was comparable, in a way, to the breathtaking finishes that Carl Lewis used to produce on the track. It always appeared as if Lewis was hitting the afterburners over the last 20 metres of a 100-metre sprint, leaving his rivals for dead. In fact, film analysis showed he was actually *decelerating*, but at a much slower rate than the other guys. In other words, he was holding his form far better than they were. In swimming, as in athletics, a loss of form in the final stages of a race is catastrophic. (When Ian mowed down Grant Hackett so spectacularly in the 400 at the Worlds in Perth, Hackett said later that he'd 'stopped at a music store and picked up a piano'. Ian, by contrast, had produced a negative split.)

Three nights after his victory over Klim in the 200, Ian took possession of the 400 freestyle. Fiddling a bit with his normal race plan, he passed Hackett this time just after the 250-metre mark, kept a bit of an eye on him, and stayed a metre ahead for the rest of the race. It was significant that this little experiment didn't, for once, produce a new PB, while Ian said afterwards he was hurting like hell – far more than he had in Perth. Obviously, then, he'd be going back to the tried and true formula. You can't beat mathematics.

In between those two races, though, Ian swam for the first time at this level in the 100 freestyle. He wasn't even tipped to figure in the placings but, incredibly, he took a full second off his PB, touching in second place behind Klim in 50.36. It was almost certainly the fastest 100 free ever swum by a 15-year-old. And it made Doug Frost's eyes light up, because by now his aim with Ian was to train firstly for the 400, then come down to the 200, which was not such a big adjustment, and finally down to the 100.

To go in the other direction, Frost reckoned, was pointless. The only people who really gave a damn about the 1500 were Australians; the rest of the swimming world practically ignored it. More importantly, if you couldn't swim 100 and 200 free, you weren't going to get a shot at the 4 × 100 relay, the 4 × 200 relay, and the 4 × 100 medley relay. And if that was the case, you were never going to come away from a big meet – say, for instance, the Sydney Olympics – with a swag of medals. That was how Mark Spitz had bagged his legendary seven golds in Munich.

Well then, if that was the thinking, why wasn't Ian trained as a 100-200 freestyle swimmer in the first place? After all, it wasn't as if he was especially built for the 400 – his size and power would have fitted him in nicely with the sprinters – and it wasn't as if the 400 free was the blue-riband event in swimming. That had always been the 100 metres freestyle: no question about it. The only sensible answer is that Doug Frost was really a middle-distance coach, and so was Chris Myers, and they had simply taught Ian what they knew best.

It wasn't long, perhaps another year or so, before Ian began to believe this himself. What he says about it now is fairly unequivocal: 'Looking at all the data and everything I've learned about myself as a swimmer, if I'd started off under a different program I'd probably be a 100-200 swimmer, and never even have done the 400. I think that's what I'm more suited for.' But he doesn't criticise Doug for limiting his capacities as a swimmer: 'If you gave me a list of ten coaches I could have been with at the time, nine of them would have done the same thing with me. Australian coaches were all doing virtually the same programs, including Doug, which is why Australia has been lacking in certain areas for so many years. Most Australian coaches don't understand sprinting at all.'

≈

No-one in the Thorpe household questioned Christina's mental toughness after she bombed out at the Atlanta Olympic Trials. It was just a case of bad luck, the way things worked out. Having spent a total of eight months out of the water in 1997, she trained like a demon for these Comm Games Trials, putting her body through extreme stress. The sets she churned out at the Sutherland pool were way superior to any of her rivals'. She studied her motivational quotes on the bedroom cupboard. *You've done the hard work*, she told herself. *Now have fun.*

Still on the comeback trail, she mightn't have been quite as fit as she was back in 1996, her expectations not quite so high – but the field was wide open. The women's 400 and 800 free were weaker than they'd been in years. But Christina swam poorly, again, and couldn't crack it for a place. After the trauma she'd suffered at those Olympic Trials, she just couldn't get her act together in a race situation. There was always a mental barrier when she got up on those blocks, although she still didn't recognise it at the time. She just couldn't explain it.

Christina wasn't about to give up yet, though. This, she told herself, was only a stepping stone to her real goal: Sydney 2000. Ian spent a lot of time consoling her. Having already been through so much together in their young lives, they were as closely bonded as siblings could be. But he did still enjoy punching her on the arm – all the time, really hard.

12

'I FEEL LIKE QUITTING'

BY 1998 THERE WAS MONEY IN SWIMMING – fairly serious money – but only for the absolute elite. For that, the athletes and their minders could thank three people: Craig McLatchey, the dynamic young executive director of Australian Swimming who dragged the culture of the sport into the modern era, leaving a few elderly casualties behind along the way; head coach Don Talbot, who professionalised the swimmers' approach to their work with a set of rules that no other sport would have worn, such as the total ban on alcohol for all athletes throughout an entire meet; and media director Ian Hanson, who taught raw recruits how to do a passable impersonation of Kieren Perkins, the ultimate role model, every time a camera or microphone was waved anywhere near them. The princes and princesses of the pool were so clean, you could hear them squeak a mile away.

The next move was to fill up the calendar with events that would maximise sponsor exposure, such as the Telstra Grand Prix series, and made-for-TV fare like the Qantas Skins. With the great resurgence in

Australia's stocks after the Worlds (seven gold medals out of a total of 20, as opposed to two gold out of 12 at the Atlanta Olympics) and with the imminent arrival of Sydney 2000, sponsors were clambering to get on board. The TV networks were especially keen to turn the best of the swimmers into their own exclusive property. In the space of a decade, the sport of swimming was transformed.

In the middle of the Comm Games Trials, on 29 April, Catriona Dixon wrote that Ian was well on the way to joining Perkins, Susie O'Neill, Samantha Riley and Michael Klim at the top earnings level. She mentioned contracts already in place worth about $200 000, plus bonuses over the next three years. Ian told the *Australian*: 'I'm very surprised at how much money I can make. I can't believe how much swimming has progressed.' On the same day, Dave Flaskas informed the *Telegraph*: 'We're still talking to a few people, but basically the shop is shut. Ian has to concentrate on his preparation for the Commonwealth Games and then the Olympics.'

Obviously things weren't entirely rosy in the Thorpe camp. Flaskas had made that comment in response to a series of fairly intense phone calls from Ken Thorpe, who was upset that Ian's training was being disrupted as he tried to service all the requirements of his new sponsors. IQ had signed up both Channel Seven and Uncle Toby's on 1 April, adding to the existing arrangements with Qantas and Sydney Water, who'd come on board at the end of 1997. As well, there was a one-off, lucrative deal with the Australian Dairy Corporation. Fair enough – in making all these moves IQ was just doing its job. But when Westpac was added as a sponsor on 1 July, things got really difficult.

In theory Ian's contracts required him to make a total of about 50 personal appearances in a year. Even though four out of five of them were in Sydney, with all his other commitments to training and schoolwork and media appearances and responsibilities to Australian Swimming, plus the constant need for *sleep* . . . an older athlete might well have coped with the load, but for Ian it was just too much. Apparently he'd not fully understood that he was at liberty to knock back any appearances that conflicted with his training and racing schedule. In fact, athletes very rarely fulfilled all their sponsor requirements; it was typical of Ian, the perfectionist, to take everything literally. And being a polite and eager-to-please 15-year-old, it hadn't occurred to him to make his problems known to the people in Brisbane. He maintained cordial relations with IQ throughout; as far as they knew, he was perfectly happy. Meanwhile, the pressure continued to mount.

Then when it came to doing the actual appearances, Ian hated all the palaver he had to endure. He had no problem with any sponsor who was using an intelligent promotion to get real leverage out of his presence – he *liked* that idea – but most of this stuff, he reckoned, was just pointless. He felt like a cardboard cut-out. Nor was it a lot of fun dealing with boozed-up corporate types who'd sidle over and insist on comparing foot sizes with The Freak. It was all so galling and humiliating, so unbelievably *crap* – and nothing to do with the person Ian saw himself as being. Even the media at this time couldn't seem to get past the now size 16 'flippers', no matter how much Ian made clear his annoyance.

The triangular management system was also proving unwieldy, with the result that in the day-to-day running of things, Dave Flaskas was mostly left out of the loop, knowing very little about what was going on. Ian didn't go out of his way to enlighten him.

Ken and Margaret never knew the half of what Ian was going through either, because he didn't tell them. They knew only the mechanics of the situation – the bare facts. It was in Ian's nature to shield them, to a large extent, from his emotional life. He reckoned, as well, that he ought to have been capable of dealing with all these problems himself. *At the age of 15?* 'Yes. Age to me has always been just a number. I've never used it as an excuse for anything. I was at the first stage of gaining independence.' Also, this was basically about swimming, and there was a tacit agreement already in place that swimming was rarely, if ever, discussed in the Thorpe household. Ian would handle this his way.

At least there was some respite in early June when Ian went on his first trip to Europe on the Mare Nostrum tour. This was a series of grand prix events where the prix was anything but grand, but which provided good race practice in unfamiliar environments, so it was valuable experience for swimmers and coaches. That was why Australian Swimming footed the bills.

First stop was Monte Carlo, which Ian adored. The pool was fantastic, the atmosphere glamorous, the hotel a treat. There he won the 200-400 double, in the process meeting and beating the 200 free bronze medallist from the Perth Worlds, Pieter van den Hoogenband. They chatted a while and got on well. Ian had no particular premonitions about the likeable Dutchman.

It went downhill from there. The troupe moved on to what Ian figured must have been the least salubrious part of Barcelona. The food was inedible, the hotel a hovel. They had to go to Planet Hollywood or the Hard Rock Café to get anything they could swallow. Thorpe won the 200-400 double again. Last stop was Canet, a tiny town on the beach, virtually in the Pyrenees. It might have been a really pretty part of southern France, but it wasn't, and the pool was freezing. Same result, though: Thorpe swims, Thorpe wins. Ian's first Mare Nostrum tour was a clean sweep.

And, despite the various tribulations, it was fun. What 15-year-old wouldn't want to be gallivanting around the world with a bunch of mates at someone else's expense? Even so, the rules were fairly strict: just like at major meets, if you wanted to go anywhere outside the hotel you had to get approval from your personal coach and from a manager, and then sign yourself in and out. It was easier just to sneak out and back, 'especially when people were being unreasonable', according to Ian. At big-time events, though – anything from Comm Games up – Ian would never leave the hotel while the competition was on. There'd be time to look around later.

≈

In early July, *Sydney Morning Herald* columnist Peter FitzSimons offered a mock 'Share Market of Sport Report' to usher in the new financial year. Of Ian Thorpe he wrote: 'Buy big, buy early. This swimmer is no longer mere speccy stock, as it has already been realised that he is probably the Next Big Thing in sport. Yet he is still undervalued on current market rates.'

With his preparation for the Comm Games in Kuala Lumpur, Malaysia, now moving into the critical 'quality endurance cycle', the pressures on Ian were building in intensity. He was taking on a heavy six-event program at these Games: the 100, 200 and 400 free, the 4 × 100 and 4 × 200 relays, and, at the request of Don Talbot, a speculative shot at the 200 fly at the end of the meet.

The heat was turned up a few notches when Ian showed up for a 'Hot Bodies' photoshoot for *Cleo* magazine. The ladies who ran the adult women's glossy had adjudged Ian Thorpe to be among seven prominent Australians who sported perfect bodies. Decked out in just a pair of undies and a singlet, Ian was feeling decidedly uncomfortable with the required poses and the choice of camera angles. So determined was the photographer to capture the entire box and dice that Ian's first move was to ask his driver to come up and have a look at the shots.

In any case, because Ian was only 15, before the photos could be published they had to be sent to Ken and Margaret, who could not believe anyone would think this was appropriate exposure for an adolescent boy. In the end, after protests had been fired across *Cleo*'s bow, the shots were tastefully cropped just below the waistband. Ian wasn't so greatly perturbed, but Margaret, in particular, was furious.

Dave Flaskas realised by now that as far as Ian Thorpe's management was concerned, the triangular process he'd put in place with IQ was never going to work. They were doing their job diligently, but from far too great a distance. It was just an ill-conceived idea. The attempted merger between GSI and IQ was not gelling anyway. Again, that was neither party's fault. IQ was (and is) reputed to be a very good management company, as high-profile clients like Grant Hackett and John Eales would attest.

Ian Thorpe just wasn't like other athletes. He was *different*. It was only at this point that Dave Flaskas fully understood that himself. 'It took me a long time to realise,' he now reflects, 'that this was a very special boy – a boy who didn't crave adulation at all. If anything, he would shun it. In a lot of ways this whole adventure was a very personal journey for him. He knew he had a gift, and he wanted to see how good he could be – but he didn't have any real expectation of a return. Even then he had a clear vision of what he was about.'

≈

The year 1998 took a massive upturn for the Thorpe camp when Michael Williams was given the all-clear just before the Games and, to everyone's delight, Flaskas succeeded in getting the boy and his parents to Kuala Lumpur with the help of Ian's sponsor, Qantas, and Telstra. Michael, just a week after having the main chemotherapy tube removed from his chest, was still bald, white as a sheet of paper, and round-faced – the Malays couldn't stop photographing him, thinking him to be an angel or a ghost – but all the signs were that he was going to make it. It was an inspiration and thrill for everyone involved, not just Ian, to see the youngster up in the stands next to his mum and dad and Ken and Margaret, his head painted green and gold, his heart overflowing with gratitude.

Margaret was feeling a bit the same way after Ian presented her with something very special that he'd picked up at the team's staging camp in Singapore. Thorpe was already an inveterate shopper, loved bartering with the dodgy traders at Lucky Plaza, and remembered that he'd promised his mum as a little boy: 'One day I'm going to buy you a ring.' When the day arrived many years later, the ring would be a sizeable blue sapphire encrusted by diamonds.

Instead of replicating the 'gold medal room' arrangements of Perth, this time the officials put Ian in with the real old heads of the team – Phil Rogers, Chris Fydler, Matt Dunn and Perkins. All the talk was again about that 200 free world record. Ian genuinely figured he'd have to break it this time to beat Michael Klim, and he said so. But he wasn't all that confident of doing it, and as the race approached, he started to hose down expectations, saying he'd be happy just to swim a PB.

Gennadi Touretski, the enigmatic Russian guru who'd guided Alex Popov's stellar career and was now in charge of both Klim and the Australians' 4 × 200 relay team, observed: 'The 200 metres is the most difficult distance. It requires absolute technique and absolute control.

It is the oldest world record for that reason.' Touretski's view was that the 100 free was swum more on pure talent, but the country with the best 200-metre swimmers was the one with the most effective swimming program. Hence he placed a huge amount of stock on the Aussies finally breaking the 4 × 200 record, which had, ironically, been set by the Unified Team in Barcelona in 1992 under the direction of Gennadi Touretski. When he talked, people in swimming listened.

The same could be said of Duncan Armstrong, who'd only just missed the 200-400 double in Seoul. Armstrong agrees with Touretski: 'It's because you have to do so much more training – twice as much, or more, as the 50-100 metre guys. Those guys don't get a huge amount of respect in the training pool because they're out before the 200-400 swimmers do their main set. To swim the middle-distance events means a huge time investment for athletes and their coaches.'

There's an underlying culture in swimming that those who do the most work deserve the greatest rewards. Hence Armstrong dismisses the 50 free completely: 'It's a joke. Everyone thinks: "Come on – do a bit more work and you might win something worthwhile".' He concedes the 100 free is the blue-riband event in the general public's eyes, but reckons it's the middle-distance swimmers who are really the masters of the sport, because they need the most demanding mix of strength, stamina and courage. 'It's just a given that that's where the big boys are – because the distance guys come down and the speed guys go up, so it's a sort of meeting ground where you get your most even test of who really is a good swimmer. If there was a 300-metre race it would stop all argument – whoever wins that is the best swimmer in the world.'

If Ian felt that way at the time, being ranked number one in the world in the 200 and 400 would have restrained him from saying so. But he wouldn't dispute the idea that the 200 free, like the 400 metres on the track, is the most painful of the freestyle events. On the track you can watch 400-metre runners tying up over the final 50 metres or so, their massive leg muscles riddled with lactic acid as they wobble all over the place in a madcap dance to the death. The same sort of thing happens towards the end of the 200 freestyle. It's just not as easy to see.

In Kuala Lumpur, the 200 free turned out to be nothing like what Ian had envisaged. He led all the way, with Michael Klim not even posing a threat. But the scoreboard had malfunctioned, and it wasn't till the 150-metre mark that the splits finally registered, announcing that Ian was under world record pace by 0.12 seconds.

The hundreds of Aussies in the crowd at the Bukit Jalil pool, including Steve and Mark Waugh, were out of their seats and roaring, but in the end Ian missed the mark by one-hundredth of a second – the smallest margin recognised in the sport. There was a wry smile as he surfaced and looked at the scoreboard – 1:46.70. It wouldn't be the last time he'd be taunted by the clock, but it seemed Ian Thorpe's annexure of the 200 freestyle record was about as inevitable as gravity.

So was an Australian gold medal in the 4 × 200 relay, with Klim and Kowalski having taken silver and bronze in the individual race. It was purely a question of whether or not they could break the record. Ian was a bit disappointed in his lead-off swim of 1:47.48, but brilliant efforts by Kowalski and Klim, with a solid contribution from Matt Dunn, got them under the target by a bare 0.09 seconds. Ian Thorpe had become the youngest man ever to hold a world record. Grant Hackett was the luckless one this time, missing out in a swim-off for the fourth spot.

The 100 metres was notable for the fact that it was Ian's first swim over the distance at a major international meet. He nailed another PB, 50.21, and missed the bronze medal by a whisker. Ian told the press he had a strong desire to add the 100 to his regular program, and picked up another gold swimming the third leg in the 4 × 100m relay. That was gold medal number four. Earlier in the same evening, Ian had taken his first real crack at a record all the experts regarded as the best in the men's book: Kieren Perkins' 'unassailable' 400-metre mark of 3:43.80, set at the Rome World Championships in 1994. Perkins had slaughtered the strongest 400 field ever assembled in that race. It was reckoned by many to be the greatest individual swim in history. The great KP personally cherished it more than any other performance, and no-one since had come within two seconds of that standard.

Ian had ruled out any chance of a new record before the event . . .

but then, swimming just the way he'd trained to do, he found himself passing Hackett at 150 metres and charging all the way to the wall to touch in . . . 3:44.35, just over half a second outside his target. A record people thought would last for at least another decade, maybe even a generation, was suddenly carrying a death sentence.

Ian Thorpe, not yet a 16-year-old, 192 centimetres tall and the heaviest athlete in the team at 95 kilos, was now recognised as the hottest swimmer in the world. Don Talbot went further: 'I don't have a good enough vocabulary to describe his abilities. He may be the swimmer of the century . . . It's genetics gone bloody crazy.' Ian didn't appreciate Talbot's statement at all. The 'swimmer of the century' idea was ridiculously premature, he thought, and insulting to all those who'd achieved far more over their long careers, while the last comment sounded uncomfortably close to the f-word. When the national coach didn't seem to acknowledge how much hard work had gone into producing Ian Thorpe, how could he expect anyone else to?

≈

Ian was tired, although in reasonable physical shape, when he got back from Kuala Lumpur. But emotionally he was all over the place, realising that he was returning to face the same pressures and often humiliating rituals he'd left behind. With the effective breakdown of the GSI-IQ merger, Ian was no longer being managed in any real sense from Brisbane, and hadn't been since before the Comm Games began. He was a free-floating entity. It was up to Dave Flaskas to rationalise the whole set-up, and fast.

But one of the first things Ian had to endure on his return was the Trial School Certificate, which he'd had to defer because of the Games. Even though he always viewed the correspondence thing as just a means to an end, and even though he did pretty well studying in isolation, the inevitable drop in grades was hard to take. No-one ever said perfectionism was easy. It was always, of course, Ian's greatest strength – and his greatest weakness.

It didn't help that one of the anomalies in Australian swimming was the fact that the national short course titles were always held immediately after the major international event of the year. Ian would give the whole thing a miss in later years, even though it was supposed to be compulsory. At this stage, though, he didn't feel he had that sort of leeway, so he turned up in Perth just a week after the Comm Games had finished, and broke his first individual world record, in the 400 free. But this was only short course racing, and in the state of mind Ian was in, he couldn't even get all that excited.

So the public face of Ian Thorpe was a boy with unlimited potential (no tabloid could resist a headline like 'THE WORLD AT HIS FEET'), smiling and waving from one of a cavalcade of convertibles as 50 000-odd people lined the streets of Sydney and Melbourne to acknowledge the feats of their Commonwealth Games heroes. Not that he didn't appreciate the overwhelming support, as ecstatic devotees hurled confetti, streamers, flowers and phone numbers at him, but inside he felt distressed, knowing that things simply had to change, and so he made a phone call to Dave Flaskas and his exact words were: 'I feel like quitting.'

How close did you come to doing it? 'It's not a question you can answer. Either you do it or you don't do it. I didn't do it.' You can be certain, says Dave Flaskas, that it was close.

For Christina, though, the time had finally come. After missing the Commonwealth Games she swam on for a few months, but she had chronic shoulder problems by now, and then a severe back strain which was going to keep her sidelined for a couple of months. *Fitness lost is so hard to recover*. She was just so frustrated by it all. 'I put my faith in the Lord,' she remembers. 'I asked if I was making the right decision, and something said yes.'

Of course, Ken's great concern was that she'd come to regret it, having never really fulfilled her potential. But she didn't. It was the toughest of decisions, but the right one. She felt that a burden had been lifted from her shoulders. Ian was saddened because he knew exactly how hard she'd worked, but he didn't try to talk her out of it, knowing that would be pointless. There was nothing more personal, be believed, than a swimmer's decision to quit.

David Flaskas knew that too when he drove to the Thorpes' house one evening to finally sort things out over dinner. The GSI merger with IQ was about to be formally wound up. The Ian Thorpe conundrum was in no way a catalyst for the breakdown, but it was extremely convenient, because it meant David could put the question directly to Ian: who did he want to go with? Naturally, Ian chose to go with the Sydney-based outfit that he'd selected in the first place.

To their credit, IQ accepted this development without any dramas, and agreed to have the contract annulled. In a show of good faith, they walked away from a significant amount of money in commissions owed. Dave Flaskas then had some very delicate negotiating to do with the existing sponsors – basically, he told them they'd have to back off in terms of their expectations – but he worked through each contract and eventually found solutions that satisfied everyone. It took several months to sort everything out, and none of the companies left the fold.

After consulting with Ian he immediately introduced the GSI version of the 'New Deal'. Firstly, any new sponsor would have to comply strictly with Doug Frost's requirements – that is, 'The Rules'. Secondly, any new sponsor would somehow have to fit in with what Ian as a person was about (although, Flaskas jokingly says, a barrel full of money would never hurt their chances). Thirdly, and most importantly, how was the new sponsor going to make life any more *fun* for Ian Thorpe? After all, Ian took no short cuts and made no compromises to be the athlete he was. So when he didn't have his head submerged in water, Flaskas reckoned he ought to be enjoying himself as much as was humanly possible. Ian couldn't have agreed more.

The New Deal got Ian's life back on the rails, but it alone was not going to guarantee his survival as a swimming celebrity. After all, it was not as if Ian Thorpe was exempt from the pressures that had afflicted Holland, Wickham, Gould, Lewis, or any of the other prodigies of the sport. As far as media attention was concerned, Ian was certainly getting more, by this stage in his career, than any other Australian of comparable age.

The paper talk was already of a possible four gold at Sydney 2000 – in the 200 and 400 free, and the two freestyle relays – and in speculation beyond that, the name Spitz kept on cropping up. Was Ian

Thorpe going to reach his peak as the next Mark Spitz in Athens in 2004? Of course, the writers would always rein themselves in with the addendum that it was unfair to make such comparisons, like labelling a young batsman as the next Bradman. But still . . .

Fortunately for Ian, his singular goal in swimming – to become the very best he could be – precluded worrying about how he might compare with any other swimmer, past or present. He wasn't concerned with anyone else's expectations, only with whatever satisfaction he gained from his own performances. He couldn't influence how anyone else performed, so there was no point even *thinking* about the opposition, let alone trying to psyche them out with trash talk or whatever. All he wanted was to do better, each time he got into the pool, than he'd done before. Two words summed up his entire swimming philosophy: personal best.

That didn't mean, though, that he failed to appreciate the public's massive interest in him. If he chose to look at it negatively, it would have been *pressure*; but by looking at it positively, it became *support*. He enjoyed having that support. Besides, he was the one who was getting out of bed around 4 am, stumping up for the ten two-hour pool sessions (which often went for two and a half hours) plus five sessions of weights work and running every week; he knew better than anyone how much he was putting himself through, so his own expectations of himself were always far greater than other people's.

These were the principles that helped insulate Ian from the fate of so many other prodigious swimming talents. All those hours of churning up and down the pool had afforded him plenty of time for introspection. He'd applied his considerable intellect to the issues in front of him – and the result was a clear, simple understanding of what he was about. He never wavered from those principles – much to the chagrin of journalists, who were (naturally) always trying to get him to say something different. But why should he? Unlike Kieren Perkins, who'd traditionally done the scribes' work for them by putting a new spin on the same old question, Ian wouldn't bother. The Answer was The Answer – and if you'd been around a while, you could always anticipate it before you even asked the question. For example:

Question: 'Do you think you can win the 200-400 double at this meet?'

Answer: 'I'll be very happy as long as I can do a PB in both events.'

Question: 'Would you like to be known eventually as the greatest swimmer ever?'

Answer: 'I'm only concerned with my own performances, not with anyone else's.'

And so on. Mix and match the Thorpe maxims, and you had an answer for any question you could think of about swimming. It drove the journos nuts – especially because Ian would always appear animated and interested, and was scrupulously polite toward them, both in press conferences and in the 'mixed zone' after races, where they'd get their early quotes to meet deadlines. So they didn't even get to criticise him for his attitude. Over the years he developed a way of presenting his answers in a shiny package so that they *sounded* interesting, different, sometimes even revelatory – but when you opened up the box, it was always the same thing inside. That was exactly his intention.

On top of that, he always told the truth, so that nothing he said could ever come back to haunt him. Although some time down the track he'd not hesitate to address a controversial issue, such as doping, he was never silly enough to air any personal gripes in the media. If he had a problem with anyone – swimmer, coach, administrator, journalist, whoever – he'd always deal with it privately, one on one. And, most crucially, he decided very early on that there were certain things that he wasn't going to share with the rest of the world. He'd put all his cards on the table, and turn them all over – except one.

It was not a card that *60 Minutes* would have paid big bucks to see. Just stuff about how he interacted with family and friends, what he was really like as a person – how he lived, in a sense, his inner life. There was no problem talking about likes and dislikes in food, clothes, movies, music, whatever. But he saw no need to turn his entire personality into an open book. Keeping that one card face down, he knew, would be the key to maintaining his sanity, whatever the trappings of celebrity might bring.

It was also a means of dealing with his natural shyness. In fact, the persona he adopted at press conferences was purpose-built – not by some media trainer, as many people suspected, but by himself: 'In doing all these press conferences and interviews I was expected not to be shy, so my way of dealing with it was to become a character that I'm normally not. I still believed in the answers that I gave – but I was kind of doing it as someone else. I've got no problem admitting that.'

He doesn't like to admit, though, that he's not naturally relaxed about being in the public eye – unlike, say, a guy like Grant Hackett. The *Australian*'s swimming writer, Nicole Jeffrey, is closer to Ian than anyone reporting on the sport now, and has known him since he was a young boy. She says he does a very good impression of making himself look unstressed, 'but only because he's developed protocols to deal with everything. His coping method is to make everything formal – to put everything in boxes. When things are taken out of the boxes, then you see that he's not comfortable.'

This is hardly surprising, and hardly a criticism. Usually there's time for a swimmer, or any sportsperson, to develop a relationship of trust with the media before their fame erupts and suddenly everyone with a camera or microphone or tape recorder is thrusting it at them constantly. For his own protection, it was natural Ian had to find ways to keep some sort of distance. The thing he objects to is the idea that he consciously formulated a plan to do that – he reckons it just spontaneously developed – and that he would become anxious about having to improvise when things went off the rails. 'Obviously I prefer the protocols to be clearly defined,' he says. 'But when things are mixed up, I think I deal with them even better. I just don't like it that way.'

Most people could never understand, really, what it would be like to be recognised, and possibly impinged upon, by EVERY person they came across: everyone they knew, and everyone they didn't know. Life for Ian became a constant process of calculating the angles: *There's Nicole Jeffrey. I should say hello to her. But will she want an interview? I haven't got time. If I stop and talk, how many autographs does it look like I'll have to sign before I can get moving again*? And so on, and so on . . .

all the time. And every action, every utterance, would become the subject of somebody's judgement.

It's very hard for an adult celeb, even with the best of intentions, to deal with these constant predicaments; but what if you've just turned sixteen? Ian handled it mostly by dismissing the problem and getting on with doing what he had to do. No doubt that could make him seem aloof at times, but that was a price he couldn't avoid paying. In a different world he'd have said hello to everyone, every time; as it was, he tried as far as possible to recognise people, one way or another.

There was, too, the other side of the fame conundrum. There are so many things that most of us have to muddle our way through as we grow up; for a 16-year-old who's among the world's best swimmers, they're either taken care of by someone else, or they don't apply. For instance, Ian never had to go to a party and make small talk with people who didn't know who he was. Public skills can be nurtured in this environment, but emotional skills can be retarded. It *had* to affect him to some extent, because this was his reality, and he knew no other.

The sporting world is full of grown-up spoiled brats whose egos have soared into the stratosphere; how much harder, again, for a 16-year-old to avoid all of those pitfalls! It certainly helped, in Ian's case, that he really didn't see himself as anything special. He had a talent, but it was far from unique – only in the top ten percent among swimmers, he reckoned. He did nurture it with great care and attention, but the talent was a mere accident of birth, and the perfectionism an inbuilt characteristic. In a sense, he was all set up to succeed in his particular field, but that didn't make him better, he thought, than anyone else.

As far as friends and family were concerned, he never allowed fame to change him in the slightest. He was so good at ensuring he was never treated as anyone special that his closest friends – Simon Cowley, Kirsten Thomson, Craig Stevens, Danielle Woods and the rest of the crew from the Sutherland pool, and guys like Ryan Barclay and Nathan Page – would simply forget that he was famous. When they got organised to go to the movies or down to the mall to go shopping,

Ian was the one who had to remember that under some circumstances, things could get a bit unusual. He really liked that.

Maybe the most important thing in Ian's survival kit was the fact that he wasn't obsessed with swimming. It's one thing to be a perfectionist, another to be consumed by one pursuit at the expense of all else. That's what destroyed Steven Holland. He'd gone to the US five months before the 1976 Montreal Olympics to train and study, but did none of the latter at all. 'I lost the race [the 1500 metres] in Montreal before I even got up on the blocks,' he admitted, 'because I was just stuffed from concentrating on nothing but swimming.' That was why he became a strong critic of Ian's decision to quit school: 'If this kid just does swimming and nothing else, he won't last beyond the Sydney Olympics,' Holland warned.

He needn't have worried. Ian had an extremely diverse range of interests. He was up to his ears in swimming for roughly 30 hours in a normal training week, and enough was enough. Hence the unwritten rule in the Thorpe household: no talk about swimming. After finishing his correspondence year, Ian read books voraciously, researched via the Internet constantly, and became erudite on a wide range of subjects including economics, modern and ancient history, geography and architecture. 'Swimming is a small part of my life,' he says. 'It isn't the thing that makes me who I am. I've been successful at it, but also at other things. I've brought more of my personality to swimming than the other way around.'

The one certainty is that Ian Thorpe tiptoed through the minefield of precocious sporting celebrity better than anyone else. He broke the mould. He survived where so many others had not; and then he prospered, spectacularly.

13

THE HACKETT ASCENDANCY

IAN HAD HIS HEAD BURIED SO FAR into the books in the final months of 1998, he hardly came up for air. He missed the Trial School Certificate because of the Comm Games, so he had to do those exams on his return, then follow directly with the School Certificate. In mid-November he had to sit for his English and maths papers, one after the other, at 35 000 feet en route to a World Cup meet in Rio de Janeiro.

It was reckoned to be the first time anyone had done an exam on a plane, and Don Talbot, an ex-teacher, wasn't mucking around in his role as exam supervisor: he actually set a stopwatch on the student, who was constantly interrupted by swimmers wanting to know if they could help. As well, Ian discovered there was a whole slab of questions in the maths paper on a subject he'd somehow missed out on. Could anything be more galling for a perfectionist? It turned out he scored in the second band for maths and the top band for English. Under the circumstances, it was going to have to be good enough: a means to an end. Young Thorpe's formal schooling – at least for the foreseeable future – was over.

Like the Mare Nostrum grand prix tour, results and times on the FINA World Cup tour (FINA is the sport's international governing body) don't matter anywhere near as much as in the big four events. It's short course racing to start with, and really just another means of filling up the swimming calendar so sponsors get exposure and no-one forgets who's who in the four years between Olympics. Again, Australian Swimming footed the bills because it was good experience for young swimmers.

But coaches don't like their swimmers to lose. Don Talbot's philosophy had always been that it was not about how well you swam as long as you won, as often as possible. He suggested to Ian that he should set out to win the 400 freestyle in Rio without going too hard. So Ian decided to depart from his usual approach of swimming as fast as he could, just to see how it felt.

Of course, he won easily, but in a very slow time – and felt totally let down. He'd never been so disappointed with himself. He'd challenged the other swimmers in that race, but he hadn't challenged *himself*, and so it wasn't any fun. That day he decided he would never again focus just on winning. If he was swimming at a state or metropolitan championships as part of his preparation for a major meet, then it would usually make no sense to bust his boiler – but whenever he was on the big stage, whenever it counted, he would go back to striving for a personal best every time he hit the water. Nothing less would satisfy him. It was a principle he and Talbot would always disagree on.

Although he wasn't supposed to leave his hotel on Copacabana Beach, there was no way Ian was going to travel to such an exotic destination without sneaking out to have a look around. In any new place he always liked to wander some distance into the backblocks, seeking out authentic experiences. As far as he was concerned, fate would determine whether he was going to get mugged, drugged, or whatever.

In Rio the juxtaposition of fabulous wealth and abject poverty stunned him, although the vibe was that the rich and the poor seemed to be having an equally marvellous time. Walking along the beach at Copacabana, and nearby Ipanema, Ian was gobsmacked. Why would such deeply religious girls want to wear thong bikinis to show off almost every inch of their bodies? 'It just seemed so bizarre,' he recalls. 'And their bodies, especially at Ipanema, were to die for.'

It was on from that scene to Edmonton, Canada, where the outside temperature was way below zero, but you could stay nice and warm in the world's biggest shopping mall: another form of heaven. Last stop on this tour was College Station in Texan oil country, where Ian was freaked out by the number of guns he saw. It didn't look to be the sort of country where you'd go hunting. Why the need for all that heavy metal?

In Brazil, Canada and Texas, even though the competition was classy, it was the usual deal in the 200 and 400: Thorpe swims, Thorpe wins. He won over 100 metres in Edmonton, too, which was encouraging for his sprint ambitions. Even more so was the amount of support he was getting from spectators, especially on the last two legs of the tour. They all seemed to want to adopt him as one of their own.

He arrived home, exhausted, on 6 December. Two days later, *US Swimming World* named Ian Thorpe the 1998 Male International Swimmer of the Year. He was the youngest ever winner. Michael Klim, who'd been given the honour for 1997, was the only realistic alternative. He'd begun with a very big bang at Worlds, but faded as the year progressed. Since Ian spent none of his spare time reading about swimming, he knew nothing of *Swimming World* magazine, and had no idea of the significance of this announcement until it was explained to him: he was as close to being *officially* the world's best swimmer as it was possible to get.

The following day, Ian was named the Junior Male Athlete of the Year at the 1998 Australian Sports Awards while, ironically, the senior title went to Klim, who also won Telstra's award for the Australian Swimmer of the Year. Obviously it all depended on how far back the adjudicators' memories wanted to stretch. The awards rolled on into the new year – NSW Athlete of the Year, *Daily Telegraph* Sports Star of the Year – but although Ian naturally made the right noises about all these awards in the press, he really wasn't much interested. If your only objective was to become the best swimmer you could possibly be, how much could it matter what place you were supposed to occupy in the sporting pantheon?

Reflecting on all the years he spent with Ian Thorpe, Doug Frost found himself able to make just one main criticism: that Ian frequently failed to turn up to awards nights where he was himself the recipient of the main honour, for instance NSWIS's award for the Swimmer of the Year, which he always won. (However, he did allow that Ian would always show up when Doug Frost was being honoured by the Coaches' Association, and that was something he much appreciated.)

Ian didn't want to offend anyone, but he really didn't enjoy standing under the spotlight while unfamiliar people in suits showered him with hyperbolic praise. It was just embarrassing. In fact, by this stage he would go into a full-on cringe whenever he saw his face in the media, which meant he rarely read the papers and selectively avoided the swimming news on television. There were, however, some awards he'd come to cherish in the future – but they weren't the ones that were confined to swimming.

Ian Thorpe didn't earn anywhere near enough money in 1998 to make *BRW* magazine's authoritative annual Sport's Rich List. But Susie O'Neill, ranked 21st among Australian sportspeople, made an estimated $1.2 million, while Klim and Perkins were also slotted in the top 50 – so the money really was there, by that stage, for those who were well established. Ian's time would come but, again, it was not a subject he ever fretted about.

What did matter to him was the whole issue of doping. He'd seen and heard enough on the circuit by now to want to make a stand, especially on the subject of erythropoietin (EPO), which he believed had long been the swimmers' drug of choice, along with human growth hormone. No test existed then for either drug, but blood rather than urine seemed to be the key avenue, and Ian wanted to be the first swimmer to voluntarily give a blood sample so that when the appropriate tests and protocols were finally developed, he could prove he'd always been clean. He wanted others to do the same, and for people to take note of those who refused. No-one in the sport saw fit to adopt the idea. 'I don't want anyone in the world ever to put a question mark over my name,' he said.

≈

When he'd turned 16 back in October 1998 and got his L plates, Ian went driving almost every day, mainly with Ken, in the family's old manual Camry. Then, in December, Mazda came on board as a sponsor, so the family car was now a new Mazda 626. The Thorpes were genuinely thrilled; they never took any of the material rewards of their son's success for granted. And when Ian bought a new set of Taylor Made golf clubs, he was ecstatic.

Dave Flaskas was concentrating on taking the family out of the public domain. Ken initially took a big step back. Then Margaret, aka 'Media Marg', who'd done countless interviews as the mother of the iconic superstar, was eased out of the firing line. All the Thorpes wanted to do was live their lives as normally as possible. Flaskas himself would do the essential media, while Ian became increasingly inaccessible for one-on-one interviews.

Catriona Dixon was still a confidant, though, and it was she who learned that Ian's paternal grandfather, 82-year-old Cec, had passed away at the same time Ian was about to compete in January's FINA World Cup meets in Sydney and Hobart. Ian was grateful for the chance to say goodbye, and Cec's wish was that he not attend the funeral, but go and beat the world's best in the pool instead – which was exactly what he did. The parameters of Cec's ageing mind had narrowed to the point where he didn't really understand what his grandson was achieving, but he knew it was something significant, even if it had nothing to do with cricket. Cecil Thorpe was a patriarchal figure, and Ian was not as close to him as he was to his other three grandparents – even though they still saw each other every week. 'I didn't really know him as a man – I knew him as my Pop,' Ian now reflects. 'He didn't have a huge influence on me.'

Ironic that Ian should use those words, since Cec had inadvertently influenced his entire life. At the time of Cec's passing, Ian was only aware that his Pop had exerted a fair amount of pressure on Ken Thorpe the young cricketer. Now that Ian has come to understand the whole story, he fully agrees that if it weren't for Cecil Thorpe, and the attitude he adopted with Ken, and Ken's response to it, then very likely he would never have continued with his swimming. If there'd been any more pressure to succeed, any less emphasis on enjoyment, he'd have walked away. That was his nature.

Despite Ian's genuine grief, the story in the water was as normal: Thorpe swims, Thorpe wins. He now carried an aura of invincibility in middle-distance freestyle, no matter what the size of the pool. With the Pan Pac Trials looming, it was considered almost a fait accompli that he'd slice that last hundredth from Lamberti's 200-metre record, and shake Perkins' 400 mark right down to the ground.

Grant Hackett, the 1500 metres world champion who, in the absence of Thorpe, would have been the undisputed Boy Wonder of international swimming, was having to fend off suggestions that he was cracking under the pressure exerted by Ian's legendary finishes. 'There is no mental glitch in me,' he told the press. 'The problem is Ian's ability to swim the final 100 metres of a 400-metre race in 53 seconds. I swim it in 55 seconds, and that's on world record pace – so there's nothing much I or anyone else can do.'

And yet, despite the amplitude of the stakes in their high-profile rivalry, Ian and Grant were still the best of buddies. 'It's not as if we're trying to fight a war,' the laconic Queenslander would say. After heats in the morning, they'd normally head to one or the other's room and order some food, then get stuck into the PlayStation. In the marshalling area before races, they were always cracking each other up. Hackett could usually even manage a quip after Thorpe had once again swum over the top of him: 'Why'd you have to go and do *that*?' Even their coaches had a jovial relationship. Denis Cotterell would often say to Doug Frost, tongue-in-cheek: 'This is how we're gonna win the race. What're you gonna do about it?'

Conversely, Kieren Perkins enjoyed a bit of psychological warfare. He would play mind games, especially with Hackett, and as it became increasingly clear that his time at the very top was finished, he resorted to them more often. But he was prepared to admit that one swimmer in the world left him in awe, and that was Thorpe. Still, Perkins had the mindset of a champion, so he was not going to give up on winning the 400-1500 double at the Sydney Olympics. A swimming writer described his ambitions as 'bordering on demented'.

A solid blow to the hopes of the sport's multi-event champions came when FINA announced it was scrapping the depressingly downbeat 'B' finals, and adding semi-finals in all strokes in events from 50 metres to 200 metres at the Olympics in order to pad out the eight-day program. For someone like Ian, who was now trying to add the 100 free to his repertoire at the highest level, it was obviously going to make things tougher. The only consolation was that the Aussies were going to duplicate the program exactly, so the swimmers would have three shots at getting their preparation and meet strategy right: the Pan Pac Trials, Pan Pacs in August, and the Olympic Trials in May 2000. Mistakes would inevitably be made in event selection and in the vital warm-up and warm-down process between events. As always for the athletes, who were among the most resourceful of people, it was a case of sink or swim.

So it was that at the Pan Pac Trials at Brisbane's Chandler Aquatic Centre in late March, Ian really started to hone his act for the Olympics. The countdown had begun. It started with the 400 freestyle final on the evening of day one. As always, he stuck to the even-or-negative split formula, and this time passed Hackett at 250 metres. Would another swimmer pushing him over that last 150 have made a difference? It was an academic question: no-one was capable, certainly not Kieren Perkins himself, who was ten seconds behind.

When Ian hit the wall and looked up at the time, the clock was taunting him again: he'd missed the great KP's record by 0.05 seconds. Instead of just smiling this time, he laughed. It was as if the gods of the sport had decreed: 'You're not getting these records just yet.' He thought at that time, and still does, that it was a good thing. Better not to just have everything handed to him on a plate.

When the crowd took their seats to watch the final of the 200 free two nights later, it seemed everything was set for them to witness a slice of swimming history. They did. Not only did Ian Thorpe miss out on Lamberti's record, he didn't even win the race. He reached the wall at the front of the field at the 150 mark, just outside world record pace, and then Grant Hackett turned the cosmos upside down, coming home over the top of Ian and just touching him out – but still

0.3 seconds shy of the record. Hackett had said before the race he'd been doing a fair bit of sprint work in the hope of making the 200 final for the first time, and maybe securing a spot alongside the golden boys on the relay team. Obviously he was incredulous at the result.

What with all that talk of an imminent world record, Thorpe admitted afterwards: 'There was a lot of pressure surrounding the race.' But he added: 'I didn't feel it. I had a bad race.' Maybe he wasn't fully aware of the effects of that pressure. His psychological armoury may not have been as impregnable as he'd imagined. Perhaps he didn't want the talk of pressure to be construed as an excuse. (No amount of questioning by the author would reveal anything because Ian had actually forgotten that Grant beat him in that race, and needed to see the proof of it in print.)

The Hackett ascendancy was relatively brief – only a matter of weeks – but it was glorious. The following night he decided, just five minutes before the start of the 4 × 200 club relay, to swap positions from anchor man to lead-off swimmer and have another crack at the record. These relay events were very low-key affairs, and about half the patrons had already filed out of the venue when the moment many had been waiting ten years for arrived: Hackett touching in 1:46.67, breaking the world record by two-hundredths of a second. Ian was genuinely thrilled for his mate, as Grant would have been for Ian, because it was a record that clearly belonged in Australia.

For Ian the pivotal event of the meet was his 49.98 swim in the 100 metres. Doug Frost had always made a big deal out of writing down short and long-term goals. Ian had given it away long ago, believing the whole idea pointless – but if he'd been writing anything at the start of 1999, it would have been: 'Break 50 for 100 free.' However, Klim and Chris Fydler had beaten him home, and there was still a chasm between Ian and the best sprinters in the world, who were down to the low 48s. But with three Australian men now under 50 seconds, Gennadi Touretski predicted Australia could break the 4 × 100 free record, and soon.

In less than a week the circus had moved on to Hong Kong for the World Short Course Championships. Ian was very sick when he lined up for the 200 free, suffering from a bad migraine and frequent vomiting, yet still managed to hack 0.36 seconds off Lamberti's nine-year-old world record – the oldest in the short course books. Talbot described this effort as 'one of the greatest swims of the year'. Ian needed injections afterward to control his nausea.

He now held the 200 and 400 world short course records, but Hackett, who hadn't been able to swim in that race because of a disqualification in the Trials back in September in Perth, fancied his chances of bettering Ian's mark as lead-off swimmer in the 4 × 200 relay. He never got the opportunity, as an official bungle saw the Australians kicked out of the final. Hackett was furious, while Don Talbot manfully took the blame.

Anyway, Grant used his righteous anger to good effect with an incredible performance in the 400 free. He destroyed Ian Thorpe's world record by a full five seconds, with Ian coming in just half a second behind him. Hackett had gone out like a man possessed, while Ian swam his usual measured, mathematical race, foot poised on the accelerator pedal, stomping on it at exactly the right moment to launch his explosive finish. It was just that this time, Grant had taken a fraction too much water from him. Ian couldn't have swum the race any faster.

That particular race showed graphically just how soft short course records were at the time. Nonetheless, at that point Grant Hackett could have credibly laid claim to being the world's best 200, 400 and 1500-metre swimmer. No-one had ever won all three events at Olympic level, but the talk was of Hackett giving it a shot. He'd suddenly catapulted himself from the no-man's-land of 1500-metre racing, where he was unchallenged, close to the heart of multi-medal territory; now he was speculating on what he might be capable of achieving in the 100 free.

But by the middle of May, at the Telstra Grand Prix meet in Canberra, the status quo in the 200-400 double had returned: Thorpe 1, Hackett 2. And so it would remain. For no apparent reason, the spark that had ignited Grant Hackett's period of pre-eminence extinguished itself.

≈

'The Sanctuary at Voyager Point' is the sort of place you'd imagine gated communities in America must look like. In this newly created suburb on the largely unsettled southern side of the Georges River, the houses are all mansions – most of them tasteful, some spectacularly vulgar – and when you drive in via the one access road, you expect to be challenged by a sentry and asked to state your business.

Ken and Margaret loved the place, and Ian was looking to slash his travelling time to the Sutherland pool. They did the sums and figured that by buying one of the display homes, with all the furniture thrown in and including a fully grown garden, they'd save about 80 grand and a whole lot of aggravation.

Ken sold the ancestral home in Milperra, and Ian topped up the difference. It was a large contribution, but Ian considered it to be a mere gesture of gratitude for all that his parents had sacrificed for him. Margaret was chatting to Catriona Dixon at the Chandler pool in March when she couldn't contain her excitement anymore, leaned over and whispered: 'Ian's just bought a house for me.' They didn't actually move in until August 1999. After that, Ian had the luxury of getting out of bed as late as 4.15 am to be in the water by 4.45. On Wednesday and Sunday mornings, when he didn't have to get up and train, he'd set the alarm anyway – just for the sheer pleasure of turning it off and drifting back to sleep.

Ian had a new sponsor long before then. Telstra, the telecommunications giant, had come on board in March and through their Lifeline service, which was a telephone refuge for distressed and often suicidal young people, Ian found he could make a real contribution. As a 'Lifeline Ambassador' he raised the organisation's profile and spearheaded a national 'Dine For Life' event, where people were urged to hold dinner parties and lean on their guests to cough up for the charity. Ian knew how to work the publicity angles pretty well by now; his own dinner party, held in the water at the Chandler pool in Brisbane with the guests in black ties and swimsuits, became the public face of Lifeline Awareness Week.

Ian's support of the Cancer Institute had been low-key, but with the Telstra connection he was now a known philanthropist, and that meant dealing with a constant barrage of requests from charities – including appearances. Every fortnight he'd sit down with Dave Flaskas for half a day as they systematically combed over every aspect of his life – swimming, private and philanthropic.

Not surprisingly, the charity thing started getting out of hand. Rather than deal with all these requests for memorabilia or donations or appearances on a random basis, it was obvious there needed to be some sort of consolidation. It was Flaskas' idea to set up a foundation of some sort, with an emphasis on Ian's main interest: helping disadvantaged young people. They started assembling the expertise required to get the thing up and running.

By around April 1999 Flaskas felt he had the Thorpe portfolio on a fairly even keel. Ian's philosophical survival kit was also fully operational, so everything seemed okay. But for David there was the gnawing suspicion that Ian was really lonely – and that, being Ian, he wouldn't say anything about it.

It was true, although Ian thinks 'isolated' would be more accurate. People he'd known for a long time were no doubt intimidated by all the publicity surrounding him. Some may have thought he'd outgrown them, but that was never the case. 'The interactivity I'd have liked to have had with other people just wasn't there,' Ian recalls. For a boy who'd always loved just quietly chilling out in a group where he felt he belonged, that was hard to handle.

He no longer had any contact with the school, so all those peripheral friends – not the closest ones like Ryan and Nathan – he'd never get to see anymore. And when Ian had available time, Ryan and Nathan usually didn't. The natural evolution was that pretty soon Ian's best friends were all swimmers. Even though they weren't into discussing swimming – like Ian, they all reckoned enough was enough – everything was still always *about* swimming, one way or another. No-one else could really understand what the swimming life was like – and even other swimmers could never understand what Ian Thorpe's life was like. It was a difficult and sometimes painful period of adjustment.

There were times – but not often, and never for long – when he wished he could be someone other than Ian Thorpe, celebrity swimmer. The reality was that he was still learning to be the person he'd become, and that was an ongoing process. At the same time, he was anything but ungrateful. In a *Sunday Telegraph* magazine article that appeared on 25 April, Ian said: 'It may have been a long transition, coping with all the fame and whatever, but I wouldn't have it any other way now.'

Things that he initially couldn't handle, he simply came to terms with. Like coming home from a successful meet, walking through the Arrival gates, and hearing the crowd cheering and screaming his name. 'Boy I hate this,' he'd think. But eventually he came to appreciate it. Australian people supported their swimmers like no other nation.

And he absolutely refused to become reclusive. He'd be at the cinema every week, either on Saturday afternoons or Sundays, he'd go out to dinner anywhere in Sydney, and he was always happy to stop and give an autograph. Occasionally people would interrupt him in the middle of a meal, but not often. People would sometimes make insulting comments within earshot, and a thousand times he felt like saying: 'I've got eyes and I've got ears' – but he never did. He'd retain his dignity. And he'd be damned if he was going to compromise his lifestyle on account of a few idiots.

At night he was much more cautious. Private parties were no problem. There were some periods in the calendar when swimmers could let their hair down a bit, but it wasn't a good look for Ian to be drinking in public, and not really feasible for him to be hanging out in bars or nightclubs, although occasionally he'd go out with friends on a Saturday night. Alcohol, or the lack of it, was never an issue with Ian anyway. 'I'm his best friend,' says Ryan Barclay, 'and I've never been drunk with him.'

From the age of 15 onwards, Thorpe would always go out and party after a meet, at home or overseas – but never all that hard. He put a lot of thought into his outfits; Guess and Calvin Klein were his favourite gear, and he cared about looking good. When he was with close friends he loved geeing them up – being 'a bit of a smart-arse', according to Simon Cowley – but even when he had several drinks under his belt, he had an innate sense of what was appropriate, and he never stepped over the line. He was always in control of himself, with the happy knack of knowing how to be both silly and sensible at the same time. All his friends agree on that. There's only one point of contention: would Ian front up to a girl he fancied at a party and just start chatting?

Simon Cowley: 'No. He's too quiet. He doesn't take punts like that.'

Kirsten Thomson: 'Yep. Not arrogantly – but he's very confident in himself.'

Ian Thorpe: 'I'd hesitate at first. Depends how keen I was.'

≈

In early June 1999, Ian went on his first altitude camp in Colorado Springs in preparation for the Pan Pacs, to be held in Sydney in August. (Altitude training is a legal way of increasing the oxygen-carrying capacity of the blood. EPO does much the same thing illegally.) He roomed with Simon in a flea-bitten hole of a hotel, trained like a demon for three weeks, covering 300 kilometres in that time, shed four kilos to get down to 92, and was reported to be 'flying in the water'. Ian knew enough not to get carried away. He'd had a great preparation once before, only to perform well below his own expectations. But he looked at his times in that Colorado pool, and he was more than quietly confident.

Dave Flaskas' mind was taking flight at the same time. For a man who'd only been peripherally involved in athlete management until late 1997, he wasn't afraid to think on a grand scale: 'I've never wavered in my belief – and I was ridiculed in the early days – that an Australian swimming star could become an international icon.' If guys like Wayne Gretzky and Lance Armstrong could be idolised in Australia when their sports hardly registered a blip on the local scene, then why the hell not? Flaskas felt strongly that Australians had always domiciled their best athletes, taking them to the world only once every Olympiad, unless they happened to be tennis players or golfers.

His first move, back in January 1999, was to try to register the brand name 'Thorpedo', since it was being bandied about by everyone, but he ended up in an infuriating trademark bunfight with a sportswear outfit called Torpedo that dragged on, incredibly, until late 2003.

Anyway, David was already thinking about how to market Ian Thorpe internationally – but he knew that wouldn't happen until iconic status had been achieved, and that wouldn't be until after the Olympics. And it wouldn't happen by accident either; a lot of strategic groundwork would have to be laid. David was frustrated when people consistently overestimated Ian's earnings in speculative articles. The *Telegraph* reported in July that 'the big sponsors have signed on and the dollars are rolling in'. Thorpe wasn't short of a quid by now, but the real money was overseas.

Not long before the Pan Pacs meet, Ian decided he needed to escape from the city, so he set off in the Mazda, with Margaret on board, to visit his accountant, Mark Sheridan, out in the mid-western New South Wales town of Young. At Sheridan's father-in-law's property, after an abortive attempt at horse-riding while Margaret and all the in-laws looked on, Ian was placed on a little 90cc tiddler of a bike while Sheridan explained the workings of the clutch, accelerator, gears etc. You could hardly see the machine with Ian on top of it, but he fanged it across the paddock, through an open gate, then up into another paddock, out of sight . . . and then, suddenly, *no sound*.

They all raced after him, and found him some distance away with his shirt ripped open and a sizeable cut across his chest, standing next to a bent-up bike. 'I didn't see that log,' he said sheepishly, pointing to a nearby stump as everyone panted relief. The next morning Sheridan's father-in-law was up in that far paddock when he discovered a piece of Ian's shirt stuck in the barbed wire fence. What had apparently happened was that Ian had hurtled full-bore into the fence because he didn't know where the brake was, and he was too embarrassed to say so. It was hardly his fault, though, because his instructor had forgotten to tell him.

An injury right then would have had all sorts of repercussions. Channel Nine had decided to take a huge punt and televise the Pan

Pacs live for the first time ever, largely because of the presence of Ian Thorpe. And if Ian hadn't made it there in one piece, the 1999 Pan Pacs would not have been hailed in some quarters as the most exciting swim meet ever held.

14

THE PERFECT RACE

THE PAN PACS WEREN'T AN OFFICIALLY recognised 'test event' for the Olympics, but they followed the Olympic program exactly, they were held in the Olympic venue at Homebush, and every attempt was made to replicate the Olympic experience.

The International Olympic Committee times everything in its schedules down to the minute – sometimes even 30 seconds – and it wasn't quite possible to go that far. For one thing, there'd be an extra 12 000 seats available in newly erected stands the following year, changing the whole configuration of the place. And of course, there was no Olympic Village yet. The Dolphins took up residence in the Stamford Hotel in North Ryde, a 25-minute ride from the Aquatic Centre in Doug Frost's decrepit minibus. Ian roomed with his good mate from the Sutherland squad, Craig Stevens.

But there was one all-encompassing constant: Don Talbot's furious obsession with Australia beating the Yanks and becoming the world's number one swimming team. (In Talbot's autobiography the subject is mentioned about 50 times.) The idea of swimming as a team sport, which the head coach fostered incessantly, had really caught on by then. The best evidence of this was the fact that any Australian would swim a mile through raw effluent to be part of a relay team, some even sacrificing individual ambitions in the process. That was never the case in the pre-Talbot era, although Ian thought the credit belonged at least equally to the team's psychologist, Clark Perry.

However, Thorpe personally didn't care much at all about beating the Yanks. Since he didn't care about beating anyone or anything other than his previous best time, why would he? There was one exception, of course, and that was the relays, where Ian Thorpe was as passionate, if not more so, than anyone. He really loved being part of a gang on a mission.

But anyway, according to Ian Hanson, at the staging camp at the Sebel Hotel in Melbourne (aka 'Camp Talbot' on account of the boss's rigid disciplines), Thorpe, Klim and Hackett made a huge difference to morale, pumping everyone up and making the rookies feel at home. It was ironic that Ian would adopt the role of mentor, since he was the youngest male on the team – and remained so, incredibly, until the Commonwealth Games in 2002.

On opening night at the Sydney International Aquatic Centre, before a crowd of about 4500, the second final on the program was the men's 400 free. There were so many Thorpes in that crowd – his parents, grandparents, uncles, aunts, Christina, plus Michael Williams and his mum and numerous other friends and supporters – and they were there every other night when Ian was on the big stage. It was a home game for Team Thorpe.

Three swimmers would contend: Thorpe, Hackett, and South African Ryk Neethling. All three got to the 200 mark in a virtual straight line. Ian, a touch in front, split in 1:51.03 – eight-hundredths of a second ahead of Perkins' record pace. And then he started to put the pedal down. In the first 20 seconds of that third 100, he edged out by a full body-length. And then he floored it, knowing that he was now capable of exactly 150 metres of full-bore sprinting while still holding his form at the upper limit of pain management.

Ray Warren called it: 'He's coming down to complete his third 100, and the split we're looking for is 2:48.15 . . . He touches . . . He's 1.86 under world time!'

Daniel Kowalski, expert commentator: 'This is absolutely incredible . . . They said Kieren's world record is probably the best in the book, and this guy is going to absolutely *annihilate* it, which is scary for the rest of the world . . .'

Ray Warren at the 350-metre turn: 'He's put four body-lengths on Neethling and Hackett . . . Here he comes. The crowd roars. They're pushing him down the pool. [In fact, amid the general din of racing, it was the first time Ian ever actually *heard* the noise of a crowd.] The world record, set in Rome in 1994 – 3:43.80 . . . is he going to do it? *Thorpe comes in. Thorpe touches.* WORLD RECORD! 3:41.83 – he's taken almost two seconds off it! This is absolutely sport at its best.'

Ian shook his right fist high in the air three times. He then paused, removed his goggles, and waved to the crowd, almost regally, smiling broadly. Grant Hackett had just hit the wall, ten metres behind him. The camera panned to Doug Frost up in the stands. Along with everyone else in the picture, Frost was going berserk. 'I haven't heard a roar like that many times in sport,' said Warren, the veteran rugby league commentator whose hyperbolic style had done a lot to popularise swimming on Nine's coverage.

Ian had swum 1:50.80 for the second half of that 400: a negative split, but almost dead even. *The perfect race.* He climbed out of the pool, gave Doug a big bearhug, then headed for the poolside interview with Nicole Stevenson. But the mike wasn't working. All that was broadcast, for the first ten seconds, was a male voice from somewhere asking lackadaisically: 'When's this 200 gonna be on?' It was a ponderous anticlimax. When the sound finally cut in, Nicole was asking: 'It's just over 12 months to the Olympics. How much faster do you think you can get?'

'Who knows?' was Ian's smiling reply.

Then it was straight to the warm-down pool, where he had about 12 minutes before the medal presentation – enough to burn off most of his built-up lactic acid over about 600 to 800 metres of slow freestyle. After the presentation, Ian walked under the traditional tunnel of upraised arms – a guard of honour from his team-mates – and standing at the end of it to shake his hand was Kieren Perkins. He really appreciated the gesture from the great man.

A quick press photo with Margaret and Ken followed, then he was immediately back in the warm-down pool to swim out the last remnants of lactate before preparing to anchor Australia's 4 × 100m freestyle relay team. This was all very tight timing: just over an hour passed between the finish of the 400 and the start of the relay.

Margaret had been jumping for joy immediately after the 400 metres, but Ken had assumed his now customary state of calm observation. Sure, there'd been some overt emotion from him back at Worlds in Perth, when Ian was still just a kid. But Ken had for some time been saying he wasn't going to get really excited until the Olympics. 'I guess I've known this was coming since he was a 12-year-old,' he told a reporter. It was his way of dealing, in public at least, with the whole phenomenon.

The general press reaction was less muted, as one superlative followed another. The scribes had no lack of quotes to work with. Talbot called Ian 'the greatest swimmer we've ever had'. Frost cut loose with: 'I think Ian is the best swimmer the world has ever seen.'

The American commentator Rowdy Gaines was most interesting on the subject. Gaines had been the 100 metres free champion in LA in 1984, but his view was that the 400, which he also contested as a youngster, was the greatest test of athletic ability in swimming. Back when he'd swum the distance, 'it was so much about pace, getting into a feel, timing. When you take a look at Ian's swim and break it down, he went into a balls-out sprint at 250 – and I have never seen anything like that. If you look at the great ones – Salnikov, Gross, Wodjat – they've all been great second-half swimmers, but really, the last 50 is when they went balls-out. Even Kieren was more of an even pace kind of guy. I have been around swimming a long time and it's the most amazing swim I've ever seen, hands down.'

All talk aside, there's a supposedly objective measure put up by the International Swimming Statisticians Association (ISSA). They use a formula based on comparisons with what other swimmers have achieved to give each world record a points rating – a measure of historical dominance. Ian had shattered Perkins' record by almost two seconds, and Perkins had destroyed the previous record, held by the Russian Yevgeny Sadovyi, by 1.2 seconds. Most importantly, no-one else apart from those two had even been close to Sadovyi's 1992 mark of 3:45.00.

Put all that together and the Thorpe swim was calculated by the ISSA at 1023 points. By comparison, Perkins' much-lauded 1500 record was worth 1018, Popov's electrifying 100 free record was rated at 1017, and the American Mary T. Meagher's legendary 100 and 200 fly records, set as far back as 1981, scored 1014 and 1016. In other words, Ian Thorpe had produced, as near as anyone could figure it, the greatest swim of all time.

≈

The 4 × 100 freestyle relay was sacred territory for the Americans: since it was established in 1964, over a span of 23 Olympic, World Championship and Pan Pacific appearances, they'd never lost in that event. As far as they were concerned, defeat was unthinkable.

Michael Klim led off to get the team into clean water and swam a 48.73 – the first Australian ever under 49, the sixth-fastest of all time, and a siren call to his team-mates that the Americans could be beaten. Jeff English and Chris Fydler fought to maintain a very slight lead, so that Ian Thorpe, the middle-distance specialist, the guy who'd finished third at Trials in the 100, hit the water just an arm's length in front of the Americans' anchor, Jason Lezak. Any betting man would have jumped on the Yanks.

Ian matched Lezak to the wall, then began to pull away. When he touched in 48.55 – the fastest-ever relay split by an Australian – Lezak was half a body-length behind. The Australian team's effort was just under a second outside the world record. The Americans were left in abject disbelief. History had been made for the second time in the one glorious night.

Oddly, the media didn't make a huge deal out of that victory. There seemed to be a lack of recognition of its significance. Admittedly, the

American team was not all that strong. They were missing their best sprinter, Gary Hall Jr, who'd been diagnosed with diabetes, and their next great 50-100 metres man, Anthony Ervin, was still on the way up. Jason Lezak was a good swimmer, but not good enough at that stage to be an individual 100 metres medallist at world level. Also, it *was* only Pan Pacs, not the Olympics – and until you'd beaten the Yanks at the Olympics, you hadn't really beaten them. They always grew an extra leg for the five-ringed circus.

But still, Ian was thrilled with his time, and even though he suspected by now that the training he was doing wasn't helping his sprinting, his first thought was that he would probably still make the Olympic final in the blue riband event. In any case, that first swim as anchor of an Australian 4 × 100 relay team was the genesis of a major part of the Thorpe legend. Even though Ian has never been a 100-metre specialist, he's been one of the greatest relay anchormen ever. He wins when he has no right to win. He swims over the top of guys who should beat him every time. There are two memorable examples, as we'll see, that simply defy belief. But *why* is he so good at it?

Firstly, he is calm. A lot of swimmers freak out when they're not just swimming for themselves, but carrying the hopes and dreams of others. In Australian teams the lead-off man might be the fastest, but the anchorman in any relay team always has the greatest pressure on him. He knows exactly what the situation is, and therefore what he'll have to do to win. Ian enjoys that pressure. Like one of his heroes, Michael Jordan, he always performs in the clutch. His skill levels are high – starts, turns, touches – and when it really counts, he executes them superbly.

He has one of the fastest relay changeovers of any swimmer, and yet he never breaks. Instead of wasting time by looking down to watch their team-mate hit the wall before taking off, swimmers are taught at age-group level to calculate when it will happen by observing the swimmer's stroke. So they *guess* when to go. They're allowed to jump the start by three-hundredths of a second, and Ian goes close to that all the time. He just misses the incoming swimmer's feet as he dives over the top. It seems incredibly risky, but he never blows it.

Because he's swimming last, the field is spread-eagled by the time Ian hits the water. That means he doesn't have to deal with the surging wave that always hits him in an individual 100-metre race because, being a middle-distance specialist, he can't get out as fast as the sprinters and is always behind his opponents at the turn. Coping with their massive wash as they hit the wall before him sets him way back. For instance, his split time of 48.55 in this Pan Pac relay would translate to 49.25 with an extra 0.7 seconds added to allow for the flying start – but his PB for 100 then was 49.98. (Thorpe hadn't worked all this wave theory out at the time, which was why he was so impressed by his relay time.)

Then there's the intimidation factor. Ian doesn't try to intimidate anyone – it's not his style – but when you're up against the man who's regarded as the world's best swimmer, you know that sometimes he can do magic. And every swimmer knows Ian Thorpe will cover the second 50 faster than them, because of his superior aerobic capacity – remember, the 100 metres is 35 percent aerobic – so they'll tend to head out like startled rabbits in the first 50, spin their wheels in a slight panic, and – *Where is he? Is he coming?* They get themselves distracted worrying about him, and tend to lose form, just a little bit. Just enough.

Finally, like anything in swimming, the touch is a practised skill. In those last few seconds, if it's close, Ian will always be the one who's charging from behind while the other swimmer is fading. It's a fact of swimming life that when that happens, and the two competitors both stretch desperately for the wall together in that final stroke, nine times out of ten it's the charger, not the fader, who gets the touch.

≈

Ever since the new Aquatic Centre at Homebush was opened five years previously, Telstra had offered a cash prize of $25 000 for the first swimmer who could christen it with a world record. Ian was handed the cheque after the relay medal presentation, and at the subsequent press conference, someone enquired as to what he was going to do with it.

It was an uncomfortable moment, because Ian didn't really want the world to know that he'd decided to split the money between the Children's Cancer Institute and Lifeline. He hadn't discussed it with anyone, including Dave Flaskas, but as always, he answered the question honestly. And so immediately afterwards, Margaret and Ken were fished out of the crowd onto the pool deck by a Channel Nine camera crew and asked what they thought of their son's gesture. Nonplussed, Margaret told the interviewer: 'Well, that's the sort of person he is.'

Ian didn't want that to happen at all. To him it was just a piece of bad reality TV. The reason he'd decided to donate the money was that it detracted, he felt, from the purity of the performance. One of his pet hates is having to stand on a dais to receive an oversized cheque plastered with the logos of companies who are trying to get leverage from one of his efforts in the pool. These days he actually refuses to do it.

Although 25 grand was at the time a sizeable sum to Ian, he'd have earned more than twice as much as that from incentives for breaking a world record written into his various sponsorship contracts. But that wasn't the point. The point was this: 'I don't like receiving money for swimming. I don't consider swimming to be work. The money I keep for myself is money earned from sponsor appearances. I feel I've worked for that money. It's that simple.'

Everything else is not money he considers, in a sense, to be rightfully his. That includes all kinds of unexpected cash and prize bonuses, money from things like sales of children's books and memorabilia, and even occasional appearances for non-sponsors where he's paid large amounts. As soon as Ian's foundation came into being straight after the Olympics, all this extraneous wealth was funnelled directly into it. Since people were forever coming up with new ways to throw money at Ian Thorpe, it amounted to a lot.

≈

The 200 metres was unique at the 1999 Pan Pacs, in that there were three Australians capable of breaking Grant Hackett's world record – Thorpe, Klim and Hackett himself – and under the rules, only two of them could make the final. It had been predicted for some months that this was a race where the record could go twice in succession – in the semi-finals and the final – as the Big Three went head to head.

Klim powered in the first semi on the evening of day two, missing the record by just 0.15 seconds and announcing: 'That's the best I've ever swum the 200 . . . and I think I can go even faster if I get the chance.'

Ian, feeling a bit the worse for wear after a night of broken sleep, and having spent the entire morning doing interview after interview with local media and ESPN in America, was up against Grant in the second semi. As they hit the wall at 100 metres almost simultaneously, Ray Warren was obviously disappointed: 'Aaah . . . they've gone outside world record time by 0.52 – so really it's now just a race between Thorpe and Hackett.'

But it wasn't. Ian simply changed up to top gear, charged away in the third 50, and then: '. . . *Thorpe – world record last night! Is it world record again? YES IT IS! He's done it again!*'

Ian looked up at the scoreboard, saw that he'd shaved a third of a second from Hackett's mark to take it down to 1:46.34, and then inaugurated a gesture that was to become his world record signature – making fists with both hands and shaking them together for a moment. He didn't even smile, though. He seemed determined to finish the job.

Doug Frost was preoccupied with pointing his video camera at the scoreboard while Ray Warren declared: 'Ladies and gentlemen, you're looking at the new legend.' Ian padded over to Nicole Stevenson and commented on how disappointing it was that only two Australians could make it through to the final. Grant Hackett was the one to miss out. 'But they're the rules and it's something we're going to have to get used to.'

'Can you do it again tomorrow?' Stevenson enquired.

'Who knows?' Ian said again, laughing.

Hackett reportedly told Ian after that race: 'Congratulations. Well deserved. I should never have held the record in the first place.' It sounded like the burden of guilt had been lifted from his shoulders, as if he'd stolen someone else's record and stamped his own name on it.

The final was billed as a clash of the titans: Thorpe, the world record holder, against Klim, the world champion. It was wishful thinking, really, because it was already clear that Ian Thorpe was swimming against himself at this meet. Klim took it out bravely, under Ian's new record time, but when Ian drew level at 100 and started to pull away again, in the third lap, it was only a matter of checking the clock. Ray Warren: 'World record Sunday, world record Monday. Will it be a world record Tuesday? *He comes down to touch – YES! OH YES! He has done it again!*'

The margin was huge. Ian's new world mark was a neat 1:46.00, with Klim a full body-length behind. The crowd had been rampant enough on the first two nights, but this time every single spectator stood, cheered, clapped, stamped their feet, jumped up and down, screamed to the heavens and at each other. It was a monumental din, almost drowning out the strains of 'Land Down Under', which somebody had deemed to be the unofficial soundtrack to an Australian world record.

Ian stood, unsmiling, nodded acknowledgment toward the stands, and held up his right arm as if to say: 'That's enough. Please.' Very subdued, he climbed from the water, gave another single wave and smiled shyly, almost embarrassed. Really, the level of adulation was getting out of hand. Frost was nowhere to be seen. Ian told the poolside interviewer, Rob Woodhouse: 'Coming into this meet, I'd never believe I'd be able to do this.' And then, accompanied by that marvellously warm and evocative European-style standing-stomping-slow handclap, he was gone.

Pan Pacs 1999 was an especially intense meet for Ian. The routine was unwavering: up at 6.30 am, breakfast at 7.00 (cereal, various fruits, toast and jam, pineapple juice and yoghurt), into 'the Dougie van' by 8.00 to head for the pool, warm up, swim heats, warm down, have a massage (by up to three people simultaneously), head back to the hotel for lunch by noon, sleep. Occasionally chat with Craig Stevens or with Grant and Michael, who were also sharing a room.

Then the team meeting at 4 pm for Talbot's motivational speech (which would invariably address the need to beat the Yanks in the overall pointscore, the gold medal tally *and* the total medal tally), back into the van, warm up, swim, poolside TV interview, 'mixed zone' interviews, warm down, medal presentation, press conference, compulsory drug test for breaking a world record. Stand around for as long as it takes to work up a pee into a bottle. Maybe there'd be a second event that night, which would involve another routine of warm up, swim, TV interview, mixed zone interviews, warm down, medal presentation, press conference. Finally, back into the van, pasta dinner at the hotel, and ready to hit the sack by 10.30.

There wasn't a lot of leeway for mucking around there. Normally Ian wouldn't go into an Australian team camp without his mini-DVD player. He might watch endless reruns of *Austin Powers* films and crack everyone up on pool deck with his Powers dance impersonations – or something like that. But not at this meet.

For a long time now, everyone in the Thorpe camp had accepted a strict rule: *don't call him, he'll call you*. Ian might be asleep, and sleep was always crucial. The rule applied across the board, including Mum, Dad and Dave Flaskas. At this meet Ian had been calling David and his wife Michelle on their speaker phone each night before bed. David would offer congratulations, but then they'd chat about anything other than swimming. Ian always avoided the subject.

Most swimmers would have bothered to watch themselves setting a third consecutive world record on the TV highlights. Ian wouldn't even turn the set on because of the saturation swimming coverage. The only other option for winding down was to surf the Internet, which Ian had been doing for a while before he called the Flaskases that night. By then it was around 11 pm.

David congratulated him again. He said thanks, then launched into a discussion based on two subjects he'd been researching on the Net: the Kosovo tragedy, and a comparison between worldwide spending on weapons of mass destruction as opposed to the total amount spent on childhood illnesses. 'If you were able to spend all that money on investing in children's futures,' Ian was saying, 'so that they were educated, healthy and productive, then the need for weapons of mass destruction would diminish because the disparity in wealth would begin to diminish . . .'

While the rest of the country – and the entire swimming world – was focusing on the extraordinary feat of a 16-year-old breaking three individual world records on consecutive nights, Ian was explaining in depth the problems associated with fixing the runway at Kosovo's main airport. Even David Flaskas, who by now understood very clearly that Ian Thorpe was not an ordinary person, was finding the conversation a bit surreal.

Immediately after the 200 metres final, Don Talbot pre-empted any cynical reaction by saying it was very likely people would not believe Ian Thorpe could swim so fast without doping. This led to the strange scenario in which Margaret was defending her son against suggestions that suggestions were going to be made. The reality was that Ian refused even to use any kind of food supplements or vitamins – a rarity among athletes – in case they were contaminated, and wouldn't even risk taking an antibiotic if he was ill. He wasn't just careful about drugs; *paranoid* might have been more accurate. But, sadly, Talbot's comments turned out to be prescient anyway.

The following night it became four world records in four days. The 4 × 200 relay team, led off very fast by Thorpe and this time including Klim, Hackett and Bill Kirby (a butterfly specialist who'd beaten off a spirited challenge from Matt Dunn and Todd Pearson for the fourth spot), slashed a full three seconds from the Australians' own record set in Kuala Lumpur. The *Telegraph* immediately launched a campaign to come up with a moniker for the unbeatable team – something like the 'Mean Machine' – but all it yielded was a laugh when one reader suggested 'Thorpe, Klim, Hackett And Some Other Bloke'.

Just prior to that race, though, whatever hopes Ian had nurtured for his sprinting were set back when he could only manage 49.71 in his semi-final, the third-fastest Australian behind Klim and Fydler. Under Pan Pac rules, that meant no spot in the final. He was improving – but very slowly. And he still hadn't worked out why his relay splits were so much better by comparison.

As Ian's feet, now maxed out at size 17, were being photographed next to those of a petite Japanese woman journalist for her Tokyo newspaper story (some things weren't worth getting upset about anymore), Flaskas was wading through 57 requests from as far afield as Norway and Brazil for 'ten or 15 minutes' with the undisputed male megastar of the sport. Dave was obviously happy to put the Thorpe footprint on all sorts of new territories, with Ian doing media spots throughout Australia, on German radio, BBC television in England, ESPN and NBC TV in America and French television. But he wasn't soliciting any sponsorship deals; Ian was all booked up, and maybe looking to cut back – except for the little matter of tying up a swimsuit deal, which would be announced in the following week.

Ian's world records had landed sponsor bonuses of $150 000, which led to total earnings for 1999 of $750 000. Among athletes in Olympic sports, only Cathy Freeman, Michael Klim and Susie O'Neill would pull in more that year.

His program was over, but naturally Thorpe stayed on to support the team. One night he was swamped by an army of 20 or so autograph-hunting girls, and had to be shepherded into the pool manager's office and out a side door, where he was confronted by another mob of starstruck fans. This was new territory for him – nothing like the real hysteria he would face in a couple of years' time, but good practice anyway. He started signing 'Thorpey' because that was what everyone was calling him, and he liked it.

Christina Thorpe was having something like the opposite experience. Of course she'd found it hard to adjust when she retired, but people generally reckoned she'd coped well with Ian's burgeoning fame. When people asked if she was Ian's sister, she'd reply: 'No – he's my brother.' It confused them and amused her.

But this Pan Pacs meet in Sydney was swarming with people she used to compete against, and it was all a bit too close to home. She didn't show her sadness to Ken and Margaret, but there were times when she did cry in the arms of her husband-to-be, David, and asked: '*Why him? And not me?*' It wasn't jealousy – just that she'd tried so hard, and hadn't reached her potential, and it was all so frustrating. She didn't go swimming once in 1999 and 2000. But she was very, very proud of her little brother.

As for the hopes and dreams of Don Talbot, they were reduced ultimately to the outcome of the last event on the program: the men's 4 × 100 medley relay. At the final changeover the US team was just fractionally in front, with Klim to swim against the American Neil Walker. Walker held off the Australian by the barest of margins – 0.17 seconds – but it emerged that Michael had jumped too soon anyway, and the Aussies were disqualified. It was shockingly close for the Yanks: 13 gold medals each to the US and Australia, with the total medal count 35-32 to the Americans, and the team pointscore 391-372.

Talbot was shattered, but there was consolation in the fact that the team was well positioned for the Olympics. An unprecedented 12 world records were broken – two more than at the drug-tainted 1994 Worlds in Rome, where the Chinese women were booed out of the pool. The Australian men's team had established itself as clearly the best in the world, and the overall Pan Pac times were far superior to the recent European Championships in Istanbul, where Pieter van den Hoogenband, now known as 'The Flying Dutchman', had picked up six gold medals.

No doubt the Channel Nine executive who'd punted on the Pan Pac coverage was being toasted many times over in the network's boardroom as spectacular ratings figures were recorded. The sport of swimming was flying high. No more so, though, than the poker-faced father of the conquering hero, who now had a new set of spectacular videos to watch at home. Of course, Ian has never seen Ken cry as he pores over those tapes again and again. He'd never, ever be in the same room when that was happening; even if he heard a tape being played, he'd turn up the music in his bedroom to drown out the commentary.

But Christina has seen Ken's reaction many times. 'Dad only has to watch Ian get his medal and he'll have tears,' she says. 'He's probably the most emotional of all of us.' Ian knew his father was from a generation of Australians who didn't put their feelings on show. But he knew that Ken was very proud of him – maybe as proud as any father has ever been – and that when the videos were rolling, his heart would be laid bare. Ken doesn't mind admitting it either. 'I just think,' he says, 'that we've been so blessed by God to have him as our son.'

15

'THERE'S NO MONEY IN SKIN'

WHEN THE TUMULT OF THE '99 Pan Pacs had died down and the overflowing message banks of Dave Flaskas and Ian Hanson had at last been emptied, David began to implement a very selective strategy to keep Ian's profile bubbling away internationally – the aim being, as always, to market him to the world after the Olympics.

He could hardly fail to notice that Ian's website had been deluged by messages from Japanese fans; the numbers of adoring emails and other correspondence ran into the thousands. And these Thorpe devotees kept sending presents and fan mail long after the event was over. Flaskas filed this unexpected development under 'Immediate Action Post-Olympics'.

In the meantime, Ian's sponsorship portfolio had to be rationalised, but none of the existing contracts would be broken. Some would just be allowed to drop off the twig. The wider objective was to get him a clear passage to the Olympics with minimal distraction. Apart from sponsor commitments, the approach was to do as close as possible to nothing, except for a brief World Cup tour in Europe early in 2000, some altitude training in Colorado, and fulfilment of Ian's Olympic obligations. 'Keep it simple' was the motto.

In hindsight, nothing in the world – absolutely nothing at all – could have been more damaging to that aim than to get involved with a swimsuit manufacturer that was not Speedo, the official supplier to the Australian Olympic team. Ian's long-running battle for the right to wear rival company adidas' wrist-to-ankle bodysuit was an arduous, distracting, time-consuming, infuriating process. It ended up with Thorpe becoming embroiled in an international power struggle between sportswear giants and between heavies at the top level of Olympic politics; it drove his manager to the point of emotional exhaustion; and incredibly, it almost cost Ian his place in the team. It was one hell of a bunfight – and, as it turned out, only the biggest in a long list of distractions in the year leading up to the Olympics.

To begin this story, we need to rewind about five months. Flaskas had been very sceptical when Rob Mills, the adidas marketing director in Australia, approached him about a new swimsuit concept back in March 1999. Of course, signing up with adidas would give Ian's image a global reach, aligning him with a major international company which sponsored superstar track athletes like Haile Gebrselassie and Ato Boldon – but adidas had never been a player in swimsuits, and there'd be no way Ian Thorpe would become a high-profile clothes horse for an inferior outfit just for the sake of a sponsorship contract. That would obviously have been crazy in a sport where victories could be measured in microseconds.

By the time Pan Pacs were looming, swimmers everywhere were suddenly sporting all kinds of unusual garb. The international push was led by Speedo, with Michael Klim chosen to be their number one test pilot in Australia. At Pan Pacs Klim was wearing a revolutionary neck-to-ankle wetsuit-type outfit that Speedo claimed to be a quantum leap in reducing water resistance, or drag. FINA had no problem with this, even though it appeared to directly contravene the association's own rules, which said 'no swimmer should be permitted to use or wear any device that may aid his speed, buoyancy or endurance in competition'. Why else would anyone pay big dollars to wear one of these new-fangled suits, if it didn't do any of the above?

Well then, you might ask, why would FINA allow them? Fast-forward to the World Championships in 2003, with Speedo and adidas sharing the naming rights sponsorship while superstars like Pieter van den Hoogenband were wearing Nike swimsuits. Nike and adidas were the big two internationally, now making massive investments in a sport that had previously been dominated by Speedo. (For adidas it wasn't primarily about selling ultra-fast swimsuits to elite swimmers; that was only a tiny proportion of the market. The object was to create a 'halo effect' for the brand. If adidas suits were good enough for the world's best swimmers, then their standard cossies had to be good enough for you and me.)

Anyway, the cat was already out of the bag. In 1992, pre-Barcelona Olympics, Speedo had produced a new fabric called 'S2000' which was supposed to reduce water resistance. Ireland's Michelle Smith had turned up in a rubbery neck-to-knee Speedo 'Aquablade' suit back in 1996 at the Atlanta Olympics, which was said to produce 23 percent less resistance than the standard swimsuit and eight percent less than the S2000 material. By 1998 the Aquablade was being worn by several high-profile swimmers including Susie O'Neill – and not a lot of acrimony had surfaced. The level of controversy surrounding the latest suits was simply a result of how radical they looked.

When the ball was first lobbed into its court, FINA had refused to act. The more loose ends they left in their interpretation of their own rules, the more power they could wield. Their basic justification was semantic, but admittedly logical: if swimsuits were to be included under 'devices', then the only way to ensure compliance with their existing rules would be to make everyone swim naked. The reality was that FINA's rules had been overtaken, in a literal sense, by developments many years beforehand, when woollen outfits gave way to silk, then nylon, then lycra. So, now it was a free-for-all.

In the 12 months leading up to the Olympics, millions of words were expended on whether the new suits should be outlawed. The great Australian swimmer Murray Rose summed it all up when he quoted an anonymous swimsuit manufacturer who'd pointed out the obvious: 'Mate, there's no money in skin.'

Critics said the aesthetics of the sport were not well served by a line-up of eight swimmers wearing different outfits ranging all the way from lycra briefs up to complete wrist-to-ankle 'shark suits'. What were we supposed to be cheering for – the athlete or their garment manufacturer? And what about lesser swimmers who couldn't get hold of a suit to compete on equal terms with the favoured ones? Swimming would never rival ball games as a spectator sport, but at least the minimal equipment had always given it a gladiatorial quality. Doping technology aside, no Olympic sport could offer a more level playing field – until now.

Forbes Carlile, the venerable Australian coach, put the anti-suit position succinctly: 'Advances in technology should be confined to advances in coaching, training, nutrition and pool designs which provide equal benefits for all swimmers.' FINA should have drawn an arbitrary line in the sand.

However, no swimmer in his right mind was going to spend 30-odd hours a week in training, then refuse on principle to wear a performance-enhancing outfit when everyone else was. Thorpe's approach was understandably pragmatic. As far as he was concerned, if the suits were declared legal by FINA then not only was he going to wear one, but he would choose whichever brand he wanted – regardless of whatever deals had been done by someone else: in this case, Australian Swimming and Speedo. That was typical of him. And when Rob Mills gave a Power Point presentation to Ian and David in June 1999 which explained the concept behind the radical new adidas bodysuit, Ian was immediately smitten.

The adidas suit evolved out of alpine skiing. It had nothing to do with water resistance. The concept was about muscle compression: a suit so tight it stiffened the body so it would penetrate water like a dart, and limited muscle oscillation, so that the onset of fatigue would be delayed. Ian was never a hard-bodied athlete; like most great swimmers, he was smooth-muscled. But his muscles were also bulky, and he figured they would compress spectacularly. He was right. He could see that reducing drag might make a swimmer *move through water* faster – but the promise of the adidas suit was that it could actually make him *swim* faster.

Thorpe was initially snowed under with info from Speedo which, he recalls, 'talked about friction drag, surface drag, line drag – to me it all meant nothing.' The adidas view was that swimmers created so much turbulence in front of them when they swam, the drag factor was irrelevant. (Ian reckons if the 200 freestyle were swum entirely underwater, he'd have gone with Speedo.)

He didn't get to try on an adidas suit until Rob Mills dropped a prototype in to the hotel in Melbourne where the team was in camp prior to Pan Pacs. Having at last climbed into it, his first concern was that the fabric, made of Teflon-coated lycra powder, would restrict his arm movement – so he tried revolving his arm, and it spun around so fast he ended up knocking out the ceiling light and cutting his hand. The elasticity in the thing was astounding. It felt like it was propelling his arm around for him. That, he figured, could not be a bad thing.

There wasn't any time for proper testing, so Ian wore ordinary sluggoes when he smashed Perkins' and Hackett's world records at Pan Pacs. Only a few days afterwards, on 1 September, the adidas deal was announced. Ian said he'd tested the suit a few times, and added: 'In my first session back after Pan Pacs I trained with it half the time. When I took it off, it felt like trying to push a semi-trailer through water.'

But Catriona Dixon wrote in the *Telegraph*: 'Don't expect to see him in it when he bids for an Olympic gold medal in Sydney next year . . . As part of the Australian Olympic team, all athletes must sign an agreement to wear the official uniforms supplied. This would mean Thorpe would have to wear a Speedo suit.'

The battle lines were clearly drawn by the Secretary General of the Australian Olympic Committee (AOC), Craig McLatchey: 'Speedo has been a supplier of high-tech costumes to every Olympic team in history. Adidas know we have an agreement – we have to protect Speedo's rights . . . We will ensure Ian has a swimsuit that is complementary to his performance goals and meets all of his technical requirements.'

It was puzzling that adidas had reportedly decided to sponsor Ian for 'a big six figures' over three years, when the rules would seem to limit him to wearing their suit only at meets where he wasn't representing Australia but the SLC Aquadot swimming club. In reality, though, the deal wasn't all that big. It was purely about the technology. Dave Flaskas was very disappointed when Speedo's marketing director, Tim Lees, at one stage stated: 'If it's about winning gold medals I'm sure Ian will be wearing Speedo. If it's about cash, maybe he will wear something else.'

'The adidas offer,' Flaskas asserts, 'was nowhere near what we were offered by other companies, including Speedo. Their last offer, made around the start of Pan Pacs, was very substantial – but even their initial offer was more than what we accepted from adidas.' Beyond that, adidas didn't know where the whole thing was heading, but in any case Thorpe was signed up to wear a range of the company's gear – tracksuits and such – rather than just the suit. If he didn't get to wear it at the Olympics, then so be it.

However, the adidas crew had determined that if the suit could be classified as 'specialised equipment' – that is, if you could prove it was of benefit to an athlete's performance – then under the IOC charter that athlete couldn't be compelled to wear one brand over another. The rule had only previously been applied to equipment like vaulting poles and running shoes rather than 'apparel'.

But wouldn't that directly contradict FINA's rules, which were supposed to *prevent* an advantage in speed, buoyancy or endurance? If you took all the legalistic and semantic nonsense out of it, *of course* it would. The whole thing was a logical absurdity, and everyone knew it – but as Dave Flaskas points out, it wasn't his job to worry about parallels between FINA's outmoded rules and the US Army's Catch 22. He was quite aware of the specialised equipment clause when he was quoted in Catriona's article about the apparent problem of Speedo's sponsorship of the Olympic team. 'We'll cross that bridge when we come to it,' he said.

So began a gigantic leap into the unknown. Ian first wore the suit, as he was allowed to do, at the Australian Short Course titles in Canberra a week after Pan Pacs. The early version seemed to provide no obvious benefit, but still it was all the media wanted to talk about. Ian got so fed up with it, he called Dave Flaskas to ask him to come down and drive him home so he could avoid having to face any more reporters. Dave recalls settling his client into the car, then absent-mindedly enquiring: 'So . . . how did you find the suit?' Ian was furious, while Dave wondered how he could have been so stupid.

On 14 September Flaskas made a formal request to the AOC to have the adidas suit classed as specialised equipment. That meant the Thorpe camp would be required, in a few months' time, to show scientific proof of a benefit from Ian's use of it. While Craig McLatchey at the AOC bristled and Flaskas tried to allay any hostility, semi-secret testing of the suits began immediately and continued at obscure times every few weeks, with the major modifications being rearrangement of seams and a continual tightening of the fit.

Eventually, several months down the track, the suit was sufficiently tight that its benefit was obvious to Ian: he had to steel himself for a wave of pain when he took the thing off after a hard session, as the lactic acid, held in check by muscle compression, was released all at once. If a lactate reading had been taken right at that moment it would have gone through the roof.

≈

Just after the Canberra short course meet, Ian was quoted for the first time in the press on his desire for a girlfriend: 'His ideal woman would have a strong sense of her own identity. The swimmer also wants a girlfriend who is intelligent, happy-go-lucky, sporty and fun.'

Subsequently he spoke of how hard it would be for him to run his extraordinary life and have an actual steady girlfriend. 'I never considered it unrealistic,' he now says, 'but I always thought it would be difficult. I kind of accepted that. At the same time I always thought someone would come along who'd be perfect, ideal. That was always in the back of my mind, but I never pushed it and was never concerned.' Ian had occasional involvements with girls from around this time onward, but always kept them away from media attention. On the one hand he was very protective of the privacy of everyone in his life, including girlfriends; at the same time, he loathed the idea of any girl being hunted down by the gossip mags and offered wads of cash to 'tell all' about her relationship with Ian Thorpe. Apart from the pool, home was the only place where Ian was able to do as he pleased without being pestered by the media. He wanted a fulfilling private life, like anyone else; and he could see that in his case, that meant it would have to be entirely private. Otherwise, he reckoned, the media's intrusion would be 'just another thing that would be kind of working against me.'

At the same time, unbeknownst to Thorpe, he had been adopted by the gay community as a pin-up idol. Apparently they liked his style. In avant-garde suburbs like Newtown in Sydney, the poster shops were full of him. Had he been aware of it at the time, he says it wouldn't have particularly bothered him: 'I appreciate the fact that they appreciate me.'

Kerry Stokes, boss of the Seven Network, certainly appreciated Ian. Embarrassed by the frugality of the Seven sponsorship contract, Stokes decided to reward Ian's Pan Pacs performance by giving him a premature 17th birthday gift of a manual Audi A4. The gesture was unexpected and overwhelming. That was the car Ian drove after he got his P plates, although Mazda, still a sponsor, also weighed in with a specially modified MX5 sports car. The accelerator and clutch pedals were shortened to accommodate the driver's legs. Never a hardcore revhead like Grant Hackett, Ian still did a pretty good job of fanging through the gears. It was one of the few sensual pleasures his lifestyle allowed.

≈

From September onwards, the countdown to the Olympic Games began in earnest. In a formal sense it kicked off with the AOC's 'One Year to the Olympics' dinner in Sydney. Ian took centre stage that night and said to the assembled throng: 'People often ask me what my inspiration is. It's not something I can write down – but I can show you.'

Gary Smith, the American writer who chronicled this narrative in great detail, described the ensuing scene: 'He exited the stage, and Michael Williams materialised. Standing in a single spear of light, the 13-year-old boy opened his mouth and spoke, but no words came out. He hesitated, mortified – had he lost his voice again? – then started over, but all that filled the hall was silence. The audience, baffled at first, sat hushed, then broke into applause. The microphone was dead, but the boy with the massive tumour was standing there, free of cancer for a year, alive.'

The story of Michael Williams was quite well known in Australia, via a TV documentary that went to air the previous year plus the occasional magazine article. People often asked Ian how his little mate was travelling. But when Smith's extraordinarily emotive feature appeared in the November 1999 edition of US *Sports Illustrated*, Ian Thorpe's image internationally was bathed in a dazzling light. The story of the young cancer patient being inspired and nurtured through his ordeal circulated rapidly throughout the swimming world. Its impact was profound. The Americans, in particular, began to hold Thorpe in awe. Their number one 200 freestyle swimmer, Josh Davis, felt compelled to photocopy the piece and hand it around to all his friends. He told a reporter: 'I admire Ian, not just for what he's done in the water but for what he's done out of it. He's got what we want, but here he is with priorities in his life. He really is ahead of the rest of the human race, and not just physically.'

On the streets of Sydney, as the colossal reality of the city's host status for the 2000 Olympics started to sink in, people were getting seriously hyped up. Australians are not known for collective hysteria, but Flaskas observed: 'It's got to the stage where Ian definitely can't stand still in public without being mobbed.' That wasn't quite the literal truth, says Ian now, but it was close. 'It was a very different time. It was all the same things I deal with now – photos, autographs, people wanting to chat – but it was just that *everyone* wanted to be doing it. Everyone was just so excited about being part of the whole thing.'

If things ever got too crazy, he could just withdraw. But Ian's approach was to savour the atmosphere, not run away from it. After all, a hometown Olympics was only ever going to happen once in his lifetime.

≈

One day at the end of October, Ian was jogging through the Royal National Park near Sutherland when his foot landed awkwardly on a rock and twisted through 90 degrees. Walking was very painful, running no worse, so he ran back to the pool because that would at least be quicker. When he took off his shoe, the swelling was horrendous – so he figured he'd move the fluid around a bit by swimming. He did a full training session. Next morning the ankle was still very swollen and tender. Ian trained again, had the injury bandaged heavily, and then jumped in the Westpac helicopter to make an appearance for his sponsor just down the coast at Wollongong. Christina, who was by then working for GSI, suggested that he have an X-ray just to be sure. So he did, with the results due in later that day.

When Thorpe was halfway through his afternoon pool session, Doug Frost took a phone call from the doctor. Ian had snapped a bone in his ankle in half, and every movement was forcing the two remaining fragments further apart. 'Get out of the pool now!' screamed the coach.

This episode turned out to be far from a disaster; in fact, it was almost certainly a blessing. Ian only missed three training sessions altogether. People had swum with fibreglass casts on their arms before, but no-one could remember anyone training with their leg in a cast. Ian did that for two weeks, then had the ankle placed in a compressor splint, which he wasn't supposed to walk on. But, of course, he did.

Anyway, the injury necessitated a lot more work than usual in the gym. Ian already had a specialist weights coach, Richard Beesley, but Doug Frost's influence had always prevented him from putting Ian on a serious program. Coaches traditionally have a potent fear of their swimmers 'bulking up', the reasoning being that water is much denser than air, and thus added bulk would be counterproductive, even if it came with an increase in power. Hence the weights sessions had been a fairly perfunctory exercise – but this new development shifted the balance of power, and Richard was given his head. He had Ian working really hard – not only on his shrunken calf and quad muscles, which he'd been unable to use for six weeks, but also prior to that on his upper body, using the heaviest weights Ian could handle. His arms and shoulders and chest were virtually transformed.

Thorpe swam at 92 kilos at Pan Pacs, and weighed 96 kilos at the end of this brief period of intense gym training. The extra weight was all upper body muscle, and he added another couple of kilos by the Olympics. Ian has never had a fear of bulking up, and experience supports him: 'Every time I put on weight, swimmers will say, "What are you *doing*?" – and then I'll swim as fast or faster than before.' Since a kilo weighs only one-tenth that amount in water, Ian thought the extra power would more than compensate. (And with the ultra-tight suit holding everything together in perfect streamline, he seemed to be on safe ground.) The latest science supports this view: swimmers who are paranoid about stepping into a gym have got it wrong.

When Ian made his comeback swim on 12 December at the NSW Metropolitan Championships, he was vindicated. It was only six weeks since he'd snapped that ankle bone. With the preparation he'd had, Frost would have settled for a 3:50 swim in the 400, but Ian pulled out a time of 3:45.96. It was a sensational effort. 'I think I'm more in balance now,' Ian said of his reconstituted body. 'I relied on my kick so much in the past.'

The plan was to do some hard racing in Sydney and Hobart, then head to Europe to terrorise the best swimmers there on their home soil seven months prior to the Olympics. 'I want to frighten the life out of them,' Doug Frost declared. However, only a week later at the Dutch winter championships, Pieter van den Hoogenband overtook both Hackett and Klim with a 200 free time of 1:46.58 – just half a second outside Thorpe's world record. The Australian champion had only recently described the Dutchman as his favourite swimmer, 'because he just doesn't give up'.

At the FINA World Cup meet in Sydney on 18 January, Ian produced his reply. Swimming in his very tight adidas outfit, and without having tapered at all, he still managed to lower his own

200 freestyle short course world record. 'I already felt in my heart I was wearing the right suit,' he remembers. 'But after that, I felt it in my mind as well.'

≈

Back in November Ian had fronted up at the opening of Fox Studios in Sydney in a radically cool all-white Versace suit. It was his first public fashion statement, as they say in the trade, but he'd always been interested in the subject, always wanted to look his best when he was out and about, and by 1999 he was hanging with an older, more sophisticated crowd. He was becoming his own man, growing into himself, and his decision to teach himself French that year was part of his personal growth. It had nothing to do with swimming, nothing to do with self-promotion – in fact that was the whole point of doing it. Along with his interest in haute couture, it was a means of self-expression. When the time for annual awards rolled around, Ian cemented his fashion plate image by wearing a slick charcoal-silver shirt at *New Idea* magazine's People's Choice Awards. Henceforth his appearance would become a preoccupation in the fashion media.

The readers of the gossip glossy had voted Ian Thorpe their inaugural Australian of the Year. He was chuffed about it. 'I take more pride in awards voted on by the public than just a panel of experts, and I also appreciate it more if it covers all sports, because I'm pleased that swimming is getting that attention.' He could have added that the magazine's readers were obviously recognising him for qualities other than being a good swimmer, because the people's choice for 'favourite male sports star' was Pat Rafter.

A much more established award was the title of Young Australian of the Year, where achievers from all walks of life were considered. Again Ian was very gratified, although he believed sportspeople were given too much of a head start in the voting for such honours.

At the purely sporting level, he cleaned up in 1999: *US Swimming World* recognised him as the world's best again, Telstra's Australian Swimmer of the Year Award followed (with Frost picking up their coach's award), and Ian was named Male Athlete of the Year at the

Australian Sport Awards and winner of the ABC Sport Star award. Undoubtedly, Ian Thorpe sat atop the pantheon of Australian sportspeople across the board, and was not too far from the pinnacle internationally.

The American International Athlete Trophy Award – previously known as the Jesse Owens Award – was presented to the person judged by the International Amateur Athletic Federation to be the world's greatest athlete in an Olympic sport. With its long tradition and enormous scope, this was regarded as the most prestigious honour in the sporting world. Thorpe was voted fourth in 1999 (behind cyclist Lance Armstrong and track stars Maurice Greene and Hicham el Guerrouj) in a country whose own top swimmers went largely unrecognised. Although he was never much focused on awards, the significance of that was not lost on Ian. He found it really surprising.

But the honour which was of greatest importance to him, then and even to this day, was the 'Don Award' – otherwise known as 'The Sport Australia Hall of Fame Sir Donald Bradman Award Presented to the Athlete Who Has, Through Their Example in Sport, Most Inspired the Nation'. It meant so much because, as Ian told an *ABC Sport Monthly* interviewer years later: 'My grandfather [Cecil Thorpe] had just passed away, and he was a keen cricketer, as my father was, and he was never capable of understanding my achievements in the pool, because he just didn't understand swimming. But he understood cricket. If he'd been able to see me win that award, in Don Bradman's name, that would've kind of hit home to him a bit – because I hold the Don in such high regard, and so did he.'

Bradman accompanied the award with a personal letter to Ian, which was framed and hung on his bedroom wall. 'Arrogance is tolerated by the Australian public,' the great man wrote, 'but never admired. That is something not needed in sport.' It was a warning that was close to superfluous in Ian's case.

But if he wasn't arrogant, he was still capable of being very cheeky. In December the Telstra Australian Dolphins were formally introduced to the Prime Minister, John Howard, at a function at Parliament House in Canberra. This was the first of several contacts Thorpe would have with the PM, who was a real fan, having sent personal congratulatory faxes to Ian on each of his world record swims at Pan Pacs. As Howard was led along the line of swimmers by an aide, he reached Ian, shook his hand and said: 'Congratulations. Fantastic. Is there anything we can do to help you?'

'Yes,' said Ian. 'I don't understand why I have to pay the same taxes as everyone else, but I don't get to vote yet.' The aide kept moving right along: 'Prime Minister, this is Susie O'Neill . . .'

There's an amusing photo of the PM looking quizzically back over his shoulder at the young swimmer. 'I'm sure,' says Ian, 'that I was respectful and addressed him as "Mr Prime Minister" – not "Johnny" or something. But I think it was a legitimate comment. I don't understand it when I don't get to have a say in things.'

He didn't mind chancing his arm a bit, young Thorpe. Most people don't seem to have his knack of getting away with it.

16

THE GERMAN OFFENSIVE

IAN WAS DESPERATE TO SWIM A THIRD individual event at the Olympics, on top of the 200-400 double. Otherwise his program would be over on day four. But he was ranked only third in Australia in the 100 free with a PB of 49.71, and wasn't too confident he could overtake Klim (48.73) or Chris Fydler (49.42) for the second slot in the blue riband event. So at the NSW Open championships, which were held in late January 2000, just prior to the European World Cup tour, he entered the 1500 freestyle for the first time. The idea was to swim an Olympic qualifying time in case he couldn't make the cut in the 100. With the 1500 scheduled on the last night of the program, he figured he'd have nothing to lose.

Thorpe didn't believe he could just cruise in and swipe the 1500 from under the noses of Hackett and Perkins. But he didn't like sitting in the stands at meets, and he knew that he could swim the long-distance event well because of all the endurance work he was doing in training. The decision was coolly received by Doug Frost, who wanted to stick with the 100-200-400 treble, and especially by Kieren Perkins, who said: 'The kid is under enough pressure as it is . . . If he's got any sense he'll stick to the shorter events.' No doubt that would have raised a chuckle or two, even though Perkins was man enough to admit his fear: 'Ian might get in the water and blow us all away in his very first swim.'

As it turned out, he won the race easily in a time about five seconds faster than his goal, and well inside the qualifying standard. But he was bored senseless and wanted to get out halfway through the 30 laps. The race just wasn't interesting. But the point was that Ian figured by now, from his research and conversations with other swimmers, that he was not training to be a sprinter: he was training middle-distance/distance, rather than middle-distance/sprint. In other words, he reckoned his program was really targeted at the 400, rather than the 200, where he believed it should have been.

It's all about swings and roundabouts. Remember, no-one had ever won the 100-200-400 treble at world level, and in the modern era few have even attempted it. Ian was the *only* athlete in the world who was swimming that program – and he still is. (For Ian, a 'win' would actually be a PB in all three events at the one meet – that was precisely his aim, then and now – but even that would always be very tough.) While the three races are within a reasonable range on the aerobic/anaerobic scale, it's extremely difficult to make incremental gains at both ends of that scale. That's because when you train aerobically, you build endurance but sacrifice fast-twitch muscle fibre, which is what makes it possible to move your arms and legs *faster*. If you can retain perfect technique, using all your power efficiently, and move your arms and legs faster, then obviously you're going to swim faster.

So the key to sprinting is to do plenty of fast-twitch work in training, which means lots of swimming at absolute race pace, with plenty of rest between sets. Quality over quantity. Sprinters have very specific muscle-building programs in the gym, and don't train anywhere near as long in the pool as middle-distance and distance swimmers – but what they do in the pool is crucial.

With Ian's training focused on the 400, his muscles were so broken down by endurance work that he *couldn't* flick on the speed button: 'I'd do a set that was specific for the 400 – say, ten 400s at a certain pace – then after that I'd try to do sprints, but I'd be so fatigued I'd never be able to get up to a real sprint. I'd still be going as fast as I could, but what I was really doing was training my body to swim for 350 metres, then another 50 metres as fast as possible. So as far as the 100 was concerned, my body wasn't trained to get that first 50 out – it was only ever trained for back-end speed.' As we've seen, because of the surging wave effect, getting out there at speed in the 100 is vital.

It's hard to say exactly what Ian knew, or believed he knew, and when he thought he knew it. But over time he became convinced that Doug was not a coach who could train him for speed, and that as long as he stuck with him, he'd never be able to swim 100 metres as fast as he possibly could. (Others thought the same – notably Kirsten Thomson, a sprinter who left Frost in 2001 for several reasons, one of which was to find a program that would hone her speed.)

The old-school coach was very concerned about creating muscle bulk, mainly because of the water resistance theory, and was clearly no expert on gym programs. He had Ian doing some speed drills amongst the endurance work but, according to Ian, 'We did a little bit – not much.' Frost's justification was, as Ian has said, the basis of Australian swim coaching theory at that time: 'I always thought it was better to build that aerobic base rather than sprint the life out of him too early. And that base carried him through – not only to swim well over distance, but to swim fast as well.' Most of the time they kept on ploughing that familiar middle-distance furrow. Plenty of quantity, not so much quality.

There was good science to support the idea that aerobic training done before puberty would benefit an athlete for years to come. However, Doug Frost himself points out that the world's fastest sprinters, Alex Popov and Pieter van den Hoogenband, haven't raced beyond 200 metres since they were kids. Popov only contests the 50-100 double. Obviously they weren't going to jeopardise what they had. Frost believed that if Thorpe could win the 100, 200 and 400 at world level, 'that would go down in history and *never be repeated*'. He considered it would be 'much more remarkable' than Mark Spitz's seven gold medals at Munich in 1972, because Spitz had only raced over the sprint distances. (He won the 100-200 free, the 100-200 fly, and the three relays.) In Ian's words, 'The 100, 200 and 400 are like different sports. That's the only way you can describe them.'

But what Frost doesn't seem to acknowledge is the obvious corollary: that by targeting Ian's training primarily at the 400, he'd made it more difficult for his prodigy to win multiple medals. No doubt he would find the suggestion offensive; but although Ian Thorpe has never made this observation publicly, the logic of it seems inescapable to him now: 'That makes sense. It's like he's criticising what Spitz did because he took the easy way to seven gold medals.'

≈

When Ian and Doug landed in Sheffield, England, on 28 January for the first leg of their three-stop World Cup tour, they learned that the main target of Frost's intimidation campaign, van den Hoogenband, had decided not to tackle Ian until the Olympics. Within a couple of days that was the least of their concerns.

The German men's head coach, Manfred Thiesmann, standing on the pool deck at Sheffield's aquatic centre, was asked by a freelance journalist: 'What do you think of Ian Thorpe?' Thiesmann's response stunned the swimming world: 'A lot of people suspect that he dopes. I was sitting on the coaches' bench in Sydney [when Ian lowered his 200 free short course world record] and almost everyone was asking, "How is this possible?" There's a lot of scepticism about him, but we can't prove it, so you can't blame him. We all know that Lamberti was pumped up and his times stood for ages, but Thorpe is not only passing them – he's passing them by seconds. He is a world apart, like the sun and the moon. I acknowledge that he has the best physique for a swimmer – his hands, his feet, his shoulders, his narrow waist, his muscles are very soft – but I am still suspicious.' It was all over the London *Times* within hours.

At the ensuing packed press conference, Ian was cool. Don Talbot had warned him this was going to happen one day, and he was prepared for it. He said: 'I know I have never taken anything and I never will, and I don't understand the concept of taking drugs. It is inexcusable.' When he called his parents at home, Ken and Margaret were more angry and distressed than their son.

Although Ian had always wanted to be the first to front up for any kind of test that would prove his innocence, the fact was the existing urine tests could only pick up stimulants, anabolic steroids and their masking agents, and there was as yet no blood test that could detect synthetic human growth hormone or EPO. Ian had already volunteered to give a sample of his blood in advance of any new test that might be developed for those substances; what more could he do? 'Here we go again,' said Ken to Dave Flaskas. 'The innocent having to prove their innocence.' That was always his perspective on the world.

It may have been inevitable, but the stupidity of Thiesmann's claim was still staggering. When swimmers and coaches openly and collectively accuse other teams or individuals – say, for instance, the Chinese women's team during the Worlds in 1994, or the Irishwoman and triple gold medallist Michelle Smith at Atlanta in 1996 – it's because they understand their own sport. Ill-informed commentators often accuse them of hypocrisy or sour grapes, but almost invariably they're proved right in the end, because they know what's possible, what's unlikely, and what's not possible without illegal help. They know that swimmers with no track record – no cumulative history of dominance – who make colossal gains in a short space of time are candidates for suspicion. Especially if they have lousy techniques. They knew in early 2000 what the sport's most authoritative commentator, *US Swimming World* editor-in-chief Dr Phillip Whitten, bothered to spell out: 'There is absolutely no reason to suspect Ian Thorpe is doping. Detailed underwater stroke analysis shows he has extraordinary technique. In addition, he exhibits none of the physical signs of drug use. His physical attributes, natural talent, excellent coaching and superior technique entirely account for his superb performances.'

Thiesmann's subsequent apology, with an oblique suggestion he'd been misquoted, was incredibly lame: 'I have never said at any time that a member of the Australian team has tested positive for drugs. I became advised about an article in a newspaper and I apologise. I know that Ian Thorpe is tested regularly but never positive.' Dave Flaskas has not forgiven the German coach. He reckoned the man should have been disciplined by suspension from the Olympic Games. He also found it interesting that Thiesmann's half-witted slur had been cast just prior to the second leg of the World Cup tour: Berlin.

The Germans had spent $250 million building a beautiful 3000-seat state-of-the-art underground pool called the Europasportpark in the old East Berlin – ironically, the former location of the most appalling systematic doping regime in history – to showcase the sport. But there was not a lot of goodwill going around on the opening night of the FINA World Cup meet.

Ian Thorpe was tapped on the shoulder and informed he'd be required for drug testing after he won the 100 free in a personal best time. It was 3 pm. An hour later Ian won the 400 free, then reported to the drug-testing room at 4.30 and produced a sample, which was accordingly divided into 'A' and 'B' specimens. But he could see something was wrong with the whole set-up. Ian was one of the most frequently drug-tested athletes in the world, averaging almost one test every fortnight since his Pan Pacs breakthrough. He knew the procedures backwards. The samples were supposed to be sealed immediately in tamper-proof containers to be shipped off to the lab, while the athlete signed a form confirming the procedure had been correctly followed.

The German Dr Eide Luebs of FINA's Medical Commission informed Ian, American backstroke star Lenny Krayzelburg and three other swimmers in the testing room that he didn't have the required containers with him – so he was going to take the samples home, presumably stick them in the fridge, then send them off the following day. After all that had just gone down only days beforehand, he must have been out of his mind if he thought Ian Thorpe was going to sign over an unsealed sample. It was just ludicrous.

Trailed by his chaperone, Ian left the testing room with both bottles clutched in his hands and headed straight for Don Talbot, who was sitting in the athletes' grandstand. 'I need you. Can you come with me?' he asked earnestly. Ian explained the situation to Talbot on the way back. Krayzelburg emerged to confirm it: 'They aren't doing it

Ken Thorpe, cricketing prodigy, aged 14.

Ken and Margaret Thorpe tying the knot, 14 January 1978.

Ian in the backyard at Milperra, aged 9. No-one ever said he'd play cricket for Australia.

Already a formidable swimming package, Ian at the NSW Championships in 1992, towering over his opposition.

Newspix/Gregg Porteous

With Michael Williams, aka 'Uncle Fester', in 1998. Ian's friendship and support helped Michael to beat an incredibly aggressive cancer, but the inspiration flowed both ways.

Adam Pretty/Getty Images

Elation after smashing Kieren Perkins' long-standing world record for the 400 freestyle at the Pan Pacs in 1999. Experts ranked this the greatest single performance by any swimmer.

Tom Un

With big sister Christina at her wedding on 4 March 2000. Ian made an emotional speech about love, and later stripped down to his boxers.

Clive Brunskill/Getty Images

On his way to another world record and his first Olympic gold in the 400 freestyle in Sydney, the 17-year-old Thorpe annihilates the field.

Nick Wilson/Getty Images

Exulting in the triumph of his 400 free victory in Sydney. His head in another space altogether, Ian couldn't recall doing this and was shocked when he saw the video.

Newspix/Brett Faulkner

The moment when the 4x100 freestyle relay at the Sydney Olympics was won. Thorpe makes a sensational changeover from Ashley Callus while America's Gary Hall Jr is slower off the lane four block.

Allsport UK/Getty Images

With Grant Hackett out of sorts early in the Olympics, Todd Pearson and Bill Kirby stepped up to help Ian and Michael Klim blow the opposition away in the 4x200 freestyle relay. This event is reckoned to be the genuine test of a country's swimming program.

Scott Barbour/Getty Images

At the post-Olympic parade in Sydney, Ian felt pangs of loneliness amid the frenetic celebrations. A trip to the US and Europe revived him.

The American International Athlete Trophy – formerly the Jesse Owens Award – recognises the world's greatest athlete. Ian won it for his performances in the Worlds in 2001.

Meeting Japan's flamboyant Prime Minister Junichiro Koizumi in March 2002.

A karate lesson in a Tokyo dojo with two world champions, Kenji Midori and Norichika Tsukamoto. 'Go on, Ian – kick me really hard ...'

Newspix/Anthony Weate

With long-time coach Doug Frost at the zenith of their partnership at the Fukuoka Worlds in 2001. Ian left Japan with six gold medals.

Newspix/Brett Costello

Day one of the new regime: Ian and Tracey Menzies entering the Sutherland pool for the morning session, 14 October 2002.

Ian's manager and friend Dave Flaskas and his wife Michelle: along for an emotional roller-coaster ride.

Shortly after this photo was taken during Ian's visit to a Shanghai primary school in September 2002, the kids got over-excited and the Thorpe camp had to beat a hasty exit.

With Ping-Ping, a student from the Beijing Zhiguang Special Education School for orphaned, autistic and intellectually disabled kids. Funds were distributed to the school via Ian Thorpe's Fountain for youth Trust.

In April 2003, Thorpe went with journalist Jeff McMullen to visit remote Aboriginal communities in the east Katherine area of the Northern Territory. Ian's Trust committed half a million dollars to help relieve chronic ill-health in the local population.

In Athens with Ernie Dingo for a 'Great Outdoors' special one year out from the 2004 Olympics. No-one was backing the Greeks to put on such a magnificent show.

Adidas

Testing resistance to his latest adidas bodysuit using Audi's wind tunnel in Ingolstadt, Germany, in January 2003.

A world of emotional pain straight after the infamous false start at the Olympic Trials, March 2004.

Jon Buckle/Getty Images

Ian congratulates his friend Craig Stevens after Craig had qualified for the Olympics by finishing second to Grant Hackett in the 400 free at Trials. A month later, Stevens handed the swim to Thorpe.

Newspix/Gregg Porteous

Chris McGrath/Getty Images

In the team. Ian in the traditional celebration of his selection in the Australian Dolphins, bound for the Athens Olympics.

Newspix/Gregg Porteous

At the Australian team's pre-Olympic staging camp in Sindelfingen, Germany, Tracey Menzies gets technical.

Newspix/Gregg Porteous

Crossing paths with Pieter van den Hoogenband at the Dolphins' first training session at the Athens pool. Their clash in the 200 free lived up to its billing.

Pierre-Philippe Marcou/AFP/Getty Images

Ian reckons no tears flowed during the emotional moments after his victory in the 400 freestyle at the Athens Olympics. Even so, the relief is intense.

Tim Clary/AFP/Getty Images

American phenomenon Michael Phelps (right), a medley and butterfly specialist, showed a champion's courage to take on Ian Thorpe and Dutchman Pieter van den Hoogenband in the 200 free in Athens – but has to settle for bronze.

Mike Hewitt/Getty Images

A bronze medal and a personal best in the 100 free at the Olympics – vindication for coach Tracey Menzies, and hence the big smile.

Daniel Berehulak/Getty Images

Not so much relief but sheer ecstasy: Thorpe wins 'The race of the century' in Athens, the 200 freestyle.

the right way.' Talbot suggested they enlist the support of the American coach, Jonty Skinner. They found Skinner and all three went back to argue, along with Ian, their case against the farcical procedure. But the FINA representative there, Chief Olatukombu of Nigeria, Dr Luebs and other German officials denied there was any problem.

At 5.10 pm Talbot and Skinner instructed Ian and Lenny and another American swimmer, Ashley Tappin, not to hand over their samples. British head coach Deryk Snelling gave the same advice to his swimmer, Stacey Houldsworth. Kazakhstan's Yermakova also decided to wait. Ian was using a mobile phone (which wasn't strictly allowed) to tell Dave Flaskas back in Sydney what was going on. Flaskas could hear Talbot yelling obscenities in the background. It was hot and sweaty in the tiny room. The athletes weren't allowed any food. An English manager smuggled in a bit of sustenance while the stand-off continued. Finally, at 6 pm, one of the German officials left to call the police.

An hour later, they still hadn't arrived and Yermakova, tired and hungry, threw in the towel. 'I'm not that important,' she said, signing over her sample. At 7.20 pm, four police officers arrived and agreed to cover the samples with official seals cross-signed by the athletes. Supposedly that would make them tamper-proof. Still very unhappy with the situation, the remaining swimmers reluctantly agreed, while the German officials whined about the amount of trouble they were causing. Thorpe didn't leave that room until 8 pm. He'd been in there for three and a half hours.

Back at the hotel, he rang his manager again and said: 'I just want to get out of here and come home.' His migraine headache was shocking. Flaskas counselled Ian to talk the situation through with Don Talbot, hoping the head coach could find the right words. Talbot himself had spent an uneasy night, and after contacting the President of Australian Swimming, Terry Gathercole, decided he was going to try to have the samples discarded.

In the morning Ian got through his heat of the 200 metres and then began a protracted conversation with Talbot up in the grandstand. Nicole Jeffrey, the only Australian reporter there, watched him shake his head over and over as Don, then Doug, then Don and Doug together tried to convince him to swim in the afternoon final. It went on for about an hour. As far as Ian was concerned, if he wasn't going to swim well on the back of all that stress and sleeplessness, then why should he swim at all?

That was still his position when he came back from lunch. More discussion. Then Talbot did something that was highly uncharacteristic of him. He said to Ian: 'I've never given a swimmer the opportunity to pull out before, but I understand what you've been through these past few days, and I'm going to give you the choice.' Those were precisely the words of wisdom required. It meant a lot to Thorpe that he was being shown that degree of independence and respect by a famously authoritarian figure. He decided that if he was going to swim, he *would* swim well. He told Talbot: 'I'll swim – but I want to do it in my new suit. If I can do that, I'll promise you a world record.'

Talbot's eyes lit up. But there was a slight problem, of course: Ian wasn't allowed to wear the suit because he was representing Australia. He just happened to have an unbranded version in his bag, which he'd been testing privately. But he reckoned he knew the rules like the back of his hand, and although he might cop a slap on the wrist, the only person who'd be liable to get into any real trouble was Talbot – 'and he kind of *doesn't* get into trouble'. In any case, the head coach gave Ian the nod. It was a maverick moment for both him and Thorpe, and a defining moment in Ian's life.

Fuelled by his anger, he swam the 200 freestyle final in a blistering 1:41.10, annihilating the field and breaking his own short course record by one and a half seconds. To this day, he rates that the greatest swim of his life – better even than the 400 free record at Pan Pacs when he shattered Perkins' longstanding mark. Nicole Jeffrey cornered him afterwards and said: 'This morning you were the most miserable kid I'd ever seen – what happened?' Ian replied: 'I decided I wasn't going to let it affect me. I just realised that if I flinched now, I'd maybe flinch again in the future when things got tough.' The experience cemented in Ian's mind all that he'd learned about the power of positivity. This was mental toughness in extremis. He'd be drawing on that account again.

Ian rang Flaskas on his mobile and said: 'The Germans have just told me I've won a prize for the best performance of the meet. It's a canary yellow left-hand drive Jeep Cherokee. What should I do with it?' Flaskas replied: 'Drive it straight into lane four and leave it at the bottom of the pool.' Ian, seriously: 'That's not very mature, David.' He decided to have the car sold and the proceeds, around $50 000, donated to UNICEF.

Most gratifying of all was the reception he received from the crowd at the medal presentation: 'I can remember standing behind the dais as they announced the winner, and the Swedes started a standing ovation, and then it spread and everyone stood up and started cheering and clapping, and the announcement seemed to go on and on, and throughout that time they just kept on cheering and clapping. I have never been so moved in my entire swimming life. It was like a huge slap in the face to Thiesmann, to their officials, and everything that had happened.' The rest of the victory ceremony was temporarily postponed as the crowd continued the uproarious celebration, refusing to resume their seats.

Thorpe shook the hand of the second-placed swimmer, Hungarian Bela Szabados, and said: 'Good swim.' The reply has stuck in his mind: 'Only one problem. I wish I wasn't swimming it. I wish I'd been able to watch *you* swim it.' Under the circumstances, and in that highly emotional state, Ian was no doubt affected by the quality of the sportsmanship Szabados displayed. And the German people's response showed what they thought of the incompetence and vindictiveness of their own representatives. In fact, Flaskas received numerous letters and emails addressed to Ian from German fans explaining their embarrassment.

Last stop on this extraordinary tour was the pretty little town of Imperia, on the Italian Riviera near Monte Carlo. Ian had never been to Italy, and the contrast with the oppressive atmosphere in Berlin was stark. He was ridiculously spoiled by the matronly cook, inevitably named 'Mama', at the little hotel where the Australian party stayed. The coffee was superb, the Italian journos asked all kinds of oddball questions (for once), and Ian just loved the girls: 'They've got the biggest heels, and they scoot around on their Vespas honking their horns and yelling abuse at people. When they get really upset they take their helmets off before they start screaming, and they look absolutely *perfect*. Then they just walk off, very dignified. I like their style.' Thorpe actually lost a race in Imperia – the 100 free, by a whisker – but it hardly mattered.

Still, the Italian sojourn was just a glimmer of light, nothing more. Ian found he had to confront a range of emotions on his return, and it wasn't easy to process what had gone on. At first, he said at the press conference in Sydney on 14 February, he was angry, then frustrated, 'then for a while I thought it was quite humorous'. But at that stage he was in denial, trying to laugh it off. 'And then it dawned on me that it *did* hurt. There's no way that I can prove my innocence at this stage, and that's what hurt me.' Like a great many athletes the world over, Ian was sweating on the scientific breakthrough that would see the introduction of blood testing in time for the Olympics.

He became even more paranoid than before. He would not drink water unless it came from a sealed bottle, sip any other swimmer's water at training, drink from an already opened can of soft drink, eat unwashed fruits and vegetables, accept any edible gift, or buy packaged food that was opened or damaged. Dining at a restaurant, he'd get a friend to order his intended drink, then do a swap.

It didn't help his state of mind when FINA, having conducted its own investigation into the testing debacle in Berlin, and having considered numerous detailed submissions including one from Ian Thorpe, concluded on 3 March: 'No violation of the FINA doping control rules . . . has taken place. Without correct knowledge about the FINA rules, competitors and coaches should not interfere in the procedures at the doping control station.' That was typical of them.

Frost was furious, Talbot even more so, while Australian Swimming backed Ian to the hilt. But the Thorpe and Flaskas show had already moved on, not even bothering to comment. By that stage it was early March, and they were up to their ears in the great swimsuit showdown.

17

THE SWIMSUIT WAR

WHILE THE YEAR 2000 WAS FULL OF pressure and at times outright rancour, with the upcoming swimsuit saga only the most prominent on the list of distractions, there were good times too. The best of them was Christina's wedding to David Williams on 4 March. First, during the speeches, Ian surrendered to a wave of pent-up emotion when David simply thanked young Michael for being there. For being alive. It didn't happen often, but the tears flowed freely at that moment. And when Ian spoke, his eyes were downcast and his voice quavered as he launched into a reading from the Bible on the subject of love: what it is, what it means. There was still, despite all his sophistication, a refreshing bashfulness in the 17-year-old's demeanour.

Afterwards the five boys – the groom and his four groomsmen, including Ian and Michael – did a choreographed strip down to their custom-made matching boxer shorts, to the strains of 'Man – I Feel Like A Woman'. Given the seriousness of Ian Thorpe's public image,

Australians would have been stunned if they'd been privy to that performance.

Straight away, as always, it was back to business. The first phase in the tortuous process of getting the adidas product ratified – gathering data to show the performance benefit of the suit – had already been done. Back on 20 December 1999 the adidas crew had booked out the Homebush pool and supplied a range of suits for testing: the latest adidas full-body suit, various Speedo drag-reducing suits, and 'placebo' suits – full-body outfits made of lycra especially for this exercise. All of the costumes were unbranded. Ian Thorpe and four other squad swimmers from the Sutherland club were the test pilots.

The crucial participant in this exercise was a former East German swimming biomechanics expert who spoke very little English but whose military precision and attention to detail guaranteed a robust objectivity. This gentleman had learned a couple of words very well – 'MAXIMUM EFFORT' – and he screamed them with bloodcurdling menace as the swimmers belted out their fastest possible 30-metre sprints in each garment. Underwater cameras and high-speed cameras mounted on the pool deck monitored every move.

The data covered speed through the water during the dive and dolphin kick underwater, speed on the surface of the water, drag calculated at higher and lower speeds using rubber cables for resistance, effect on body position in the water, and quite a bit more. As far as adidas was concerned, the evidence gathered would make a compelling case for its bodysuit to be classed as specialised equipment. The presentation was to be made to the AOC in a couple of months.

Correspondence between Craig McLatchey at the AOC and Flaskas began cordially enough the following day, with the bureaucrat requesting details of Ian's 'technical requirements' so that Speedo could fashion him a suitable outfit, and politely including another copy of the 'Team Membership Agreement', which 'contemplates the requirement for Ian to participate in a Speedo swimsuit at the 2000 Olympic Games'.

However, by the middle of February, just as Ian returned from Europe, several shots had been exchanged and the heat was on. Naturally adidas wasn't going to supply confidential details of a suit it had spent years developing, and anyway, the adidas muscle compression principle was totally different to the Speedo drag reduction concept – so how exactly was Speedo proposing to copy it? Finally the crucial meeting was set up for 25 February, with Ian Thorpe, Dave Flaskas, Rob Mills and adidas' biomechanics expert Ciro Fusco presenting their test data to McLatchey and Herb Elliott, the AOC's Director of Athlete and Corporate Relations.

Part of that meeting involved Thorpe giving a detailed lecture on the history of men's swimsuits, demonstrating that with each innovation the improvement claimed by the manufacturer had actually been greater than what was being claimed this time around. That historical progression was the basis of Ian's later argument: if any swimmer wanted to challenge the legality of his suit, he wasn't worried because whatever suit they were going to wear would have to be declared illegal under FINA's rules as well. Although Ian knew those rules were in need of an urgent overhaul, that wasn't *his* problem.

The adidas submission was so technically impressive, according to Rob Mills, McLatchey sportingly declared he couldn't fault it. So the runs were on the board. Speedo simultaneously switched tack, claiming they were about to introduce a new-generation suit in mid-March that 'would blow him [Thorpe] away'. Ian agreed, naturally, to test the new Speedo suit when it became available, and reckoned that should he choose to wear Speedo, he would not have any problems from adidas. That was quite true. Although the stakes were very high, there was no requirement for Ian to wear anything other than the suit of his choice. At the same time, Speedo said they'd accept Thorpe's decision in any event and not call in the lawyers.

As soon as the new Speedo suit, manufactured from a secret material that mimicked shark skin, was launched on 15 March, the company promised to make 150 outfits available to the Australian Olympic 'shadow squad' before Trials in May. But there'd be another 300 swimmers competing at those Trials. Already there was an obvious inequity, not to mention the fact that only a few favoured swimmers – including Klim, Susie O'Neill, Matt Dunn and Grant Hackett –

would have their outfits 'laser fitted', while the rest had to grab them off the rack. It was all too shoddy.

At the same time, the public was getting very hyped up because Speedo apparently claimed an overall performance advantage for its new shark-skin suit of three percent. This had the tabloids creating graphical representations of swimmers miles ahead of their previous best times, with the 1500 metres diagram showing Kieren Perkins almost a full lap in front of a struggling figure in a pair of sluggoes. The record books would have been obliterated overnight if that were the case. The majority of journalists railed against the implications of the coming revolution. A few welcomed it with equal vehemence.

Nothing like that ever happened, of course. (Arguably it was all just a journalistic misunderstanding of what Speedo had actually said.) But it was apparent the Speedo suits provided some advantage, with 15 world records falling in Athens at the World Short Course meet on 16–19 March. Obviously it *did* seem to matter whether or not you could lay your hands on one – regardless of what the adidas boffins thought.

Meanwhile, AOC President John Coates had lent his considerable weight to the debate, warning that any swimmer who was wearing old-tech gear at the Olympic Trials and didn't make the team might take court action. Top swimmers could be disqualified. The same, of course, could happen at the Games themselves, with a beaten swimmer appealing to the Court of Arbitration for Sport (CAS). Coates, one of the sharpest legal minds in the sporting world, would prefer to nip any such chaos in the bud. He wanted FINA to explain exactly how it had arrived at the conclusion the suits were legal under its rules. Otherwise, he'd be seeking an 'advisory opinion' from CAS on the legality of the suits.

What followed was a comedy of bureaucratic manners. Coates wrote eloquent letters to FINA's Algerian President, Mustapha Larfoui, explaining in great detail the internal contradictions in the swimming association's rules. Larfoui replied with no more than a few sentences that dripped contempt. John Coates would normally be an unbackable favourite in any game of contracts at 20 paces, but FINA wasn't playing. They refused to recognise that the AOC or CAS had any say in the matter.

Part of Coates' enquiries concerned the methods FINA had employed to actually test the legality of the suit. FINA's General Secretary, Gunnar Werner of Sweden, had claimed that tests were conducted, but 'declined to give details of the process', according to a news report. That line came unstuck a few weeks later when Australia's FINA representative, Roger Smith, admitted no tests ever took place. They hadn't even bothered to submerge one of these newfangled suits in the water to see if it came up for air.

Coates decided to turn to the CAS for an advisory ruling. He asked Rob Mills to provide technical details of the adidas suit for CAS to consider. Mills refused, saying he believed adidas had correctly followed the FINA approval process. There was paranoia in the air. Coates then wrote to Flaskas, urging him to get Ian to reconsider his position. He warned that his legal advice was that if CAS found that FINA had no authority to approve the bodysuits, all of Ian's performances in it, including at the Olympic Trials, would be void. In other words, he could be *out of the Olympics*.

The previous day, Rob Mills had written to Herb Elliott, pointing out exactly which Olympic marketing rules it was going to comply with and which it would contest. 'Adidas has planned a comprehensive marketing campaign featuring Ian and the full body suit,' he told Elliott. Well, *of course* they had. Elliott replied the next day: 'I trust adidas would not take any action which would put Ian in breach of his Team Membership Agreement.' In other words, he could be *out of the Olympics*.

All this critical correspondence took place in the space of a couple of days: 21 to 24 March. How hot could it get in this kitchen? Meanwhile, Don Talbot wanted Coates right out of the picture, believing the AOC's 'scare tactics' were seriously unsettling his swimmers. 'If we don't wear the long suits we can forget it,' he said after the Athens event. He later added: 'I would rather win the medal and if someone wants to challenge me to get it off me, let them try.'

No-one was playing with Johnny. Dave Flaskas accepted all along that Coates' motives were honourable and his arguments couldn't be faulted: 'Sometimes it was reported that John was trying to stop Ian from wearing the suit. At no time did we think that.' But Flaskas and Thorpe had mapped their course, and there was no turning back now. Even so, Dave reckoned there were times when the pressure exerted had him wondering whether to throw in the towel. He asked Ian: 'Mate, do you want to go through with this?'

'If it gives me one-hundredth of a second . . .' was Ian's reply. So they pressed on.

Time was precious, because the Speedo suit had to be properly evaluated by Ian according to his agreement with them, and the Olympic Trials were fast approaching. The testing was set down for 27 and 28 March, with technical presentations from the biomechanist and the fabric expert, plus a session of swimming and feedback. All parties agreed Ian's choice would have to be made by 10 April at the latest.

It wasn't a complete charade. Thorpe was quite willing to have his views turned upside down by the new Speedo suit – but that was extremely unlikely. He just didn't think the principle made sense. By contrast, he recalls the first time he wore the adidas suit while actually training: 'I was doing a warm-up and I found I'd done a 400 about 20 seconds faster than I'd normally do an easy 400 – and I thought: *how did I do that*? Because I just wasn't tired.' Little wonder that he was prepared to put it all on the line.

Anyway, adjustments to the Speedo suits were required. The process would continue. But Speedo didn't meet the 10 April deadline for delivery of the altered suits for testing. By 13 April, with exactly one month to go until Trials, Flaskas was getting jumpy: *where are the suits*? Meanwhile, Rob Mills at adidas, now convinced that the AOC's motive actually was to protect Australian swimmers from legal action, about-faced and agreed on 30 March to provide all the technical information Coates had requested for CAS. Coates duly lodged his submission to CAS on 7 April, 'seeking an advisory opinion on whether swimming's full-length body suits conform to FINA regulations'.

Coates had still not reckoned on FINA's obtuseness. On 19 April Gunnar Werner was quoted as saying: 'If the opinion goes against

FINA then we don't care; it is just an opinion and we couldn't change the rules anyway because it needs the entire congress to do that and the proposals for that agenda have closed.' That was the degree of concern FINA was capable of showing for athletes whose entire careers and livelihoods could hinge on these deliberations. Werner went on to blame the whole thing on Ian Thorpe: 'As far as I understand, it is an internal problem with Ian Thorpe, who does not want to swim in Speedo.' Could that statement have had anything to do with FINA's finding, following its enquiry into the German drug testing farce, that Ian should have shown more respect for its officials?

Finally the altered Speedo suits arrived. The timing was lousy. But even though he was already moving into his Trials taper, Ian tested them rigorously over three days at the Sutherland pool in late April while AOC heavies and Speedo reps looked on. Ian gave it all he had in those tests, which included endurance work – a scenario that didn't please Doug Frost at all – but it would have taken a miracle to change his mind by then. On 28 April GSI issued a press release announcing Thorpe's decision to go with adidas. The Speedo people were hardly thrilled, but they were satisfied the testing had been genuine, and generally they acted honourably in wishing Ian the best of luck.

On the same day, Coates made it official that the AOC would classify the suits as specialised equipment. Perhaps his motivation was to demonstrate he was on the athletes' side before CAS brought down its opinion, which was due within days. And again, on the same day, the AOC produced an official protocol for bodysuits which was, naturally, designed to shut adidas out of the promotional picture as far as possible. That marked the opening of a whole new front in the swimsuit war.

On 2 May – only 11 days before the Olympic Trials – CAS handed down its advisory opinion, which was that it didn't have the authority to examine whether FINA's decision to approve the suits was valid or not. The way was left open for any individual to challenge a bodysuit wearer in court – maybe at Trials, maybe at the Olympics. In other words, swimmers had no more certainty than they had when the whole question was raised. *They could be stripped of their medals*. The entire gabfest had been useless.

In reality, the only person who might have sued at the Olympic Trials was freestyle sprinter Chris Fydler, a lawyer in his other life who'd always opposed the suits on principle and continued to point out all kinds of potential problems associated with their 'legality', none of which has been resolved to this day. But no-one wanted to know. The coaches and officials at Australian Swimming were furious at the way this drama had played out, leaving the team divided and confused for the first time since the iron rule of Don Talbot had begun. 'TAKE YOUR CHANCES' was the headline on the *Telegraph*'s story. Like everyone else, that's what Ian did.

≈

As the Trials loomed, Ian became anxious, testy, dark, moody – very unusual for him. 'I haven't been the best person to be around,' he admitted. His training sessions were a closed shop. Even Channel Seven, his sponsor, didn't have the contractual right to interview him, and at Ian's request their film crew was eventually barred from the pool. 'A camera in your face is the last thing you want when you're hurting,' he says. 'You can almost *feel* that zoom.'

That was an apt metaphor for the entire nation's attentions. As far as the media were concerned, the Sydney Olympics were very much 'The Thorpe and Freeman Show'. With Cathy out of the country most of the time during the protracted build-up, that left just one. Ian was often door-stopped at the pool gates, harassed by media everywhere else. 'No day of the week was easy,' he reflects, 'and it got harder and harder going into the Olympics.' But apparently he thrived on the situation: 'When things get difficult for me, I seem to be able to cope at my best.'

Having experienced his sister's agony in 1996 at close quarters, Ian repeatedly stressed he was taking nothing for granted before he lined up on 13 May in front of 6000 spectators at the revamped Homebush pool, in his now ultra-tight bodysuit, for the first of his Trials events, the 400 freestyle. Thorpe went out in an incredible 1:49.1 for the first

200, two seconds under world record pace, leaving Grant Hackett five body-lengths behind and commentator Ray Warren in a state of rapture as he neared the finish: 'Is he going to get under the record? In he goes . . . 3:41.33! He has done it again! You are a *freak* [that word again], Ian Thorpe! You might well be the greatest ever . . .'

Hackett, a full ten seconds off the pace, was still swimming after Ian had stood, removed his goggles, and waved a dignified acknowledgment to the crowd. Ray Warren was simultaneously gushing: 'They say Spitz was great . . . We know Dawnie was great . . . But has anyone ever been better than this boy?'

Ian told Nicole Stevenson in the poolside interview: 'The best part of that swim was that I was able to gain selection for the Olympic team.' He repeated the phrase twice: '*I've gained selection . . . I've gained selection . . .*' In the context of Ray Warren's comments, it seemed almost ludicrously humble. But his father had always deemed representing your country at the Olympics to be the greatest honour for any athlete. As Ian had stated back in primary school, that was his singular ambition. And of course, anything *could* go wrong, even if you were Ian Thorpe. You could, for instance, be thrown out for a false start . . .

Ian called and consoled Grant Hackett, who was utterly dejected. Then he gave the adidas suit a ringing endorsement: 'I felt a higher body position. That might be mental . . . and then throughout the race I felt a lot better with my stroke.' What more could you want from a swimsuit? But of course, he'd only swum half a second faster than he'd managed in his lycra briefs a year before – and at 195 centimetres, he'd actually grown three centimetres since then. Whatever the benefit, it was obviously not *that* big a deal. And to play it up too much would detract from his own performance – which was always the dilemma for all the suited-up swimmers, especially when they were looking to break world records.

They kept on tumbling for Ian. When he emerged onto the pool deck after the semi-final of the 200 free, having taken 0.31 seconds from his old world mark, he shook Doug Frost's hand over the media fence, but the coach seemed to be affecting an air of nonchalance as he studied the sheet of paper in his hand intently. He didn't even look up. It seemed somehow comical.

Ian knew he still had some juice left in the tank after that semi-final, so he wasn't too concerned about facing up to the strongest 200 freestyle field ever assembled, at any level, the following night. But just before the race started, he felt the onset of a crippling migraine. He hadn't had one since Berlin back in February. (*Stress-related? Food allergy? What was it?*) He struggled with waves of nausea as he stood on the block. And then, when he dived in, his goggles immediately filled with water. Hadn't he bombed out when that happened in a crucial race once before, years ago? Could he swim with water in his goggles *now*?

It could have all come unstuck right there. Olympic Trials: no second chance. And here was Michael Klim, trying to steal the race (as usual), but this time he was taking it out faster than ever, a full second under Ian's new record pace at the 100. An athlete's existence is defined by how he responds to this kind of situation. Ian might well have started thinking about whether he could grab second place. Instead he somehow stuck with Klim all the way, fighting to control the concurrent pain of the migraine and the lactic acid. Finally, after 175 metres almost toe-to-toe, Michael fell away. In those last few strokes Ian blitzed him by well over a body-length and raised the bar just a little higher again, at 1:45.51.

Thorpe chatted poolside with Rob Woodhouse on camera for about a minute. His head was still aching like mad, but he wasn't even puffing. Then Woodhouse turned to Michael, who was *still* trying to catch his breath. 'He's just awesome,' panted the man who'd only recently won seven world championship medals and been hailed the world's greatest swimmer.

So these Trials had turned out to be an exact re-run of Pan Pacs '99, with Ian setting three world records in the same events on the first three nights. It was enough to wind Ray Warren all the way up: 'Ladies and gentlemen, boys and girls – you are watching a man they'll be talking about centuries from now . . .'

Even before the 200 semi-final was swum, Doug Frost announced he was putting Michael Klim's 100 freestyle Commonwealth Record of 48.73 'on notice'. It really annoyed Ian. He knew there was no reason to believe he would suddenly lower his PB by at least a second. And even if it *were* likely, why carry on about it before the event? Increasingly, Doug was saying one thing, Ian another, and reporters snapped up whichever statement would sell papers. Mostly that would be Doug's. And there was the extra burden of dealing with the first three or four questions at the press conference, which would address whatever it was Doug had said. 'So then I'd have to either contradict my coach,' says Ian, 'or figure out a way to hose it all down. This happened all the time.'

After qualifying third-fastest for the 100 metres final behind Klim and Fydler, Thorpe said that he would 'definitely' swim the 1500 if he couldn't place first or second to secure an individual swim in the sprint race at the Olympics. Talbot disapproved. So too did Frost. But Ian was insistent, teasing everyone with: 'I'm a little bit curious about it.' No wonder, considering what he believed about the way he was being trained.

As it turned out, he swam fourth in the final, missing his PB by 0.03 and trailing well behind Klim's quicksilver 48.56. In fact, he only beat the fifth place-getter, Todd Pearson, by the barest margin – one-hundredth of a second – to take the last priority placing in the 4 × 100 relay team. If he'd finished a fingernail slower, there *may* have been another way onto the team, but not necessarily. And, as usual, he was stone cold last at the turn.

Ian still wanted that third individual swim at the Olympics. He brushed past Denis Cotterell, Grant Hackett's coach, on the way to the warm-down pool and told him he was going to swim the 1500. Word got around quickly: Thorpe vs Perkins vs Hackett would be a heady mix over that distance. Thirty minutes later he'd changed his mind and pulled out. Frost had weighed in with a flat-out refusal to countenance the idea. As long as he was coaching a boy who wanted to swim the 100, he wouldn't be swimming 1500 metres as well. Ian had no great attachment to the long-haul event, so there was no need for a showdown.

At the press conference Thorpe said: 'I don't think swimming the 1500 and perhaps training for it would let me swim the 200 and the 400 to the best of my ability . . . It just isn't something I want to get into.' Of course not: the race was boring. Ian wanted to swim *fast*. Perkins admitted he was relieved: 'I'd be lying if I said I wasn't.' Hackett went to bed none the wiser, having not spoken to his coach that evening.

≈

A week after Trials, Ian was sitting opposite Andrew Denton, one of the sharpest comic minds in Australia, in front of a packed audience in a Channel Seven studio. The gig was part of his sponsorship agreement with Seven. There'd been so few opportunities for the Australian public to see what sort of guy the 17-year-old Ian Thorpe really was, and people were curious. Pretty much all they knew was that if you asked him the same (serious) question, on the pool deck and in press conferences, he'd give you the same (serious) answer. *Every time*. Ian still had no great need to dispel that image.

But Denton, naturally, took another tack. After a hilarious segment in which he commentated on a pack of boy dolls swimming in a simulated race (because Channel Seven didn't have the real footage), Kieren Perkins appeared on a giant video monitor.

Andrew: 'You sent Kieren a hero fax as a kid . . . Do you remember what you said?'

Ian: 'Hi. My name's Ian. I'm nine years old and you're my hero. Please send me a letter back.'

Andrew: 'And did Kieren send you a letter?'

Ian: 'No, he didn't. [*Perkins laughing on the monitor.*] That's why there's so much tension between us now . . .'

The audience loved it. Ian obviously had comedic timing. Denton pressed on . . .

Andrew: 'What was it like meeting the Queen?' [Ian had been given a formal introduction during a state visit in March.]

Ian: 'I don't know if I should say what I think of the Queen . . .'

Andrew: 'We all have an urge for her we can't control – right?'

Ian: 'Speak to John Howard about that.'

Denton looked shocked. The audience guffawed. Then Christina Thorpe appeared on the set to inform everyone that Ian was a total slob. On the giant screen appeared footage of an outrageously messy bedroom. The audience gasped in disbelief.

Ian: 'That's not my room. That is *not* my room . . .'

People were in two minds whether to believe him or not. It was intriguing. (Actually, an adidas film crew had shot the footage one day out at the Thorpe house, at Denton's request.) Then Christina started into an anecdote about a quite recent fruit fight between herself and her brother. 'She always tells it wrong,' Ian insisted before butting in with his version, lingering long over a description of how he'd rubbed this squished-up banana right through his sister's hair, then sat down to await her response. Christina was so mad she threw a fork at him that stuck right into his knee and drew gushes of blood when he yanked it out. He told the story so well, in such delightful detail, the audience was by now enraptured.

So – the light bulbs went on all over Australia as Denton's show monopolised the ratings. Ian Thorpe was not just a humble, articulate, serious bloke who could swim fast. People would henceforth come up to him in the street and say: 'Mate, I didn't realise you were a funny bastard as well.'

18

'THE QUESTION EVERYBODY'S ASKING'

THREE YEARS PREVIOUSLY, A MEETING with Alex Popov was enough to get Ian excited. Now it would take a bit more than that . . . like having Nicole Kidman in a leather catsuit slinking right across a crowded room to fix him with a radiant smile and announce: 'I just *had* to meet you.' It was at the premiere of *Mission: Impossible 2* at Fox Studios, Nicole and Tom were apparently big fans, and Ian was blown away: 'I was just freaking, thinking: "*Wow. Wow*. This is Nicole Kidman."' Within a matter of months, he'd have a gaggle of movie stars eating out of his hand. Meanwhile the press wanted to know all about Ian's date, a stunning brunette model from Melbourne named Kinga Burza. 'We're just getting to know each other,' he told Catriona Dixon. No further questions, please.

Altitude training in Colorado in June during the 'aerobic phase' of his preparation opened Ian's eyes to the level of celebrity he'd already attained in the US. He knocked back a host of media requests and concentrated on churning out the heavy work over three weeks while

Doug got very annoyed about the amount of 'spying' going on. US Swimming officials camped on the pool deck and wrote down every lap time, every stroke rate. 'I told them to piss off,' says Doug. But Ian wasn't worried about it. He knew if his rivals didn't have their act together by now, no amount of skulking around would make any difference.

Arriving back in Australia to begin his 'quality endurance cycle' in early July, Thorpe was by now almost inured to the massive pressure on him. A market research outfit had found 79 percent of Australians nominated Ian Thorpe as the athlete they most wanted to watch at the Games, with Cathy Freeman second on 41 percent. While the rest of the country whipped itself into a frenzy, Ian just tried to stay focused on his mission: to push himself in training to the absolute limit, to embrace every ounce of pain and understand that it alone was his insurance against failure. *Only the pain of a hard workout can save the agony of defeat.* 'I *like* the pain,' he said. 'I know there has to be a point at which I'll have to back off – but I haven't reached it yet.'

When Dave Flaskas asked him what he wanted to achieve for himself at these Olympics, Ian fixed his manager with that same look of inflexible determination he'd once given his primary school teacher, Paul Butler. He'd raised the bar just a notch: 'All I want is *one* Olympic gold medal. Just one.' Once he'd accomplished that, he could then start thinking about another one.

Ian remembers one session when the aquatic centre's workers hadn't arrived to turn on the lights, so he slipped into the pitch blackness of the pool and swam away, counting his strokes, knowing exactly when the wall was coming – *tumbleturn and push* – his every sense automatically attuned and totally at one with the water. In such sublime moments it was possible to grasp and reaffirm for himself the purpose of it all.

To Ian, that purpose was *not* to achieve some form of transcendence via the pursuit of 'greatness'. He never thought that the remainder of his days would be somehow more meaningful because he'd once been a great swimmer. But he did concur with this statement, from P.J. Mullen's *Gold in the Water*, reflecting on the athlete's journey, rather than its end-point: 'It is noble because one of the most important things to do in life is to at least once chase a dream with every ounce of power and conviction we can muster.'

'Greatness' involved comparing yourself to everyone else, and that was not the point at all. Only a few could ever aspire to 'greatness' in any field – but every person could aspire to be as good as they could possibly be. 'The most important thing,' Thorpe believes, 'is learning about yourself, via your successes and failures, in striving toward that goal. I think that's more important than achieving the goal itself. It's not just about self-esteem; it's more about self-awareness. It's not about taking great pride in what you do; it's about learning what's important.'

It just so happened that Ian Thorpe was one of those few whose talents made greatness a possibility. But his was a philosophy of inclusion: he wanted people to understand that by totally committing to some kind of goal, and by refusing all temptation to lose focus, the satisfaction that resulted was immensely greater than the sacrifices involved. Not just in sport, but in all of life. Not just for Ian Thorpe, but for *everybody* – including every kid who'd ever contemplated suicide because they could not embrace their own intrinsic worth. That was the message he tried to convey in all of his work with Lifeline, and the philosophy behind the modest little book he would write for children and adolescents in 2002, *Live Your Dreams*.

Because Ian adhered so faithfully to these tenets, it was all the more disappointing when his performances were again questioned. On 13 July the German swimming team captain, Chris-Carol Bremer, reportedly told the newspaper *Die Welt* that uncommonly large hands and feet resulted from the use of human growth hormone. Bremer didn't mention Ian by name, but hardly needed to: 'If we are dealing with hGH, as the Australians are accused of, then one of the symptoms in athletes is that everything is huge. Hands and feet are unusually big.'

Asked directly about Thorpe, Bremer replied: 'I am not commenting on this. But people should know which physical abnormalities are caused by certain doping methods, and make their own minds up from that.' Bremer was a doctor. He ought to have pointed out that only extremely excessive use of hGH could cause enlarged extremities, and that would also cause severe facial abnormalities – none of which were evident in Ian Thorpe. And anybody with or without a medical degree would be aware that heredity could easily account for Ian's outsized hands and feet. His mother had size 11 feet, his father size 13, although neither was six feet tall. Even Christina wore size 10 shoes. Bremer's subsequent letter of apology to Ian, in which he claimed to be the victim of a journalistic ruse, was almost as lame as Thiesmann's. The claims were pathetic and laughable.

But where was the long-anticipated blood test for EPO and hGH? Ian reiterated that he wanted to be the first athlete in the world to submit to a blood test to prove his innocence. French and Australian scientists were working separately and frantically on an EPO test – the French with urine, the Aussies with blood – but they were facing a 2 August deadline to produce evidence that their tests were mistake-proof. The Opening Ceremony would be held on 15 September, so the IOC couldn't have pushed it much further.

The Australian Sports Drug Agency (ASDA) had launched a 'True Champions Passport', with Ian Thorpe and wheelchair athlete Louise Sauvage as the figureheads, which recorded all the dates and results of Australian athletes' urine tests by ASDA. It had some symbolic value, but everyone in the sporting business knew that among privileged athletes, the drugs of choice were the undetectable ones. Of course.

As it turned out, the IOC's Medical Commission approved both the French and Australian EPO tests – the catch being that an athlete had to fail both tests to be deemed positive. The Australian blood test could detect 'markers' (indirect indicators of EPO use) up to three weeks back, but there were grave doubts about how it would withstand a legal challenge, and three weeks was still plenty of notice for drug cheats to stop before they came to Sydney. And since the French urine test could only detect EPO use during the previous 72 hours, no-one was going to be silly enough to get busted and thrown out of the Games.

But at least the EPO tests now existed (although still there was nothing for hGH), so there was a platform for swimming to move forward on the whole question of cleaning up illegal drug use. That is, if FINA really wanted to.

≈

Prior to the Olympics, Murdoch's tabloid press began producing a weekly liftout, 'The Olympian', under the editorship of veteran sportswriter Phil Rothfield. In late July, before the swimmers went into their two-week staging camp in Melbourne, Catriona Dixon was instructed by Rothfield to do a phone interview with Ian for a long story headed: 'IAN THORPE'S MOST REVEALING INTERVIEW'. Within the double-page spread there was to be a sidebar – 'The World According to Thorpe' – which would address, in a modified question-and-answer format, how Ian felt about a range of issues: 'On Olympic Expectations, On Being Called a Freak, On Life as a Millionaire', and so on. The last of these ten items was to be Ian's response to the heading: 'On the Rumours that He's Gay'.

Speculation about Ian Thorpe's sexuality had reached a crescendo by this time. It was just about impossible, according to Catriona, to have a conversation about him without the question being raised. *Everyone* wanted to know the answer. So Catriona's reasoning was that the issue had to be broached sometime – why not do it with a person Ian could trust, someone who'd known him since primary school and had never written a bad word about him? She felt strongly that it was the right thing to do.

Ian couldn't believe it when she asked the question. 'Is this on the record?' he said.

'Yes,' said Catriona. 'This is not just me and you talking. This is part of the interview.'

'I can't understand why people would say that,' Ian said. 'I don't know why they would say such a hurtful thing.'

Reflecting on that interview now, Ian says: 'It was kind of a shock hearing it come out of her mouth, and I can only say how disappointed I was that it actually got to that point. I mean, she *knew* the answer to the question – she just needed it on the record. I thought it was crap and I wasn't going to partake in it. If you're going to ask such a question, use a trash writer – don't use a swimming writer . . . If you're going to do that with swimming writers, you ruin their relationship with the swimmers, so you're never going to get a decent story. I was so disappointed in her . . .'

When Catriona told Rothfield the result of the interview, she was concerned he'd run an 'I'M NOT GAY – THORPE' style of headline on the front page. Well, *of course*. Her boss was a hard-nosed tabloid man. He was hardly likely to bury such a juicy tidbit at the bottom of a sidebar in a feature story. But in any case, how appropriate was it that such a question would appear in a publication called 'The Olympian', and in a modified 'ten questions' format? As far as Dave Flaskas was concerned, it was ridiculous and abhorrent.

After Ian told Dave what had happened, he was straight on the phone to Catriona the following morning as she was driving to work. He said he was very concerned, and so was Ian, that she'd asked the question. Catriona was upset by Ian's reaction, but still convinced it was a reasonable approach to the issue. Flaskas said: 'Dicko, I ask you not to run that.' She justified her position: 'But I think it's important. It's the question everybody's asking . . .' David disagreed absolutely. Catriona faced a dilemma. She told Flaskas to leave it with her.

Catriona asked herself whether she wanted to waste the six years she'd spent nurturing the newspaper's relationship with Ian, and at the same time demolish her personal friendship with someone she had a great deal of respect for. She thought not. She told Rothfield the situation and insisted that she didn't want to go ahead with that question. A decision was reached not to run it. There were nine questions instead.

In the end, it didn't cost her the friendship with Ian or his manager. Both of them understood the position she'd been placed in. But she still thought the Thorpe camp was 'crazy' not to address the issue: 'I'm surprised they didn't just stamp it out. Just come out and say: "I'm not gay. Yes, I like fashion. And no, I don't have a girlfriend. Would you have a girlfriend if you had to get up at 4.15 every morning and lead the life I do?" He could have done it with Channel Seven, or written it in his own column in the *Australian* . . .'

Ian would never have done any such thing. Of course he was aware of the rumours – he could expect to hear all kinds of innuendo directed at him whenever he went out – but he just could not see the value in dignifying the whole subject with a response. Nor was he going to compromise his strict privacy policy in order to satisfy people's prurient interests. 'I'd rather have to deal with this speculation every day than have to live a life where I'm hounded all the time about who I'm seeing and what we're doing. It's a part of my life that I want to protect as best I can.' That was probably not a perspective likely to be adopted by the average young Australian male – but since when was Ian one of those?

So he made his choice, and would stick with it until he decided it was appropriate to talk about what was happening in his personal affairs. At the same time, Ian was genuinely perplexed as to why it was such a big deal. 'I don't see why everyone has an obsession with it,' he now says. 'I just can't understand it. I was a bit shocked and taken aback with this episode – but it didn't affect me. Those kinds of things only make me stronger. Whatever's dished out, I take it and move on. That's the only way you can approach things like that.'

(He'd obviously moved on a long way by the time he filmed an ad for AMP which aired in August 2002. Nine famous faces were asked the question: 'What are you looking forward to?' Ian's smiling response: 'I look forward to the day when Kylie takes over the world.' Kylie Minogue is a famously known gay icon, and Ian was deliberately fanning the flames of speculation, just for the hell of it – because by then it really didn't bother him what anyone thought. At all.)

≈

Doug Frost had two swimmers at the Olympics – Ian Thorpe and Kirsten Thomson. Since all three of them were Olympic debutants, Ian decided to get three special commemorative rings made in the shape of the Olympic symbol. Doug was extremely chuffed to receive his ring. A few tears were shed by the hard man as he boarded the plane for Melbourne with Ian and Kirsten.

'He was a bit shocked,' Ian recalls, 'because it meant so much to him being recognised as our coach. Mostly he didn't get that kind of personal response from his athletes – actually being thanked for something he'd done. Some people might have become a better person, or a tougher person, as a result of swimming with Doug, and he didn't often get to hear about it.' Frost was apparently still emotional when a journo asked him about his ring the next day.

Don Talbot was taking no chances with his swimmers, who were forbidden to leave the Sebel Hotel without reporting to the duties officer so their whereabouts were known day and night. They were not allowed to go anywhere in a car or cab. All strenuous activity, apart from their taper training, was out. Kieren Perkins had strained his hamstring before his first Olympics in Barcelona in 1992, where he'd 'run around like a kid in a lollyshop'. There'd be no repeat with Ian Thorpe, who was tightly wrapped in cotton wool. Security guards shadowed him and some other big names around the clock.

Talbot's staff were instructed to build confidence with words of encouragement whenever possible. 'Great swim this morning,' one of them reportedly told Grant Hackett. 'Thanks,' he replied, 'but I had the morning off.'

When journalists asked Ian how much pressure he was under, his responses were typically low-key: 'Things don't change at the Olympics. The water temperature's the same. The distances are the same. There's the same number of competitors.' In other words, logic told him it was actually just another meet. He even confessed he was 'a bit confused about the whole Olympic thing': what was he supposed to be feeling? Everyone else was walking around with their heart-rate ten beats above normal – but not Ian. 'I'm not nervous at this stage,' he said.

It seemed to get under Perkins' skin whenever he heard Thorpe talk about 'just another meet'. At a press conference held before the team left for the Olympic Village on 9 September, he declared: 'Ask him after the Games if he feels the same way. People just don't realise the Olympics are different to anything else. The World Championships are easy. The Pan Pacs – easy. All meets are easy compared to the

Olympics. Comparing the Pan Pacs to the Olympic Games is like comparing the Melbourne Cup to Race 5 at Oodnadatta.'

Perkins was entitled to be more wary than anyone of what the Olympic cauldron could do. At Barcelona, seven men had started their events as world record holders, and six of them were beaten. Perkins, in the 1500 metres, was the only exception. He liked to point out that in the 100-year history of swimming competition at the Games, only 17 percent of the swimmers had recorded personal bests. The occasion was just too much for a great many athletes. Perkins was furious when the AOC proclaimed it 'expected' nine gold medals in the pool (including three from Ian: in the 400 free, the 200 free, and the 4 × 200 relay). As far as he was concerned, the 'bean counters' should back right off.

In his mini-biography of Ian Thorpe, *Early Days*, swimming writer Will Swanton pointed out that outrageous upsets were almost the norm at the Olympics. The great West German Michael 'The Albatross' Gross landed at Seoul in 1988 as the world record holder in the 200 free over the previous five years. The red-hot favourite in the event, he was downed by 46th-ranked Duncan Armstrong, who produced a once-in-a-lifetime performance to break the world record while Gross finished fifth. Four years before that in Los Angeles, unheralded Queenslander Jon Sieben swooped from seventh at the halfway mark of the 200 fly and shot past the unbackable favourite, Gross (again), to take the gold medal in a time *four seconds* quicker than his previous best. An astonishing effort. Who could predict which swimmer would somehow magically harness the potent energy of the Olympic experience – and which would succumb to it?

One thing Ian knew for sure was that the biggest mistake he could make would be to get overexcited about the occasion, or worry excessively about the outcome of his races. He approached these Games exactly as he'd always approached a big-time meet. If you believed you were already doing everything the best possible way, why change anything? And if people knew all there was to know about Ian Thorpe's mindset – all the things that collectively made him so mentally impregnable – he'd have been the *last* Olympic debutant they'd be concerned about.

Ian received his Olympic blazer during a ceremony at the University of Western Sydney, a short drive from his ancestral home in Milperra. Margaret and Ken were, of course, in attendance. His mother spoke of how her son had achieved his childhood dream, so she didn't care if he won gold, silver, bronze or nothing. Ken told a pressman that he 'couldn't have been more stoked' if Ian had just been handed a baggy green cap.

Then it was on to the Olympic Village, where Thorpe shared a room with Michael Klim. Michael had been one of the major disappointments in Atlanta in 1996, failing to make the final of the 200 free after going in as world number one. Perhaps it was thought that he might offer some useful words drawn from his experience. But for the younger man, it was more important that they were great mates and would have more fun just mucking around together in their room, rather than having to wander around the Village looking for entertainment. It was somewhat reminiscent of Perth at the Worlds in 1998. Ian got ready for a good time.

≈

Was there room for one more hurdle, one more test of Team Thorpe's mettle before the opening of the Big Show? Just one more.

Back on 19 June John Coates had written to Ian, requiring him to sign a document that absolved the AOC of all responsibility if any athlete without a bodysuit decided to legally challenge his results at the Games. Ian read it carefully, found it a touch unnerving, but knew that with swimmers of all nationalities at the Games intending to turn up in all sorts of new-tech gear (which they did), the entire world wasn't going to be turned upside down by a court decision. Public opinion wouldn't have allowed it. Thorpe signed the document, and gave it no more thought.

In the backroom, though, tensions were mounting on another front. Adidas had a sizeable promotions budget and obviously wanted to get some mileage out of their 'victory' on the bodysuits, and the

AOC was equally determined that the extent of that victory would be so minuscule you couldn't detect it with an electron microscope. That was their job: protect the sponsor.

Because of a special deal advantageous to Nike that had been brokered in the US concerning the rights of the big apparel companies, adidas thought they were entitled to a similar concession in Australia. They had a plan A, which involved running their award-winning ads (showing Ian racing against a seal) right throughout the Oympics – with no reference to the athlete being an Olympic swimmer. Plan B involved a range of 'point-of-sale' material (cardboard cut-outs taken from the TV ad, 'Thorpedo' T-shirts and so on) that the company wanted to use in sports stores around the country to market its association with Ian.

The AOC nixed all those plans in a letter to Rob Mills dated 31 August. Phone calls laden with threatening overtones followed. GSI's client manager Frank Turner wrote to Rob Mills, urging him to comply with the AOC's ruling. A crisis meeting was held at the International Olympic Committee's hotel on the Wednesday before Friday's Opening Ceremony on 15 September. Adidas was very disappointed with the outcome, but their first response was to drop plan A, knowing that if Ian Thorpe were to be dragged into a legal bunfight on their company's behalf at this stage, it would be a PR disaster. But they already had all this point-of-sale gear set up in sports stores, and they believed they had a legal right to keep it there. The AOC didn't.

Phone conversations continued to rage around the clock between the AOC and adidas, although technically the party who'd breached the Team Agreement was Ian Thorpe. Dave Flaskas wasn't privy to any of these 11th-hour discussions, so he didn't know how heated things had got until the day before the Opening Ceremony, when AOC lawyer Simon Rofe called him. Flaskas thought he was going to say: 'It's been a tough fight, but good luck', or something similar. What he said was: '*Dave, Ian's accreditation to the Games can be withdrawn unless adidas pulls down all its point-of-sale material nationally.*'

David called Rob Mills. It was a 'pretty heated discussion', as you'd imagine. 'Rob, please take the stuff down,' said Flaskas.

'We're within our rights,' Mills replied.

'Rob, *please* take it down.'

Mills said he'd think about it and ring back later. He did, finally, and said: 'Okay.' He didn't want to put the Thorpe camp, and in particular Ian's beleaguered manager, whom he considered a friend, through any more trauma. Frantic activity followed around the country, in the hundreds of retail stores where the Thorpedo's cardboard image smiled benignly at unsuspecting customers. Meanwhile, Flaskas considered how close he'd come to a total meltdown.

He told neither Ian nor Doug Frost anything about this final pre-Olympic drama. They didn't need to know there was a possibility of them being frogmarched out of the Olympic Village. When Ian found out about it after the show was over, he was furious at what he saw as the AOC's bullying tactics. He knew that any legal action against a bodysuit wearer from a swimmer was highly unlikely to succeed – but this was a bit different.

The IOC heavyweights did not have much of a track record when it came to backing down in games of brinkmanship. So far as they were concerned, the Olympics would always be larger than any individual. And this was an issue that now involved the two biggest corporations in sportswear: adidas and Nike. Adidas had been official sponsors of the Olympics for three decades. Now, for the first time, it was Nike who were the official Olympic sponsors, rather than masterful ambush marketers. The shoe was (literally) on the other foot – and when an outfit with that much clout decides to flex muscle, any outcome is possible.

But could anyone even *begin* to imagine the uproar that would have followed the forced removal of Ian Thorpe from his hometown Olympics?

19

'THE BEST DAY OF MY LIFE'

WHEN HE FIRST ARRIVED AT THE Olympic Village, six days before the Opening Ceremony, it was hard for Ian to keep a lid on his excitement. To him the atmosphere was something like the frenetic flavour of New York City, multiplied several times over. The food hall, which seated 7500 of the 11 000 athletes at a time, was the length of a football field. It was a blast to think that many of the world's most famous athletes were sitting in the same room, but highly unlikely that Ian would run into any of them, because there were just so many anonymous ones. You couldn't possibly go looking for sporting celebs, even if you were inclined.

On the other hand, one famous athlete – Ian Thorpe – was constantly exposed to autograph-hunting, handshake-grabbing, snapshot-seeking athletes from countries he'd never heard of. It was hard to deal with, especially at breakfast time, when on one occasion athletes from Gambia, the Philippines and Tanzania insisted on turning his morning encounter with a cereal bowl into a film shoot.

He just had to get used to it. Track stars Maurice Greene and Ato Boldon sought him out and they had a chat in an interview room, and he spotted the tennis-playing Williams sisters one day, but otherwise it was simply an ocean of multicoloured, hard-bodied, hyped-up humanity.

A couple of days after moving in, Ian was granted one of his fondest wishes when he, Kieren Perkins, Grant Hackett and Hayley Lewis were the first athletes to be tapped on the shoulder at the pool and asked to surrender some blood for EPO testing. The swimmers generally thought it was a joke that both blood and urine tests had to be failed to register a positive – but nonetheless, it was a start, and there was room at last for some optimism.

The Aussies had the best accommodation in the Village, Ian reckoned. Their demountable houses surrounded a sort of village green known as Boxing Kangaroo Square, which sported a giant TV screen. It was big enough to accommodate all the Australian team, who'd gather around each night to support every competing Aussie. To experience that patriotic camaraderie was an incomparable privilege.

Thorpe watched the Opening Ceremony on the big screen with the rest of the swimmers. It was an unwritten rule that you didn't march if you were competing next day. Westpac had given Dave Flaskas the chance to buy absolute premium front row tickets for himself and his wife Michelle. Ian watched as the cameras panned from Muhammad Ali to Greg Norman to Bill Clinton to . . . Michelle Flaskas. He called her on the mobile: 'Nice outfit you're wearing.' It was worth a laugh. Then he got into a 'bonding shave-down session' with Klim and Hackett. Ian went to bed at 9.30 and slept well.

It would have been hard to miss the headline on the morning *Telegraph*'s 'Olympian' liftout: 'INVINCIBLE'. It covered a shot of Ian Thorpe leaping from the blocks. He refused, as always, to regard it as extra pressure; instead it was *support*. 'But I thought it was ridiculous. You can't say that about anyone. I just kind of dismissed it.'

The bookies at Centrebet didn't think it was ridiculous. For the 400 freestyle Ian was the hottest favourite of all Olympic athletes at 20-1 on. His best time was, after all, more than 12 metres ahead of

America's world number two, Klete Keller. (The same odds were offered for the US men's basketball team, which did win, and Susie O'Neill in the 200 butterfly, who didn't.)

Ian got the bus to the pool, arriving at around 9 am, and warmed up in a lane next to Hackett. Then he checked the TV to watch the Australian triathletes, who weren't considered 'invincible' but were expected to dominate their inaugural Olympic event. The men bombed out completely, with the women returning just one silver. The Aussie shooters were also off target, which meant Thorpe would be gunning for his country's first gold medal that evening. *Still* he felt no nerves.

Just after 11 am he swam his heat of the 400 free with minimal effort, in a pair of briefs, and broke the Olympic record. That was reassuring. During their taper before a big meet, swimmers duplicate what's worked for them in the past. Some lose their edge if they rest more than three days, while most (including Ian) continue to scale back the work over three weeks. But sometimes their bodies don't exactly adapt in predictable ways. Sometimes, inexplicably, they 'miss' their taper, and once that happens, it's just about impossible to recover. The meet will be a write-off. That's what Ian meant when he said: 'The hardest swim is always the first, because there's a question mark over what's going to happen.' If you can break an Olympic record while in cruise mode, you know for sure you haven't missed your taper. Ian Thorpe's odds shortened to 50-1 on for the final. That *was* ridiculous.

For some years, Ian had been telling the media he'd swap all of his achievements for an Olympic gold medal. It may have been something of a contradiction, since he'd always said he was only concerned with surpassing his own performances rather than with winning. But in any case, it encapsulated how *all* swimmers felt about the Olympic Games. They did not dream of fast times or perfect strokes; they dreamt of Olympic gold: the most immutable of all symbols, the most precious of all metals. And so it seemed to Ian a little puzzling that even as the climactic hour of his life approached, he felt extraordinarily calm. He'd been hearing about 'the Olympic buzz' for so long, but he still hadn't really felt it. Of course, he didn't want to be burning adrenalin all day long; he remained determined not to let himself get overstimulated. He was just very surprised at how well he was handling the task.

He called to check on how the family was travelling. Christina was, as always on day one of a major meet, a nervous wreck. 'Just have fun,' she said, trying to sound cool. 'This is your moment.' Ian ate some pasta for lunch and drifted off to sleep.

At 6 pm he caught the bus back to the pool, with the race due to start at 7.15. Will Swanton was the one journalist observing his demeanour during the warm-up, and wrote in *Early Days*: 'Thorpe slid quietly into the congested training pool like a crocodile preparing for the kill, his eyes shifting left and right, sizing up his prey, his stroke long and strong and ominous. The only thing that separated him from public view was a thin blue curtain hanging between the training and main pool. But hope drifted over to him, hung above him, all around him.'

Every movie star, rock star, sport star, business heavyweight and politician of note had taken their places inside the Aquatic Centre alongside three generations of PMs: Howard, Keating and Whitlam. (Where was Hawkey?) Even Chelsea Clinton, representing her father, had found her way into the audience, flanked by a posse of security men. The reconfigured grandstands were filled to their end-stage capacity of 18 000 – an unprecedented crowd for a swim meet. Five million Australians were tuning in on TV, astronomical numbers around the globe.

Ian walked to the change-room and began the arduous task of squeezing into his dark blue, tighter-than-skin costume. It took around 15 minutes. Hackett, who was strangely off-colour and hadn't swum well in the morning, finally zipped him up. Still Ian felt nothing unusual: no nerves. He walked up the tunnel behind South Africa's Ryk Neethling and turned left, only a few paces now from the pool deck, his ears tuning in to the gentle, consistent hum emanating from the massed audience. At the precise moment when he emerged into view, the announcer intoned: 'Ladies and gentlemen, please welcome competitors for the final of the Olympic men's 400 metres freestyle.'

And the *noise* . . . it was unlike anything Ian had ever heard at any swim meet. Hope, fear, apprehension, euphoria and anticipation all bundled into an incomprehensible wall of sound – people screaming, laughing, clapping, shrieking, jumping up and down and praying to God, as if they personally were about to be subjected to an exhaustive examination of their own mettle. Ian glanced toward the towering western grandstand and observed the energy of thousands of foot-stomping, fist-clenching Australians bellowing: 'Go, Thorpey, go!'

Was it possible for him to ward off the excitement any longer? Did he *want* to? After all, he'd dedicated so much of his life to the prospect of standing in this particular place at this particular time, in order that he alone should carry the aspirations of his countrymen in an age-old symbolic quest for supremacy. Ahead of him: less than four minutes in which to define forever his existence as an athlete. If that was not thrilling beyond belief, then what was the point of it all?

He felt the Olympic buzz. But still, he could not afford to entirely succumb to it. Not yet. 'I couldn't let *that* be my moment,' he recalls. 'That wasn't what I was there for.' Even though the atmosphere was extraordinary, Ian had expected it, he was prepared for it, and he allowed it to infuse his body and energise him for just three seconds . . . then, back into total focus.

Doug Frost was nervous. He told Swanton: 'I think every time he jumps in here he probably feels like he owns it. I hope he does this time around.' Talbot was nervous: 'It's like being in a colosseum: Kill! Kill! Kill! You know what I mean?' You'd have thought it was Talbot's first Olympics, not the last of a dozen. But even he had never seen anything like this, the crowd cacophony having now morphed into a stereophonic chant. From the one side: '*Thorpey! Thorpey!*' And from the other: '*Aussie! Aussie!*' And then, eventually, quiet. Onto the blocks. 'Swimmers, take your mark.' GO.

Ian was fifth away off the gun – just to be safe – and yet still surfaced well in front of the field, having employed the strongest underwater dolphin kick in swimming. He sat marginally ahead of his own world record pace at every turn, with only one swimmer, Italy's Massi Rosolino, even capable of staying in the frame. Intermittently the crowd would chant: '*Thorpey! Thorpey!*' Heading up to the 250 turn, the Italian issued a serious challenge, ranging almost to within a body-length of the leader – and he stayed there until they reached 300. But Ian's next 50 was so powerful, so masterful, that by the time he got to the final turn, the result was way beyond doubt.

The last 50 metres was an exquisite mixture of pleasure and pain. He allowed himself the briefest of glances left and right as he came off the wall (something he would very rarely do in a race), and then he actually *smiled* all the way to the finish – accompanied, of course, by a roar that could have been heard from the bottom of the pool – *knowing* that as soon as he touched, he would be the Olympic gold medallist. What a luxurious feeling that must have been.

Thorpe beat Rosolino by almost three seconds in a new world record of 3:40.59 – three-quarters of a second better than his old mark. The rest of the field converged almost in a straight line, but so far back they were almost at shouting distance. While the Italian was going berserk – jumping up and down on his lane rope and waving hysterically, such was his joy at taking silver – Ian was the Zen master. He first looked heavenward and mouthed the words 'Thank you' – the only time he has ever done that. Then he stood, double fist-pumped a few times to acknowledge the world record – no smile – and just momentarily curled his upper lip in an uncharacteristic gesture of defiance.

Then he hauled himself out of the water and into a world he later described as surreal. It was as though everything around him had stopped, snap-frozen into a black and white frame. Only he appeared to be animated, and only he appeared to exist in colour. He seemed to be watching himself as if he were another person – an automaton. Time almost stood still, but not quite; he knew he had to act in some way, but didn't know what to do: 'Because you've never been able to experience euphoria like this before, your body and mind don't know how to respond, so it seems like you just stand there and do nothing for a while.' (Cathy Freeman later described an identical experience after winning, under incredible pressure, her 400 metres gold medal on the track.)

Ian then did something he has never done before or since. He stood and faced the throng, directly in front of Ken and Margaret and

Christina and the Flaskases and all his other family members and supporters – although he didn't actually *see* any of them – and he arched his back and raised his arms into the air and pumped his fists skywards in triumphal exaltation. The crowd revelled in it. When Ian saw it later on the videotape, he had no memory of that moment at all, and it shocked him.

≈

The night was young, and the 4 × 100 metres relay awaited in just an hour's time. Thorpe had to do his poolside interview, in which he described how he'd reacted when confronted by the fervour of the crowd; then the mixed zone interview – no more than a few minutes; then straight to the warm-down pool to cover about a kilometre's worth of slow laps before being hauled out to the medal presentation (and if ever there was going to be a joyful tear, then surely this would have been the time, as the flag was raised and the anthem played – but no); then a slow walk around the pool deck, stopping every ten metres or so for press photos with Rosolino and the bronze medallist, Klete Keller, while Margaret clambered down to the railing to try and catch Ian's bunch of flowers, but couldn't get close enough for her son to chance his suspect throwing arm. The cameras panned continually to Ken Thorpe, who seemed, even by his standards, unusually subdued. He was just drinking in the atmosphere, like a sunbathing lizard.

Then it was straight into the press conference, where Ian was asked exactly who it was that he'd thanked at the moment of victory. The answer was God, for the gift he'd been given, and Mum and Dad and the rest of the family for their enormous contributions, and his coach and manager for theirs, and everyone else who'd supported him . . . but mostly it was a thank-you to whatever benevolent force it was that stopped a person from spending all his life in the pursuit of a singular goal, only to somehow blow it at the critical moment. 'I was giving thanks,' he said later, 'that I hadn't fallen flat on my face.' You'd have been excused, at the time, for wondering just how that could happen.

There'd been such an air of inevitability about the 400 metres – particularly with Grant Hackett struggling to find any sort of form, and finishing only seventh – that the result was almost overlooked when set against the amazing drama which was to follow that night. It shouldn't have been. It was a monumental achievement for a 17-year-old Olympic debutant. Not only was it a world record, but in the wider context, Ian's level of dominance was what inspired US head men's coach Mark Schubert to say: 'The guy's in a completely different league to everyone else.'

Perhaps that level of dominance ought to have been even greater. Massi Rosolino amazed everyone by his effort in clocking 3:43.40 – so much so that one journalist was moved to ask him directly whether it could be attributed to performance-enhancing drugs. 'They can test me all they like,' replied the amped-up Italian, 'but all they'll find is parmigiana and spaghetti.'

Fair enough – but that may only have been because there was no approved test for illegal use of human growth hormone, even though ascertaining *possible* abuse was not that difficult. Rosolino was one of 61 Italian Olympic athletes (out of 538) who'd registered abnormally high levels of naturally occurring hGH in tests secretly carried out just before the team left for Sydney by the Italian Olympic Committee's head of research, Alessandro Donati – the same scientist who had exposed rampant drug abuse in pro cycling in the mid-1990s. The findings were initially suppressed by the Italians, but they came to light just days after the Games ended.

Debate over those test results still rages in swimming circles. Rosolino vehemently asserts his innocence, and of course is entitled to keep his medal and his reputation. But if you erase him from the picture, just hypothetically, and look at the gap to the following line of swimmers headed up by Klete Keller – the challengers are a full *15 metres behind* when Ian Thorpe touches the wall. Ian now says of that race: 'Recently I was reminded that I'd annihilated a field at Olympic level – and that had never actually occurred to me . . . I always just look forward, and forget what's happened in the past . . . But I think in the light of history that performance will be viewed differently.'

Dave Flaskas agrees. For him personally, the relief and elation following that win were directly proportional to the amount of aggravation he and Ian had suffered in the previous 12 months – from the broken ankle to the drug allegations to the German testing debacle to the ongoing swimsuit drama and its near-cataclysmic final act . . . along with a great many lesser hurdles along the way. When Ian's hand touched the wall, David also spontaneously gave thanks to a higher power. 'I was so emotional I can't tell you how I felt. There was no way of expressing it,' he recalls. But as everyone around him went racing down to the railing to get closer to the conquering hero, Flaskas found himself transfixed, in a sort of reverie, just staring ahead . . . until a woman sitting behind him reached over, tapped him on the shoulder and said earnestly: 'You must be so *proud* of your son.' David had swapped seats with Ken, which had caused the mistaken identity – and with that the spell was broken; Flaskas was bursting forth with laughter and relief. But the moment was about to be overtaken and almost submerged, in the space of one crowded hour, by an unforgettable piece of sporting theatre.

≈

There was some hesitancy about Thorpe being positioned as anchorman in the 4 × 100 relay. A kind of hush descended when the team positions were announced during the afternoon rev-up session before the swimmers boarded their bus. What if Ian were to swim a bad 400 on his Olympic debut? How would that affect his confidence? He was Australia's fourth-fastest 100-metre swimmer at Trials, and everyone knew he'd be lining up against the American Gary Hall Jr – a renowned relay swimmer, then owner of the fastest 100 relay split ever, winner of two Olympic relay gold medals already and one of the greatest sprinters in the world. Hall had won double silver at the Atlanta Olympics in the 50 and 100 free, having managed to beat himself in the 100 when he got tangled up at the wall and missed his touch.

Against that, Ian Thorpe was yet to swim a great 100. There was no real awareness, at this stage, of his extraordinary capabilities as a relay anchorman. That story was yet to unfold. But he *had* already anchored Australia to its first-ever win over a weaker American team at Pan Pacs

'99, and there was a feeling – perhaps more of an optimistic prayer – that lining up against a champion of Thorpe's stature might just intimidate the American. Some kind of hocus-pocus had to be conjured from somewhere, because on paper the American team, never once beaten at the Olympic Games, wasn't going to be beaten this time either. They were just a bit too fast.

The Aussies did have one thing figured out: the Yanks always tended to overswim the first half of their relay splits, then died a little in the second half. If you could get a lead on them and make them chase, that would exacerbate their tendency to go out too hard. So the Australian tactic, put forward by relay coach Doug Frost and ratified by Talbot, was to swim the team in reverse order of their finish at Trials: Klim, Fydler, Callus, Thorpe. And to instruct them never to panic, because they would fall behind on each leg, and then come back to close the gap.

Gary Hall Jr had been *the* story of the Olympic build-up, at least as far as swimming was concerned. A likeable extrovert, Hall was also a mentally tough individual, having been advised by doctors to give up swimming 17 months before the Games after they'd diagnosed diabetes. Five months later, on a regimen of daily insulin injections, he was swimming faster than he had in Atlanta. Just a few weeks before the Opening Ceremony he produced a website entry that read in part:

> *Olympic Diary. August 22, 2000. Phoenix, Arizona.* I like Australia. In truth, I like Australians. The country is beautiful, and the people are admirable. Good humour and genuine kindness seem a predominant characteristic. My biased opinion is that we'll smash them like guitars – but the logic in that remote area of my brain says it won't be so easy for the US to dominate the waters this time . . .

By pulling out the 'We'll smash them like guitars' line in isolation and giving it saturation coverage, the Australian media demonised Hall. It was absolutely disgraceful journalism, but the tabloids had their villain. He wrote in a later website diary entry: 'It got people mad. It made people laugh. It got me in trouble. Good God, I thought I was going to be killed . . . I felt like I was Australia's most hated man.'

It was actually Ian's idea for his team-mates to perform an air-guitar send-up of the Americans if they managed to beat them. And as soon as he said it, he wished he hadn't. Making fun of the vanquished wasn't an Ian Thorpe thing to do. But anyway, he didn't think it would matter . . . because he alone of the foursome did not believe they were going to win. Despite his habit of relentless positivity, he just couldn't see it happening.

The other three, according to Ian, wouldn't accept the possibility of losing. Ashley Callus had startled everyone at the orientation camp in Caloundra, Queensland, after the Australian team was selected. Each member of the entire Dolphins squad had been asked to stand and declare his or her intention at the Games. Callus viewed himself as the rookie whose failure could prevent his more illustrious team-mates from winning a historic gold medal, so he got to his feet, stared down at the others and announced: 'My name is Ashley Callus and I'm going to the Olympics to win a gold medal, so you blokes better pull your fingers out.' (Callus was, incidentally, a member of the Currumbin Surf Club, which had boasted Duncan Armstrong and Jon Sieben among its brethren. They were not scared, these Queenslanders.)

Thorpe's prognosis for the relay changed quickly after his victory in the 400. His confidence was soaring. He was now an Olympic champion, so in a sense the pressure was off him – but he'd also inspired his relay team-mates by demonstrating what an impact they could have on that seething, fire-breathing mass of 18 000 Australian fans. Callus and Fydler had been sitting side by side during the 400. Callus later said: 'Once he hit the wall and we saw "World Record" and the crowd just going nuts . . . it was like being buzzed by a cattle prod. We were ready to fire.'

When Ian left his press conference there was just time for him to squeeze into a dry bodysuit. Everything had been timed down to the minute, but he was in a real hurry to get that suit on, which was why, all of a sudden – *rip!* – it busted open at the seam. There were only 15 minutes to go before the race. It would take about 15 minutes to get into a *dry* suit. No-one had ever attempted to get into a wet one. But it was either that, or swim in his sluggoes, or in a torn bodysuit.

Frantic SOS calls went out on assistant manager Lyn Fowlie's walkie-talkie: 'No, I'm not joking – he's ripped his suit!' Ian's bag was found somewhere in the warm-down area and rushed to the change-room. He fished out a wet and forlorn-looking adidas bodysuit. Three people worked feverishly to help shoehorn him into the thing. The process was exhausting. What effect would that have on Ian, mentally and physically? No time to worry about it. The other swimmers were out on pool deck, the introductions about to start, and – where was Ian Thorpe? He raced down to join them, got there just in time for the big intro, and they all went up as a team. They were ready to rumble.

Michael Klim was on fire, scything down the pool with his unusual straight-arm stroke, reaching the 50-metre turn first, and opening up a lead of 0.7 seconds over the American Anthony Ervin by the time he hit the wall . . . and then Chris Fydler was away, with America's Neil Walker in hot pursuit as Ian glanced at the scoreboard, which displayed the split times for only a few seconds. Klim's time read 48.18. Was that a world record? Ian couldn't be sure – he wasn't really up on the numbers in the 100 – and you wouldn't want to tell your room-mate he'd just broken a world record if he hadn't, so he looked again: *48.18*. Then it was gone. 'I think you just broke the world record,' he screamed at Klim, barely audible above the general commotion, as Klim in turn was screaming at Fydler to get motoring. 'Are you sure?' Klim eventually hollered back.

'Pretty sure.' He was right. Popov's record of 48.21 in the blue riband event had been eclipsed, but that momentous achievement was obliterated by the crowd's hysteria as Neil Walker gained on Fydler and looked to be drawing away . . . until, just as Frost had predicted, the Australian clawed his way back brilliantly to give Ashley Callus an arm's length start on Jason Lezak. And again, the same story on the third leg: Callus overtaken on the way out, but pulling back inch by inch as the crowd saw the dark-suited figure climb onto the block and began to scream: '*Thorpey! Thorpey!*'

The two giant anchormen stood side by side, Ian swinging his arms rhythmically as Gary Hall Jr – the villain of the piece, and *loving* it – kissed his biceps and scowled theatrically while Ian tried to block out the incredibly distracting din so he could concentrate on guessing the precise millisecond when Callus would touch. The Australian hit the wall just 0.25 seconds ahead – a barely discernible margin – but Ian's changeover was *sensational.* He knew it had to be.

Even so, Gary Hall Jr overtook his rival so quickly in that first 50 – his arms, it seemed, were moving at twice the speed of Ian's – and turned to emerge three-quarters of a body-length in front. The American sprinter was away, the crowd's hopes in freefall, while Channel Seven's race caller Dennis Cometti became more and more hoarse as the final lap unfolded: '. . . Hall is in front. What can the champ muster? A gold medallist earlier tonight . . . *Now* he's digging deep. The crowd is roaring. Their hero is coming home. Will it be a fairytale? Thorpe is coming out after Hall. They're matching strokes now. Thorpe on terms with Hall . . . They've got about 15 metres to swim . . . Thorpe is overhauling him . . . *Hall and Thorpe . . . Thorpe's in front . . . Thorpe and Hall . . . Thorpe goes in – AUSTRALIA WIN!*'

How? How did he get there? How could a middle-distance specialist who'd never swum better than high 49s and couldn't crack it for an individual swim in the 100 free – and who'd just an hour previously finished the fastest 400 ever swum – mow down an outright speedster who would go on to take gold in the 50 free and bronze in the 100 at that same Olympics? People will replay the tape of that last relay leg and wonder about it for as long as the Olympic Games are staged.

But the ingredients were all there: the nerveless determination, the very fast changeover, the faultless skill in the tumbleturn (Ian later said it was the best turn in a 100 he'd ever done), the lack of a surging wave to contend with, the unmatched aerobic fitness, the total maintenance of form, the refusal to panic, and finally – the touch. Thorpe was coming; Hall was fading. In the end, there was the length of an outstretched forearm in it: 0.19 seconds. The Americans had broken their own world record by almost a second and a half, yet lost the Olympic 4 × 100 free relay for the first time ever. Expert commentator Andrew Baildon was taking the whole context into account when he called Ian's 48.30 split 'the greatest Australian relay leg in history'. Not forgetting Klim's world record, what Ian Thorpe had done in that race was the absolute essence, the literal embodiment, of what it means to be a champion.

No-one would ever see him that excited again. Somehow he knew without checking the board that he'd got the touch, even though the last moments had been a blur. He was out of the water and into the bearhug embraces of his mates in a flash, screaming 'Yeess!' and pumping his fists and just about going berserk with Klim and Fydler and Callus, who then started thrashing their air guitars in the direction of the Americans. Ian gave a couple of cursory strums, then thought better of it. Meanwhile, Ken Thorpe had gone over the top, standing and punching the air and signalling 'number one' high above his head. That was an unprecedented scene.

Pandemonium is a barely adequate word to describe the atmosphere at that point. The joint was ROCKING. Legend has it the pavers outside the Aquatic Centre were actually undulating from the sheer amplitude of the celebrations inside. Could that be right? Workers at the pool reckoned it was.

The Americans were admirable in defeat – none more so than Gary Hall Jr, who told the subsequent press conference: 'Everybody who bought a ticket definitely got their money's worth. I consider this to be the best relay race I've ever been a part of. The last 50 metres, I went after it. I doff my cap to the great Ian Thorpe. He swam better than I did.' (Even that was not *literally* true, as Hall's split was actually six-hundredths of a second faster than Ian's.) Far from being a villain, Gary Hall Jr was a class act.

Although he's lately come to reassess his earlier swim in the 400, Ian still automatically nominates that relay as the highlight of his career. At the press conference he said simply: 'It's the best day of my life. The best hour of my life. The best minutes of my life.' A lot of the spectators seemed to feel the same way. After the medal presentation they lingered long at the exits, as if hoping for some sort of encore to the immense drama they'd witnessed.

Sydney is a hard-edged city, but the Olympics had infused the populace with a generosity of spirit that seemed to be enchanting – and never more so than on that famous opening night at the Aquatic Centre. They actually sang 'Waltzing Matilda' with gusto as the trains came to the Olympic Park station to take them home. That, too, was unprecedented.

Ian boarded the bus back to the Village and switched on his mobile, which told him he had 48 new messages. One was from his mum, who'd gotten in early: 'We're extremely proud of you and we love you.' Then there was one from Tom Cruise and Nicole Kidman, who'd been watching on TV in Florida and both reckoned it was 'awesome'.

What followed was a junkyard of garbled noise as Margaret and Christina sang 'You are the champion of the world' while riding on their courtesy bus back to the luxurious Channel Seven hospitality boat moored in Sydney Harbour, then passed the phone around so everyone could have a screech into it. Ian was doing interviews on his own bus while getting a friend to download all this racket so he could check the rest of his message bank. (He finally called the next day and told them they were all idiots and couldn't sing anyway.)

At the same time, Ken Thorpe was making his own way quietly home on a standard Olympic bus, having knocked back the chance to share with Margaret and Christina in Kerry Stokes' harbourside largesse. It wasn't his scene: 'I'd rather just be a normal, simple person.' At any other meet, Ken would get to mix with all the other swimming parents, and experience their highs and lows as the events unfolded – but Channel Seven had graciously provided a swag of tickets for the extended Thorpe clan in a completely different area. Although he was grateful, of course, Ken was disappointed that he couldn't be with all the people whose hopes and dreams he'd shared over so many years.

Nor did he want to become the 49th caller on Ian's mobile. It wasn't necessary. 'He knows how I feel,' he told a TV interviewer. 'This is the ultimate for me as a father. I just get so emotional seeing the flag go up and hearing the national anthem . . . He knows how much that means to me. He's given me that tonight, that feeling, and it's something I'll never forget as long as I live.'

What more could happen that evening? As Ian walked to the entrance to the Village and handed over his accreditation pass, it failed to register on the computer, and the security alarm went off. It turned out someone had made a copy of Thorpe's pass for a souvenir, which meant the original one had been invalidated. It was not as if the official didn't recognise Ian Thorpe, but still he was bound to ask: 'Have you any ID?' Ian said yes, and pulled two Olympic gold medals from his bag. It sounds apocryphal, but that's exactly what took place.

There was time for a late dinner, so Ian headed for the food hall. A few Australian athletes who were sitting together spotted him as he walked in, and spontaneously stood and applauded. Then a few more stood up, and then some more, in a sort of snowball effect, until eventually almost every athlete of every nationality who happened to be in that enormous building was on their feet, clapping and cheering.

'I guess it went on for about ten seconds,' Ian recalls. 'I don't know. I would've been embarrassed – I kind of smiled and acknowledged people, then got my food and sat down as quickly as possible . . . But I was quite taken by it, and it kind of felt to me that this was what the Olympics were all about – that athletes could recognise my achievement and be pleased for me, just as I would've been pleased for someone else.'

When Thorpe at last returned to his room he found Michael Klim, the Olympic veteran, still all shot up with adrenalin and buzzing like crazy. A lot of athletes say they can't sleep at all after they've broken a world record, which is not surprising. But Ian is infamous for falling asleep in mid-conversation when he's really tired, and Michael was still babbling excitedly about that historic relay as his room-mate happily nodded off. Unlike a lot of the Australian swimmers, who found it almost impossible to come down from the euphoria of day one at the Olympics, the double gold medallist slumbered like a baby.

20

NEVER MAKE AN EXCUSE

COMING INTO THE GAMES, Pieter van den Hoogenband was having to deal with at least as much expectation from his countrymen as Ian Thorpe. He was the undisputed superstar of European swimming, world-class over 50, 100 and 200 metres, owner of the fastest 100 and 200 relay splits in history – and just to make the residents of his quiet home town in southern Holland even more fixated, no Dutchman had ever won an Olympic gold medal in the pool. On top of that, he'd suffered the misfortune of finishing one place out of a medal in both the 100 and 200 free at Atlanta in 1996, so he had the sympathy vote wrapped up – and he was also a hell of a nice guy. *Everyone* wanted a piece of him.

Little wonder the 22-year-old medical student was happy to escape to the anonymity of a Newcastle base, a couple of hours' drive north of Sydney, where he could go about his preparations unnoticed, clocking sizzling training times only he and his coach knew about as the Games approached. In *Early Days* Will Swanton aptly likened him to an eel lying in the weeds, waiting to strike. Just five centimetres shorter than Ian, he was 27 kilos lighter: a sprinter whose power-to-weight ratio and high body position in the water seemed to allow him to skim across the surface with a very fast stroke rate, but apparently minimal effort – the antithesis of the Thorpean combination of heavyweight power and ruthless efficiency.

'Hoogie' (as he was now genially referred to by the local media) talked up Ian's gold medal prospects in the 200 at every opportunity, perpetuating the idea that the Australian was invincible: 'Ian Thorpe is so strong. His personal best is still a second ahead of mine so I'm not really thinking about the gold. I just want to make a medal and stand on the podium.' Then he blew his cover completely on the second night of the program in the 200 semi-final by shaving 0.16 seconds off Ian's world record. He was down to 1:45.35. Suddenly the Lying Dutchman was forced to come clean: 'I'm swimming so fast it's unbelievable.'

But so too was Ian Thorpe, who looked to be doing it easily, so smooth and controlled as he touched just two-hundredths short of Hoogie's new record in the second semi-final. He smiled when he looked up at the clock. Somewhere else, according to Centrebet's news release, a punter wasn't smiling. He'd placed $30 000 on Ian Thorpe for a return of just $600.

Dave Flaskas was concerned from the moment Ian walked out on pool deck the following evening, at 7.10 pm, for the final. He looked a bit pale, and somehow smaller, as he stood in unfamiliar territory behind the block at lane five, while the Hoogie Man entered the imaginary corridor of favouritism behind lane four. Channel Seven shifted its underwater camera to Ian's lane in a show of faith, but the whole vibe was different from opening night. Hoogie's outfit stretched only from the waist to the knees; bare-chested, he seemed to be signalling that he needed no high-tech help to bring down the man in the dark blue suit.

There was no question the Dutchman was a far better sprinter than Ian. A few days later he would win gold in the 100 metres, defeating the legendary Popov for a second time. But this race was twice that distance, with the aerobic factor playing an even bigger role than it did when Ian mowed down Gary Hall in the relay. The assumption was that if Ian Thorpe was there or even thereabouts at 150, it would be all over: nobody in the world could match the Thorpedo's fitness and supercharged kick in that last lap.

Things looked good when van den Hoogenband led by only four-hundredths at both the 50 and 100-metre turns. By the time they got to 150, they were dead even: not a split second between them. Surely the stage was set for the local champion to come powering home. They went in lockstep up the last lap, stroke for stroke, but when Ian reached for the overdrive button, it just wasn't there. Hoogie kicked away in the final 25 metres and equalled his one-day-old world record, while Ian trailed in almost half a second behind. For the first time in memory, he'd failed to improve on his preliminary times in a final. Eighteen thousand spectators were stunned; what they'd seen didn't make any sense. Even the swimming writers – *especially* the swimming writers – were in shock. Among the annals of disappointment in the life of Ian Thorpe, this was the Big One – or at least, so it would have seemed to everyone who'd witnessed that scene. It was clear that having been hailed as invincible by a nation besotted, Ian was going to define himself indelibly by the way he reacted to this defeat. How would he handle it?

While van den Hoogenband gazed at the scoreboard in amazement, then across at his father, Cees-Rein, who looked to be on the verge of a heart attack, Ian climbed the lane rope and gave his conqueror a hug and a congratulatory word. He then padded over to poolside interviewer Linley Frame and said simply: 'I didn't swim as well as I would have liked to. He just swam so well, and I wasn't able to match it.' Five million Australian viewers might have been screaming at Linley to ask *why not?* But the rookie interviewer wasn't up to it.

In the mixed zone straight after that, Thorpe said: 'I feel very privileged to swim in that race. I thought I might go a bit faster, but the ball doesn't always fall in your court.' Softly, he added: 'I can't win every race I go in.' Asked about the possible effect of all the pressure on him, Ian replied: 'I'm not going to break a world record every time

I swim. That's just not going to happen, and everyone has seen that tonight. I couldn't have given anything else. I hurt a lot at the end.'

He would later reflect that he felt genuinely happy that Pieter, a man he liked and admired, could experience the same elation Ian had felt himself after his all-conquering Olympic debut. Coming from just about any other athlete, it would have sounded hollow, perhaps even laughable. But Ian had that rare quality of magnanimity – always had done, even as far back as primary school – and people could sense that he genuinely meant it. He means it just as much now when he says: 'I really wish everyone in the world could experience that amount of joy. Even if only once.'

The 17-year-old Ian Thorpe had shown Australians how to deal with their shock and disappointment. But not everyone, it seemed, was up to the task. People didn't want to let go of their emotional attachment to the myth of Thorpe's invincibility. In fact, it seemed there was only one person in the entire country who didn't want to make an excuse for Ian, and that was the man himself.

Some of the stuff that was trotted out was wildly off beam – but there were persistent rumours of an illness, and people who'd watched Ian swim for a long time had no doubt that there was substance in them. Nicole Jeffrey recalls: 'He's never made an excuse and never will. But I think he was sick. It was such an uncharacteristic swim . . . people were shocked. Even though he only swam half a second below his new PB, everyone believed he was ready to *smash* that time . . . Thorpey at this stage was just starting to take on the big programs, and he'd developed a bit of a pattern of crashing with his health towards the end. He'd done it in 1999, and it wasn't so surprising to see it happen in 2000.'

Finely tuned athletes are always on the verge of sickness, because they put their immune systems under so much stress. Swimmers are especially susceptible, spending all that time immersed in cold water, and there are some in the Australian team who are legendary for finding a 'trapdoor' every time they perform poorly at a meet. By contrast, Ian Thorpe has an almost pathological aversion to making any excuse. Partly it's to do with his upbringing, but mainly it's his own response to the adversity he faced with his chlorine allergy as a kid. Logic decreed he should never have been a swimmer in the first place, but he persisted – and the only way he could do that was to ignore the way he was feeling, and train as hard and swim as fast as he could anyway. Which is exactly what he continued to do. So it became ingrained in his value system: *never make an excuse*.

Journalists continued to enquire about his health; Ian continued to say he was fine. No-one believed him. Only Dr Brian Sando, the Australian team's medical director, could solve that mystery. He searched his records and confirmed for the author that Ian had visited him on 18 September (the day of the 200 final), and again on the following day, and again on 22 September. He said confidentiality rules prevented him from giving details of the reasons for the patient's visits – unless Ian would agree. ('At the time,' Dr Sando recalls, 'Ian was anxious that nothing be said about these things, because it may have been construed as an excuse.') Predictably, Ian would not agree to have the details released. Fair enough.

But Dr Sando didn't remember that he'd already let the cat out of the bag. An AAP report went out on the wire service, dated 21 September 2000: 'Ian Thorpe has an upper respiratory tract infection . . . "He wouldn't have been competing at as high a fitness level as he would have liked," Australian team head doctor Brian Sando told reporters . . . Dr Sando said Thorpe started to feel the effects of the infection on the afternoon of his 200m race on Monday . . . Symptoms of the infection include a sore throat, headaches, runny nose and a slight fever.' So there it was, in black and white – but somehow, inexplicably, the report wasn't picked up by the papers in any major way. Even now, years after the event, Ian still prefers to sidestep the question: 'I can laugh about that . . . the second it [the defeat in the 200 metres] happened, everyone made every excuse possible – it was extraordinary. Upper respiratory tract? Someone might have seen me coughing or something . . .'

Everyone connected with Ian knows that whatever the actual situation, he'll say he feels fine. That's just his way. But he will admit that he has very rarely hurt as much as he did after that race. He'd been to the warm-down pool to try and shake the lactic acid out of his legs, but they were roaring with pain, and he couldn't disguise it because it was making him feel sick, and he didn't want that to be the front page photo because he knew how it would be construed. So he went back to the change-room, slumped against the wall, and waited for relief. Doug Frost told the author: 'He collapsed in that change-room. They called me down and I rushed down there. He passed out – couldn't breathe.'

'I was hurting,' says Thorpe, 'but I never passed out.' In any case, you can be sure it was not pleasant. But eventually he recovered, then remembered he had a commitment to fulfil for Olympic Aid, an athlete-driven program that raises money to help disadvantaged children play sports. Two Aboriginal sports scholarship holders and one leukaemia sufferer got prime seats to watch the 200 final, and were then led to a small room at the rear of the Aquatic Centre, where they waited for Ian to walk through the door. In he came, chatted with the youngsters – including 13-year-old Cameron Ellis, who'd undergone intensive chemotherapy for ten months – then donated a specially autographed bodysuit to Olympic Aid for an online auction that ended up raising $100 000, and contributed another $10 000 cash prize he'd received from Gatorade.

Before the 200 metres final was staged, Ian had made a special request to see his family some time that evening. This was a difficult logistical exercise for an athlete of his profile, given the tightness of Olympic security. (Some less prominent swimmers could just change into an anonymous tracksuit and slip quietly into the crowd to see their folks, but not Ian Thorpe.) There was only one place it could happen – in the office of the general manager of the pool complex – and not until about 9.30 pm. Ian waited. In walked Ken and Margaret and Christina, and after he'd embraced them all, Ian said: 'Mum – I'm okay.' He knew they'd be worried about how he was coping with the events of that night, and he was coping just fine.

The meeting lasted only ten minutes at most, because Ian had to get down to the press room, but it gave him a real boost to see that his family were so happy for him. It was also a very strange encounter, as

Ian recalls, because he just couldn't find the right words to describe how exciting it had all been. 'However I tried to explain it,' he remembers, 'it didn't come out as good as it actually felt. It was like when you have an amazing dream and you want to explain all the details to someone, and they say: "Is that all?"'

By the time Ian got to the press conference it was late, but he didn't really notice that there weren't a lot of journalists in attendance. The following morning, Jeff Wells wrote in an unusually narky article in the *Telegraph*: 'Thorpe, meanwhile, lost even more sheen with the world media by not turning up for his press conference. Most had abandoned the wait after 90 minutes.' That situation should never have been allowed to happen. The implication that Ian Thorpe was a sore loser, in the context of what actually went down that night, was simply wrong, and could easily have been avoided with better management. Ian wasn't even aware of Wells' story at the time, and doesn't consider it a big deal. But Ken Thorpe took everything to heart – so much so that he should have adopted Catriona Dixon's advice years before and stopped reading the papers. Of all the articles ever written about his son, that's the one that *still* burns him up, even now.

≈

The 4 × 200 metre relay on day four really *was* a 50-1 on proposition. Only a heart attack by one of the quartet could have stopped the Australians. Ian, Michael Klim, Todd Pearson and Bill Kirby broke the world record yet again, giving Ian his third gold medal. Dan Kowalski had missed the cut and Grant Hackett was having such a lousy meet that he too had to sit it out in the grandstand, but somehow got himself together enough on the final day to stop Perkins from pulling off an Olympic treble in the 1500.

Ian was given one more swim to complete his program – a freestyle leg in a heat of the medley relay. But just before that, he arranged to host Ken and Margaret for lunch in the food hall at the Village – a rare privilege for parents, who weren't supposed to be allowed in there until the meet was over. Ian had only been able to show them his 200 metres silver medal, so he took them down to the team vault and extracted the three gold ones with his name on them.

Olympic medals are much larger, and heavier, than people imagine. 'If ever you hold an Olympic medal,' wrote P.J. Mullen, 'you feel how quickly it draws heat from your hand until the alloy is warm. The medal draws from you, just as you draw from it.' If you're an outsider – not intimately connected with the athlete concerned – and you happen to get hold of their Olympic medal, it can induce a feeling of trespass so powerful that you feel compelled to return it straight away. Olympic gold medals are almost magical.

Even that meeting with Mum and Dad lasted only an hour in total, and like the ten-minute encounter a few nights before, it was a special indulgence. Normally a swimmer would be isolated from all personal contact with friends and family for the duration of any major meet, and that even included Trials. It's difficult for the uninitiated to wrap their minds around this. In a sport where parents are an integral part of the whole process of producing a world-class athlete, the moment of highest emotional pitch finally arrives – and they're separated from their children by an impenetrable wall of security. Unavailable to the athlete himself is the kind of intimacy that all people crave when they're standing atop the pinnacle, at the very zenith of their existence.

Ken: 'He's always got a big program and his time is limited. We don't want to make it any harder for him.'

Margaret: 'We were thrilled to be able to see him, but you prepare yourself not to. If we get to see him during a meet, it's a bonus.'

Ian: 'That's how it is at every competition, but I'm used to it, and so are they – and if you can't deal with it, you can't do this. Don't even try.'

But because of that, you'd imagine, there must have been some kind of 'emotional debrief' after the event, especially after the Olympics: a time to just kick back with the family in the lounge room, watch a few race videos (even if only once), and just talk about how things *felt*. Not in the Thorpe household. The family has never watched a race together. Ian would prefer to talk about the people he'd met, the fun experiences he'd had, the things that he'd learned. The racing was up there on the video screen for all to see if they wanted to – so what was the point in ruminating on it?

He would swim, and then he would move on. That's why there were no trophy cabinets in the Thorpe household at Voyager Point. Just a closed room full of stuff – all of it of priceless sentimental value, and most of it littered across the floor like the trail of dirty clothes and junk in Ian's bedroom. He wanted to live in a house, not in a shrine devoted to himself.

≈

Ken Thorpe now reckons there was divine intervention in Ian's loss to Pieter van den Hoogenband: 'I believe if he'd achieved all his goals, there'd have been nothing further to strive for.' Ian may not necessarily put it down to an act of God, but he agrees that if he had accomplished everything he possibly could have at those Olympics, he'd very likely not have gone back into the water: 'I realised I wasn't satisfied with that 200, because I reckoned I could swim faster than that.' So there was the plan: another four years of commitment, with no turning back.

A journo asked at the press conference after that superlative opening night: 'Was Don Talbot right, Ian? Are you the swimmer of the century?' Ian wasn't having himself on. He replied: 'It's something I can't justify, can't accept until I achieve a lot more.' It turned out he wasn't even judged to be the swimmer of the meet, let alone the century. That was van den Hoogenband, who won the blue riband 100-200 freestyle double, set a new world record for the 100 free (47.84) as well as the 200, took bronze in the 50 free, and produced the fastest ever 200-metre relay split to get the Dutch team a bronze medal in that event as well. It was enough for him to edge out Ian in *US Swimming World*'s voting for the 2000 Swimmer of the Year.

The Australian medley relay team ended up winning silver behind the Americans, and heat swimmers also receive a medal, which left Ian Thorpe with a total of three gold and two silver medals: the most by any athlete at these Games, and on face value, the greatest single Olympic haul ever by an Aussie. But all medals are not of equal value, and Ian didn't need anyone to tell him that.

He had one individual gold and one silver. That didn't begin to compare with Shane Gould's achievement of gold medals in the 200 free, 400 free and 200 IM, silver in the 800 free and bronze in the 100 free at Munich in 1972. Of course, it was not in the ballpark with Spitz's four individual golds in a total of seven from Munich; nor did it stack up well against Matt Biondi's 50 and 100-metre freestyle golds plus three relay golds and an unlucky butterfly silver and 200 freestyle bronze at Seoul in 1988. To swim 400 metres and 100 metres so brilliantly on the same night, as Ian did, was something very difficult, and very special – but it surely didn't make him the greatest ever. On the path to immortality, he knew he had taken only the first few steps. He never allowed the sort of hubris that sells newspapers to cloud his self-judgement.

As for Don Talbot's dream of world domination, this time it was never a contest. The American swimmers won 14 gold, 8 silver and 11 bronze; the Aussies collected 5 gold, 9 silver and 4 bronze. Talbot reckoned the Dolphins had become so overexcited by the opening night heroics of the men's relay team, they just couldn't bring their adrenalin down and get their minds back on the job. A lot of experts agreed with him. But the bottom line remained: as far as the Yanks are concerned, it's all about the Olympics. And until you've beaten them there, you haven't really beaten them at all.

≈

After the swimming program, which takes up the first week of the fortnight-long Olympics, it was party time. Getting in and out of the Village was a bureaucratic nightmare, but worth it if you wanted to enjoy yourself, and Ian did. He got to various events during the early evening, mainly the athletics, then slotted into whatever sponsor function he had to attend. Then he'd zip across town to News Club, which was an old wedding reception set-up in Kings Cross that News Ltd had hired to entertain clients. It wasn't the standard commercial sell – 'Everyone will be there' – at all. The club was a very casual (invitation-only) affair at first; but at every Olympics, one place becomes known as *the* place to be, and this was it.

Everything was free, bands like INXS and Savage Garden provided the entertainment, you could sit back and just chat with anyone or no-one – and it got to the point, eventually, where if you weren't somebody special you weren't going to get a look-in. Ian met a lot of well-known people there and had a great time just about every night. Almost 18, but not yet able to hold an alcoholic drink in front of a camera (unless it was a vodka and soda disguised as mineral water), he was poised and comfortable among the doyens of society. After all, he was far more famous than any of them.

From a Channel Seven corporate box at the Olympic Stadium, sitting alongside Chelsea Clinton, Ian watched Cathy Freeman's run in the final of the 400 metres. Perhaps he alone in the crowd of 100 000 could have fully understood the unspeakable relief Cathy felt as she crossed the line in front. Thorpe the swimmer and Freeman the runner had been the nexus of Australia's Olympic hopes; and as Ian watched her stunned and uncomprehending reaction, he knew it was the same surreal experience that he'd had on his victorious opening night. Like him, she simply didn't know what to do. He felt very happy for her.

Ian mentioned to Chelsea over the ensuing dinner that he was planning to be in New York City in a few weeks' time. 'You should come over to Washington and I'll show you around the White House,' she said. He wondered if she could possibly be serious. He was going to find out.

That same evening, Thorpe had his first ever experience of Japanese hysteria. There was some background to this. Dave Flaskas had been approached by executives from TV Asahi, which was the Japanese Olympic broadcasting network, and had met with them each night before the swimming began. Asahi was number one in news and current affairs in Japan, but a lightweight in sports/variety shows.

Dentsu, the world's biggest ad agency, advised Asahi that the best move to beef up its programming would be to strategically promote swimming as a major sport. The Japanese people had a great liking of swimming for fitness; they had some up-and-coming stars who could be relied upon to revive the sport domestically; and they happened to be hosting the next World Championships in Fukuoka in 2001, and the next Pan Pacs in Yokohama in 2002. TV Asahi had secured the rights to those events and needed a figurehead to lead the push, and so Dentsu set out to identify the likely top medal winner at the Olympics and to work with Asahi to make that athlete the face of swimming in Japan.

Not surprisingly, they couldn't go past Ian Thorpe – especially since the Japanese had a historic and well-remembered record of great distance swimmers back in the era of Murray Rose, whose great rivalry with Tsuyosi Yamanaka had made him an icon in Japan. So the connection with Australian swimming was already there. When Ian delivered at Homebush, Asahi's already planned promotional push was green-lighted. But what began as a hard-headed commercial enterprise turned eventually into something else entirely – a relationship of genuine mutual affection which had been presaged by the overwhelming response of the Japanese (especially young girls) to Ian's performances at Pan Pacs '99.

After Cathy's medal was presented and the anthem was belted out by the enraptured multitude – who could have imagined such patriotic scenes in this bashful country even a decade ago? – Ian and David were transported by golf buggy to TV Asahi's gigantic headquarters at the International Broadcast Centre. As Ian walked in he received a standing ovation and was showered with gifts – but that wasn't all: 'People were screaming and pushing each other and being hysterical; they'd touch me and then start crying . . . it was just bizarre.' Thorpe wondered what the hell he'd gotten himself into. Why was this happening? He might reasonably have imagined it was some sort of orchestrated adulation for the benefit of TV Asahi – but it wasn't. Now that he's gained a far deeper understanding of Japanese culture, he understands it was simply a reflection of the enormous respect they had for him.

The network did a live hook-up back to Tokyo, with Ian hearing the questions translated via an earpiece. It wasn't easy, but he got better at it, and the process of relationship-building with TV Asahi and the island nation to the north began from there. It was to prove immensely rewarding for Ian, and not just financially.

≈

The singular honour of carrying the Australian flag at the Closing Ceremony was handed to Ian Thorpe as the country's best-performed athlete. That was an emotional time for Ian, especially since he'd missed out on marching at the Opening Ceremony. Reflecting on the whole experience, he would always say that just being at the Games was his career highlight: it most definitely wasn't 'just another meet'. But especially in light of all he'd been through in the previous 12 months, he was severely drained by the end of it, and in need of some powerful rehab.

Ian didn't even bother to ask for a special exemption from the Australian Short Course Championships, even though the meet was supposed to be compulsory. He'd spent some months planning a long break from the pool, including the trip to New York and on to Europe, and he wasn't interested in anyone's attempts to stop him.

The ten days from the Closing Ceremony to his departure for the US turned into a mindless blur. It was a time of exhausting overstimulation: emerging from a hotel room to do a parade in Sydney, then a plane flight to Melbourne and another parade and another hotel, then back home chilling out and visiting Michael Williams, then an obligatory appearance on Channel Seven with Andrew Denton and Cathy Freeman . . . and all against a backdrop of people (naturally) wanting to be at him, wanting a piece of him and, worst of all, wanting to talk about swimming with him. Somewhere in all the frenetic activity he called Kerry Stokes and asked if he'd mind if Ian traded up the A4 for an Audi TT – the radical-looking sports car – as an 18th birthday present to himself. That was fine, but he doesn't even remember driving to an Audi dealership and buying the car.

The one memory that remains crystal-clear was of riding in a convertible as the cavalcade of Olympians paraded past the Education Department building in Sydney. There were signs in big bold letters all over that building congratulating athletes who attended public schools – 'KIRSTEN THOMSON, KIRRAWEE HIGH' was one of them – and Ian felt a sudden and powerful yearning to be an ordinary kid at high school, studying for his exams and mucking around with his mates. It was a pang of loneliness, amplified loud by his strung-out condition.

The last thing he wanted to do was bask in the adulation of well-wishers, even though he appreciated their support. There was nowhere he could enjoy himself; he had to get away. The urgency was so great that even though his birthday was on 13 October, the planned flight for 15 October was brought forward three days. Ian had a quiet celebratory dinner at home on the 11th, boarded a plane for Los Angeles with Michelle Flaskas the following evening, and turned 18 somewhere over the Pacific Ocean. It might not have seemed a satisfying way for any young man to reach his majority – let alone one who was semi-rich and very famous – but that didn't matter. Ian was about to embark on a journey that somehow developed its own extraordinary momentum, until it became an odyssey that would have been beyond the imagination of any other 18-year-old Australian.

21

THE BIG APPLE

IAN'S ADVENTURE HAD ITS BEGINNINGS when he wandered for the first time into an Emporio Armani store in Sydney early in 2000. People like Ian Thorpe don't go unrecognised anywhere, and soon he found himself being introduced to the general manager for the Italian brand in Australia, Mary Chiew. He bought some clothes and declared himself thrilled with them, while Ms Chiew was equally taken by the young man's demeanour. She decided to ask Giorgio Armani's people in Milan if she could introduce Ian to their boss at the upcoming 25-year Armani Retrospective at New York's Guggenheim Museum in October. She sent a welter of information about him, along with a letter of recommendation. This was standard procedure – the first step in becoming a 'friend of Armani'.

This exhibition was a hell of a big deal in the fashion world, and Ian was the only Australian on the celebrity guest list. But the Armani thing was not a sponsorship: the fashion house doesn't sponsor anyone. Ian still had to pay for his clothes – albeit at a generous discount. In return for being a head-turning model in the famously upmarket label, Thorpe would be catapulted by the Armani connections into a world of glamour and sophistication internationally. He was about to take the initial step.

But first there was a little sidetrack. Since Ian had decided to leave three days earlier than planned, he'd been invited to stop over in LA and appear on Jay Leno's top-rating *Tonight Show*. Such are the ways of celebrity that the show's producer had somehow found out the Aussie swimmer could have some time to spare on the way to New York.

Since he'd crossed the International Date Line, it was still Ian's birthday when he settled into the studio audience shortly after checking into his hotel. Leno pretended he'd 'only just found out there's a special guest in our midst'. But Ian was already wired for sound when he was hauled up on stage to 'co-host' the program. That's showbiz. Some fuss was made of his birthday, then he read some cue cards with aplomb, found himself trading a few gags with one of the guests, comedian Drew Carey, and generally enjoyed himself.

The audience reaction surprised him; it was obvious that just about all of them knew who he was, and their applause was enthusiastic. That 4 × 100 relay race had been front page news, not back page, in the *New York Times*, and it was a fair bet the footage of the 'Thorpedo' storming over the top of Gary Hall Jr was embedded in the minds of a lot of Americans. There were several people offering congratulations as Ian and Michelle wandered the streets of LA, killing time before they linked up with Dave Flaskas, Mary Chiew and a gaggle of Aussie fashion writers in the Big Apple.

Armani had put the whole crew up in the ultra-swank Intercontinental Hotel, with Ian's suite looking straight down onto Central Park. He'd always wanted to be at the epicentre of this buzzing metropolis – its architectural magnitude just excited him – and there could be no better way to do it than to be cruising up to the Guggenheim in a limo with his entourage, then striding the red carpet (which was actually blue) behind Cuba Gooding Jr while the swarming clusters of international press kept screaming 'Thorpey' as they waylaid him into a zigzagging sequence of interviews and photo ops. It seemed to take him forever to run that gauntlet (which is apparently the fashion world's recognised measure of status) – not that this was of great importance to Ian. While everyone else was there being seen, his main interest was the actual exhibition. He found it fascinating.

Afterwards, he was surrounded by models and movie stars at a private dinner party hosted by Armani. Apart from the famed designer himself, he met just about everyone who was there to be met: people like Billy Crystal, Michelle Pfeiffer, Glenn Close, Meryl Streep, Lauren Hutton, Lauren Bacall, Claudia Schiffer, Martin Scorsese and others. The actress Ashley Judd made the biggest impression on him, admitting she'd followed all his Olympic events and recounting how she'd read articles that poetically described the beauty of his swimming style.

It surprised Thorpe that these people seemed just as excited to meet him as he was to meet them. Mary Chiew offers: 'He was new on the scene, people admired him, and he was delicious-looking.' Sharon Krum, writing in *Harper's Bazaar*, went a shade further: 'Ian Thorpe floated through that party – where celebrities were lining up to meet him – like he owned it.' Even allowing for the prerequisite puffery of these fashion glossies, it was beyond doubt that the Thorpedo 'arrived' that night.

The fact was that even though he was a genuine movie buff and admirer of most of the people he encountered, he'd gone past the stage of being star-struck. All of these celebrities, thrust into the public eye by whatever talent they possessed, were basically no different from himself. Nicole Kidman might have caused him to tremble at the knees not too long ago, but he'd chatted with Elle Macpherson at a party following the Olympics, and presented Kylie Minogue with a platinum album just before the Games were over. He'd even asked her out on a date, which she'd been unable to accept because of a prior commitment. The boy from Milperra was obviously not scared.

Immediately, doors began to open for him. He had to extend his stay in the city when he was invited to the *Vogue* Fashion Awards, to be staged a couple of nights later. Scenes from the hilarious movie *Zoolander*, starring Ben Stiller, were filmed there using the actual audience as extras. He met 'lots and lots of famous people, but no-one that interesting', and then found himself at Jennifer Lopez's after-party at the Hudson Hotel. He spoke briefly with J-Lo and other celebs, but when the supermodel Heidi Klum was introduced to him, he almost went into meltdown again. 'She is one of the most beautiful women I've ever seen – and she was incredibly nice to me. I thought: "Why the hell is she talking to *me*?"'

Perhaps she thought, like Mary Chiew, that Ian looked 'delicious'. He'd certainly grown into his prominent features – the very broad mouth, the large aquiline nose – as he'd matured, so that his face had softened and become more handsome. Asked to produce a smouldering look on magazine shoots – as he was when doing an exclusive for *Harper's Bazaar* just the day before the Armani bash – he was now capable of doing a pretty decent job (although maybe not as good as Ben Stiller). No doubt it helped having three gorgeous swimsuit-clad models artfully arranged around him at the time.

Ian and the Flaskases flew on to London via Milan and Venice. Ian got a warm reception when introduced to the crowd at half-time at a home game for his favourite football team, Tottenham Hotspurs. There were meetings with various agents and a partnership was formed with a London-based outfit, Fresh, to handle the swimmer's European profile in the lead-up to the 2002 Manchester Commonwealth Games.

Having already dined at the famed Nobu restaurant in New York part-owned by Robert de Niro, Thorpe continued his education in Japanese-style haute cuisine at the London version of Nobu. These early culinary adventures were the genesis of his later fascination with all things Japanese.

Business completed, Ian had always intended to go back and squeeze a bit more juice out of the Big Apple. But before that he got a message from the Armani connections suggesting he return to LA to be photographed by the (late) legendary Herb Ritts for *Vogue* magazine. The fashion icon was apparently not going to be outdone by its rival, *Harper's Bazaar*. But . . . well . . . who *exactly* was Herb Ritts? 'Don't you *know* who he is?' came the reply. They didn't really, although Ian had heard of him. Anyway, they decided not to pass up the opportunity, so Ian and Michelle headed back to the West Coast.

Ian wasn't disappointed in the Ritts photos, which he described as 'beautiful'. The photographer had him in all sorts of contorted poses, but the cover was simply shot in an elevator – no background – with a shadow across his face so all that was clearly visible was one eye. Maybe it was a case of beauty being literally in the eye of the beholder, but Ian believed it captured something unique to himself.

There was an added bonus. Thorpe had been saying publicly for a long time that one of his all-time fantasies was to somehow make a cameo appearance on his favourite TV show, *Friends*. Elle Macpherson, who'd appeared on the show, put in a strong recommendation, but nothing came of that. So he was resigned to sitting in the studio audience with Michelle, watching the show being filmed, when he spotted Sarah O'Hare, whom he'd been friendly with ever since the opening of Fox Studios. Somehow Sarah convinced the producers to bounce one of the extras in favour of Ian, who was thrilled to appear for just a couple of seconds sitting in a café chatting over a mug of latte. He was still just a kid at heart.

He proved it on his last day in LA, when he was reluctantly dragged along to Disneyland by Michelle. Ian thought the whole idea was totally uncool. 'We'll only be here for an hour,' he told their driver. However, six hours later he was still refusing to call it a day, having been on all the scariest rides and even posing for shots with Mickey Mouse and Donald Duck. They had a special escort, organised by one of Jay Leno's connections, which meant they went straight on to every ride without queuing. Supposedly this is a service that does not exist – but in America, unlike Australia, celebrity makes its own rules, and a single phone call can change everything.

It was lucky Michelle had plenty of energy, or they'd never have cut it as travelling companions. Ian treated *every* place like it was Disneyland, racing from one attraction to another, hardly stopping to eat. It was always just: 'Let's get another Jumba Juice.' (This was an America-wide fruit juice franchise – like eating at McDonald's, only quicker.)

'Please,' Michelle had once begged in mock exasperation, 'can't we just STOP and have some real food?' No. She swears they got through three days in LA – breakfast, lunch and dinner – on practically nothing but Jumba Juice. Same deal in New York. 'I've never met anyone,' she reckons, 'who fills every second of his day like Ian does, and gets so much excitement out of it. And it rubs off. He has an amazing ability to build that passion into you.'

But there comes a time when any sensible person has to pass the baton. It was picked up by Kirsten Thomson, who was travelling with her sister and brother-in-law to New York. Ian had arranged to link onto the connecting flight with them in LA. He forked out the cash for an upmarket hotel, then launched another week-long assault on his favourite city. They went ice-skating in Central Park, got lost on the subway, visited the Statue of Liberty, did a hundred other things. And then, with two days before he had to head home, Ian fished out the phone number and secret prompts that Chelsea Clinton had given him.

It was really nowhere near the forefront of his mind throughout that week, and he was still hesitant about the whole idea, but . . . what the hell? He dialled the number, negotiated the maze of passwords, and ended up leaving a message on the First Lady's voicemail: 'It's Thorpey here. Give me a call at my hotel.' The President's daughter got back to him in five minutes. Next day he and his three companions were on a plane to Washington. They checked in to another ritzy hotel, then found themselves out the front of the White House, taking snapshots like any other tourists . . . until it was time to actually go in.

The security was, of course, extreme – but once they got past it, Chelsea proved an excellent tour guide, showing them parts of the house that nobody gets to see, and explaining the importance of everything in the context of American history. Ian was fascinated. But the kid in him demanded that he have a photo taken of himself sitting in the President's chair in the Oval Office.

Finally they wandered out into the Rose Garden, and Chelsea had just begun to explain its significance when all of a sudden there was a commotion, snipers appeared on the roof, there was a police car, two more cars behind that, then the President's car, with a car either side of it, another car behind, another police car behind that, and finally an ambulance. 'Oh . . . Dad,' said Chelsea. 'You're home.' Ian was amazed by the lack of formality as Bill Clinton introduced himself, they had a bit of a chat, then mucked around throwing a tennis ball for the dog, Buddy, to chase after. Weightier matters beckoned Mr Clinton inside, so he said goodbye while Ian tried to remember whether he'd straightened out the mess he'd made in the Oval Office.

Then he began to reflect on what a marvellous thing it was to know that the President of the United States 'had a common respect for myself, for the people I was with, and for my country. It was a very proud moment for me . . . It made me homesick. I remembered to ring my mum, who I hadn't called for ten days.' It was time to go home.

≈

Fitness lost is so hard to recover. That's why most swimmers will baulk at the idea of taking anything more than two weeks off at any time in the yearly cycle. They're paranoid about getting out of shape. Ian hadn't planned to get back into the pool until early December, which would have meant a break from swimming of two and a half months: an unheard of period for an elite competitor. So there was criticism – most of it covert, but a good deal of it aired on talkback radio – of Thorpe's five-week overseas jaunt. In swimming circles it was regarded as massively self-indulgent. Swimming's code of behaviour demanded rigorous austerity. To be seen swanning around the globe in the most glamorous of company was the antithesis of the sport's ascetic ideal. Had Ian Thorpe lost the plot? Was he going to have his head turned by all this glitzy nonsense? Had he forgotten what made him famous in the first place? Swimmers just didn't do this sort of stuff.

It was as if the sport's one collective fear was that its finest practitioners would all suddenly come to their senses, climb out of the pool, towel down and do something more fun with their lives instead. Don Talbot spelled it out in his autobiography: 'The longer a swimmer stays out of the water, the harder it is to get back.' And after a very long period, so the conventional wisdom went, it was just about impossible. But Ian Thorpe – Renaissance man, international jetsetter, fashionista and self-taught intellectual – was also, first and foremost, a *swimmer*. Having landed back in Sydney in mid-November, he was on deck at the Sutherland pool within 24 hours. He felt overweight and extremely unfit. He just couldn't wait to get back into his routine, to start feeling good in the water again.

Ian sensed the air of disapproval, but he didn't let it worry him too much. He'd been warned to expect it. He began by doing something just as radically different as the long break itself. Instead of the standard approach of gently easing himself back into the work – three sessions a week, then five, then seven for a few weeks – he went all-out, doing the full ten swim sessions in the first week and the full dry land program as well in the second. He did 50 kilometres in week one, then 60, then 70. By Christmas he was back to full fitness, and absolutely raring to go. His objective for 2001: to swim every event faster than ever, but especially the 200 metres freestyle.

The effect of Ian's trip on his psychological well-being was so positive that he resolved to take the same sort of break every year – and every year he'd hear the same disapproving noises. People just didn't get it. Ian Thorpe was the most dedicated trainer in the Australian swimming team. He *never* missed a session. His entire life was about self-denial. He'd turn down more invitations in a week than most people would receive in a year. But then, when the major event on the calendar was all done and the medals all won, he had a powerful need to ditch the stick and grab some of the dangled carrots instead. And as he did so, he would be visibly reinvigorated. People close to him would describe the transformation as 'startling'.

Perfectionism is a characteristic of most elite swimmers. They all live in a hermetically ordered environment under the dominion of time: the time they get up, the time it takes to have breakfast, the time it takes to get to the pool, the times they do in their training drills, the time they get to recover before the next time they train, and the time they go to bed. A person as perfectionistic as Ian Thorpe could, if he were not careful, become unhinged by the relentless hegemony of time, and by its corollary: the obsessive desire to swim faster every single time he raced.

And so the more disorganised and unstructured the end-of-year adventure, the better. That's why the first one was so perfect: it was the precise opposite of his normal clockwork lifestyle. He could pick and choose whatever he wanted to do. But even then, he still had to discipline himself to take a break from his self-discipline. He had to learn to relax. It started with the smallest details – like learning that he didn't have to fill out the early-morning breakfast room service menu because he had the option of wandering down, late, to the dining room instead. And learning that he could then decide whether to go for a light jog – or not – depending on how he felt. And so on. It was hard for him to do. But psychologically, he felt it was vital that he have these normal experiences to establish some sort of balance.

Before long, though, he'd find himself falling back into the old ways. He sometimes tries to imagine what life would be like as a non-perfectionist. 'It would be so much easier,' he figures. 'But I'm not prepared to let it go. It just doesn't feel right.'

≈

It was a long time in the pipeline, but Ian Thorpe's Fountain for youth trust was finally launched on 24 November 2000 at a massive function funded by Telstra at the Westin Hotel in Sydney. The objective: 'To raise money from the public and seek support from corporations to establish and maintain a fund to alleviate illness and disease in children.'

The big end of town was very well represented among the 700 ticket holders, Channel Seven supplied footage of Thorpe's Olympic highlights just to get everyone fired up for the memorabilia auction, Prime Minister Howard gave a rousing speech to launch the trust, and Ian regaled the audience with his account of the Olympic 4 × 100 relay and with yarns about how he'd recently appeared on *Friends* and met Bill Clinton. The comedic timing he'd first displayed on Andrew Denton's show hadn't deserted him, and the vast audience lapped it up. He wound up with a special thanks to the PM for taking some time out to attend the function, considering there was a cricket Test on that day.

Nicole Jeffrey observed that with Pat Rafter and Ian Healy having their own personal charity foundations, and Cathy Freeman's already in the works, it appeared that conspicuous consumption had been replaced by conspicuous donation for the thinking sports superstar. Fair enough, but since Ian had already given away practically all the money that had come to him apart from personal sponsorships and AOC funding, he could hardly be accused of jumping on a bandwagon.

Nor was he particularly wealthy for a philanthropist. He was routinely and wrongly referred to in the various media as 'a millionaire many times over'. *BRW* magazine got it right, estimating Ian's total income for 2000 from his 11 sponsors at $1.3 million. It made him Australia's highest-paid swimmer, marginally ahead of Klim, O'Neill and Hackett, although he was only number 22 on *BRW*'s list of Australia's 50 biggest-earning sports stars.

But the building blocks for greater things were in place. Flaskas had wisely structured most of the sponsorships so they'd be up for renegotiation on or around 31 December. Ian was voted the most marketable Australian sports star in 2000, ranked equally in a survey with Cathy Freeman as Australia's most popular Olympian, and again won the Telstra Australian Swimmer of the Year Award for 2000 (with Frost winning Coach of the Year again). The biggest deal, though, was Ian's ascension from fourth in 1999 to second place, behind the US track star Marion Jones, in the American International Athlete (Jesse Owens) Trophy Award, which recognises the world's greatest athlete. Ian regarded that as the highest accolade he'd ever received. So even though he'd (ironically) relinquished *Swimming World*'s unofficial 'world's greatest swimmer' title, for the time being at least, to van den Hoogenband, there were still plenty of aces in Dave Flaskas' hand.

The time had come, as his manager had long planned, to take Ian Thorpe to the world. And naturally, Japan was the first country in Flaskas' sights. Secret meetings began in January, with Dentsu and Coke cooking up plans to make Ian the face of Coke's Aquarius sports drink in Japan, as well as TV Asahi's figurehead for the Worlds in

Fukuoka. The network agreed to spend a week in Australia in February filming a documentary about Ian. That would be followed by a promotional tour of Japan in April as a lead-in to the World Championships in July. On top of all that, Thorpe had been selected as the role model to front a United Nations-backed anti-recreational drugs campaign in Japan, to begin shortly after the Worlds meet. The slogan: 'NO – NEVER'.

When spotted by pressmen at the airport and a Melbourne hotel talking to Japanese men in suits, Flaskas insisted he was 'catching up with old friends'. He was obviously enjoying himself, knowing that if things came off right, he'd be a trailblazer on the international stage.

22

AN AUTHENTIC JAPANESE EXPERIENCE

ENTERING 2001, IAN COULDN'T SHAKE the idea that he was, for the first time, being given the tall poppy treatment by the media and public. It was nothing too overt. For instance, one paper played up the fact that in his first swim after the Olympics, at the NSW Open titles in mid-January, he was 12 seconds slower in the 400 free than his Olympic and world record: 'THORPE'S RETURN A STUNNING ANTICLIMAX'. Only the fine print revealed he was actually a bit faster than he'd been at the same time the previous year.

Ian had always been a very popular member of the Australian team, but no man can be all things to all people, and there may have been some personal issues as well. There was a tremendous amount of focus on him at the Olympics – perhaps more than some other big-name swimmers would have liked. There was the fact that he'd taken on the establishment over the swimsuit saga, and was now distinguished as the only Dolphin wearing an adidas suit (and that became an issue again, with Speedo reportedly close to refusing to renew its sponsorship of the Australian team a few months later because of Ian Thorpe's insistence on adidas). Some may have thought he was getting preferential treatment by ignoring the short course meet and other events like the Qantas Skins, and making his own arrangements as to when he would swim. And of course, anyone reading the popular press, rather than *BRW*, would have imagined him to be far wealthier than he actually was. It could all add up to a certain degree of resentment, his manager concedes. Considering the circumstances of the average journeyman swimmer, it was probably surprising there wasn't a lot more of it.

At the same time, a columnist at Melbourne's *Herald-Sun*, Jon Anderson, wrote in late January: 'Like many high-profile sportsmen before him, Thorpe's sexuality has been questioned, with rumours reaching a crescendo during the Olympics'. Anderson went on to praise Martina Navratilova and Ian Roberts, 'both of whom showed remarkable inner strength in outing themselves.' Clearly Ian Thorpe was paying the price of fame. Anderson himself admitted Ian had never commented on the subject, nor been asked about it. It was grubby journalism, and drew no response from the Thorpe camp. It certainly deserved none.

Ironically, the press had simultaneously developed an obsessive interest in Ian's relationship with Martina Hingis, whom he'd joined in a promotional doubles match at the adidas International tournament. They had dinner together, liked each other, but there was no romance – although a columnist in the *Sun-Herald* reported: 'Take it as fact – Ian Thorpe and Martina Hingis are much more than just mates.'

Meanwhile, Don Talbot had come up with the idea of fuelling interest in a non-Olympic year by setting up a 'revenge match' between Thorpe and van den Hoogenband over 200 metres for a winner-take-all prize of $1 million. Obviously if he could find a promoter willing to put up the cash, it could be recouped by worldwide TV rights. The idea got about three seconds of consideration from Flaskas, who immediately recalled the infamous 150-metre match race between Michael Johnson and Donovan Bailey to determine 'the world's fastest man'. Johnson broke down when well behind halfway through the race, with critics claiming he faked the injury to avoid embarrassment. It was a debacle.

David didn't even bother asking Ian what he thought about it. He knew that putting the emphasis on money rather than competition was something Ian would never do: 'He just sees that sort of thing as "dirty money" – something that does no good for the sport.' It might have been interesting to find out whether the Dutch medical student felt the same way.

What Thorpe was really into at the time was making his swimming life more stimulating. His plan was to add at least one other event, apart from the freestyle races, to his program leading up to the Commonwealth Games, and swim it at national level for the next three years. The first move was to enter the 200 backstroke and 200 IM at the NSW Open titles. He did okay in both events, even winning the medley at age group level. You don't forget how when you've been taught well, and Ian enjoyed himself. He actually felt like he was recapturing his youth.

However, there was a wild card introduced that year: the 800 freestyle. FINA had resolved in September 2000 to add the event to its World Championship program in Fukuoka, and would therefore be likely to add it to the Olympic program as well. It was billed as the perfect meeting ground for the two untouchables in the 400 and 1500 metres – Thorpe and Hackett – with Grant already declaring he was hot for the showdown.

But then FINA confounded everyone with its adjusted program, which had a total gap of just 15 minutes separating the semi-finals of the 200 free and the final of the 800, during which the two semi-finals of the women's 200 breast-stroke would be held. Depending which semi of the 200 Ian was in, that would leave roughly ten minutes in the warm-down pool; a bare minimum is twice that long. The Australian Championships, also Trials for the Worlds and scheduled for late March in Hobart, would naturally be an exact copy. When the program details were released on 9 January, Ian said it was obviously too hard and he wouldn't do it. By 18 January he was 'unsure' about it. By 24 February it was 'still a possibility'. By 8 March he was in.

Why? 'Probably because it *did* appear to be too hard. I thought I may as well give it a go. What did I have to lose?' Frost was agreeable; if there was a World Championship gold medal up for grabs, he'd take it. And given the way Ian felt about his training program, he *knew* he could swim 800 metres very, very fast – even though what he really wanted to do, above all else, was to swim 100 very fast. Anyway, he dropped his experiments with the backstroke and medley for the time being, and girded himself for the challenge.

It was amusing watching two good mates having their genteel version of a media stoush. 'I won't swim it as an endurance event,' said Ian in a rare bout of bravado. 'I'll swim it as a sprint.' Hackett had changed his mind about relishing the showdown, warning Ian that the schedule was too hard and he ought not to spread himself too thinly. Then he declared: 'Long-term I plan to claim the 800 and 1500 records that Kieren holds.' He later added: 'Ian's got to do two 400s, and I've got to do half of a 1500, so it might be a bit harder for him.' It was clear that Grant considered the new event to be his territory.

In the build-up to Trials, Frost had his swimmers doing race-day simulations – 'heats' in the morning, 'finals' in the afternoon in full race attire. *Sydney Morning Herald* swimming writer Michael Cowley had a mole in the Thorpe camp – his niece – and found out through her, less than a fortnight before the meet, that Ian had just swum a simulated 200 metres final in his bodysuit in heavy rain and gone close to matching Hoogie's world record. He was absolutely *flying*. Ian was shocked when Cowley questioned him about it – he reckoned training times should be private – but he admitted it was true.

So it was hardly surprising that on day one in Hobart, he swam 3:40.76 in the final of the 400 free – only 0.17 seconds outside his world record. He went out slowly, allowing the crowd of about 2000 to briefly ponder his form, then overtook Hackett by the halfway point and came home like a bullet. He felt relieved – because *you never know until that first swim* – and he felt vindicated: 'I'd shown that you can do the things you want to do, as long as you have in the back of your mind what's most important – and swimming was still my main priority.' The Thorpedo was back.

Hackett had likewise clocked his second-fastest time ever for 400 metres, so they were both fired up for the 800. Ian had no idea how to swim 800 metres – he'd never done it before, and he hadn't even done any experimental swims at training. But he knew what speed he could maintain comfortably, so he decided to do that for 600 metres, then try and crank up a big finish, just as if he were swimming the second half of a 400. Even though he was in unknown territory, he figured he'd apply his usual rule, bring down the curtain on his lane, and pay no attention to what Hackett was doing.

So, just 15 minutes after a tough 200 semi-final and a totally inadequate warm-down, Ian dived in and, as it happened, swam eyeball to eyeball with a fresh Grant Hackett for 700 metres. It was pure theatre; no-one could possibly tell who was going to kick away in that last 100. Would it be the sprinter or the stayer? Perkins had predicted, before these Trials began, that it would be Hackett. All logic, according to Don Talbot, suggested it *should* be Hackett.

But Ian started bringing in the big kick at 700, and by the time he'd finished the race, Grant was three body-lengths behind. Ian had produced a big negative split and covered the final 100 in 53.68 seconds – faster even than he'd done it in the 400 metres. Obviously he was right about the way Frost was training him, and his endurance was even greater than he'd anticipated. He'd broken Kieren Perkins' admittedly soft 1994 world record (set on the way to his 1500 record) by 4.4 seconds. Hackett, stunned and a bit exasperated, could only exclaim: 'Who comes home in *53 seconds*?'

In the post-race interview, Grant facetiously asked the crowd to feel sorry for him – it was the second time he'd broken a world record and been beaten by Ian Thorpe. Ian said he could have swum it faster if he'd done a few things differently. It was a reasonable observation, given this was his first-ever shot at the event. And he'd get a chance to prove it in July.

But that wasn't the climax of this meet. It came in the 200 final on the following night. Nobody was prepared for Ian to recover so quickly from his 800 swim. He had little competition – both Grant Hackett and Michael Klim had given up chasing him in this event – so it wasn't surprising that he led the field home by ten metres. But the time – 1:44.69 – annihilated Hoogie's world record of 1:45.35. Again he'd come home at blinding speed, a full second faster than he'd managed for the back end of his Olympic final. It was the fifth time he'd set world records on consecutive nights, and it was his 13th individual record (including nine long and four short course) – the most by any Australian male. Only two other men had held world records over such a range of distances: John Konrads in 1958–60, also at 200, 400 and 800 metres, and the tragic American Tim Shaw, who in 1975 was the world record holder in the 200, 400 and 1500 metres, only to be trained into the ground and virtually destroyed by his maniacal coach, Dick Jochums.

Ian's performances did amount to staggering stuff, but the media went somewhat overboard. Shane Gould produced a convoluted argument to the effect that 'with a semi-trailer load of want', Ian could emulate her own achievement of 1971–72, when she simultaneously held all the freestyle records from 100 to 1500. 'Thorpe's exceptional ability means the feat could also be in his reach within a year,' she concluded.

Ian wasn't buying it. He knew that although human physiology hadn't changed at all in the 30 years since Gould had dominated the world, swimming standards definitely had. He politely dismissed her column, but the *Telegraph* stated: 'It seems the only person who believes Thorpe isn't capable of matching Shane Gould's feat . . . is Thorpe himself.'

Hoogie's record for 100 metres was 47.84; Ian's PB was 49.71. Perkins' 1500 record was 14:41.66; Ian's PB – albeit that he'd only swum it once – was 15:25.06. Yet Frost was insisting it was 'only a matter of time' before Ian became world champion and record holder in the 100 – he was at it again – while at the same time Perkins was claiming Ian could rewrite the 1500 record book. 'What is going on here?' wrote Wayne Smith in the *Telegraph*. 'Thorpe can't be the world's greatest sprinter at the same time as he is the greatest distance swimmer. Can he?'

Well, no. He can't. He could have gone all-out one way or the other

– that is, training specifically for the 1500, or the 100 – and few would doubt that he was a good enough swimmer to eventually claim those records. But not simultaneously. Ian isn't ever going to delude himself; for instance, he readily recognises that the 200-400-800 world record treble, which he still holds today, is not as difficult a feat as a 100-200-400 treble would be.

Still, the Thorpedo only added fuel to the rising excitement when he surprised himself by annexing Michael Klim's 100 metres title – Klim had won it four years in a row – slashing his PB from 49.71 down to 49.05 in the process. With a decent start he'd have achieved his target of breaking 49 seconds – but still, he now had the one he wanted most, having improved his position from fourth in 2000 to first. It was the only time any man had held all the Australian freestyle titles from 100 to 800 since the days of Konrads. Chris Fydler had retired, while Michael Klim was beaten into third by Ashley Callus, and so would be denied a swim in the blue riband event at the Worlds, only six months after holding, very briefly, the world record.

Ian's results meant he would have an incredibly tough seven-event program in Fukuoka: 100, 200, 400 and 800 free, plus the three relays. However, he reckoned this was the first time he'd come through a full meet in perfect health, so he felt he was ready for it. He felt also that the burden of doubt had been lifted from his shoulders; and with so many dramas now behind him, he was primed to enter a golden period in his young life.

≈

When the Japanese talk 'saturation coverage', they don't muck around. Ian Thorpe's presence was already everywhere in Japan when he and the Flaskases landed for the promo tour only days after his record-breaking efforts in Hobart. Dentsu and Asahi had obviously done their work well. It was scary for Ian to see billboards of himself 100 times larger than life, especially when he had no clue what the writing was saying.

Now, back in the country that had so intrigued him four years earlier, it was time to crank it up a few more notches. Ian immersed himself in Japanese culture while the Japanese immersed themselves in him. During a five-day romp with the Asahi network they did news and current affairs shows, lifestyle shows, cooking shows, kids' shows, sports shows: the lot. There were magazine and newspaper articles and all sorts of other promotions as well. TV Asahi had even organised for Ian to meet the most famous man in Japan – not the Prime Minister, but the manager of the Tokyo Giants baseball team – out on the pitcher's mound just before a game at Tokyo Stadium. And the network had wound the Japanese public into a frenzy about the Worlds, so there was standing room only at press conferences when local media asked Ian about his prospects. As well, Japanese swimmers like Mai Nakamura had come through to lead a resurgence of interest in the sport in a country so long starved of its own aquatic heroes. Fukuoka 2001 was going to be *big*.

The Japanese invented reality TV many years before Westerners realised it was more fun to watch people being humiliated in real life, rather than just actors. Ian's introduction to the phenomenon was being a contestant on one of the country's top-rating shows.

Before the program Thorpe and his female opponent had to secretly nominate which were their favourite foods, and one that they could not stomach. Each would have to eat four meals, one after the other – three of which they liked, as well as the one they hated. The object was to display the highest ideal of Japanese stoicism, so that your opponent could not possibly guess which was the plate that made you feel sick. There were a couple of comedians chucked in there to keep the action moving along, the Aussie guest was wired up with a translator, and it was on.

Ian can't stand eggs, so when his scrambled eggs arrived, he covered them with sauce and hoed them down, saying he just loved them because he never gets enough time to cook them before training. It sounded plausible. But the contest turned out a draw, with both Ian and his opposite number getting it right on their second guess. It was only later, when Ian was watching a show that featured young men running full-bore head-first into a brick wall, that he realised he'd been brought in at the very benign end of the spectrum.

But he just loved how *everything* in Japan was different, so there was amusement or amazement around every corner. And he loved the perfect order of things: how the schedules for everything were even tighter than his own at home, and how there was no crime – apart from the Yakuza, who were among the heaviest crims in the world, but who seemed to know their place, just like everyone else. He loved the degree of respect people showed each other, especially in the bowing ritual; he began to appreciate the aesthetic of Japanese culture, exemplified in the smallest things, like the artistry of flower arrangements in people's tiny homes. 'I like the ritualistic nature of the society as a whole. When I'm there long enough, I start to become more and more Japanese.'

Most of all, he loved learning the intricate rituals surrounding eating in Japan: precisely what to do with chopsticks, how to serve food to others, how tea cups should be held. He'd already decided that, come what may, he would eat nothing but Japanese food on this trip: breakfast, lunch and dinner. It was a challenge. Most of the time he and the Flaskases had no idea what they were eating. Often their hosts didn't seem to know either.

The most memorable meal was their first experience in a *fugu* restaurant in Tokyo. These places serve only the poisonous blowfish, which is a major Japanese delicacy – the cleanest and purest white fish flavour. (*Fugu* chefs spend years at university learning how to remove the poison gland so that it releases no toxin; about 100 Japanese die each year from eating badly prepared *fugu*.) Anyway, the blowfish was served in several courses, and one course involved some little balls that burst in the mouth to release a truly horrendous taste. Their very obsequious hosts didn't speak English well, so it took a lot of sign language before they understood that they were eating the fish's sperm sacs. Ian got all four of his balls down. He was always the bravest of the three of them, and he really didn't want to offend anyone.

That was a good thing, because he was seriously tested when the party decamped for the last two days of their visit to the ancient capital of Kyoto, about an hour outside Tokyo. Apparently the television people wanted them to have an authentic Japanese experience before they went home, so they were accommodated in a traditional inn with its manicured courtyard, and it was arranged for them to meditate – which none of them had done before – in a beautiful 800-year-old Buddhist temple where the *shogun* had once performed his devotions. This was no tourist hangout, but a very sacred place where a senior monk, the master, showed them how to sit properly, breathe and focus. A bell rang to signify the beginning of the meditation.

The master carried a large and quite heavy bamboo pole with which he would gently tap each of them in turn to adjust their posture. After about 20 minutes or so, Ian fidgeted a bit and leaned forward. The master saw him, paced over, and just as Ian thought he was going to have his posture readjusted, the bamboo-wielding monk went *whack* – belting Ian across the meat of the shoulder. 'Wow, that's hard,' he thought. Then it was the other shoulder – *whack* – this time even harder. Michelle, sitting next to him, was shocked. The monk left the room.

Forty minutes later a bell rang, announcing the end of the session. 'Did you see that? THE MONK HIT ME!' Ian exclaimed theatrically. Then he showed David and Michelle the red welts, but they were laughing their heads off, happy to have been spared. At that moment the master returned and enquired: 'Did you enjoy your experience?' Ian reflected on that for a bit and realised that he had – but only *after* he'd been belted. 'I went straight into a real meditation then – before that I'd just been bored. The rest of the time really flew, and I realised that I'd been hearing bells and school kids laughing – but there were no school kids around. It was just the whole vibe of this place . . .'

So obviously the master knew exactly what he was doing. His next move was to ask Ian for his autograph. As he handed over the pen, Thorpe noticed he was wearing a Rolex watch. What sort of monk wants an autograph and wears a Rolex? It was typical of the endless variety of surprises offered up by this country. Ian could never get enough of Japan.

≈

Not long after he'd barely missed out on a spot at the Sydney Olympics, Simon Cowley left Doug Frost. Then, a couple of weeks after Ian's return from Japan, Craig Stevens went to the AIS to train and Kirsten Thomson joined Brian Sutton's squad at Sydney University. The four of them had been very close, and now the dynamic of the squad was radically altered. It would never be as much fun for Ian again.

Frost conceded that the two freestylers, Craig and Kirsten, probably thought they weren't getting the same attention from him as his star swimmer was. Thorpe's take on it was a bit different: 'Craig and I were doing the same program, and he's a 1500-metre swimmer. Kirsten might have had a slightly different program, but it was still basically a middle-distance program, and she's purely a 200 swimmer . . . We should all have had our programs individually tailored.'

'I don't really think Doug put Ian first,' says Kirsten now. 'But I think he figured the sessions were working for Ian, so they should work for everyone.' (She subsequently found her training sessions as a sprinter under Sutton vastly different – a lot more quality, a lot less quantity.) Both Kirsten and Simon believed that when Frost began coaching them after he moved to Sutherland in 1997, it was the best thing that had happened to them. Their young bodies could cope with the massive workload and recover quickly; but as they got older, Doug didn't adapt their programs as they believed he should. Both reckoned they were being overtrained.

There was also the problem of Doug's authoritarian approach. Both swimmers thought they should have had some input of their own as they reached their late teens – but that just wasn't Frost's way. Kirsten vowed, after she'd been made to cry when she was 14, that she would never do it again, no matter how much Doug yelled at her. Even though she believed the coach really had his swimmers' best interests at heart, and didn't intentionally go about upsetting people, he was just so difficult to get on with. Now she was 17, and he was *still* yelling at her all the time. Doug's assistant, Tracey Menzies, became the mediator whenever swimmers were in conflict with him: 'She held the squad together for a long time,' says Simon. 'Without her, a lot of this stuff may have happened sooner.'

So that left Ian – the one who'd trained harder than anyone since he was 14 years old; the one who, despite his reservations, still enjoyed the challenge of boring, gruelling sets; the one who had the ability to do whatever Doug asked of him; the one whose maturity and strength of character ensured Doug didn't overstep the mark; the one who was still producing the goods. Even so, the relationship between the swimmer and his coach cooled a little more.

On 7 May, just 11 days after the simultaneous departure of Stevens and Thomson was reported, Doug Frost became the third recipient of the highest honour bestowed by the World Swimming Coaches' Association – 'Coach of the Quadrennium' – basically for his work with Ian Thorpe through the years 1997–2000. He also became one of 14 Australian coaches, stretching back to the days of Harry Gallagher and Dawn Fraser, elevated to the rank of Master Coach. At the same presentation, the Rookie Coach of the Year was named: Tracey Menzies.

≈

Ian's portfolio was going through a process of rationalisation; in other words, the ante was upped. Sydney Water, one of his earliest sponsors, dropped off at the end of 2000. Mazda finished up in March 2001, with Audi conveniently replacing them in May. Westpac finished at the end of June, but the long-running saga was the battle between the Seven and Nine networks for Ian's signature.

Seven's original contract was up in March, and Nine pitched hard for him, given they had the rights to every major event apart from the Olympics and the 2002 Commonwealth Games. Negotiations dragged on until the end of June, with very big dollars on offer this time around. Finally the Thorpe camp opted for another four years exclusively with Seven. Ian's loyalty was with Kerry Stokes, who was happy for him to explore his creative on- and off-screen interests in television. 'Don't be surprised to see him turn up as a reporter on a lifestyle show, or as an actor,' said Flaskas. The only thing certain was that Ian wasn't going to be a swimming commentator. If he was going to be on screen, he wanted to play someone other than Ian Thorpe.

It was a bit of a departure for Ian to be heading off on a Mare Nostrum tour of Canet, Monaco and Milan in mid-June, during the 'quality phase' of his preparation for the Worlds, but Doug thought some actual racing would sharpen him up. He hardly needed it: Ian was in unbelievable shape. Even though he was in the middle of heavy training, in some races he came close to matching his world records. It was obvious to every pundit that by the time he was fully tapered, he was going to be taking a wrecking ball with him to Japan.

It didn't even bother him that just a couple of days before the meet was due to start, FINA made the astonishing decision to leave the 800 metres freestyle out of the Olympic program. 'Doug would have seen it as the loss of an Olympic gold medal, but I wasn't thinking that way,' says Ian. He was still thinking about the blue riband event: the 100 metres. This 800-metre race was just an interesting challenge, a satisfying diversion. There'd be other ways to challenge himself in the future.

23

THORPEMANIA

DAVE FLASKAS HAD WARNED IAN HANSON that there were likely to be some radical scenes at Fukuoka Airport when Ian Thorpe arrived. Hanson didn't know exactly what to expect – nor did anyone else – so he sent his right-hand man, Dave Mason, on a recon trip a few days early to check out security arrangements. Mason quickly realised there was an obsession with 'Ian Soap' in the port city, as there was throughout the country. When he got to the airport for the team's arrival, he saw that the 'barricade' he'd been told about was nothing more than a piece of rope. 'You're kidding,' he said to the Japanese security liaison man.

'Trust me,' came the reply. 'They will not go past that line.'

'Do they know you here?' Ashley Callus asked Ian as they walked out into Arrivals. When they spotted him, shuffling along in the middle of a tight pack of swimmers, the crowd of hundreds – some reckoned thousands – erupted. They were 25 metres deep, they were mainly girls, they were mainly school age, and they were all screaming hysterically. Not one of them crossed the rope barricade. Only two people did that, both of them Australian photographers.

Everyone who witnessed the bizarre scenes during the following week could think of only one thing comparable: 'Beatlemania'. It was an apt description in every respect, except for the fact that no-one got hurt. Thorpemania was a controlled form of hysteria. Like gangsters, even hysterics know their place in Japan. Sometimes it got a bit precarious, with people climbing over each other to get closer to Ian, constantly invading his space, wanting to touch him (girls) or shake his hand (boys), but he never felt in real danger because of the underpinning sense of order in Japanese society.

Still, he hadn't imagined things were going to be quite this full-on. It was a constant drain on his reserves; every moment of every day he was on show. He couldn't even look out of a bus window without having females screaming at him. A crowd of about 200, mostly schoolgirls, stood vigil outside the team's hotel all day long, which meant the other swimmers would be dropped off the bus at the front while Ian would stay on board, hidden, and enter via one of three secret routes at the back. On the way out, it was a similar game in reverse. The girls never figured out what was going on until the last day.

A few times, feeling a need to acknowledge their devotion, he'd get off the bus and walk through the mob – which was, once again, roped off. All the girls would reach out their hands, and whoever was touched by the Australian demi-god would scream even more ecstatically than the others.

At the temporary Marine Messe pool, which had been constructed in just three weeks to house a capacity crowd of 10 000, the support for Ian Soap was so boisterous it almost matched the Sydney Olympics. Fans waved 'I Love Thorpedo' signs; every kid had a Japanese flag tattooed on one cheek and an Australian flag on the other; and each time Ian stepped up to the block, the acclamation was much longer and louder than for any other athlete, Japanese swimmers included. Even Ken and Margaret, who were recognised from TV Asahi's documentary, signed hundreds of autographs and posed for hundreds of photos while queuing outside the stadium. Ian Thorpe was adopted, embraced and adored by the multitudes of a foreign country. It was simply extraordinary.

The Americans, who'd always enjoyed a measure of popularity in Japan, were bemused by the whole thing – especially when, after being comprehensively smashed by Australia on day one in the pool, they found themselves boarding a shuttle bus for their hotel that was plastered from end to end with a gigantic image of Ian Thorpe. The Aussies thought that was hilarious.

Naturally Ian came in for a fair amount of good-natured ribbing from his team-mates, who were kept in a constant state of amusement, but they also thought it was a great thing to see Japan rekindling its enthusiasm for the sport. Ian Thorpe's presence was inspirational – like the influence of Tiger Woods on golf, or Michael Jordan on basketball – so that within a couple of years, the Japanese had a world record-breaking breast-stroker and new national hero, Kosuke Kitajima, and several other medallists at the Barcelona World Championships. By the Beijing Olympics in 2008 they're expected to be a real force again.

There was only one problem with all this hysteria. Schoolgirls could naturally be relied upon to scream on cue, but run a mile if anything sexual was actually suggested to them. More mature Japanese women made it very clear they wouldn't think twice about it. Some demanded Ian take his shirt off so they could admire him. Others would take photos of his backside. Women would approach him alone or in front of hundreds of people and virtually put the hard word on him. Their approach to sex owed nothing to the Judeo-Christian tradition. Like everything else you can think of, the Japanese do it differently.

After all this investment in the fortunes of a single swimmer, it would have been the greatest anticlimax in the sport's history if Thorpe had missed his taper. But he hadn't. That much was obvious after his first final, the 400 metres. He went out in quite leisurely style, looking to conserve energy for the 4 × 100 relay, and was a full two seconds off world record pace at the 200, with Massi Rosolino and Grant Hackett right on his shoulder. At 300 he started to pull away by a body-length from Hackett, but even at the final turn he was still 0.93 seconds outside his record time, so there was no chance, apparently, of a new world record. And then he absolutely *floored it*, covering the last 50 in a miraculous 24.36 seconds. That was enough to slice 0.42 seconds off his old mark, to the astonishment of Ray Warren: 'This man has done it again! He's given the clock a start – and a beating! *Ian Thorpe . . . I ask you, is he not the greatest ever?* Look at them – they're dancing in the aisles!' And so they were. Ian was almost giggling as he checked the clock: 3:40.17. *Gold medal number one.*

Hackett, too, was a happy man, having surpassed Rosolino's Olympic time to become the second-fastest 400 swimmer in history, just over two seconds behind Ian. The 800 metres showdown was going to be very serious business.

This time around the schedule was even tighter than at the Olympics, with the 400 starting at 6.45 pm and the relay at 7.24. But again it had all been planned down to the minute. Ian answered two questions from Japanese and Australian television, got an adequate 1200-metre warm-down in while chewing on an energy bar for the first 200, and then jumped on the podium to accept his medal while still in his bodysuit. The Australian reporters would never forget the sound of rolling thunder as wave upon wave of people raced down the aisles of the makeshift grandstand to get to the railing and catch a closer look at the Aussie giant.

The pressure of the suit on his organs, even when unzipped, was making him feel ill, but there was no alternative. There were just eight minutes from the start of the ceremony to the start of the relay. By the time the anthem was played and victory walk finished, one or maybe two minutes were left. Luckily Ian would be swimming last again. He bolted down to take his place with the others.

With Gary Hall Jr missing from the United States line-up, Ian was up against Jason Lezak – shades of Pan Pacs '99. Klim, Callus and Todd Pearson got him into the water just ahead of the American sprinter. Ian Thorpe was now Australia's premier 100 metres freestyler, and as Nicole Stevenson said: 'This is one of his events. He *cannot* lose it.' And he didn't, producing his fastest-ever relay split: 47.87. He was thrilled with that time. Even with the flying start, swimming sub-48 convinced him he could, in spite of everything, be right up there in the 100. *Gold medal number two*.

There were no wild scenes this time – just a dignified all-round embrace – although it was tremendously satisfying for the Aussies to beat the Yanks for the third time in a row. Holland's team edged out the Americans, Hoogie coming home with the fastest relay leg in history: a blistering 47.02. The Flying Dutchman had experienced serious problems dealing with his post-Olympic celebrity at home, but he was obviously in good enough shape to try and repeat his famous victory over Ian in the 200.

This had already been a tough opening day for Ian, exacerbated by 40-degree heat in the middle of the day. Now there was an appointment with the media in the mixed zone, with every question and answer having to be translated, then the medal ceremony, warm-down, massage, compulsory drug test for breaking a world record, then another linguistic marathon of a press conference, into the bus to run the gauntlet of fans, dinner with Grant Hackett, and finally bed. But that was nothing by comparison with night three, which posed the challenge of the 200 semi and the 800 final.

There were exactly 15 minutes from the end of the 200 semi-final, in which Ian swam a conservative 1:47.20 to qualify well behind van den Hoogenband, till the start of the 800. But if you subtracted transit time to the warm-down pool and marshalling time, that left only eight. Doug Frost kept on drumming it in: 'You've only got *eight* minutes.' Ian raced to the pool, swam the fastest 600 metres of warm-down ever (without any of the usual rest periods and fluid intake that help remove lactic acid from the body), scoffed half a Power Bar on the run back to marshalling, and fronted up to take on a very fit, very fresh, totally focused opponent.

'Grant Hackett may be holding all the aces,' commented Ray Warren in a rare understatement. If ever he was going to beat Ian Thorpe in any race again, *surely* this was the time. Ian pulled his usual mental trick, turning a negative into a positive, telling himself: 'I'm that little bit more warmed up than usual. My body is ready to go fast. That's the mode I'm in now.' And *believed* it.

Hackett did everything right, putting it to Thorpe in the first hundred with a withering 54.54 seconds – almost two seconds faster than world record pace – and challenging him to stick with that pace, all the while hoping to pour the lactate into him so he'd have nothing to finish with. And Ian just sat on him, precisely one arm's length behind. A few times he tried to crank it up but felt himself losing efficiency, so he settled back into his sustainable pace, which happened to be exactly the same as Grant's. The others weren't in the picture.

As was the case in Hobart, it was mesmerising – 'beautiful to watch', said Warren, 'almost synchronised swimming'. It was closer to a heavy-weight title fight, with Hackett going first for a quick knockout, then trying to wear his opponent into submission with a barrage of body-blows. But when Ian was still there at 600, only 0.29 seconds behind, he must have known it was over. At 700 they turned exactly together, and by 750, Ian was one-hundredth of a second in front. If Hobart was pure theatre, this was the greatest of encores, making a mockery of FINA's decision to scrap the race at the Olympics.

Inevitably, Ian hit the accelerator in that last 50, and Hackett just didn't have enough left. He'd fought valiantly, and it was closer this time, but he had to accept that he'd yet again broken a world record and come second. Ian hit the wall only a bit over a body-length in front, but had slashed his own record by two and a half seconds. 'As a performance, in its context, it was very good,' Ian now reflects. 'But it didn't mean that much to me, because the 800 hasn't been legitimised yet.' *Gold medal number three.*

At the moment when Grant stared up at the scoreboard, he did not look happy. He rolled his tongue tersely around in his mouth, keeping his emotions in check, and he didn't smile. He'd wanted that one badly. But, as always, he was the epitome of graciousness in the post-race interviews. Not many people on earth could know what it would be like to have been the world's greatest swimmer, and a nation's most lauded athlete, but for a chance meeting between Ken and Margaret Thorpe. No doubt that's what Grant Hackett would have been – a former world record holder in the 200 free, and world record holder and perpetual world champion in the 400, 800 and 1500. No-one else could match that.

But in real life, having finally emerged from the shadow of Kieren Perkins after beating him at the Sydney Olympics – and especially after destroying his 1500 record at the end of this meet – he had been unable to topple Ian Thorpe in the 800, or the long course 400, ever since that last-stroke loss at the Perth Worlds back in January 1998. Apart from his brief window of ascendancy in early 1999, he had the number '2' stamped indelibly on his forehead. Yet not once was there the slightest sign of resentment, nor did Grant ever deviate from his line on Ian Thorpe: that he'd rather have Thorpey around than not, because the world's best swimmer gave him something to chase – and he was never going to give up.

The consistency of Hackett's personality – his relentless niceness and extraordinary humility – astonished swimming commentators just as much as Ian's. And they both really enjoyed their 'one of the boys' status among the established swimmers. But they diverged at that point. Grant was always just a big boofy bloke, relaxed and uncomplicated, while Ian, for all his modesty and friendliness, had a commanding presence – almost a regal aura – especially in the eyes of opposition swimmers. Daniel Kowalksi observes: 'Everyone on the other teams just stopped and stared when Ian Thorpe was on pool deck. It was always quite funny, and buoyant for our team as a whole. There was so much respect and admiration for him, and we fed off that. You can't help but gain confidence from Ian's presence. The way he continually strives to get the best out of himself, and the way he speaks and carries himself – it all has a profound influence on the other swimmers.'

Thorpe's position in the worldwide estimation of swimmers may have been secure, but he'd failed to endear himself to the suits at FINA. And the relationship worsened after he launched an attack on them, straight after winning the 800, for failing to test for EPO at these championships. FINA had refused to reintroduce the protocols that had passed muster through the IOC's Medical Commission at the Sydney Olympics, claiming legal and technical flaws made them suspect.

At the time he spoke only of the EPO situation, but Ian wasn't just worried about that. He reckoned that with some countries having poor testing procedures, it was obvious that a minority of swimmers with unnatural body shapes were making huge gains, and it was getting 'ridiculous' at the time. He believed it was the usual story: FINA didn't have a genuine agenda to weed out drug cheats, but preferred to protect the image of the sport.

FINA told him the following day to get back in his box. 'He should respect the position of the scientific people – people in the labs doing the job every day,' said FINA's executive director, Cornel Marcelescu. 'The swimmers should swim. This is the most important thing.'

Ian had been vocal on drugs before, but never as directly critical of the world governing body's overall approach. Ian Hanson's view, as the media director for Australian Swimming, was that the star swimmer should be leaving it for others to talk about, rather than creating problems for himself. He fronted Ian at the time: 'Why do you want to get involved in this issue? You don't need to do this . . .'

Ian replied: 'If I want to get involved in it, then I will. And I don't give a damn who you are or what you think – or what anyone else thinks.' Ian was well aware that his voice carried a heavy weight – and if he didn't speak, who would?

John Mendoza, the chief executive of ASDA, has followed the history of FINA's position on EPO testing, and of this period he says: 'It did go into a bit of a black hole after Sydney . . . FINA simply refused to engage on the issue . . . Ian had every right to say: "Hang on – we had this test ten months ago – why isn't it being applied here?" There was no test at all – neither blood nor urine. Just basic steroids and stimulants.'

Then came the media-billed 'revenge match' against Hoogie over 200 metres. 'I think van den Hoogenband can try anything he likes,' said Duncan Armstrong in pre-race commentary. 'But Ian Thorpe is in the best shape of his career at this meet.'

And so it proved. Ian was only two-tenths in front of the Dutchman at the 150, and just one-hundredth of a second inside world record pace – but his last lap was an absolute scorcher, bringing him to the wall with almost two body-lengths to spare and carving another massive slice off his record time. He was down to 1:44.06 now, having taken less than 11 months to shave the 200 record by 1.29 seconds. It had taken 11 *years* to reduce Lamberti's mark by the same amount.

Hoogie held Ian's arm aloft after the race in an ostentatious gesture. It was noticeable, as the cameras panned to Ken Thorpe in the stands, that his applause, unsmiling as usual, was particularly intense. It looked as though he personally wanted that one. If Ian did too – and that surely would have been understandable – he wasn't admitting it: 'What was significant was that I swam a PB.' It was his 12th individual long course world record, and the culmination of the vow he'd made after the Olympics. *Gold medal number four.*

And that was when it all started: the first whispers of what was to become a media preoccupation, if not a Thorpean one. Seven gold medals. *The Magnificent Seven.* The standard set by Mark Spitz in 1972 at Munich, and the one against which every multi-medallist at world level is always compared. It was now only a possibility, and a quite remote one, but the question was first posed on 25 July 2001, after Hoogie's challenge had been so comprehensively dismissed: *Can you win seven gold medals?*

'I don't think that will happen,' Thorpe responded. 'In fact, I'm certain it won't happen. I'd be happy to be wrong. I'm swimming well at the moment, but not that well.' Although Ian entered the meet ranked world number two in the 100 – his highest-ever ranking, on the strength of his 49.05 at Trials – that was always going to be a difficult event, especially with Hoogie swimming that ridiculous 47.02 split in the relay. The 4 × 200 was a still a gimme for the Aussies, even at this level; and then the final event was the medley relay, where Australia didn't really look capable of matching the Americans. The Seven seemed a long way away. One thing was certain: if he could do it, it would be a far greater thing than Spitz had achieved. Ian was now only the second man to win three individual freestyle events at Worlds – Tim Shaw in 1975 being the other. To win four – from 100 to 800 – would be beyond phenomenal. Michael Cowley wrote in the *Sydney Morning Herald* that if Ian Thorpe could add the sprint crown to the other three titles he would be unarguably the greatest male swimmer in history, and there was no hyperbole at all in that claim. For his part, Ian didn't even *know* it hadn't been done before. He never thought of asking anyone.

After the semi-finals were over, it looked a real chance. Swimming below full-bore, Ian had broken 49 for the first time with a 48.96, and qualified second-fastest behind Hoogie, who always seemed to go all-out in semis but had only managed 48.57. Anthony Ervin, the crack American sprinter, won the other semi in a slow 49.43. Ian reckoned, on the basis of his relay split, that he ought to be capable of a 48.6 . . . or maybe a 48.5.

There was drama in the morning when the 4 × 200 relay team was disqualified on the basis of a timing stuff-up and a protest by the Germans, only to be reinstated on photographic evidence shot by the media. The same evening Ian was pictured by the TV cameras yawning in the marshalling area before the final of the 100. It had been a long campaign.

Ervin went out like a madman, as if to prove his sixth-fastest qualifying time was all wrong. Out in lane 2, he'd blind-sided Hoogie, who turned second while Ian hit the wall fifth – 'Close enough if good enough,' said Ray Warren. But Ervin kept on flying out in the boonies, with Hoogie closing at the death, and Ian Thorpe charging home . . . and then . . . chaos. To the naked eye it was obvious Ervin touched the wall first, but the timing system was malfunctioning again and the scoreboard showed Hoogie as the winner, with Ian third and Ervin nowhere.

The Dutchman leaped in the air in celebration and started walking towards the cameras before the number '1' appeared next to Ervin's name, and a time of 48.33. Ian was relegated to fourth, two-hundredths of a second outside a podium finish. His time: 48.81. A new PB, but still not what he'd anticipated. *Why* couldn't he find those extra few tenths that should rightfully be his? It was just baffling. He still hadn't figured out the bit about the surging wave.

So that was the end of The Seven. There was plenty of rest for Ian before the last event on that night's program, the 4 × 200 relay. Hackett was super-quick, Klim extended the lead to almost four body-lengths, this time 'Some Other Bloke' was Bill Kirby, who swam well to put Ian in the water 0.73 seconds outside the Aussies' world best time. The only question was whether Ian could break another world record. He smashed it by almost two and a half seconds with the fastest 200 relay split in history. *Gold medal number five*.

Only two swimmers had ever won five gold medals at a Worlds meet – Jim Montgomery in 1973 and Tracy Caulkins in 1978. Thorpe's chance for the unprecedented sixth, in the medley relay, just didn't add up against the Americans. Matt Welsh would get the Aussies some sort of lead in the backstroke, but they had no world-class 100 breast-stroker, with little Regan Harrison, who'd managed a sixth in the 200 breast, up against the 100 metres bronze medallist, Ed Moses. Then Geoff Huegill, the butterfly bronze medallist, was matched with Ian Crocker, the butterfly silver medallist . . . and finally Ian Thorpe vs Anthony Ervin, gold medallist in the 50 and 100 metres – the fastest freestyle swimmer on earth.

The Americans were in lane 4, Australia in 5. Ray Warren: 'The question is, will Thorpe be level [with Ervin] when they say go? Because if he is, if you go on the 100 times the other night, he *can't* catch Ervin. Not even if your name is Thorpe.' All up, they needed a minor miracle.

Welsh put them in front, with the US in fifth spot after the backstroke leg. But Moses quickly overhauled Harrison, who then dug in and swam the race of his life to reel back the American and put Huegill in the water just behind Crocker. How did Huegill catch the silver medallist? Impossible to say. But as he motored down the return lap, Ian got up on his block early – a gigantic figure in his jet black suit – and started to swing his arms rhythmically, backward and forward, as if winding himself up for takeoff – just like he always did, only sooner. Ervin, the fastest man in the world, with at least half a body-length advantage over Thorpe in the 100, looked sideways. They hit the water *exactly* together.

As always, Ervin went out superfast, and nailed his turn. Duncan Armstrong: 'Oh, the American's got a body-length on him . . . It could be all over.'

Ray Warren: 'The Americans . . . the Olympic champions . . . They're in front. Thorpe goes for everything now. There's only 15 metres to go . . . Thorpe is mowing him down! Ervin's in front –

Thorpe is coming over him! *Ervin . . . Thorpe . . . Thorpe . . . Ervin . . . He got there! Thorpe has won it for Australia in the final leg! What a swim! How can you give Ervin a body-length start?*

Anthony Ervin could go and ask Gary Hall Jr about that. But there was more drama. The scoreboard was down. One of the teams had been disqualified. Ian, with his risky approach to the changeover, always assumed he was the one who'd broken. It had to happen some day. But when the result finally came up, it was the American, Ervin, who'd been freaked out by the big black shark next to him and jumped early. Ken Thorpe found Dave Flaskas in the crowd and said simply: 'I thought I'd seen everything.' *Gold medal number six.*

In the Australian media, the Aussies won the meet with 13 gold, 3 silver and 3 bronze. In the American media, the US won the meet with 9 gold, 9 silver and 8 bronze. The damned Yanks wouldn't give Don Talbot his moment of glory, claiming victory on the total points and medal count, rather than the number of golds. He'd waited 45 years – since the Melbourne Olympics – for Australia to be hailed as the world's greatest swimming nation again, and now found he was having to do much of the hailing himself, even though at the Olympics countries were always ranked by gold medals first. The Americans had not brought their best team to Fukuoka in 2001 anyway; it wasn't exactly the B team, but there were four world record holders missing. *You haven't really beaten them till you've beaten them at the Olympics.*

In any case, Ian Thorpe had repaid TV Asahi's investment and vanquished the best the world could possibly have offered, breaking four world records in the process. If there was a point when he could not have been any more famous in Australia – around the 2000 Olympics – the same now applied in Japan. Normally Ian wouldn't watch himself on TV, of course, but he was addicted to the ads on Japanese television. Flicking from ad to ad, he could hardly escape images of himself. And on TV Asahi, there seemed to be nothing else but Ian Thorpe.

You know you've made it in Japan when the presidents of Dentsu and TV Asahi fly especially from Tokyo to Fukuoka for a *fugu* lunch. When the Aussie team doctor found out Ian and Dave Flaskas were going to eat blowfish, she was appalled. Ian was given pills to swallow with tonic water 'immediately if he felt anything strange'. He told David they were to make him throw up in case of poisoning. 'What about *me*?' his manager replied. But fortunately there were no problems, and at the lunch Thorpe presented both presidents, Mr Narita and Mr Hirose, with didgeridoos, which they tried to play without success and to much hilarity.

Fukuoka is renowned as the home of the blowfish, and at $US500 a head, Ian didn't mind being treated to another lunch by TV Asahi execs the day after the Australian team, along with Dave Flaskas, flew out. Ian and Michelle Flaskas and Ian Hanson were picked up by a mini-bus and deposited at another famous but deserted *fugu* restaurant, where the network did a live cross to the Thorpedo speaking a few phrases of Japanese while consuming the traditional delicacy.

They'd failed to anticipate that people watching the show live would recognise the venue. By the time the party got outside there were hundreds of hysterical females in wait, and not much Japanese reserve in evidence. While the TV execs tried to push Ian through the crowd to get him onto the bus, Michelle was knocked to the ground in the melee. It was madness all around – but Hanson noticed Ian had a smile on his face as he beat a path to the door of the escape vehicle. He may have been recalling the opening scene from the first *Austin Powers* flick. That was about as radical as it got on that trip.

≈

In a comprehensive Roy Morgan poll conducted shortly after the Worlds, Australians over 14 years of age were asked: 'Who is your favourite sports star?' Ian Thorpe topped the male list with 26 percent of the vote, with Pat Rafter next on 10 percent, Steve Waugh on 5 percent and Tiger Woods on 1.5 percent.

If a similar poll had been done in Japan, there's no doubt he'd have been in the top echelon, up there with Japan's biggest sporting heroes, and with the broadest appeal of any foreigner in the country. David Beckham was to enter the field on a similar level but from a different direction during the World Cup in 2002, not so much as a soccer player but mainly as the more mature woman's sex symbol, wearing his 'metrosexuality' on his sleeve – although his subsequent misfortunes might have placed him somewhere down the totem pole now.

But Ian always had cross-generational appeal. He lived up to the sporting expectations of young and old, both in Sydney and Fukuoka, and the whole society appreciated the fact that he could beat the world and retain his humility. He was the sort of person every Japanese parent would hope to produce, particularly those who despaired of the low-achieving younger generation who, they believed, were bludging off the efforts of those who'd rebuilt the country after the war.

The Japanese were obviously used to foreign celebrities not being able to speak their language at all, so they'd hang on every word from the interpreter, and really concentrate on body language and facial expressions. They'd look to make an emotional connection – something they've definitely done with Ian Thorpe. But Ian had really applied himself to learning a bit of Japanese, and at the end of each appearance on TV he'd say a few words, always to rapturous applause. After one of his events in Fukuoka, he even did a brief poolside interview, falteringly, in Japanese. He mightn't have said much, but in Japan it's the effort that counts.

It was obvious, too, that Ian genuinely liked and respected Japanese culture. He was to return a dozen or so times in the next few years, always delving into something of interest to him – learning to slice sashimi expertly ('It's all about the knife – you need a very good one'), having a karate lesson with the world champion (who foolishly invited Ian to kick him as hard as he could), meditating, visiting the museum at the bomb site at Hiroshima. It was never just a matter of making money and getting his passport stamped; he involved himself in Japan and took great pride in understanding the intricacies of Japanese etiquette. Nothing could be more impressive to Japanese people, especially the older generation.

But Thorpe could also mix it with the trendiest youth of the country. He was never as big on the feminisation of masculinity as Beckham, but he was known to be very interested in fashion and grooming, and this Japanese generation has taken the idea of 'metrosexuality' to typically excessive levels. It's not unusual for young

Japanese men to use foundation, lip gloss, eyeliner – whatever. Ian does none of that stuff, but to a large extent he's their kind of guy.

≈

The Australian press got a bit carried away about Ian's earning capacity after Fukuoka, especially in light of the Japanese hero-worship of him. The *Telegraph* reckoned his income would sit between $3 million and $4 million in 2001, and that Flaskas was cutting deals with the Japanese that would quickly send it to $10 million annually. 'Ian Thorpe Inc' was therefore estimated to be potentially worth about $100 million by the time he retired.

Those kinds of numbers were never remotely in the frame. Flaskas knocked back several very lucrative deals on the basis of poor image fit or Ian's personal discomfort with them. But there *were* some big contracts in Japan, especially with TV Asahi and Coke (Aquarius) and the anti-drug campaign, with some even bigger deals due to cut in later in 2001, worth all up about $10 million over the next few years. Ian Thorpe was building a business empire with Dave in command, but it was never about squeezing out the last dollar. Flaskas' job was to give Thorpe every chance of maximising his earning potential, but he thought his responsibility was to ensure Ian enjoyed his life as much as possible. That had more to do with the unique experiences his celebrity afforded than it did with money.

Still, Ian was to end up earning $2.5 million in 2001 – much more than anyone else in the sport internationally. He was by far the world's most famous swimmer, and Flaskas had proved his point: that an Australian athlete with the right qualities could venture beyond the domestic market and blaze a trail for others to follow. Ian had raised swimming's profile, attracted new sponsors at home and overseas, lifted TV ratings and made the Australian titles – let alone Pan Pacs and Worlds – a viable TV proposition almost single-handedly, as well as playing a huge role in re-establishing Australia's position as a premier swimming nation. It was just about time for him to go gallivanting around the world in search of serious fun once again.

24

LIFE AND DEATH

IAN SWAM FOR THE LAST TIME IN THE short course Australian titles in Perth in August 2001 before announcing he wouldn't be bothering with the world short course event in Moscow in April the following year. He just wasn't interested. Straight after Perth he backed up for the meaningless dash-for-cash which was the Goodwill Games in Brisbane at the end of August. (This non-event was Don Talbot's final meet as head coach.) Lacking any real motivation, Ian tried to swim just fast enough to win rather than as fast as he could, and he was beaten by Hackett in the 200 free, although it was insignificant. He was tired and rundown.

But the six-week break he'd planned was going to be even more fun than the post-Olympic world tour. There was a fair bit of business, but mostly it was pleasure. First stop: New York, as a guest of Armani at the fashion house's inaugural show outside Italy. He'd also been approached by UNICEF to do some promotion for UN Children's Week, including a possible meeting with Kofi Annan. Then on to

Japan, where he was booked to do a special for TV Asahi and launch the anti-drugs campaign. After that there were sponsor commitments in Germany and Switzerland for adidas and Omega, then another Armani fashion show in Milan. Then on to England to fulfil his role as a 'Commonwealth Games Ambassador' at the ticketing launch on 1 October, followed by some free time in Paris before flying to LA to appear on Jay Leno's *Tonight Show* again, this time as a proper guest. Between all that, plenty of catching up with friends in LA, New York and Milan. If the previous year's trip was anything to go by, the really fun part for Ian would be waiting to see which new doors would be opened for him by the Armani connection.

Michelle Flaskas and Ian touched down in New York in the early evening of 10 September, the plan being to catch up with Dave a week later in Tokyo. Originally they were booked into the Tribeca Hotel, right across the road from the World Trade Centre, but had to switch to another hotel 15 minutes' walk away towards midtown Manhattan because of a double-booking.

Thorpe went for a jog in the morning to shake out the cobwebs, arriving at the World Trade Centre and stopping there for a quick coffee. He and Michelle had planned to go to the viewing platform at the top of one of the Twin Towers to take some snaps that morning, so at 8.15 am he walked back to the hotel to pick her up. While he waited for her to finish getting ready, he flicked on the TV. Both the towers were ablaze by then.

The world's best swimmer was not on the way to the World Trade Centre in a taxi before making a chance decision to go back to the hotel for his camera, thus saving his own life, as was widely reported. Nor was the Tribeca Hotel razed to the ground, as was also widely reported. However, the difference between life and death for Ian and Michelle was no more than about half an hour.

Ian rang home. His mother, woken from her slumber, answered the phone. Ian told her a plane had crashed into the World Trade Centre, he and Michelle were fine and quite a distance from the building, they figured it was a terrorist attack, she'd see it on TV in the morning, and he'd see her in six weeks' time. Apparently Margaret had visions of something like a two-seater plane banging into a building. When she saw the scenes the following morning she was terrified, but by then there was no phone connection between Sydney and New York.

Michelle rang David at home directly after Ian's call, and together they watched as the Pentagon took a direct hit and as the first of the towers collapsed. Then Ian and Michelle decided to walk towards Ground Zero to have a first-hand look. Everyone else was heading the other way. It seemed to both of them like they were in a scene from a disaster movie. As they got closer, most of the people were weeping or distraught, or wandering in a daze, covered in grey dirt. Long queues of stunned New Yorkers waited to make phone calls. After they'd walked a kilometre they could go no further, so they wandered aimlessly like everyone else. As it became known that thousands had been killed, shops closed, traffic stopped, sirens wailed, jeeps and helicopters appeared, and then there was an eerie quiet, as the city's population hunkered down in hotel foyers to watch the carnage on TV.

Ian and Michelle watched as well. Then they wandered some more. They didn't talk much. They found an open café and had lunch. They were, of course, perfectly safe. But they knew they should try to make further contact with home, and even though the phone lines were down it was still possible to queue for ages to send an email from an internet café. For some reason – Ian doesn't really know why – he sent an offhand, irreverent message to the office. Something like: 'Wish you were here. Having a great time – NOT.'

Meanwhile, in Sydney, every TV screen was filled with images depicting the city of New York as a chaotic war zone, with people running screaming as millions of tonnes of disintegrated rubble pursued them up the skyscraper canyons. The horror show was on an endless loop (including scenes of people jumping from the towers which were censored from US screens), creating an impression that was entirely different from the reality Ian and Michelle were experiencing. David Flaskas was taking frantic calls from Ken Thorpe, and Michelle's sister, and God knows who else, trying to reassure them all he'd do everything he could to get the pair out of the city. And then . . . this flippant email arrived. What on earth were they thinking over there? Didn't they understand what people were going through at home? Actually, they had no idea. Even if they were of a mind to go home, which they weren't, every airport in America was closed anyway, and the hotels were all telling people to stay put. There was nothing to do but wander some more.

So they wandered Tuesday, and Wednesday, and Thursday. They tried to give blood, but New Yorkers had lined up so deep they were turned away. They reflected on all the images of missing people that had been posted on butcher's paper, with accompanying messages and poems, some of them immensely moving. On the Thursday evening they found themselves in Union Square, where a candlelight vigil was being held and butcher's paper was laid out everywhere for people to record their feelings. There were messages of hope alongside messages of hatred and calls for revenge. People sang songs of peace. It was like something out of the 1960s.

The most emotional moment for Ian was seeing a gang of four firefighters racing by as everyone stood up simultaneously and applauded them – an act that seemed to symbolise the extraordinary support people were offering each other in a city notorious for its hard edge.

By that time the phone lines had been restored, and David called and told Michelle he'd organised a car, via a contact at the Canadian Olympic Committee, which would pick them up at 10 am Friday morning and drive them to Toronto. From there they could fly home. But Ian and Michelle really wanted to attend a memorial service that was being held on the Friday afternoon in every church in New York. They'd organised their own car to leave after the service for Canada, and then they intended to fly on to Japan and pick up their itinerary from there.

David, who hadn't slept for three days and was operating on the ragged edge of nervous exhaustion, wouldn't hear of it. He told them they had to come home straight away: 'Ian's parents want him home. *Get him home now.*' Michelle was furious with David. 'He just couldn't understand that we were okay. It was like he didn't give us credit for being able to look after ourselves.' Thorpe didn't fear for his safety, he felt strongly that he shouldn't allow what had happened to change his plans, and he'd explained that to his mother and father on the phone already.

David was insistent: the car would be waiting at 10 am, and they'd better be ready to get in it. Very annoyed at missing the memorial service, they did as instructed and made a slow ten-hour trip in heavy traffic to Toronto, where they were booked into a hotel by the Olympic Committee contact. The following morning, Michelle was on the phone to her very relieved sister when Ian looked out the window, then grabbed the phone from Michelle and said: 'You're not going to believe it. Everything's cordoned off. It's a bomb scare.' While Michelle's sister got to freak out all over again, the two of them just laughed. It was getting ridiculous.

Ken Thorpe rang the same morning, very upset, and told Michelle she had to bring Ian home. Powerless to protect him from the other side of the world, Ken and Margaret needed to physically see him safe. Ian was adamant their fears were unfounded; he was going on to Japan, and so was Michelle. The phone kept ringing. More and more argument. Finally it came down to Ken saying to his son: 'I'm not going to *ask* you again. I'm *pleading* with you – please come home – for Mum and me.'

Ian thought about everything his parents had given up for him. Was he prepared to let go of something that was so important to him – 'something that actually makes up the person I am' – for their sake? Of course he was. A few days later the pair of them flew home via Los Angeles.

Michelle and David were still at odds with each other, and they vented their anger and frustration for a long time before things finally subsided. It was a weird time for both of them as they tried to come to terms with their emotions. Ian simply resigned himself to the situation, gave his mum and dad a big cuddle, and headed for the Gold Coast to let his hair down. He was determined to have some fun no matter what.

In an article in the *Sunday Telegraph* that should have won some sub-editor a gong for worst headline of the year – 'I DON'T FEEL LUCKY, I FEEL VERY FORTUNATE' – Ian was invited to wax philosophical about his near-death experience. 'Something like this makes you question things about your own life and I've been able to do that,' he said. 'I've learnt something.' Exactly what he didn't say then, but he later spoke of realising more than ever the primacy of his family, and the need to ensure he never put anything important off till tomorrow.

Anyway, it's hard to see how his life could have been any more full than it was. Having returned from a quick promo trip to Japan, he was back in the water and training hard by 20 October, making it a six-week break as he'd originally planned. But over the next month or so he was everywhere, wearing out the red carpet at movie premieres and product launches, at the opening of an Armani store in Sydney, accepting the award as *GQ* magazine's inaugural 'Man of the Year', interviewing pop stars backstage at Melbourne's Rumba festival for the in-house TV channel, working creatively on a pilot for a mysterious non-sporting TV program with Seven, and being the promotional face of a planned $500 million 80-storey supertower, the world's tallest residential building, on the Gold Coast. This was the inauguration of his latest sponsorship deal, a five-year contract worth millions with the Japanese Gold Coast-based Sunland Group. He announced he'd bought a million-dollar apartment in the building off the plan, and was even invited to have an input into its design.

Ian Thorpe was becoming a man of many parts, the consequence being that there were the usual rumblings about his ability to focus on swimming, and concerns about how long a multidimensional personality such as his could be expected to do so anyway, considering all the options he seemed to have. There'd been sporadic reports ever since the Olympics that Thorpe was hankering to take up some course or other at uni – usually medicine, economics or architecture – but the plans always came to naught, if there were plans at all, because his hectic lifestyle made them unfeasible. Realistically, he couldn't be the world's best swimmer and do all the things he wanted to do and be a student at the same time. He accepted that eventually, and contented himself with researching his various interests on the Net, occasionally playing the stockmarket, and doing his French tutorials twice a week at home just for fun.

And that was the crucial thing – he was having plenty of fun. It had taken some years to get to the point where he actually enjoyed just about everything he was called on to do by his sponsors. His business life and his personal interests had virtually merged, so he was in a constant process of self-education. The dark days of 1998 – 'I feel like quitting' – were a distant memory. And by this time he reckoned he'd found the right balance between getting the best out of himself in the pool and occupying his extremely active mind. As always, the two aspects of his life were never allowed to cross over. The pool would always take priority over everything else, because he was still, after all, a perfectionist.

And as always, he said he'd keep swimming as long as he was still enjoying it. In his heart, he knew that would be at least till the Athens Olympics, and probably beyond that to Beijing. 'I don't know if I've reached my full potential,' he said at the Telstra Swimmer of the Year Awards, where he won the major award again. 'I want to retire knowing that in one particular year I was able to achieve everything possible.'

You could read an awful lot into that statement, and people did. He'd already achieved six gold medals at world level; and he'd announced back in October that he was considering adding either a backstroke or a medley race to his 100-200-400 free schedule at the Australian Championships, which were Trials for both the Commonwealth Games in July and Pan Pacs in Yokohama in August. (Only Pan Pacs would be featuring the 800 freestyle.) Was this an alternative way to get a shot at The Seven? A precursor to an attempt to win the same events at world level as Spitz had done? The media became preoccupied with that question from then on.

Meanwhile, 2001 was another clean-up year for awards, surpassing even the avalanche of 1999. *US Swimming World* reinstated him as the male number one, making him the first man ever to win that title three times. (Grant Hackett was runner-up.) He went to a function in Melbourne at lunchtime to pick up the Olympic Writers' Award, then straight on to the Telstra dinner, where he also won their inaugural People's Choice award. Surprisingly, he was so highly regarded in France that he went within one vote of toppling Michael Schumacher in the prestigious *L'Equipe* magazine's annual expert poll for the world's

'Champion of Champions'. Even further left of field was the announcement in a mass-selling Chinese sports magazine that he'd been voted by readers as 'Most Popular Sporting Personality in China'.

There were a pile of other awards, literally too numerous to name let alone collect in person. But the biggest deal of all was the Jesse Owens Award. Alongside the names of Edwin Moses, Carl Lewis, Lance Armstrong, Michael Johnson, Marion Jones and many others, Ian Thorpe's was inscribed on sport's most hallowed trophy for his performances in 2001. He was the world's greatest athlete.

≈

Apart from his burgeoning disillusionment with Doug Frost – something swimmers had begun to notice on pool deck in an oblique sort of way as far back as the Fukuoka Worlds – 2002 dawned cloudless for the prince of the pool. He was the current holder of three long course individual world records – 200, 400 and 800 freestyle – and two relay records – 4 × 100 and 4 × 200. He'd long been uninterested in short course racing, but still held the 200 free record in that. A lot of writers, expert and non-expert, were now routinely referring to him as the greatest swimmer ever. Some prefaced that description with 'potentially' or 'arguably'. Others limited it to 'Australian'. Some reckoned the only currency that counted was Olympic gold, others that longevity was the decisive issue. The only person who seemed to dismiss the concept entirely was Ian Thorpe. 'Judge me when I've finished swimming,' he would say. There was much more to be achieved.

At the same time, he was the undisputed darling of the media. It was nigh impossible to find a bad word written or said about him. Like Pat Rafter, he was everywhere lauded for his humanity, generosity, sportsmanship, humility . . . to the point where he considered his public image to be somewhat unrealistic. Still, he was about to learn how much it can sting when the media turns – as it inevitably will – especially when the lashing is based on an abject distortion of the truth.

At the launch of the Sunland supertower project on the Gold Coast back in late November 2001, a 29-year-old Channel Seven reporter for the *Today Tonight* program, Nicki Voss, had bowled into a carefully planned and tightly scheduled media event and created some consternation. The ink was two days old on Ian's massive contract with Sunland, so everyone was tippy-toeing around, anxious to ensure that all the reporters who'd flown domestically and from Japan could get their one-on-one interviews done with the swimming champ before he had to get on a plane back to Sydney.

When Dave Flaskas arrived following an appointment in Melbourne, the journalists had all gone, Ian was about to dash for the airport, and the PR people and Sunland execs were very agitated. They told him Voss and her crew had arrived late and jumped the queue, promising they'd need only five minutes but actually taking about 25, thus causing some of those reporters to miss their interviews. Voss had a casual, flirtatious attitude and made offensive comments, including one to the MD of Sunland, Soheil Abedian. As well, she was dressed in a sexy outfit that was all wrong for the occasion.

An embarrassed Flaskas fielded the complaints, then rang the network to tell them why they'd been poorly represented that day. He figured they'd want to know. As an afterthought – and this was in no way central to the problem at all – he added: 'On top of all that, the first thing she did was make some comment to Ian about his feet.'

Channel Seven sacked Voss, who brought an action for unfair dismissal. She was friendly with a News Ltd journalist who wrote an 'exclusive' piece in early January which suggested the sacking had happened because Thorpe had been offended by the context of her comment about his feet. A follow-up story said Seven had ended up making a 'substantial' payout to Voss. Ian was left looking like a power-wielding prima donna who couldn't handle a joke.

Voss *had* made some quip to Ian, which he can't remember exactly but had included some implied reference to the size of his genitals. He rolled his eyes but didn't respond at all, since he was not particularly offended. He hadn't instructed Flaskas to make any complaint to anyone. Now he was being pilloried in all the News Ltd publications and by 2UE radio jock Malcolm T. Elliot. *Sunday Telegraph* columnist Kate de Brito took the story at face value and opined that Ian Thorpe had 'turned into a first-class dill' who 'shows a startling sense of his own importance'. The *Telegraph* ran an editorial which began: 'Ian Thorpe, say it isn't so.' Had the paper bothered to ask him in the first place, he would have. Channel Nine ran a website poll on whether the reporter deserved to be sacked for joking about Thorpe's feet. Sixteen thousand out of 20 000 supported Nicki Voss. And on it went.

The British tabloids picked up the story and covered themselves in glory as usual. The *Sun* went with the headline: 'YOU KNOW WHAT THEY SAY ABOUT MEN WITH BIG FEET . . . OOPS, SORRY', then ran a pic of Ian in his sluggoes, inviting readers to make their own judgement . . . etc.

Flaskas' response was to feed the true story to the Fairfax press, then begin defamation actions against every News Ltd paper and Southern Cross Radio, owners of 2UE. The upshot was apologies on air from Elliot and in de Brito's column, and 'make-good' stories in the *Australian* and News tabloids, where Ian told how distressed he was that anyone would think he'd be callous enough to have someone sacked over a trivial incident. 'This is the first real issue I have dealt with where I feel I haven't had 100 percent support,' he said.

It was, and it wounded him, especially when some kids taunted him about it one day. But he told Nicole Jeffrey he would not respond petulantly by becoming a media hermit. He had far too much to lose by doing that.

25

THE MAGNIFICENT SEVEN

After toying with the idea of swimming the 200 IM, Ian plumped for the 100 back as his new event for the Commonwealth Games Trials in Brisbane in March 2002. It was hardly what you'd call a project – in training he covered no more than 750 metres of backstroke in all, only in warm-ups and warm-downs. He didn't do a single set. It was actually just about having a bit of fun, a slight variation from Groundhog Day at training, and it fitted nicely into the Commonwealth Games program. He planned to keep on challenging himself in different ways, because that would keep him interested in the sport for longer.

Of more concern to Ian at the time was the continued misfortune of Michael Klim. His good mate had been hampered by an ankle injury at Worlds, and now spinal surgery had taken him out of the picture for Trials, even though it looked like he would have been on track by the Comm Games and Pan Pacs. Ian's fortunes were tied up with Klim's, in that his absence could mean Australia surrendering the two freestyle relays to the Americans. But Ian insisted he was arguing in principle when he said Australia should overhaul its rigid selection process to give selectors discretion to choose proven performers. (Michael accepted the 'perform on the day or else' policy, which had been in place since the beginning of Talbot's reign in 1989, and wasn't complaining.)

The *Telegraph* reported: 'Thorpe claimed any athlete who placed in the top three at a Trials meet, and was then dropped to make way for an established star who was too sick or sore to compete, would accept the situation.' This was a breathtakingly naïve statement. Ian was obviously too young to remember the controversies that raged before the Talbot Rules. 'When you're dealing with human beings,' Ian observed, 'not everything is black and white.' He may well have been naïve, but at least no-one could accuse him of hypocrisy when his own human error clashed dramatically with the selection policy two years later.

Ian was swimming faster in training than he had before the previous year's nationals in Hobart and, as always, he reckoned he'd be shooting for PBs in Brisbane. Before these Trials he used a word he'd never mentioned before: 'I'm expecting to plateau at some stage, but until that happens I'm not going to accept it and I'm not going to think about it.' So the 'P' word was not, as some had suspected, taboo in the Thorpe camp. That would have been unrealistic. At 196 centimetres, Ian had finished growing by the end of 2000, so he could no longer expect improvements as a matter of course. All swimmers plateau at some stage. They can stay there for a long time, but if they continue to vary and improve their training and don't slacken off, they can eventually expect to scale the next peak, and then plateau again – and so on. That's how it works, and it's a psychological test for every swimmer when they reach their first plateau.

On opening night at Brisbane's Chandler Pool, in the 400 free, Ian blasted through the third hundred, left Hackett and the rest of the field way behind, and turned at 300 metres 0.38 seconds inside his world record mark. The bookkeepers were already reaching for the erasers when, surprisingly, Ian hit the wall in 3:40.54 – a third of a second outside the target. It was the second-fastest 400 in history, but such was the expectation by this time that the *Telegraph*'s headline read: 'NEWSFLASH: IAN THORPE DID NOT BREAK A WORLD RECORD'. It was comparable in a way with the famous headline the Poms had once printed about Bradman: 'HE'S OUT!'

What followed was a reasonable enquiry into why the pool's manager had failed to turn on the air conditioning even though temperatures had reached 36 degrees and it was like a sauna inside the place. It turned out no-one had thought of it. While Ian admitted he felt seriously drained at the end of the race, he didn't use the steamy conditions as an excuse, and was happy with the swim. Everyone assumed, though, that it had cost him another record.

So the air con was at full blast the following night for the 200 final, and giant fans were also introduced which buffeted the swimmers as they tried to hold their line. This time Ian could only manage the third-fastest swim in history – a full second outside his record. He admitted he was disappointed, considering the quality of his preparation. Since the 100 was not his pet event, it was clear this would be the first time in three years that he would fail to break an individual world record when fully prepared and tapered.

Grant Hackett used the 'P' word freely in discussing Ian's performances, and proclaimed it gave hope to swimmers such as himself and Hoogie. Considering the conditions, and the fact that Ian really struggled to recover from that exhausting opening night, it seemed premature. Frost called it a 'pause' rather than a 'plateau', and predicted that normal service would resume in Manchester.

In the 100 freestyle Ian devoured Ashley Callus again at the death to take out the national 100-200-400 treble for the second successive year – something never before achieved by anyone – with a swim of 48.98 compared to his PB of 48.81. Neither here nor there, but he was happy enough with that, he said. 'Do I change anything? I don't think so. I move on to the next meet.' But not before having his bit of fun in the 100 backstroke the following night.

Matt Welsh had won gold in this event at the Worlds in Fukuoka. Having qualified fourth-fastest for the final, Ian knew he had no realistic hope of beating Welsh. The world champion led all the way to win in 54.96, with Ian taking the silver in 55.74 – a time that ranked him number three in the Commonwealth. On the preparation he'd had, it was quite incredible – especially considering his start was, in his words, 'pathetic'. In fact, it was comical to see a still shot of Ian flopping inelegantly backwards into the water while all the others arced gracefully through the air – but his underwater work was so powerful he ended up surfacing on a par with them anyway.

'If Thorpey wants to go a few rounds with me, I'm up for it,' the feisty Welsh declared. Ian was careful to direct the press's attention toward Matt rather than himself at the post-race press conference, conscious that the world champion would want due respect. But through no fault of Ian's, the situation became increasingly aggravating for Welsh. The media's approach frustrated him. Every question directed toward him in the lead-up to the Games seemed to be about Ian. It devalued all that Welsh had achieved in the event himself. (When they finally got to Manchester the British press were so insensitive that one journo even asked Welsh if he felt 'unpatriotic' for standing in the way of Ian Thorpe and a historic seven gold medals.)

Ian never deviated from the line that Matt Welsh was the champ and he had no expectation of beating him. He was only in it for the novelty value. There was a bit of stress on the swimmers' relationship, according to Ian, but not that much, because Welsh never blamed him for the media's fixations. They stayed friends, and their mateship ended up becoming stronger.

Doug Frost, though, took a more aggressive line from the start. Immediately after the event at Trials, Frost publicly stated he believed that with a bit of work at training, his swimmer would be the number one backstroker by Comm Games time. Ian didn't bother to tell Frost to pull his head in. 'I was just so used to him saying things like that, and by then I was at my wit's end with him.' Something was going to give, and fairly soon.

≈

In the wake of the September 11 attacks, there was a sharp slump in Australia's $2.3 billion annual Japanese tourism market. The

Australian Tourism Commission asked Ian if he would act as an honorary 'Holiday Ambassador' to Japan. Ian was happy, and proud, to help out by appearing in massive outdoor and print ad campaigns in Japan, and fitting in his promotional work with his ambassadorial duties, the first of which was to meet the Japanese Prime Minister, Junichiro Koizumi, at a special reception.

Just two days after the nationals were over he flew into Tokyo. The customs man, who would surely have recognised him, asked: 'What is your purpose in visiting Japan?' Thorpe replied: 'To meet the Prime Minister.' After much bowing and scraping, Ian and his entourage were ushered through as a matter of urgency. It amused him to think what would have happened if he'd been in the US and told them he was there to meet the President. 'They probably would've arrested me for being a nutcase.'

It turned out the PM was a bit of an authority on swimming, being of the generation that remembered the long-distance duels between Rose and Yamanaka, and spent much of their time together *insisting* that Ian should swim the 1500. As a newly appointed ambassador, Ian felt he should somehow avoid telling Mr Koizumi that he was completely uninterested in the event. Diplomacy was harder work than he thought.

The very next day Ian flew to New York to accept the Jesse Owens Award at a massive function at the Waldorf Astoria Hotel. Ken and Margaret were flown over especially for the occasion, but the flight turned into a nightmare, with the pilot trying to land in atrocious weather at three different airports. Three times he employed full thrust to pull out of the landing, before finally getting the plane down in Richmond, Virginia, as the weather closed in again. Everyone on board thought they were going to die. Ken Thorpe, who already had a real fear of flying, swore he would never set foot in an aircraft again.

Ian had made a lot of very fluent speeches in his life by now, but this was clearly the highest honour ever bestowed on him and the greatest collection of luminaries ever assembled before him. On top of that, he found that his appearance on stage was to follow that of New York's iconic mayor, Rudy Giuliani, who naturally spoke superbly and received a standing ovation. It was a daunting scenario for a 19-year-old. Thorpe was anxious to include everything and everyone, so he'd written his speech in full. 'I struggle when I write things down,' he says. 'Usually it just comes. I really struggled to say what I wanted to say.' He thanked all the appropriate people and spoke with humility and insight, drawing an analogy between the trials of Jesse Owens and the tragedy of the terror attack. But the speech was halting and nervous, delivered almost in a staccato style. In any case, he was very warmly received by the audience. There was no doubting the young man's sincerity.

Ian went back to Ground Zero to reflect on his previous New York experience, before moving directly on to London and Manchester to promote the Comm Games. It was a whirlwind trip, this one. In GSI's London office they rolled out one interviewer after another in an exhausting production line. But there was some light relief when a spunky young thing from one of the tabloids tried to crank up the Nicky Voss drama all over again. 'Is it true what they say about guys with big feet?' she asked Ian.

'What? That they have to wear big shoes?'

'You *know* what I mean . . .'

'What? You need big socks to fit them too?'

The young scribe was getting really agitated, while Ian enjoyed himself. 'All your female fans out there want to know,' she pleaded.

'Let them think whatever they want,' was Ian's measured reply. Anything else, of course, would have resulted in a Fleet Street feeding frenzy.

≈

Ian's cover was blown when it was revealed in early April that his secret TV project, which he'd been filming at various times over the past four months, was a 'feel-good reality show' loosely mimicking the old *Charlie's Angels* TV series. *Undercover Angels* had Ian in the studio-based role of Charlie, directing three glamorous gals around as they performed various good deeds for people in need – stuff like decorating a nursery for the new parents of i/v fertilisation triplets, or finding a dream puppy for a young brother and sister whose dog had been stolen. Stars of the show were the three Alfa Romeo convertibles the 'angels' drove while pursuing their missions, there were other 'product placements' everywhere, and the whole deal involved local businesses donating their goods and services – while receiving massive publicity in the process.

Reactions to this unique concept covered the entire gamut. Channel Seven executives were delighted when the critics' preview screening drew tears from many of its audience. That was precisely the objective. The show's debut on 12 May was the fifth most-watched program in the country for that week – a massive ratings success. *Undercover Angels* held its ratings well over its run of 11 episodes, averaging 1.3 million viewers. The *Sydney Morning Herald*'s TV critic, Ruth Ritchie, called it 'the worst show in the history of the world'. Others expressed similar, albeit slightly less extreme, opinions.

Ian's own performance was neither great nor terrible, and it got better. As far as he was concerned, the point was that every other reality show was about plumbing the depths of human nastiness. He was aware that he and his angels were treading all sorts of fine lines, but he declared himself proud of the result, and lost no sleep over the criticisms. He was enjoying himself.

He seemed to have just about perfected the art of having fun two nights before the *Angels* debuted, when he hosted the Autore South Sea Pearls Masked Ball at Sydney's Overseas Passenger Terminal to wind up Australian Fashion Week. This one had the stamp of the Thorpedo all over it. All proceeds (which amounted to almost 160 grand) were directed to the Ian Thorpe Fountain for youth. The host got to squire a hot celebrity – in this case Sarah O'Hare, a woman he was utterly smitten with when they first met – but spent most of the night jumping on and off stage to drum up interest in auction items, crack jokes and show off his personally designed Autore pearl necklace and bracelet collection for men. Thorpe the perfectionist had taken the precaution of having one singing lesson – 'Just to make sure everything was intact' – and finished up the night belting out a duet with Katie Underwood of Bardot fame in front of the 500 mildly astonished guests. It wasn't too embarrassing.

The social scribes dubbed it 'The Ian Thorpe Show' and called it an unqualified success. Ken and Margaret Thorpe showed up in their masks and had fun, no doubt reflecting at the time that their son didn't seem to have any trouble expressing himself.

≈

On 24 May, FINA at last announced its program of surprise out-of-competition blood and urine testing for EPO. But the blood test, it was by now determined, would not hold up as a positive in court, since it only showed up 'indirect markers' going back a few weeks. The urine test, which only detected use of EPO three days back, *would* hold up legally – so obviously the ideal approach would be to use the blood test in order to try and determine which athletes to go after with the urine tests, and take as many out-of-competition spins of the wheel as was necessary to get a positive. Otherwise you'd have to be very lucky to ever nail anyone.

It was never that simple. The issues kept on shifting – from duplication of testing between different organisations, to the lack of sufficient numbers of blood tests, to the efficacy of testing in some countries and by some labs, to the lack of (expensive) EPO testing on many occasions when ordinary urine testing was done, to what looked like the deliberate targeting of known clean athletes (such as Ian Thorpe in particular) so as to make the results look good, and the fact that world champions and world record-breakers would only face urine testing without blood testing . . . and on it went. The central issue remained the same: did FINA really *want* to catch drug cheats?

Some sports, such as cross-country skiing and cycling, had decided to suspend athletes on the basis of a blood test by declaring it a 'health risk' if they were to compete, while not calling it an EPO doping violation – even though everyone knew that was the case. FINA didn't have the will to grasp that nettle. Still, the wheels of doping justice were creaking, inexorably, toward a destination that Ian Thorpe hoped would be somewhere in the vicinity of . . . Athens, 2004. But he wasn't going to hold his breath.

≈

The Thorpe family moved into a much bigger home, still at Voyager Point, on the June long weekend of 2002. By this time Ian had made the decision – firmly, positively, irrevocably – that he'd split from Doug Frost after Pan Pacs in August. He'd toyed with the idea for a long time, and almost made up his mind prior to the nationals that year. Now he realised that if he didn't bite the bullet, and soon, he was going to stop enjoying his swimming. And that meant he was going to stop swimming, just like he'd always said.

It was, of course, a twofold problem: the personality of the man, and the direction of his coaching. Ian had long since come to believe that because he was always 'Doug Frost's athlete', his coach's arrogance reflected negatively on himself. He'd also long believed that the more time he spent with Doug, the more likely he was to absorb elements of his personality – he'd seen that happen to many people in the intense confines of the coach–swimmer relationship – and he definitely didn't want that. Ian saw himself and Doug as polar opposites, and preferred to keep it that way.

'I didn't think what I got out of Doug as a person was contributing to me as a person,' he now observes. 'At the same time, he can be a very generous, caring person away from the pool . . . friendly, loving toward me, my family, other swimmers and their families . . . It might be a minority of his personality, but I wish that side shone through more. Anyone who says it's not there is not painting an accurate picture of Doug.' Still, in all the years he'd spent with Frost, the man had never really changed. There was always the inexplicable aggression, the needlessly confrontational attitude. It would wear anyone out.

On the coaching side, Frost had apparently lost control of his swimmer by the time they were heading into Manchester. Ian had decided there was a lot to be gained from a proper weights program under the direction of Richard Beesley. He'd seen the results when he'd bulked up by six kilos in the lead-up to the Olympics, and his opinion was that he could afford to trade off a tiny bit of range and flexibility for even greater strength gains. Doug didn't agree, and Ian didn't care. By the time he'd finished his prep for Manchester, he weighed almost 105 kilos – five more than at Fukuoka, where he was already the heaviest elite swimmer in history. 'Maybe,' he joked, 'I'll sink like a stone.' But he didn't think so.

There was nothing to suggest this Comm Games meet would be a doddle for Thorpe. First he'd have to shorten his usual taper so he could more easily jump back on the trampoline and produce another taper for the Pan Pacs meet only three weeks later – a ridiculous piece of scheduling. Still, the Aussies were his main competition, and they'd all be in the same boat.

Speaking of which, Grant Hackett produced a scorching swim at a Telstra Grand Prix meet in Sydney just before the team left for its staging camp in the German town of Sindelfingen. Hackett broke his own 400 metres short course record with a time that translated to a long course 400 of 3:41 – less than a second shy of Ian's world record. The three relays were virtually in the bag, but Ashley Callus would push him to the limit in the 100, and he still needed to make up over a second and a half on Welsh to match the backstroke champion's best, but he'd only been able to devote five percent of his training to the event.

Ian got an early taste of the Fleet Street mentality when, at a press conference in the camp in Germany, one of the hacks who'd flown over from England asked: 'Are you prettier than David Beckham?' Ian was nonplussed, then burst out laughing before replying: 'I hope not.' When he hit Manchester, it was to a reception from 'a mad media circus' of about 50 journalists and photographers jostling all over each other to get a snap and grab a line or two. You had to wonder why they didn't just stay in their offices, since they apparently made everything up anyway. The *Daily Express*, for example, added ten centimetres to Ian's height and reckoned his annual earnings were between 12 and 17 million pounds. Every newspaper was on Thorpewatch, including highbrow broadsheets such as the *Times*, which ran a headline: 'IS IT A PLANE? IS IT A BIRD? NO, IT'S THE THORPEDO!'

Ian never read the papers during a meet, and very rarely otherwise; but given the sort of questions he was being asked – including the ones about movie star 'friends' he'd never even met – he knew he was being mythologised. It was something that always irritated him. So many untruths had already been written about him, but it was out of hand this time around. 'What people have started to believe about me is almost a legend rather than a story – things based not on fact but on the fable of my life. One slight exaggeration is followed by another, and all of a sudden things start to get away.'

Just as annoying was the fact that the British media had him marked down for The Magnificent Seven, and it seemed to Ian ridiculous and unfair that nothing less would satisfy them. It didn't matter how many times he said it was highly unlikely he could win seven gold medals, and that was not his original aim anyway. The Poms just didn't listen, and ran with whatever suited them.

The best thing about Manchester was the atmosphere of the tiny pool. The constant musical backdrop kept the crowd of barely 2000 revved up and wildly enthusiastic. Spectators in the front row were so close they could shake Ian's hand. His mum was among them, waving her miniature Aussie flag, while Ken was true to his word: no way was he ever getting into an aeroplane again. At home, he'd have been one of the TV viewers who made Ian's *heat* of the 400 the second most-watched sporting program of the year – only the World Cup Final rated higher. Obviously the time difference would have accounted for the sizeable audience – but it was only a heat. Was everyone worried the Thorpedo was actually going to sink? He was only *joking* when he said that.

He was joking again when he came out for the final – grinning like a fool and dancing to the music. The relaxed intimacy of the place had infused him with a sense of joyous nuttiness. Could Grant Hackett do anything about it? He still refused to throw in the towel, having told Nicole Jeffrey a week before: 'I'm trying everything here, guys, and I will get there. I am persistent. I have no doubt that Ian's human.' But the human Thorpedo simply had Hackett's measure. The reality was that if Grant couldn't get a long way in front by the time they hit 300, it was not possible for him to win. And Ian, although still swimming inside his curtain, was taking out his races much faster than he used to. This time it was blistering – almost a second in front of world record pace at the 100, and it stayed there till the 300 mark. He knew that as long as it felt like he had efficiency in his stroke, he'd have plenty left in the tank to bring it home. Like the 800 at Fukuoka, it might have *looked* like a cat and mouse game, with Ian seemingly keeping an eye on Grant and refusing to give him a sniff – but it was in fact the same old tactic. That is, *no tactic*.

When Thorpe had a body-length on his rival at 300, the experts stopped watching Hackett and looked at the clock instead. It was close, but Ian got there – shaving his world mark down to 3:40.08. That was his 13th individual long course record – one ahead of John Konrads' total, one short of Dawn Fraser's. And he could have gone faster, having let his intensity slip just a fraction as he glided, rather than slammed, into the wall. That cost him the 3:40 target he really wanted to go under. But it was a relief to have swum well. He'd silenced the doubters who thought he'd gotten too big – including Doug Frost – and proved Hackett's talk about his plateau had indeed been premature.

Who could have blamed the guy for a bit of wishful thinking? As he grasped yet another silver medal, having finished three seconds off the pace, Grant finally blurted: 'To tell you the truth, it *sucks*. Here I am swimming times that no-one else in the world can do, but I'm still finishing second.' But then he went back and held his line: 'There is still no era I would rather be in than the one now – with the world's greatest-ever swimmer.'

The Brits had no doubts about Hackett's judgement. The *Times* reported: 'Surely no-one has ever moved through the water with the same bewitching combination of power and grace.' A couple of tabloids opted for a simple running count. After Ian anchored home the 4 × 100 relay, it was: 'TWO DOWN, FIVE TO GO'. Simple.

There was, however, some bad medicine going down in the Thorpe camp. The Thorpe–Frost partnership was starting to unravel, and Ian wasn't quite ready for that yet. It started the night before the swimming began, when Doug approached Margaret Thorpe and Dave Flaskas and told them: 'I don't think Ian's going to swim all that well in the 400 here – just thought I'd let you know.' The following night, after the 400 was done, Doug told the same pair: 'I think Ian will break the 100 metres world record at this meet.' As far as Ian was concerned, it was all laughable.

The swimming program was compressed from the Olympics' eight days to a tight six-day schedule, which meant the 200 final followed on the second night. In the warm-up pool before that final, there was a fairly heated discussion between Ian and Doug, and Ian made no attempt to disguise his frustration. The substance of it was that Frost was focusing, as he often did, on what the opposition was going to do – because he'd never really accepted Ian's swimming philosophy. Thorpe wanted to talk about what *he* was going to do. Other swimmers, who were constantly on Thorpewatch and aware of the general speculation about Ian and his coach, saw this incident as pivotal – whereas of course it was not. It was just very public.

Ian duly went out and won the 200, but this time he faded in the final 50 and recorded only the third-fastest swim in history. He told the reporters he was having an off-day, 'just wasn't with it' and had 'one of the worst warm-ups ever'. He also called Flaskas on his mobile, and it was clear to his manager that Ian was extremely unhappy, and that issues long simmering were at last coming to the boil.

The following night presented the 4 × 200 relay, which was of course a gimme, and then in the 100 free Ian blew away the field and produced a new PB, down from 48.81 to 48.73. It was a milestone – his first-ever major international victory in the 100 free – and it placed him as the second-fastest Australian ever behind Klim and ninth-fastest man in history. But his goal by then was 48.50. He wasn't even aware at the time that no man had ever pulled off the 100-200-400 treble at Commonwealth Games level: a very good indication of the degree of difficulty he was always facing.

That was gold medal number five. Since the final event, the medley relay, was a certainty, it all came down to the showdown with Matt Welsh, just as everyone had thought. The backstroke champion was at his wit's end with the British press as they continued to cast him as a sort of party-pooping villain, and on top of that he'd been controversially disqualified in the 200 backstroke for a false start. He was 'the Games' Mr Angry', as one paper put it.

Thorpe kept pouring cold water on his own chances of upsetting Welsh – he did it emphatically, at every available opportunity – but

Frost, fresh from telling reporters that Ian could be chasing *nine gold medals* in Athens, kept talking him up. 'I'm absolutely ecstatic about his backstroke – I really am,' he said. Welsh was absolutely over it. But there remained, always, the unanswered question: just how freakish was Ian Thorpe?

In the final Matt got to the turn first, Ian third. Ian's aerobic power lifted him in the second 50 and he passed Malaysia's Alex Lim right at the death, but he couldn't catch Australia's best backstroker. Matt Welsh first in 54.72, Thorpe winning silver in 55.38. A pretty slender margin of half a body-length in the end. Welsh admitted he'd been weighed down by all the hype, while the Brits were amazed at how graciously Ian took his 'rare defeat'. In fact, he was stoked with his performance, because it was a new PB. As he said for the thousandth time, that was his singular aim in swimming. 'I think it's a limiting attitude to be competing against other people when you can be challenging yourself,' he told the press conference. There was a sense that many among his audience didn't really get it.

Ian added the medley relay gold on the final night to his tally, making it six gold and one silver. Asked one final time at the press conference about The Seven, he said: 'I don't think it will ever be done again.'

The schedule was so tight that after two questions Thorpe was whisked away in a car with a police escort to the stadium so he could carry the Australian flag in pouring rain at the Closing Ceremony. But just as he was about to jump in the back seat, a drug test was announced. Next to him sat an anonymous chaperone, waiting for him to produce a pee. He managed to deliver a sample at the stadium, thus avoiding the need to be trailed all the way around the arena as he proudly carried the Australian standard. Meanwhile, only the Queen was permitted to use an umbrella. Her loyal subjects were soaked to the skin.

With Pan Pacs looming in three weeks, the Aussie team was straight back into the pool and hard training the following morning. The science of this was quite simple – just a matter of getting about five days of fairly heavy work done so as to produce a decent 'bounce' when the taper kicked in again. But the swimmers were highly unimpressed with the meet scheduling, no-one wanted to be on the 6 am bus after the late-night celebrations, the pool was inadvertently locked up when they got there, Ian had to do a prearranged interview with Laurie Lawrence before he could start his laps, there was no time even for breakfast, and off they scrambled in the bus to the press centre to wrap up the whole show with a gigantic press conference and photo shoot. So there was already a semi-chaotic vibe about, even before Ian Hanson said: 'Thorpey, have you got your medals, mate?'

Ian rummaged in his bag. 'Oh, no. I've got a couple – not all of them. Here's one . . . two . . .' That was it. The rest were back in his room somewhere.

The world's media were waiting – 100 pressmen, 20 cameras. Hanson took charge. A driver was called to search Ian's pigsty of a room. No luck. Then team manager Karen Stephenson was given the task of racing around the Village and rustling up four gold medals and one silver from anywhere, then ferrying them over to the press centre while Hanson stalled the photographers.

They did the press conference first. 'More questions? Does anyone have any more questions?' The scribes, used to being curbed, hustled and generally shuffled off to Buffalo, must have found this approach refreshing. Then there were the TV Asahi people, who (to everyone's amazement) had paid the full Comm Games TV rights fee just to talk to Ian Thorpe – no-one else – in the mixed zone and exclusively after this press conference. So that took up another half an hour. Hanson was starting to sweat as the shooters jostled for positions, and still the medals hadn't arrived. Finally, with a bit of sleight-of-hand, Ian was ready to pose – with two of his own gold medals, three from Grant Hackett, one from Dyana Calub and a silver from somebody or other. No-one was any the wiser.

Ian found them in the end, in another bag, wrapped up in a towel. It wasn't that he had no respect for his Commonwealth Games medal haul. Just that he was, after all, still a boy – and that's what boys are like. Actually, considering the depth of his achievements so far, it's astonishing to reflect that this was the first time Ian Thorpe wasn't the youngest male on an Australian Dolphins team.

26

THE PARTING OF WAYS

BECAUSE IAN HAD MISSED THE MOSCOW short course meet in April, he was marginally less jaded than the rest of the Aussie team when they arrived in Yokohama in the last week of August. He'd already publicly conceded that the Americans were going to win back their number one ranking at this meet. On comparative times between the US Trials and the Australians' Comm Games performances, it was looking like a slaughter. As well, they'd produced an incredibly versatile 17-year-old star, Michael Phelps, who'd broken a butterfly world record at 15 and was now being hailed as 'America's answer to Ian Thorpe'.

Still searching for his own ideal program for Athens, Ian decided to leave the 800 free to Hackett and the backstroke to Welsh. He wanted to focus on his sprinting, so it would simply be another shot at the treble – 100, 200 and 400 free – and the three relays.

As far as Thorpemania in Japan was concerned, nothing whatsoever had changed. If anything, the obsession with him was even more concentrated after his performance at the 2001 Worlds. (It was enough to turn the tourism slump around, with the Australian Tourism Commission handing the credit to the Thorpe campaign.) One observer counted six consecutive TV ads featuring Ian Thorpe. The only difference this time was that the Australians' hotel was perched very high on a hill – an arduous walk for schoolgirls up a winding road – which reduced the gaggle of hormone-fired hysterics standing vigil outside from 200-odd to about 40. There was a weird sense of deja vu, though, with everyone finding it all just as amusing as last time.

Early in the evening on day one, before the finals began, Ian Hanson was approached by Michael Cowley of the *Sydney Morning Herald*. Cowley told him that the *Sun-Herald*'s well-connected sports columnist, Danny Weidler, was running with the story, to appear the following morning, that Ian was about to split with Doug Frost. Tracey Menzies, Frost's 29-year-old assistant who also taught art at Ian's former high school, was mentioned as the likely replacement, according to unnamed sources. Cowley's editor wanted a response from Ian Thorpe, *right now*, for the paper's late edition. Cowley knew he wasn't going to get an exclusive interview, so he told the other Australian swimming scribes what was going on, and they agreed to request a mini press conference with Ian for the Aussie contingent only, after the main press conference. That would avoid turning the issue into an international gabfest in the middle of a major meet.

Hanson agreed, then called Dave Flaskas, who was at home on an intravenous drip after suffering blood poisoning from a cut leg in Manchester. Flaskas didn't know Ian's decision was a fait accompli, but he knew it was coming, and that Weidler's story would be based on good information. So all they could do was stall a definitive answer for as long as possible, and just try to get through the meet. Otherwise there'd be nothing else in the media but Thorpe and Frost, and everyone in the team would be disrupted. Hanson decided to tell Ian nothing at all until the night's racing was done.

Ian wasn't too sure about how his prep for this unusually timed meet would work out, so for the first time in his career at a major meet (unless you count the Goodwill Games), he put winning gold in the 400 free ahead of his perennial pursuit of a personal best. Thorpe covered the distance five seconds slower than his record, but quickly enough to beat Grant Hackett, and admitted afterwards: 'Grant and I just wanted to get 1-2 for Australia.' Both swimmers had to jump back in for the 4 × 100 freestyle relay within an hour.

Ian anchored that team to yet another last-gasp win over the Americans, mowing down Jason Lezak in the final few strokes. Three years after Ian had first done the job on Lezak at Pan Pacs '99, the American was still not quite of the calibre of Gary Hall Jr or Anthony Ervin over 100 – but again, he was so far in front at the turn, you had to wonder how Ian could possibly catch him. The Japanese crowd, of course, went crazy.

After the relay medal ceremony, Hanson and the team's psychologist, Clark Perry, took Ian aside on the pool deck and told him what was running in the *Sun-Herald* in the morning. Ian didn't lose possession of himself, but he was ashen-faced. 'My god,' was all he could say.

'It's my role to tell Doug, if you want me to,' said Perry.

'No,' said Ian. 'I'll tell him. He deserves that.'

First he had to smile and wave his way through a 'swimmer of the night' presentation. Then he went to the warm-down pool and did his laps, reflecting on how the whole debacle had come about. It was not a single person he'd confided in, who'd then leaked the story, as was widely supposed. Actually he'd told a few people his intentions; he wanted to share what he was going through with close friends. It was a bit of loose talk in the change-rooms that had given him away – an accidental slip-up. He had no-one to be angry with.

Ian finished swimming and beckoned Doug outside. 'What I have to tell you,' he said, 'is that it could appear in the paper tomorrow that I'm splitting with you.' Frost chuckled dismissively. Ian continued: 'From your point of view, the problem with the story is that it's true.'

Doug Frost was in shock. He was bleeding all over the pool deck. Ian told him that if he was going to keep swimming, he had to make some changes. This was one of them. Doug walked away. Then Ian had to go and front the press conference, and then the mini press conference, where Cowley invited him to comment on the upcoming story.

He could have just denied it outright, of course. That would have made his life easier in the short term. It would all come out in the wash after the event, and then the journos could have their story. But Ian just couldn't do that. He'd never lied to the press, and it simply wasn't worth it to start now. So, according to Nicole Jeffrey, 'He virtually contorted himself inside out.' The thrust of it was that he'd heard the rumour, but 'there is no truth in the fact that something has been determined. The day will come when we part ways. It might be tomorrow, it might be in ten days, it might be at the end of this meet, it might be in five years.'

'Being all experienced journos,' Nicole recalls, 'the moment he walked away we all went: "Shit – it's true. They *are* splitting".' Frost stated he would say nothing until the end of the meet. Hanson stepped in and said Ian had promised that all would be revealed in the fullness of time, and exclusively to the swimming writers, because they deserved that for their loyalty and discretion. But not yet. *Please stay cool.*

To his great credit, the following morning Doug Frost approached Ian and said: 'What are you expecting me to do now?'

'Whatever you think is appropriate.'

'Would you like me to coach you through the rest of the meet?'

'Yes – I'd really appreciate that.'

So the two men got on with it, both with as much dignity as could possibly have been mustered. Frost earned plaudits from all quarters for the way he handled himself.

Ian won the 200, but was unhappy with his effort. He'd been sloppy and distracted – not surprising under the circumstances – but still went faster than anyone else had ever done. Then he anchored the 4 × 200 team to another gold, having to overhaul America's Chad Carvin, who'd started just in front of him. (Without Klim and Bill Kirby, the 4 × 200 men were coming back to the field.) That made it four. Then came the event he was really looking to do well in at this level – the 100 freestyle. He badly wanted to swim 48.50.

The scoreboard blacked out after Ian's semi-final, which meant someone was about to be disqualified for moving before the start. Ian was nervous, but when it was revealed that the culprit was Japan's Naoki Nagura, the spectators collectively sighed with relief. They wanted a clean sweep from Thorpe-san.

Anthony Ervin had withdrawn, and Ian qualified second-fastest for the final. It was the noisiest crowd of the meet, as befitted the blue riband event. Ian got to the turn in fourth place, then beat everyone home to take a fifth gold medal. But he looked up at the time and saw that he hadn't managed a PB. At 48.84 he was precisely one second off van den Hoogenband's world record pace. Although gold in a 100 free final at Pan Pacs was nothing to sneeze at – only his second major international success in the sprint, after Manchester – that wasn't really what he was after.

The final event, as always, was the medley relay. Ian was sent in way too far behind the Americans to pull off another miracle – but he gave it everything, settling for a silver medal, with a split time of . . . 47.20. What? *47.20?* That was the second-fastest relay split in history, behind only Hoogie's 47.02. And it should translate to a 100-metre swim off the gun of 47.90 – *only six-hundredths shy of the world record.*

For a long time Ian had suspected that there was something that didn't add up – at least, not for *him* – and this was the ultimate proof. Relay swimming obviously gave him a stroke efficiency he couldn't get in a 100-metre race, and now it finally dawned on him what it was all about. *The surging wave effect.* If only he could improve his front-end speed and get to the turn with the other sprinters, he wouldn't have to battle through all that wash. Of course, that was one of the things he and Doug had been trying to achieve, in their limited way, all this time – but it was the paramount *importance* of it that was now quite clear to Ian. Fast-twitch muscle fibre was the key. A wholly new approach to training. And it was all about to begin.

Ian signed off directly after the final medal presentation by taking the mike and thanking the Japanese crowd for their support of the Australian team. It was only a 30-second speech, and unremarkable except for the fact that he did it in Japanese. The crowd, of course, went berserk in appreciation.

Thorpe rated that 47.20 split his third-best performance ever, behind the 200 short course record in Berlin pre-Olympics, and the 400 long course swim at Pan Pacs '99 when he smashed Perkins' record. The Aussies were hammered by the Americans in the gold medal count, 21–11. They had only one glorious year, by their own reckoning, at the top. Ian's year was judged on the basis that his world record-breaking spree was apparently grinding to a halt, with just one new mark set – in the 400 free at Manchester. But there were extenuating circumstances, and in his view the dreaded plateau was not yet approaching.

When someone is as good as Ian Thorpe, it's easy to lose all perspective on their achievements. In a little over a year, at World, Commonwealth and Pan Pacs level, he'd won a total of 17 gold medals and two silvers. He was unbeaten in 24 consecutive starts across the hugely demanding 100-200-400 freestyle range. He had not lost a 400 metres long course race since 1997. Since 1998 he'd lost only twice in serious competition over 200 metres. He was surely the most dominant competitor in any major international sport.

With one man standing beneath a veritable shower of gold, a whole country can forget how difficult it is to beat the world at swimming. Australia won one gold medal in the pool at the Los Angeles Olympics (Jon Sieben), one gold in Seoul (Duncan Armstrong), one gold in Barcelona (Kieren Perkins), two gold in Atlanta (Perkins and Susie O'Neill), and five gold in Sydney, with Ian involved in three of them. Of the total of 13 for Australia at 2001 Worlds, Ian was involved in six. Of the 11 total at 2002 Pan Pacs, Ian was involved in five. Unless you're as good as Ian Thorpe, gold medals at this level are very, very hard to come by.

≈

There was plenty of controversy in the Australian press surrounding the imminent split with Frost, which had all but been confirmed by the time the meet was done. Don Talbot, no longer head coach and now a consultant to Australian Swimming, was highly sceptical. But Ian had a few days of business commitments in Japan, and it would all have to wait until the promised swimming writers' press conference after he got home.

Ian had always wanted to visit the museum at the Hiroshima atomic bomb site. He'd felt awkward about asking his Japanese hosts in the past, but this time an excursion was arranged for himself and Michelle Flaskas. The museum contained such things as models of the city before and after the bomb struck, photos of survivors with horrific burns, and exhibits such as a child's bicycle reduced to molten metal, its rider vaporised in the blast. No-one could really imagine the levels of suffering inflicted, but the museum provided a shocking window into that time, and you couldn't fail to be affected by it.

It was the last place Ian wanted to be mobbed by a busload of school kids. He and Michelle had to break away from them, find the security people and eventually hide in an anteroom until the youngsters left. When they finished their tour they stopped to write in the message book, and then each folded an origami crane. It took a long time to make one. Japanese people will fold 1000 cranes to make a wish, and the smaller the cranes, the greater the wishing power, because it involves more effort. People had folded cranes using needles to make them *tiny* – and strung together 1000 of them – so all this colourful origami paper carefully arranged around the site represented a concentrated outpouring of hope for the future.

Thorpe was impressed to learn that each year, the lord mayor of the prefecture that contained Hiroshima would send letters to each country professing to have nuclear weapons, and ask that they be dismantled. 'You walk away from it as a positive experience, not the negative I expected.' What was on display at that museum, and in the rebuilding of the city itself – tenacity, strength of spirit, hope and optimism . . . these are the commodities athletes appreciate most. They are the currency that rules the sporting world. That's why most athletes abhor negativity, and if there's one message Ian Thorpe wants to convey to other young people, it's to take a positive view of life. 'We're all born positive and learn to be negative. It frustrates me that people complain, especially in this country, about what they don't have, rather than appreciating what they do have. And although we've got all this focus on terrorism, we should remember that we live in a time when there's significantly less warfare around the world than ever before. We have to look at cultivating tolerance, rather than hatred and frustration. If you're frustrated about something, *change it*.'

He was about to take his own advice on that score.

≈

Ian had spent a long time looking at dozens of potential alternative coaches, arrived at a short list of three Australian and two international possibilities, and made his final decision well before the Pan Pacs meet. It was not easy; the move was so long in the making because he thought it would be hard to find a coach who could get more out of him than Doug. 'There are a few good coaches in Australia, and he's one of them. There are very few great ones.'

It was a nerve-racking time for Tracey Menzies. She'd been counselled by Hanson and Flaskas to say nothing from the time her name appeared in the *Sun-Herald* on 25 August, and didn't actually know Ian's intentions until he returned from Japan and asked if she'd consider coaching him. She would. The decision was announced at a small informal press conference on 12 September.

Under questioning, Ian would only say (in about three dozen different permutations) that Doug had played a huge role in his success, and he'd always be grateful for that . . . but he was no longer enjoying his swimming as he had once done, so his choice was to make a change or give up the sport. And he thought the change he'd made would allow him to reach new heights. He liked Tracey Menzies' coaching philosophy, her attention to detail and her eye for stroke technique. Tracey would be entering a brave new world.

All other things being equal, Ian was bound to adhere to the Thorpe tradition and keep things close to home. Coincidentally, Tracey had started swimming at Padstow as a six-year-old under Chris Myers. At ten she moved up into Doug's squad, and swam under his direction until her retirement eight years later. She won medals at Age Nationals in the 200 and 400 freestyle, and also dabbled in backstroke, but by the time she reached Open level she was plagued by glandular fever, chronic fatigue syndrome and a blood disorder. She gave it away in her

HSC year, and started coaching under Greg Hodge at the Sutherland pool while doing a visual arts degree. That was in 1990.

Seven years later Hodge left to take up a job at the NSW Institute of Sport, and young Tracey, by then the senior assistant coach, was left holding the fort at Sutherland for seven months while Doug Frost was manoeuvred over from Padstow to become head coach. She was virtually unknown among the coaching fraternity, but had enough skill to help Simon Cowley to his first Australian breast-stroke title in October 1997. Then Doug arrived.

Tracey had great people skills, but that didn't make it easy to deal with Doug Frost. He intimidated her as much as everyone else: 'Sometimes if I had to say something to him, I felt like a nervous 14-year-old girl.' The situation arose often, because parents who had a complaint would normally approach Tracey rather than face the wrath of the head coach. As well, he had a way of making her feel that whatever she did, it was never good enough. He always seemed to be about keeping her off balance. And now, here she was taking over his one remaining elite athlete, his pride and joy – and they'd be training, still, at the Sutherland pool, right there underneath his nose. It was hardly likely to be an untroubled transition. Greg Hodge, by then Australian Swimming's 'high performance director', described it as 'a delicate issue'.

Frost put a brave face on things in the media. Contrary to reports that had him 'depressed' and 'shattered', he told the *Sun-Herald* he was very happy to have been given his life back. He was going to focus on reducing his golf handicap. He and Ian were still great mates, there were no hard feelings and people shouldn't imagine that he'd suddenly lost his meal ticket, because 'Ian didn't pay me anything. Anyone who says otherwise is wrong.'

In essence that was true. Swimmers didn't share sponsorship and prize money with their coaches, and Ian was not an exception. However, Flaskas had been successful in building a 'coach component' into some of Ian's contracts, and there was the high performance grant from the Sports Commission. But Doug pointed out he was paying off his one indulgence – his beloved BMW – and he'd show anyone the evidence if they wanted.

On the same day as Frost was protesting his serenity, the *Sunday Telegraph* had Greg Hodge putting the slipper into him. Hodge reckoned that including Ian Thorpe, Frost had lost six national-level swimmers to alternative coaches since the Sydney Olympics. Four would have been a more accurate number, the others being Craig Stevens, Simon Cowley and Kirsten Thomson. In any case, 'he needs to take stock of what he's doing and address it,' opined Hodge.

Why such a public outburst from the coaching supremo? Hodge was a fan of Tracey, and the reality was that battle lines had been drawn. Apart from Talbot, several old-school coaches – some of them long-time mates of Doug – had been critical of Ian's decision, but none more so than the legendary Dick Caine. Not a man known for mincing words, Caine was quoted in the *Sunday Telegraph* article thus: 'In six to 12 months I wouldn't be surprised if Ian Thorpe started falling to bits . . . People are too scared to say anything about Thorpe because of who he is, but in my opinion that girl will not tell Ian Thorpe what to do. Ian Thorpe will be telling her what to do.' Caine said Frost was 'heart-broken', and added: 'Like Ian, the girl was a no-name who Doug taught how to swim and then made her into a coach. He hasn't only lost a kid, he's lost a coach who he trained and brought up.'

The last statement was wildly inaccurate. But obviously it was far from irrelevant that Tracey Menzies was only the second female to coach on the Australian swimming team. (The first was Elka Graham's coach, Narelle Simpson.) There were some cantankerous members of that almost exclusively men's club, and they were going to make it as difficult as possible for her to prove she belonged. She gritted her teeth and got on with it. Her mission: to make Ian Thorpe the fastest swimmer ever. However long it took.

Before he and Tracey got down to business, it was time for Ian's annual therapeutic jaunt. A bit of business, but almost all fun this time. The business was in China, where Flaskas had cooked up a schedule with a PR outfit to consolidate Ian's apparent popularity there, do some charity fundraising and make some donations from the Fountain for youth, and get behind the Australian presence in Beijing, where billions of dollars worth of tenders were soon to be dished out in the lead-up to the 2008 Olympics. Another quasi-ambassadorial role, but Flaskas figured a foot in the door, and the chance to work up some Australian connections, could eventually lead to something even more substantial than the Japanese market.

Ian loved being in China, especially the more out-of-the-way places, and everywhere the energy of rapid development against an ancient backdrop excited him. But he couldn't expect to understand the country and its protocols by drawing on the Japanese experience. It was entirely different, as Ian discovered when he visited a school in Shanghai. He was talking to a class of 30 or 40, but word of his presence spread and kids came running from everywhere to mob him, without any of the decorum that protected him in Japan. They were grabbing him and jumping all over him. Teachers were screaming at them, but they weren't listening. It was weird – like nothing he'd ever experienced – and he had to hightail it out of the place.

At a banquet in the city in his honour, Ian got to test his culinary limits when the king snake dish was served, and he was given the privilege of downing the animal's spleen. It was a slimy green blob immersed in a 70 percent alcohol drink, and the idea was to swill the lot down in one gulp. But no-one told Ian that, so he ended up biting into the spleen, which horrified both him and the onlookers equally. It tasted disgusting. But Thorpe's iron gut prevailed again.

They told him there was a certain effect from eating the snake spleen, but they weren't going to tell him exactly what. 'Instead, you tell us what it does,' said his Chinese hosts. He woke up next morning, checked himself in the mirror, and noticed nothing unusual. The following morning, he was gasping in disbelief. 'Everything was sparkling and crisp and amazing to look at. I felt like I could see for hundreds of kilometres.'

Ian and the Flaskases moved on to Beijing, where the swimming star did all kinds of media. They took a day off from the promotional grind to visit the Great Wall and the Forbidden City – but everywhere they were pursued by film crews who'd been tipped off, and when people started crowding in on them as well, it was never enough to simply say: 'Enough.' The public recognition factor wasn't comparable to what Ian faced in Japan, but it was surprisingly high, and it wasn't hard to see how quickly it could grow. Team Thorpe would be coming back to China, for sure.

After five days they headed out to London, then Ian travelled on his own to Milan for his first Armani catwalk fashion show. It was, as with any Armani showing, a celebrity-fest, but Ian was by now a bona fide A-lister, happy to pronounce his views on the collection to Japanese and Italian interviewers. He was in his element, heading back to Giorgio Armani's place – the designer owns six mansions in a row on a street popularly known as 'Via Armani' – then dining with other guests at Nobu. Then it was off to Paris to catch Aussie designer Collette Dinnigan's showing.

At the grand Hotel Crillon, one of the most expensive in Paris, Ian was given a fantastic suite to himself at a special rate. He'd arranged to meet up with some old school friends who were backpacking through Europe, and he could see they were doing it pretty rough, so he invited them back to the hotel for a scrub-up. They tiptoed into the place, were gobsmacked by Ian's quarters, and had to be convinced it was okay to jump in the shower.

Ian would have been just as happy to be backpacking through Europe himself – he knew it was the experience that counted, and the glitz and glamour didn't actually amount to anything – but all the same, it was fun to see the looks on his friends' faces. If they'd seen him chatting with his old mate Bill Clinton in the foyer before the former president went off to lunch with the Aga Khan, it would have done their heads in.

27

FAST TWITCH

ON THE DAY IAN ARRIVED HOME from Europe, 11 October 2002, Simon Cowley announced he had unfinished business in swimming, and was coming back to train at the Sutherland pool under Tracey Menzies. He'd quit in despair in the middle of Trials that year, not knowing where his life was heading, but he had faith in Tracey's ability to get him back on track. Ian stretched his break to the customary six weeks and started training under the new regime the day after his 20th birthday.

It was a strange beginning. Tracey was hit by a barrage of cameras when she arrived, and then Frost walked into the pool with a black towel completely covering his head, as if he were facing trial. Still, the first session was great, and they both left on a high.

Doug was still officially the head coach, but the fact was he was now in charge of the age groupers while Tracey had the senior elite squad – Ian and Simon, and subsequently another freestyler, Jason Cram – so it amounted to a complete role reversal. While everyone, including Doug, was hastening to assure the media that relations between them all were fine, the reality was very different. According to Ian, 'If I was doing sprints, Doug would still be timing me. Whatever Tracey said, he'd make an obvious scoffing gesture. Or he'd walk up to the board [where the sets were written down], look at the program, and sort of say it was a load of rubbish. I mean, you could laugh at it – I *was* laughing at it – but I could see it was getting to Tracey.'

In the afternoons, Doug would come in an hour earlier than he had to, just to let Tracey know he was watching her. But he refused to ever acknowledge her presence – unless he wanted to appear gracious in front of other coaches. Yet Doug had his supporters among swimming parents, some of whom also refused to acknowledge Tracey because, they said, she'd caused the whole problem. It was a very unpleasant situation for her.

Ian wasn't going to be driven away on account of Doug's bitterness. Tracey just dug in her heels. But on top of all this weirdness there were other distractions, starting with a court case that involved a very odd couple. Taylor Martin, 27, an exotic dancer, was either a woman with an unrequitable fixation on Ian Thorpe or a scammer who was looking for a means of making a buck out of him. Whatever, her intermediary was her next-door neighbour, 32-year-old Vernon Ray Hopkins, who'd first put the wind up Ian back in January when he left a note on his car's windshield in the parking area at the pool, advising him: 'Don't wear quarter pants. Signed The Phantom.' (He meant to say three-quarter pants.) It looked to Ian like the start of every celebrity's biggest nightmare. Someone was watching him.

Three days later a second letter appeared: 'My name is Kanga. I am a 21-year-old actress. I've just moved back here after 12 months in Hollywood. I've seen you at training. Would you mind if I was to come and say hi?' Thirteen days later, another letter: 'This is Kanga again. I was wondering if you would allow me to take you out to dinner, just as friends. I don't want to know you as Ian Thorpe the celebrity, I want to know you as the funny, kind, caring, unassuming person that you are.' A mobile number was provided.

Ian was increasingly nervous and selfconscious as he walked out to his car. Three days after the last letter, Hopkins approached him personally as he was getting into the Audi, and gave him a bumblebee soft toy, a single rose and a note: 'How about dinner just as friends? Love Kanga.' At that point Thorpe was seriously concerned for his safety, and went to the police. They searched Hopkins' car and Martin's flat, and found a few videos of Ian swimming in competition. One of them was labelled 'Thorpe (Sex)'. Was there a plan to videotape Ian in a compromising situation? Or somehow sell 'their story' – whatever that was – to a current affairs program?

There were no more approaches, but it wasn't until the end of October that Ian's case seeking an AVO against the pair came to court. Martin claimed to have a degree in criminal law and represented herself, cross-examining Ian in the witness box. She later gave evidence that she used letters because she was too shy to approach him – an unusual affliction for a stripper. The magistrate found that she had an infatuation with Ian, and ordered both her and Hopkins to stay at least 20 metres from him, his home and the Sutherland pool.

The odd couple weren't at all happy with the verdict, and demanded that Ian apologise for not telling them their approaches were unwanted. 'Obviously there's people out there that's going to think we're psychos, which we're not,' said Hopkins. Then they launched an appeal against the AVO – for what purpose, you could only wonder. They lost, with the judge declaring Ian had good reason to fear them, and increasing the distance they had to keep to a more comfortable two kilometres. Incredibly, Martin stated they'd appeal again to the Supreme Court, although they were both still fans of Ian. *Why?* 'We've got a right,' she said.

In mid-November Thorpe was in the studio at ABC radio doing an interview with Monica Attard, who'd previously flagged to Dave Flaskas that she wanted to ask Ian how he felt about the gay rumours. He'd never spoken publicly on the subject. Flaskas told him that was her intention, and Ian could obviously have vetoed the idea if he'd wished. But Dave suggested: 'If you want to discuss it, I believe this is the best forum to do it in.' The general tone of Attard's 'Sunday Profiles' program was a world away from a 'ten questions' format in a tabloid paper.

In response to Monica's question, Ian said: 'You know, I'm a little bit different to what most people would consider being an Australian male. That doesn't make me gay. I mean, I'm straight. People want to claim me as part of a minority group and put labels on you, and that's not what I'm about, and I don't understand why people are like that. I think it's because . . . I try to speak as well as I possibly can. I try to be articulate. I don't put on a slang, I don't try and sound macho . . . I have an interest in fashion. I have an interest in things most people don't label as being part of the macho male thing.' He went on to say that far from being offended, 'it's the most flattering thing anyone can ever say, because if someone wants to label you or claim you as part of a minority group, it means you must have some strength in your character or in what you do.'

The *Sydney Morning Herald*'s Jacquelin Magnay put Ian's comments about being flattered in context: 'For several years Thorpe has been idolised by the gay community as one of its international icons. His bare torso features on many gay websites. And within the gay community there was a strong belief that Thorpe was one of theirs and that he was simply waiting until after the Athens Olympic Games in 2004 to reveal his sexuality.'

Surprisingly, the tabloids didn't make a big deal out of the story, although they all ran follow-up articles. Dave Flaskas told Magnay that Ian wouldn't be commenting any further, nor would he care what the response was. 'There was no agenda,' he said. 'This was no public relations stroke of genius or public relations stroke of lunacy. It was just a chat between two people.'

One of the reasons Thorpe had previously refused to address the subject was because putting it on the record would legitimise further discussion of it. He told *ABC Sport Monthly* magazine shortly after that interview: 'It's a question that I understand young people have wanted to ask for a long time, yet it's none of anyone's business – and now, with me answering that question, it almost means it's okay for people to continue asking it.' *But are you glad it's dealt with now – that you put an end to all that speculation*? 'Well, I don't know if it's dealt with. I think the same people who speculated will either believe it or won't believe it. You know, you're damned if you do, damned if you don't.' Ian still doesn't really care what people think, but now says: 'In hindsight, I probably wish I didn't answer it the way I did . . . The question should not be asked of anyone. You know, it's still out there. Nothing's changed. Out of the people who think I'm gay, I've probably changed the minds of 20 percent.'

But there has been a significant shift, according to Michelle Flaskas, who's spent a lot of time in public with Ian over the last four years. She believes Australians were waiting for him to fall from his squeaky-clean pedestal – and when it didn't happen, he grew in stature. As a 17-year-old he dealt with the strain of this torrent of rumour-mongering – which could not have been easy to do – and confirmed over the years, with his conduct and dedication to charity work, that he deserved people's respect. As a result, the constant innuendo has at last started to drop off – even if only by degrees.

Reflecting on that, Ian agrees: 'I think people are starting to understand me much better. They've kind of taken my attitude – that they don't really care. And people *shouldn't* care. Partly why all this innuendo happened was that people wanted a way to try and get at me. And it didn't work.'

≈

The year 2002 drew to a close in customary fashion, with Ian showered in awards, publications making all sorts of wild projections about his income, and *BRW* magazine getting it about right again. His earnings had jumped from $2.5 million to $3.8 million, of which only $25 000 came in prize money and about $100 000 from public speaking. The extra $1.3 million was from the renegotiation of contracts, along with a healthy Japanese infusion. Only two relatively small sponsors had been added to the existing ten – Autore South Sea Pearls and AMP Society – while the biggest was clearly adidas, with Aquarius, Telstra and Channel Seven on the next line. Sponsorship Solutions, an outfit specialising in valuing sponsorships, ranked Ian Thorpe the hottest property in Australia; they reckoned any company wanting a piece of him now could start bidding at $450 000. Mark

Sheridan still handled every aspect of his financial life, running an investment portfolio that included property, securities and managed funds.

No other swimmer was even in the ballpark with those numbers, but Ian's income was in line with his status in the sport. He was nominated again for the Jesse Owens Award – now expanded to include all sportspeople – along with Ronaldo, Michael Schumacher, Tiger Woods, Lance Armstrong, Serena Williams and Tim Montgomery. He was named *US Swimming World*'s Swimmer of the Year for the fourth time in five years. No other male has won that honour more than twice, and no other person more than three times. (Had he beaten van den Hoogenband in the 200 free in Sydney in 2000, it would undoubtedly have been a sweep of five from five.) Still, he was pushed in the voting this time by the up-and-coming American phenom Michael Phelps, who was now ranked world number one in the 100 fly, 200 IM and 400 IM.

As usual, Ian was the Telstra Australian Swimmer of the Year and winner of the People's Choice award, among others. At the awards function in Melbourne on 9 December, Doug Frost made his curtain call, being presented with the Coach of the Year award once again. He deserved to go out on a high; he had accomplished great things.

Although Ian had been very complimentary of him in his own speech, Frost somehow contrived to deliver his acceptance speech without even mentioning Ian Thorpe. It caused a bit of a stir. In fairness to him, Frost was never going to win any awards for eloquence, and when he realised his mistake he sought out his former protégé and apologised. Nonetheless, Ian was not happy that Doug had made oblique but aggressive comments he believed were designed to swipe at Tracey Menzies. It could not be described as edifying stuff.

≈

Fast twitch. That's what the new regime was all about. Ian wanted to sprint, and Tracey wanted to make him a sprinter. But there was never any likelihood in the short term of dropping the 400. Commentators kept saying he'd have to consider doing that because of his size, and the problem of stretching across the range from 100 to 400 metres. But Ian's aerobic base was so strong, it was too hard for him to walk away from his signature event. They agreed to continue to pursue the ultimate goal: an unprecedented Olympic 100-200-400 treble. Could it be done? Don Talbot reckoned that with the way Ian had revolutionised the 400 freestyle, turning it into something closer to a sprint race, he'd brought the treble into the realms of possibility. Of course, Thorpe himself never talked in those terms. He just wanted to improve his 100 metres PB, believing he was capable of much better than 48.73. If that meant he became the world's fastest swimmer, so be it.

The first move was to drop all thoughts of defending Ian's 800 metres title at the Worlds in Barcelona in July 2003. Although he still held the world record, he had no great attachment to it. They'd naturally have to focus centrally on the 200 rather than the 400, and change everything about the training routine. To begin with, there'd be more of it – a total of 35 hours per week instead of 30, but with a maximum of 20 in the pool over ten sessions, the rest on dry land: running, boxing, weights and yoga. A 20-year-old can't maintain the same workload in the water as a 16-year-old and recover as quickly.

Ian had done no running from the time he snapped his ankle bone. The weights sessions had always been a source of friction between coach and swimmer, and the boxing just a break from routine. Now both sessions would be done longer, harder and with greater awareness of the objective. Menzies wanted Ian more land-fit, with greater core body strength, less body fat and better muscle definition, standing up square rather than bow-shaped and round-shouldered, so that he'd cut a straight, clean line through the water. Otherwise she could see him losing reach and flexibility as he got older.

The Frost terminology – A1, A2 and A3 sessions, aerobic phases and quality-endurance phases and such – was replaced with a new lingo. There were still aerobic training sessions, naturally, but the emphasis in sprint work would now be on absolute race pace. There was no point in swimming the back 50 of a 100 metres at 24.8 pace if Ian wanted to race it at 24.5. He had to work his body so it would know how to race at that speed.

And he had to rest it in cycles that were conducive to hitting the right speeds. With Tracey the sessions were more intense, more specific, more mentally challenging – he had to concentrate much more on stroke count, stroke quality and how his body felt in the water – but they were less physically stressful. He didn't walk away from a session so broken down he couldn't do another good one all week. And he had more flexibility to reschedule sessions according to how his body was reacting. Rather than a preconceived series of imperatives, some of which would be frustratingly impossible to meet, it was more of a partnership based on totally honest feedback.

Tracey was heavily into the science of physiology. Instead of taking a single lactate reading, for instance, she would look at a range of readings over a period and determine the lactate peak. If the level kept going up for several minutes after Ian had stopped working, that meant he'd need more sprint work as opposed to endurance work. She was on the case. Everything was about precision. They'd look to shave a few hundredths here, a few hundredths there. For instance, Doug had changed Ian from the standard swimmer's feet-together stance on the block to the fashionable track stance, one foot splayed behind the other. Film analysis now showed that although it got him into the water quicker, it was just a fraction slower overall. So he changed back. They did similar work with underwater filming on his turns, looking to get the best possible return from the energy expended. All his swimming skills had to be refined.

Under the old regime Ian followed what was then conventional thinking about diet: plenty of complex carbs and as little fat as possible. That was when respected nutritionists thought eating fat made people fat. Now the trailblazers believe body fat has more to do with insulin, which is overproduced by eating foods with a high glycaemic index (GI): bread, pasta, potatoes and such – what Grandma used to call 'starch'. Ian switched to a low GI diet with no wheat products, ate as much fat as he wanted, and would get consistent energy in the morning from foods like nuts, rather than an instant sugar hit from toast and jam. He felt much healthier and more energetic, all the time.

It was obvious to everyone that Australia's gun swimmer was happier than he'd been in years. At a FINA World Cup meet in Melbourne in early December the swimming journos started comparing him to Elka Graham, whose breathless, bubbly press conferences were impossible for the fastest note-takers to keep up with. Training was far more encouraging and convivial to begin with, and he believed fervently in what he was doing: detraining bad habits, and reasserting his natural feel for the water. The earliest signs were good. At that World Cup short course meeting, after only eight weeks back in the water, he contested just the 50 metres freestyle for a change, made the final and swam a PB. He was twitching faster already.

Things went from good to better. Thorpe led a 16-strong team of young swimmers on a World Cup short course tour that began in Paris on 17 January 2003. There he lost to Hoogie in the 100, but swam brilliantly in the 200, only three-quarters of a second outside the world record he'd set in Berlin. Then in Stockholm, Ian had a night out at a gala dinner with the 20-year-old Swedish Princess Madeleine, organised by high performance director Greg Hodge, and promised the princess a fast time if she came to the pool the following day. He delivered a 400 metres effort that missed Hackett's world record by just 0.05 seconds. It was a PB by over a second, and thrilled Ian as much as it did his royal guest.

The following day he entered the 200 IM as a 'fun event' – the first time he'd raced a medley since he was fourteen. His winning time of 1:56.00 ranked him the short course number two in the world, the sixth-fastest of all time, a whisker outside Matt Dunn's Australian record, and within 1.35 seconds of the world record. Considering he'd done no medley training whatsoever, it was just astonishing – and only served to highlight what a tragedy it was that Ian had left behind the form strokes all those years ago.

Although there'd been speculation he might shoot for the 400 IM at the Athens Olympics, as well as the 50 free, Menzies said straight away he wouldn't be adding a medley swim to his schedule for the Barcelona Worlds. He was just mucking around. Naturally, however, people got excited, and immediately there was talk again of The

Seven. Or even The Eight. And Ian himself hadn't ruled out swimming eight events in Athens. It was just that he was thinking of eight swims, rather than eight gold medals. By the time they reached the third leg of the tour, Berlin, Ian was having to tell the press once again that he didn't believe Spitz's record could be equalled, and he wasn't intending to try. 'It's not possible – I've been saying that for three years,' he declared. Then he swam a PB for a short course 100. He was on fire.

These were the happiest of times. Tracey Menzies had quit the art teaching job at the end of the year to devote all her time to her elite squad. In spite of the difficulties she faced, Tracey was loving the challenges posed by the learning curve she was on. As she was ascending the Eiffel Tower with Ian on the first leg of this trip, she found herself suddenly overcome with tears. 'Why are you crying?' he asked.

'I'm just so happy,' she said, 'because of this opportunity you've given me – to be doing this with you, and doing this with my life.'

'You're nutty,' said Ian bashfully.

'No, I'm not. And if I don't get another chance to say how privileged I feel, I'm saying it now. Just so you understand.'

Then Ian got sick, and everything changed. It was probably in Europe that he picked up the virus, because as soon as he got home it was obvious to Tracey that he was struggling to get through their sessions. When she enquired as to his health, Ian would reply that he was fine. That was his way. But he just wasn't the same person. Eventually he called one morning to tell her of severe headaches and fever. He had pathology tests and was diagnosed with viral encephalitis, a type of brain inflammation. The doctor ordered him to do nothing but rest until he felt better.

Ian was out of the water for seven days and couldn't train properly for another three weeks after that. So he was in and out of the pool throughout the month of February – a period when he should have been in consistent heavy training leading into his three-week taper for Trials, which started at Homebush on 22 March. Heading into her first major meet with Ian, Tracey was suddenly cast into unknown territory; the normally straightforward calculations turned into a complicated equation as she tried to nurse her swimmer through enough work to get a reasonable taper effect. It was a lousy preparation.

So, what did Ian do? He refused to acknowledge any problem, of course. *Never make an excuse*. He certainly *looked* to be in great shape, having stripped three kilos of fat from his frame, so he was down to 102, and comparatively ripped. As he unfurled the newly impressive body at a final pre-Trials hit-out in Canberra, Ian said he'd had a great preparation and the changes Tracey had made were *wonderful*, so he'd be very surprised and disappointed if he didn't swim at least one PB. That meant world records were in the frame. Not only that, he'd changed his mind about the 200 IM and was adding it to his program with a view to swimming it at Worlds if he could handle the workload.

Could he possibly have put his new coach under any more pressure? Surely it was a fine thing to believe in the power of positivity – and Ian had swum very well through pain and stress and illness before by exercising his mental toughness – but he'd never been *this* sick before, for so long and at such a critical time, and he was after all only human.

Tracey prayed that somehow it would turn out all right, but always there was the pressure of the coaching fraternity's scrutiny. While she had her supporters, there was no getting away from the fact that several among them were death-riding her . . . not just out of loyalty to Doug Frost, and not just because she was female, but also because her new-school methods threatened an old ideology based on blood, sweat and tears.

There were times when Tracey wished she'd taken on anyone other than Ian Thorpe. She understood, though, that he wanted so badly to do well at this meet – primarily to vindicate her, but also himself. And the only way Ian knew how to make that happen was to will himself into it. Although she might have wanted to say: 'What about *me*?', Menzies knew that was not her role. She had to bite the bullet. To stand alongside Ian, and actually talk up his chances so his confidence would be buoyed – that was the biggest test of character she'd ever faced.

For his part, Ian understood that he had a responsibility to Tracey, and that to make an excuse would have eased the pressure on her – but he really did believe in the power of mind over matter: 'I am *not* going to allow myself not to perform well just because I don't feel well. I'm bulletproof to the extent that a lot of things can be thrown at me, but it's about how much I'm prepared to let them affect me. *I really felt I could swim well at that meet . . .*'

And he did swim well – somehow. But not as well as he'd been suggesting he would, and thus not as well as everyone expected. For Ian Thorpe a good swim was a world record; a poor swim was still among the all-time top ten. It was a fairly fine line, and as far as the pundits were concerned, he was on the wrong side of it at these Trials.

In the 400 final he beat Grant Hackett by only half a second in 3:42.41 – his slowest swim at nationals in four years, and more than two seconds outside his world record. 'I've had a really good preparation, so I don't know what it is. I guess I just had an off swim,' he said. No comfort for Tracey, but the press spared her an inquisition . . . not for long. In the 200 final he beat Hackett again, but was even further off the pace, clocking 1:45.35 compared to his record of 1:44.06. 'I would have liked to have swum a lot faster,' he said. 'I'm pretty disappointed.' *Well then, Tracey, what's going on?*

She talked all around the subject, and managed not to spill the beans. It was very tough. Ian wasn't pulling back on his expectations or dropping any hints; on the contrary, he declared: 'I still feel like I should be performing well. Sometimes you just don't go as well as you'd like.' Tracey was left to make the observation that Ian was trying too hard for her sake, and needed to relax. Although she actually did believe that this was a secondary problem for Ian, apart from the illness – she could see that his stroke was tense and lacking fluency – it sounded lame. Although Greg Hodge raced to her defence, and so too did Ian, you could almost hear the derisive chuckling of crusty old men.

Before the final of the 100, Ian announced he wanted to post a time that would equate to his 47.20 relay split at Pan Pacs. So the *Australian* did the sums and headlined: 'THORPE HOPES TO BREAK 48'. Hoogie was the only man ever to go under that mark. No doubt there was something in Ian's mind telling him he could do it, *willing* him to do it . . . but really, how much pressure did he need to put on Team Thorpe?

As it turned out, Ashley Callus had him beaten for 99.95 metres of that race. With 20 to go Ian was half a body-length behind and looked out of it, but somehow he managed to conjure a dead heat with an admittedly lucky touch. The time: 49.05. In reality it was an incredibly courageous effort – one of his best ever under the circumstances – but nobody knew that. It looked slow. And he'd beaten Callus convincingly at Trials in 2001 and 2002. It must have been hard for Tracey to swallow the *Sydney Morning Herald*'s report: 'The measure of Thorpe's sprinting abilities is that he could only match the efforts of a virus-riddled Callus . . . who has only been able to do half of his usual training.'

Ian changed tack slightly, claiming that he'd made significant adjustments under Tracey and couldn't expect to see the benefit for another six months. There was truth in that statement, too – any new program would take a year to yield its full value – and it would have washed if he'd made it *before* the meet started. In every paper the bone was being pointed, subtly or unsubtly, at Tracey Menzies.

There was some relief for her when Ian produced a PB by a second in his 200 IM semi-final, then slashed that by another two and a half seconds in the final while demolishing the World Championships bronze medallist, Justin Norris. His 2:00.11 broke Matt Dunn's five-year-old Commonwealth record and placed Ian fifth-fastest in the world in the previous 12 months. He was less than two seconds outside world record time: extraordinary. Greg Hodge called it 'one of the truly great swims of all time when you think about it'. He'd be brushing up his medley act and taking it to Barcelona for sure.

Looking back on that meet and the way he approached it, Ian observes: 'I did the right thing because that's the right thing for me. It's not the *easier* thing to do. That's always there, but I refuse to do it that way.' If Tracey Menzies was coming along for the ride, she was going to have to get used to the fact that Ian Thorpe thought he really *was* bulletproof. She'd taken a few slugs herself, but she held firm, and in the end she was standing tall beside him.

28

THE NEW PHENOMENON

IT MAY HAVE BEEN GOOD FOR MENZIES to be subjected to a trial by fire, but it was also superfluous. Ian's health secrets all had to come out in the wash, because the Australian team members had an obligation to swim at the inaugural 'Duel in the Pool' against the USA in Indianapolis on 6 April – only a week after Trials – and Ian had already applied to Australian Swimming for an exemption on health grounds before Trials began. The Australian team doctor, Jeni Saunders, had backed up Ian's plea with a letter outlining the diagnosis and agreeing with him that the long flight and further competition so soon after his nationals program were likely to endanger his preparation for Barcelona in late July.

Maybe Ian thought that somehow he could withdraw from this high-profile meet without having his motives questioned or his reasons scrutinised. Not so: he was the main Australian drawcard, and there were sponsors and telecasters in the mix. So of course his reasons had to be aired publicly. And given the way he'd been talking himself up all through Trials, it was hardly surprising that his withdrawal on medical grounds was greeted with scepticism by some Australian coaches, officials and senior swimmers. It was a messy situation – one that put even more pressure on Tracey from those who thought Ian was wriggling out of his obligation. In team meetings, coaches were saying directly to her: 'There's a set of rules for one, and another set of rules for others.' It's doubtful the same people would have been bailing up Doug Frost with their opinions.

Ashley Callus pulled the pin along with Thorpe, and their announcement was followed by withdrawals from five others, including big guns Liesl Jones and Geoff Huegill. The Duel in the Pool was turning into a fizzer, and resentment against Ian's stance grew – as if he were somehow responsible for the domino effect. Kieren Perkins, newly appointed to the Board of Australian Swimming, cast doubt on Ian's motives and claimed that real leadership of the team was now being assumed by Grant Hackett.

Thorpe could have bolstered his position by staying at home. Instead he travelled to a remote part of the Northern Territory to visit Aboriginal communities, then after a week's rest he headed with Dave Flaskas to Japan, where he'd just picked up two new sponsors in Sony and Konami Sports Clubs. After a bit of promo work they chilled out for a few days on the resort island of Okinawa. Meanwhile the Aussies were predictably flogged by the full-strength Americans in Indianapolis, and the whole affair opened a wound that has never really healed. At the heart of it is a fundamental conflict between the welfare of high-profile athletes with exhausting programs and the natural desire of Australian Swimming to promote the sport so that it's visible as often as possible, not just twice a year at the nationals and the big international meets: Comm Games, Pan Pacs, Worlds, Olympics.

It's in the athletes' interests, obviously, that the sport grows itself – but someone like Ian Thorpe is not being too precious by suggesting to officialdom that if they want him to swim massive programs and carry off a swag of gold medals, they need to allow him some discretion in deciding what his body can and can't do. For instance, Ian has no doubt his decision to miss the Moscow world short course meet in

April 2002 helped him get through that year's ridiculous schedule at Comm Games and Pan Pacs – while others with heavy programs, including Grant Hackett, got sick.

At the launch of his high-tech DVD – *Ian Thorpe: Beneath The Suit* – Ian put the issue squarely on the table, calling on officials to examine the workload because it was causing illness and injury. Two weeks beforehand, at the end of May, he'd slogged through another obligatory grand prix meet in Cairns, and he'd had another bout of sickness three days later. In truth, doctors weren't absolutely certain what was wrong with him, the diagnosis of viral encephalitis being just 'the most logical explanation' for the range of symptoms showing up from time to time. He was always having to monitor himself, looking for signs of fatigue and fever. The year had started so well, but everything was being compromised by this mysterious illness.

≈

The Board members of Ian Thorpe's Fountain for youth Trust provide their services free, so that all the money collected is actually spent in the field. In its first couple of years of operation, the trust contributed to research on childhood illnesses and to projects such as Beijing Zhiguang Special Education School, supporting orphaned children with disabilities. But as tens of thousands of dollars in funds grew into hundreds of thousands, what the Board needed was a single clear focus. It got that when Ian invited former *Sixty Minutes* reporter Jeff McMullen to join his trust.

McMullen knew from his own experience that by far the sickest and neediest children in Australia were living in remote Aboriginal communities. He'd been out there many times. Ian had a particular concern about young people and suicide, and Jeff told him in these communities there was such depression and despair that children sometimes hanged themselves. McMullen agreed to talk to leaders in the major isolated communities in Cape York, Western Australia and central Australia, and report to the Board on what the trust could do.

He found that in central Australia the health situation was worse than when he first went there in the 1960s. Generations of neglect had led to a catastrophic cluster of illnesses known as 'syndrome X' – the result of childhood malnourishment which produced adults who suffered from hypertension, diabetes and heart disease simultaneously, and who died on average 20 years younger than white Australians. In the US, by contrast, Native Americans had closed the health gap so that their life expectancy was only a few years less than that of white Americans.

Jeff told Ian the most important role for him was to go and meet the Aboriginal leaders and publicly champion the cause. He had a brief rest after nationals to gather his strength, then off they went with cameraman David Brill, a former colleague of McMullen's, flying to Darwin and then on to the Territorian town of Katherine. They stayed in a motel and drove hundreds of kilometres in different directions each morning.

What Thorpe saw over four days in those remote places stunned him. He was amazed at how sick people were in general – adults were staring at death in their 30s and 40s – and especially how small all the children were. Up to 80 percent of the kids suffered some degree of deafness – the result of chronic inner ear infections. He was shocked to learn that Medicare didn't exist for these people. He thought it was for all Australians.

It was obvious the problem had to be attacked at its roots. The Fountain for youth Trust formed a partnership with the Fred Hollows Foundation and the Sunrise Health Service Aboriginal Corporation to help fund a primary health care and education system to improve birth weights through nutrition, look after young mothers and screen infants for illnesses. Ian told those partners they could count on this being the focus of his trust for the next three years, and committed a total of about half a million dollars.

But that was obviously a tiny fraction of what was needed. The Australian Medical Association estimates $300 million has to be budgeted for special health projects for the entire outback Aboriginal population. Ian's bigger contribution was to get the 'exclusive' story onto the front page of the *Sunday Telegraph* under the headline 'WE HAVE TWO AUSTRALIAS'. The tone was aggressive. Ian Thorpe 'accused Australia of ignoring the plight and shocking living conditions of Aboriginal Australians'.

Brill's footage was also aired on a Channel Seven special, *Race Against Thorpe*, which was set up as a prime-time fundraiser for this particular cause later in the year. It looked more like something you'd expect to see on TV Asahi, with Roy Slaven and H.G. Nelson commentating as teams of celebs and no-names were pitted against Ian Thorpe in a race over 1000 metres, and in Ian's view it was hardly great television – but it rated spectacularly and did the job of getting the message across. McMullen reckons the political impact has been strong in an area that's never had a high-profile champion before. Politicians know it's perilous to ignore a heavy-hitting sports star on a mission.

What Ian wants white Australians to understand, above all, is that 'people shouldn't accept bar-room conversation about what's going on out there – that Aborigines are drunks who waste their lives away, not wanting to go to school, not caring about their children. That's just totally inaccurate. Local indigenous people *are* creating projects to help themselves. We also make the assumption that we're throwing a lot of money at the problem – but we aren't, and a lot of what we do spend is caught up in the bureaucracy.'

One evening at twilight the three white men found themselves at a place called Edith Falls, outside Katherine, lighting a fire and throwing a few snags on the coals. Soon they were surrounded by Aboriginal families, with kids challenging Ian to swim in the billabong because the crocs in there were 'only freshies – they don't eat much', and of course after he ran out of excuses he ended up in the water with them, and saw the thrill it gave them to be sharing a part of their lives with this famous man they'd seen on television. 'That's when he's at his best – in that easy, relaxed, sharing environment,' McMullen observes. 'And the elders sat there on the edge of the falls, just smiling at the idea that this 20-year-old had bothered to make such a journey, and was intending to speak up about what they'd told him. Ian was looking around and seeing: *this is my country, these are my people, part of my family* – and once you see it, you can't walk away from it.'

Ian knows he needs to do more with his gift than simply collect gold medals and world records. But he's not seeking a more all-encompassing 'greatness' for himself by transcending personal glory; that's not the point of it at all. He just wants to make a difference, and knows that he can. 'I'm not going to change the world,' he says. 'But what I hope I can do is change attitudes, so that in future these people's lives will improve. And our own lives will be better by doing that.'

≈

The sporting media always want a drama, and drama needs rivalry. Hackett and van den Hoogenband had proven themselves extremely worthy opponents, but they were never cast by Ian as 'rivals', in spite of the media's occasional attempts to generate some heat. As he said a thousand times – to the point of exasperation – Ian didn't understand rivalry. If the whole idea of the thing was to become the best swimmer he could be, what did it matter where anyone else fitted into the scheme of things?

With the arrival of the 18-year-old American Michael Phelps, number one ranked in the 100 fly and world record holder in the 200 fly and 200 and 400 IM, the press in the run-up to Barcelona Worlds became obsessed with the question of who was the world's greatest swimmer. The only person in the swimming milieu who was genuinely uninterested in the answer was Ian Thorpe.

Phelps, a 193-centimetre racing snake who spent half his time on dry land eating to try and bulk up, was a brash kid from a small blue-collar mill town in the east coast state of Maryland. (Coincidentally, he had a very talented older sister who just missed the US team for Atlanta '96 and whose subsequent Olympic dreams were snuffed by chronic injuries.) He'd been schooled to adopt a more humble approach by his 37-year-old coach, Bob Bowman, who admitted the attitudes he'd tried to instil in his prodigy were drawn directly from the Ian Thorpe book of maxims. Michael was actually a nice enough bloke and Ian liked him, but the American stoked the media fire by making it clear that he *was* interested in the answer to the big question, and he'd be doing his darnedest to prove in Barcelona that the answer was Michael Phelps.

It was never going to be a meet where Thorpe would replicate his six-gold haul from the Fukuoka Worlds. To start with, the competition would be tougher across the board, with the Americans fielding an Olympic-strength team. Ian wasn't entering the 800 free, in which he still held the world record, and to have any chance of pulling off both freestyle relays Australia needed a fit and firing Michael Klim. (The multiskilled Klim was a forlorn figure at Trials, this time unable to swim because of a recent shoulder reconstruction. He hadn't contested a major meet since Fukuoka in 2001, and Ian made a good luck gift to him of a ring he'd had specially made for himself after the Sydney Olympics.) On comparative times, the medley relay also looked well out of reach for the Australians.

Ian went into Barcelona ranked third in the 200 IM, and some parts of the press, ever-vigilant for *the* story of the meet, put forward the idea that this was the race that would settle the issue of who was the world's best swimmer. It was absurd. Michael Phelps, medley specialist and world record holder, up against a bloke who'd swum the event once at an open long course meet. It would make as much sense to suggest that Phelps should be in a swim-off for the title against Thorpe in the 400 freestyle.

At the same time, Don Talbot was firing Phelps up by claiming that he had great potential but hadn't done anything much as yet, and that people who were saying he was better than Thorpe were 'out of their minds'. Meanwhile, both Hoogie and Hackett were talking about their sensational preparations, so the pressure was going to be on Ian even in his signature events. There was a consensus that the four-time unofficial world's greatest swimmer was at a critical point in his career: it was even conceivable he could come away without a gold medal.

You wouldn't have known it to look at him. People couldn't remember when they'd seen Ian more relaxed and happy. As long as he kept improving, he'd remain that way. But all this discussion about rivalry butted up against a related issue, and that was the question of what Ian Thorpe should be happy with. Coaches and officials wanted medals, especially gold ones. As far as they were concerned, the object of racing was to win. As far as Ian was concerned, the object remained the same: to swim faster than ever before. Medals were fine if they happened, but not the point.

As he was still maturing, hacking slices off his best times whenever he got wet, there was no conflict at all. But there had to come a time, it was widely thought (or at least, hoped), when Ian would see that he needed to manage himself through a meet in order to maximise his medal haul, rather than go hell-for-leather in every event. That time, it seemed, should be around about now.

Tracey Menzies certainly thought so, and believed the realisation was dawning on Ian. Don Talbot had once addressed the question when he was running the show. Talbot told Ian he was glad to hear he'd been talking about gold medals, not PBs or world records. Thorpe replied that if that was how he'd been quoted, it was a gross misrepresentation. 'That's not what I'm about,' he said yet again. No matter how many times he repeated himself, most people didn't seem to want to get it.

And he *still* won't relent on it. Other coaches have also tried to influence him, 'and I'm prepared to think about it,' he now says. 'But at the end of the day, it's rubbish. I won't accept it. I'll stop swimming before I do that.' It would be pointless, according to the Thorpean world-view, to keep on swimming as long as he was still winning gold medals for Australia, regardless of the quality of his performances – like a declining rugby warhorse who uses guile to cut corners and get through a game. It would be pointless because it would be about *dominance* as opposed to *excellence*, and Ian has no interest at all in dominance. If it came to that, he'd have to move on.

And so he and Tracey were talking somewhat at cross-purposes as they headed to Barcelona from their staging camp in Germany. Although his health was not 100 percent – he was still having tests to try and learn more about this virus – Ian was telling the media he hoped to be swimming 'nothing less' than his best times. Meanwhile Tracey was publicly hosing down expectations and privately wondering why Ian chose such odd times to talk his prospects up. 'My job as a coach,' she says, 'is to teach Ian that he's placing undue pressure on himself. To voice that is to open a can of worms, because the world expects him to meet his own expectations, and if he doesn't, people think he's failed . . .' If that is in fact her job, then she still has the work in front of her.

≈

The 2003 Worlds, distinguished by a fun atmosphere with occasional bursts of chaos, were held in a temporary indoor pool with crowd capacity of about 7000, while the outdoor pool used for the Olympics in 1992 served as the warm-up facility.

Tracey gave Ian free rein to swim the final of the 400 as he saw fit. Hackett stuck with him for the first 250 but couldn't hold the pace and came in a few seconds behind, wondering why he hadn't done better. Ian's winning time was 2.5 seconds outside his record. Not that bad, not that great. He pronounced himself 'pleased' with the swim, although he'd taken it out slower than he wanted to. Menzies was relieved to chalk up a gold medal.

Then, swimming in lane eight after almost missing the final of the 4 × 100 free relay, the Australians were touched out for the bronze medal by France, with the Russians beating the US to gold. Without Klim, and with Callus still unwell, the world champions were battling to stay in it.

Although she was warmiy embraced by the swimmers and support staff, it was obvious at this meet there was still a coterie of coaches death-riding Tracey Menzies. The message would get back to her in subtle ways – never delivered to her face – and no doubt some would suggest she was paranoid. But the team's media officer, Dave Mason, was happy to go on the record when asked if her perceptions were accurate: 'Definitely. I saw Tracey under huge pressure in Barcelona, with a lot of the older coaches waiting for her to fail. I saw her being subjected to unfair comparisons with what Ian had done before, with a lot of people being nice to her face and then putting her down.' Ian saw and heard it all too. He says the anti-Menzies clique actually wanted to instigate new coach selection criteria that would oust her from the team. Under the existing system, based on Ian's international point score, she was the first coach picked. 'Most people,' Thorpe observes, 'wouldn't be able to deal with the expectations put on her, even with the support of everyone on the team. But among coaches she was quite isolated . . .'

How small-minded were these people? Possibly it had to do with an observation made by Don Talbot in his autobiography, published in late 2003: 'Australia has the lowest-educated coaches in the world compared to other high socio-economic countries. The average level of education of our coaches is probably the end of primary school. Some have gone on to do their School Certificates and Higher School Certificates, but at this time I can't think of a single coach who holds a university degree.' If he'd thought harder, he'd have come up with at least one: Tracey Menzies.

Hoogie threw down the challenge with a 200 freestyle qualifying time 0.78 faster than Ian's. Everywhere there was talk that he was primed to repeat his victory at the Sydney Olympics. Tracey was feeling immense pressure at that point. She found herself a seat in the back of the stands, readying herself for the final. A Spanish gentleman who spoke little English recognised her as Ian Thorpe's coach, and befriended her.

Van den Hoogenband hurtled off the block and hit the 100-metre turn ahead of world record pace. But Ian was right thereabouts, and at 150 he exploded off the wall, brought in the big kick . . . and sailed past the Dutchman to win by more than a body-length. Up in the stands, the kindly Spaniard leaned over, kissed Tracey on the cheek and said: 'That was a very tough one for you.' She cried tears of joy and relief. Then she headed downstairs and ran into Hoogie's coach, Jacco Verhaeren, who gave her a hug and said: 'I'm happy for you. That was great.' She cried some more.

Thorpe's time was 1:45.14, a bit over a second outside his world mark. He stopped at the media mixed zone and did one interview in English for Channel Nine, one in fluent French, and another in halting Japanese for TV Asahi. Tracey met him in the warm-down pool and asked if he was happy with his time. He said he wasn't. She could have become upset at that moment, considering the load she was carrying. But she took a step back, realising Ian wasn't being nasty. He was just disappointed, having focused so much of his training on the 200, and having brought to Barcelona his relentlessly optimistic nature. She told him to look at the performance in the entire context of the year he'd had. It was a good swim.

Ian told the press: 'I felt like I should have been able to swim a lot faster than what I did.' If that's what he thought, that's what he was going to say. Tracey just had to get used to it. Doug Frost, interviewed back in Sydney, stated magnanimously: 'He probably wants to break world records and prove that his move has been worthwhile, but I don't think that's important . . . Probably at some stage he's going to plateau a little.'

The fact was, though, that no freestyle swimmer at this meet was as fast as they wanted to be. Ian wasn't going to say anything tantamount to an excuse, but Grant Hackett had no such reservations, describing the old-fashioned lane ropes in the temporary pool as 'absolutely horrible'. They weren't doing the job of absorbing the turbulence, so in freestyle sprint races, in particular, the washing machine conditions were almost comical. The effect seemed to be much less significant in the form strokes. It made Ian's swim in the 100 free semi-final, when he knocked two-hundredths off his PB to get down to 48.71, all the more impressive. Significantly, it was a race he was able to lead from start to finish, avoiding the worst of the wash, with both Hoogie and Alex Popov qualifying faster in the other semi-final.

There was also a young bull on the charge at this meet, and nothing was going to get in his way. Michael Phelps broke his 200 fly world record in a semi-final, backed up to win gold in the final, then squared up against Grant Hackett to lead off the American team in the 4 × 200 relay just 45 minutes later. Hackett had won bronze in the 200 metres, but Phelps swam past him to give the Americans a lead and a chance to finally wrest this relay from the Aussies' iron grip. They didn't, because Ian Thorpe hit the water for the anchor leg dead level with them and swam the second-fastest 200 relay split ever . . . but all the talk was about Phelps. The butterfly and medley specialist had suddenly become the fourth-fastest 200 freestyle swimmer in history. Was there anything the kid couldn't do?

In the final of the 100 free, Ian got to the turn a full half-second behind the leader, Popov, and couldn't make up the gap on the way home. He needed still more front-end speed. But it was pretty close: Popov first in 48.42; Hoogie second in 48.68; Thorpe third in 48.77. Ian was mowing them down so fast at the end, another ten metres would have got him a win. As it was, he was now only a third of a second away from becoming the first man in history to win the treble at world level. When he got out of the water and fronted the mixed zone, he was *glowing*. And as he stood on the dais with those two great swimmers, he felt deeply privileged: not only was it his first medal in the 100 free at the ultimate level, but he was part of the most decorated podium in the history of swimming.

And yet, all achievements at this meet were being swept away by the brilliance of Phelps, who broke another world record in the semi-final of the 200 IM. Ian had to back up after the 100 for that race with only one event in between, giving him only 17 minutes of recovery time, and still managed to qualify fifth-fastest for the final, three seconds behind the American. But it was obvious Phelps was never going to be threatened by a medley hobbyist. He was far too good for that.

On the following day Phelps broke the 100 fly record to become only the second man ever, after Spitz, to hold four world records simultaneously. The buzz around him was as great as it had ever been for Ian Thorpe. Then came the 200 IM final 'showdown', with Phelps incredibly slashing his new record by a further 1.5 seconds. He was on another planet as a medley swimmer at 1:56.04 – but it was equally amazing that Ian Thorpe, swimming the event for only the second time, edged out the Olympic champion, Massi Rosolino, to take the silver. It was another PB for Ian, taking him well under his target of two minutes. Again, he was more than happy with the result. He had three gold medals, a silver and a bronze.

But Phelps, the new phenomenon, was at this point looking a near-certainty for five gold and a silver. Then, just as he seemed unstoppable, he was stopped – by his unheralded countryman, Ian Crocker, who took his new 100 fly record away and beat him to the gold by a whisker. That also put him out of the medley relay final, but he got to pick up another gold medal anyway by swimming in the heat. Then he cleaned up the 400 IM in yet another record-busting time. Four gold medals and two silvers was Phelps' final tally, but more significant was his total of five individual world records at the one meet. That had never been done before, by anyone. And he didn't just shave those records, either. He slaughtered them.

Ian's program ended on a sour note when Australia's medley relay team was disqualified after winning their heat for an illegal change between the backstroke and breast-stroke legs. It would probably have been another medal for him, but not gold: the Americans smashed their own world record in the final. They came away with the number one team title again, with 11 gold medals to Australia's six, reinforcing the fact that Fukuoka 2001 was a mere aberration.

Ian has often said his performances all come down to interpretation, which is why he doesn't really care how people rate them. Nonetheless, this meet was widely regarded as around par for him – neither here nor there. 'I never thought it was a bad meet,' he reflects. 'But it wasn't a great meet.'

He'd set the bar so high and, at face value, Thorpe's Barcelona haul didn't compare with his six golds at the Fukuoka Worlds in 2001. From another perspective, he got closer to achieving his central ambition – the 100-200-400 treble – than he did in 2001, and against better opposition. There was no Popov at Fukuoka. He swam a PB for the 100 free in a pool everyone agreed was lousy for freestyle swimming. Ranked fourth in the world in that event, he came third.

Miraculously, he entered a novelty race, the 200 IM, and beat the Olympic champion. Ranked third in the world, he came second. He couldn't do anything about his team's lack of firepower in two of the relays. And as even Doug Frost admitted, it was only to be expected that he'd level off in the 200 and 400 free. However, Frost told the author: 'My *mother* could have coached him to improve his 200 IM and 100 free times.' The jury was still out on Tracey Menzies.

With all eyes cast immediately toward Athens, it wasn't long before the Phelps camp started taking direct aim at Ian Thorpe's signature events. The 'Baltimore Bullet', as he was known, reckoned he wanted to go one-on-one with the world's best on the biggest stage. Americans love the idea of a gladiatorial confrontation, but would Phelps really jeopardise other near-certain victories to satisfy his and his countrymen's desire for a showdown? As good as he was, he would have to make significant gains in the 200 and especially the 400 free to match it with Ian. Phelps wasn't going to announce exactly what he'd decided until after the US Nationals in early July 2004, but he kept the idea afloat.

However, on the evidence of Barcelona the man to watch was van den Hoogenband, who produced a mind-boggling freestyle split in the medley relay of *46.70* on the final day of competition. That told everyone Hoogie had missed his taper by a couple of days. It looked like he was again going to be the biggest threat to Ian Thorpe at the Olympic Games.

29

'THORPE BEATS THE DON'

AS USUAL, IAN SKIPPED THE SHORT course titles at home and flew from Barcelona with the Flaskases to Athens to make a special pre-Olympic episode of *The Great Outdoors*, along with Cathy Freeman and Ernie Dingo. Local dignitaries called a press conference because they wanted to present Ian and Cathy with medals for their 'contribution to tourism', but the athletes themselves were unavailable because they were doing the film shoot . . . so there was total confusion, although they managed to sort it out in the end. Would that become a familiar story of the 2004 Olympics?

Then the three of them flew to London, where Ian was lionised in a BBC documentary called 'Born to Win'. The Brits were lumping him in with their own David Beckham, Jonny Wilkinson and David Coulthard for this series, which was oddly magnanimous of them. He had time to catch a Robbie Williams concert before heading to Tuscany to join a bunch of English and Swedish swimmers, including his friends Mark Foster and Therese Alshammar, for a holiday at a rented villa in a town called Arezzo.

Thorpe was a man of the world by now, but this sojourn was different because for once he'd decided to drop his compulsion to organise things and just go with the flow. In the plane he pulled out his guidebook and looked up 'Arezzo', which was described as 'determinedly grim'. *What?* Actually it was nothing like that. It was medieval, rustic, but beautiful, and they had a great time. After a week Ian had to come home to join aerial skier Alisa Camplin as co-host of the 'One Year to the Olympics' dinner on 13 August.

The following morning Don Talbot launched his book at the famous old North Sydney pool, and Ian was slated to deliver a speech. He reached into the pocket of his immaculate leather coat and pulled out . . . the speech from the night before. So, there was nothing to do but wing it. He talked about how most of the impressions people had about Don Talbot were negative, and about how most of the discussions he'd ever had with Don were disagreements, and . . . all in all, it was a very unusual speech for a book launch. But he also found plenty of positive things to say, and Talbot, who was now a supporter of Tracey Menzies, took it well. He'd done a lot of straight talking himself in his time.

Ian didn't feel he needed his customary six-week break. After a fairly cruisy first week of training, he was back into it full-bore. His main focus this time, instead of doing the extended international jaunt, was to bed down the purchase of his spectacular new split-level waterfront home not far from Cronulla. He knew he'd miss the convenience of Margaret's round-the-clock maintenance, but it was time to spread his wings. The sale was settled on 12 September and he moved in straight away.

You get a lot of house for $2.9 million: panoramic views, four bedrooms, formal lounge and dining rooms, rumpus room, jacuzzi, four-car garage, boatshed and jetty . . . and a swimming pool. Unlike most 20-year-old blokes, Ian knew his way around the kitchen, could whip up something tasty at any time, and made coffee like the connoisseur he was. But he never remembered to clean up after himself, and when it came to doing the laundry, he'd just dump it all in the back of the Audi and drive home to Mum's. He wasn't that different, really.

≈

'THORPE BEATS THE DON'. On 19 September, the *Telegraph* ran with the results of a two-month reader poll to determine 'Sydney's Greatest Ever Male Sports Star'. Ian Thorpe had 'knocked Bradman from his perch – albeit by a narrow margin'. (What would Cecil Thorpe have had to say about that?) The time was always going to come when memories of cricket's most compelling legend would begin to fade, and perhaps the witnesses to his feats were getting too old to bother about voting. But Ian felt awkward; he really would have preferred not to win this poll. Hence he put a lot of thought into his acceptance speech for the function at Star City. 'It doesn't sit all that comfortably,' he said. 'I'm a great fan of Sir Donald's, and he remains one of the world's and Australia's greatest sportsmen. So while it is pleasing, especially as the award was voted by the public, it's also quite strange and I don't know how to take it.'

There appeared to be no limit to Ian's popularity. His own range of Autore pearl jewellery for men was a smash hit. He put out a collection of 'IT' underwear designed to his requirements – which he personally modelled at the launch at David Jones in the city – and the stock disappeared in no time. (He could have called them 'Thorpedo' undies, having finally won the right to use the trademark after a protracted court battle, but good taste prevailed.) The clincher was a poll by the *Sun-Herald* asking readers who they'd most like to have over for dinner on Christmas Day. Ian Thorpe was the first pick, followed by John Howard and Nicole Kidman. People had been saying for a while that in the eyes of the Australian public, the Thorpedo had transcended sport. That seemed to be the proof of it.

As his 21st birthday approached on 13 October, Ian marked the occasion by reflecting on his life for the *Sydney Morning Herald*. It seemed to have been divided into three parts: the period before he entered the Australian team at age 14, then the period between 14 and 18, and then the years from 18 to 21. The middle period was 'a fantasy world, and it was strange . . . It was about learning how to deal with it as best I possibly could . . . the expectations, the rubbish and the good things that come with it – being able to enjoy the person I actually am, instead of the person everyone thought I was.' The final period was most satisfying. 'In the last three years, I've done the most with and gained the most from my life, outside the pool, in the pool . . . Right now, I'm probably the happiest that I've ever been.'

He recognised very clearly the importance of not having overbearing parents. Had Ken and Margaret been heavy-handed, 'I would have walked away from the sport a long time ago. You just can't handle that extra burden.' On that score, he believed he would know exactly when he'd finally scaled his personal Everest and become the best swimmer he could be. 'I have this feeling that when I do swim that way, I'll just *know*, and that will be it . . . And then I'll say: "Get out now".'

Ian wanted to show his new place off to all his family and friends, so he hosted a traditional 21st party at home. Of the 100-plus guests, about half were the core of family members who attended every major Thorpe gathering. Ian didn't invite them because he had to, but because he wanted to. He thanked them all for their influence, great or small, on his life.

The following week he had another 21st party – this one a more youthful bash for his closer friends in and outside of swimming – at the old Mortuary Station, where corpses used to be taken in bygone times. The theme was Mod Goth, and Ian only expected people to come in black, but most of his guests had gone to amazing lengths with their outfits. It was a raging party, just as he'd wanted. But there was a time when he found himself talking quietly with Grant Hackett and Michael Klim about all the great experiences they'd had together, and it seemed an appropriate moment to tell those guys how much their friendship meant to him. He told them he didn't want them to think of themselves as his *swimming* mates; they were his *mates*, full stop.

They'd been the backbone of Australian swimming for seven years, these three young men. They'd been subjected to enormous pressure, constantly in the limelight – and yet not a cross word had passed between them. Their mutual respect was potent and enduring, but it was about more than that. It was about genuine friendship. So when it was announced that Grant Hackett would share the 2003 Telstra Australian Swimmer of the Year Award with Ian Thorpe, they both could not have been happier. They'd each won three gold, one silver and one bronze medal in Barcelona, and if ever there was a man who deserved to have his time in the sun, it was Grant.

At the awards function in Melbourne on 1 December, Ian was joined at his table for the second time in three years by one of swimming's most glamorous females, Amanda Beard. The American breast-stroke champion was in Australia for the Qantas Skins and World Cup meets at the end of November. The *Sun-Herald* reported that they avoided public displays of affection, but 'tongues were wagging' when they were spotted holding hands under the table.

Apart from the attempt to hitch Ian up with Martina Hingis, which was just wishful thinking by the media, this was the first time he'd actually been romantically linked with anyone in the gossip pages. And he's prepared to admit: 'I *am* very keen on her – but it's ridiculously hard to pursue. Timing's terrible, distance is terrible – everything is going against it.' When the *Sun-Herald* followed up Amanda in the US a week later, she said much the same thing. A pity.

In many ways, the awards night was a vindication for Tracey Menzies. The newest member of her elite squad, Amanda Pascoe, made a touching speech about how the other three swimmers and their coach felt like family to her. Thorpe got up and said it had been a very tough year, and that there'd been some people who were supportive, and more people who weren't supportive – and those people had made it difficult, not only for himself but for his coach. So he thanked Tracey for showing the personal qualities he always believed she had, and which she'd needed to get through the year. His purpose was to make clear this message: *if you're feeling a little bit of guilt, that means I'm talking to you*. 'A lot of the time,' he observes, 'those coaches don't realise I know what's going on.'

Nonetheless, the bottom line remained: Ian was now sharing a domestic title he'd owned for four consecutive years, and internationally he'd dropped from first to fourth in the pecking order, according to *US Swimming World* – behind Michael Phelps, the unanimous choice for Swimmer of the Year, Japanese breast-stroke record-breaker Kosuke Kitajima, and the reborn Alex Popov. Ian may have had little or no interest in such things, but the rest of the world had plenty. And in the end, the responsibility fell squarely on the shoulders of his coach. Although Tracey had influential supporters, the background noise of her existence was still the sniggering of grumpy old men.

'I've had a good year,' she said at the end of it. 'A hard year, but a good year.' She was bearing up. Thorpe had a good enough year to pocket $3 050 000, according to *BRW*. A bit down on the previous year's earnings, with Telstra pulling the pin on its sponsorship back in February. But there'd be new and very lucrative horizons opening up in 2004.

≈

In an Olympic year, there could be no stinting on preparation. Circumstances had prevented Ian from doing any altitude training in 2002 and 2003, even though it was a proven winner for him. This time around he'd be doing two stints in Arizona: one in November 2003, a sort of aerobic training booster, and another in late May leading into the Games in August.

Ian got straight off the plane from the US at the end of November to swim on the same day at Homebush in the Qantas Skins. He still managed to post a PB for the 50 freestyle. He was looking good. He trained hard and well throughout the summer, loving his work – even the sand hills running – and enjoyed learning to surf at Cronulla. He'd been at it for well over a year, and revelled in the challenge: being almost six and a half feet tall doesn't help when it comes to getting up on a short board. Sometimes he'd paddle out in the channel off the heaviest break on the Australian east coast, Shark Island, and just sit and watch the expert surfers getting barrelled in a spectacular aquatic show. It would be a long, long time before he'd be good enough to take on the Island, but he looked forward to that day.

At the NSW Open in January, Ian swam in the 19 years and over 200 free and cruised to the wall more than six seconds outside his record. That was about par for the course in the middle of heavy training, but Tracey was curious. She got Ian to suit up and go all out in the Open 200 free, just to see where he was really at. His time of 1:46.65 was faster than he'd ever done outside a major competition.

The coach was so happy with that, she pulled him out of the meet. There'd be no need for any more racing before Trials.

Ian's only dilemma was his program. He wasn't happy with the amount of strain he'd put on himself by swimming the 200 IM at Worlds, and the Athens program was going to be the same: a lousy 17 minutes between the final of the 100 and the semi of the medley. It was more of a problem, though, that he'd have to swim the medley heat the same morning, and he reckoned that would again take the edge off his freestyle final. A pity, since the medley experiment had been really enjoyable . . . and so he vacillated right up until the entry deadline for Trials.

Talbot was urging Ian to stick with the medley and have a shot at The Seven, but in the end the die was cast: a six-event program at most, including the 100, 200 and 400 free along with the three relays. A major consideration was Athens' energy-sapping heat, especially since it looked likely there'd be no roof on the pool. Ian wanted to make sure he could swim as fast as possible in the relays. So all the experimentation with backstroke and medley events had come to naught, it seemed. The public may have viewed it that way, but as far as Thorpe was concerned, it was all about having a bit of fun. 'It's almost unacceptable to have fun in [professional] sport,' he observes. As he'd said a hundred times, he was never interested in The Seven. Everyone had just gotten carried away with the idea.

That left the Spitzean feat to the only other man on the planet who might have been good enough. In December Ian had said for the umpteenth time he believed it could not be done. Speedo in America garnered massive publicity by offering Michael Phelps $US1 million if he could prove that opinion wrong. Phelps had every intention of giving it his best shot – he was even talking about The Eight – but still wasn't letting on exactly how he'd go about it. Not until July.

For Ian the focus now was on whether he could pull off the Olympic 100-200-400 treble for the first time ever. He might have been relentlessly positive and supremely optimistic, but he still didn't think so. Even though he felt he was training with a coach who understood sprinting, he was yet to overcome the effects of all the endurance training he'd done. There wasn't time, he didn't think, to rebuild all that fast-twitch fibre before the Olympics. He *knew* he could do much better than 48.71 for 100 metres. He reckoned 48-low would be well within the frame, but you'd need to go under 48 seconds to win in Athens.

Tracey thought the same. She also thought Ian needed more experience racing the 100, because in that event he had to practise his new skills over and over in the race environment. Everything they'd worked on had to be done perfectly: the start, the stroke, the breath pattern, the turn, the finish. In terms of stroke mechanics the 100 free is not a mini version of the 200, but another event entirely. Nonetheless, they were making progress. Ian told his coach he felt smoother and more efficient in his stroke than ever. He wasn't holding as much water on his back as he used to. He was standing straight and square, as Menzies wanted him to, and his body composition was much better. His first 15 metres of the sprint had not improved much, but his next 25 had. He needed to get through that first 50 in 23-low to be some sort of a chance and, according to Tracey, he was homing in on the target.

They both realised, though, that if Ian wanted to achieve his greatest ambition, he might have to drop the 400 freestyle after Athens. *Swings and roundabouts.* But at this stage he still had a huge amount of aerobic ability socked away in the bank, and he'd be spending some of it to try and win another Olympic gold medal in his signature event. Although there was always talk, before every meet, that Grant Hackett was about to bounce Ian Thorpe off his pedestal in the 400, it simply never happened. Thorpe would be a very warm favourite to repeat as Olympic champion.

≈

In late January 2004, a couple of months before Trials, Ian's financial brains trust unveiled a deal that had taken a few years of planning, and which had the potential to take him out of the very comfortable category and into the realms of the seriously rich. It was not a straight sponsorship but an equity deal with the So Natural food group, which markets soy-based products and owns Paramount Seafood. Ian was given five percent of the Australian company's shares to start with – worth $1.1 million up front – with a chance for that to run to

20 percent if the partnership was a 'moderate success' and up to 50 percent if it did better than expectations.

The deal was a complicated arrangement which involved selling two products into the Asian market: a Thorpedo-branded water-based sports drink to be released in Australia in August and a bit later in Japan and China, and a Thorpedo-branded canned seafood product due to be launched in Australia and Japan in December. Expected turnover all up in the first three years was $50 million. This was the first time any Australian company had given equity to a celebrity in exchange for their name and image. The licence for both products would run for 15 years and cover Australia, New Zealand, Japan, China, Hong Kong, South Korea, Singapore and Taiwan. A massive potential market, with So Natural perfectly placed to take advantage of Ian's cult following in Asia.

Naturally he wanted to explore other equity deals because they'd continue to earn him money long after he finished swimming. Meanwhile the Sony sponsorship in Japan was extended to China, with Ian signing up to do a series of commercials for that market before the Olympics. It looked like being the publicity breakthrough in China that Flaskas was seeking, with Ian also slated to tour Japan and China as a 'Sony ambassador' after the Games. The celebrity approach was not one the electronics giant normally went for, but with Thorpe's pan-Asian appeal they could see enormous potential, and Flaskas didn't have to squint too hard into the distance to see where all this might lead. In the meantime, Ian had already bought an apartment in Beijing off the plan, in a building plastered with his image and the greeting: 'Welcome. I am Ian Thorpe, your new neighbour.' He was way ahead of the game, with the pundits comparing his business exploits with those of the Great White Shark. He wasn't likely to blow the Shark out of the water just yet, but the Thorpedo brand was about to be fired up at last.

Ian felt qualified, anyway, to get stuck into FINA for its 'Jurassic' efforts in the area of marketing the sport. At the same press conference to launch the Australian Championships, he mentioned again his concern that the strict sudden-death selection policy could result in the best athlete, under some circumstances, missing out on the Olympics.

'I think there should be a five percent leeway if an athlete has an injury or illness. They should have the opportunity to fight for their position.' Had he been able to foresee the future, he would certainly have included 'other extenuating circumstances'.

In the lead-up to Trials, Speedo unveiled for the media its new-generation suit, the Fastskin FSII, on 9 March. A question was asked from the floor by media director Ian Hanson: *Would Ian Thorpe swim faster in one of these new suits?* Of course he would, according to the US biomechanist, David Pease: 'We've shown it is the fastest suit.' Speedo's managing director, Rob Davies, jumped in with the claim that 'tests proved' this was the fastest outfit, and the second-fastest was the original Fastskin, and they'd tested every single suit they could get their hands on.

Dave Flaskas was very angry that Ian had obviously been singled out, when he was only one of four swimmers who'd be applying to the AOC to wear another brand. Glenn Tasker, Australian Swimming's CEO, agreed the question was 'unsuitable' and the biomechanics boffin should have declined to answer it. 'There is no scientific evidence Ian would swim any faster in the new suits,' he said. Not only that, there *couldn't* be any such evidence – not unless Ian was involved in the testing himself. The idea was nonsense.

To begin with, the suit Thorpe wears is unique to himself, and he wears each outfit only once, because they always stretch just a little. Before Trials he'll be measured over every part of his body three separate times, and the measurements adjusted so that exactly the right degree of tightness is achieved in the right places. For instance, the latest suit compresses his quads so much they measure four centimetres less than normal. That's a huge difference. If he can peel a suit off, he'll give it to a charity to auction as memorabilia. But if they get the measurements just right, he has to cut himself out of the garment – so it's completely useless. How could anyone test such a thing? The suits are now so tight he couldn't possibly get one on wet, and even though he's an expert, they *still* take 15 minutes to climb into – whereas these days he could get into one of the early models in five. The outfits are made by a woman in a small town outside Milan, the only place in the world where the stitching can be done. The material for each suit is worth about $300, but since Ian is one of a minuscule bunch of athletes wearing them, the actual cost per suit all up is closer to $40 000. Is this specialised equipment, or what?

The AOC had been rubber-stamping Thorpe's applications to wear the adidas suit ever since the drawn-out drama prior to Sydney 2000. Now Speedo had its new-generation gear up and running, the company wanted to go down that road again, insisting that the protocols provided for comparative testing. John Coates at the AOC wasn't having any of it. There would be no testing, he ruled, since it would be too disruptive to the swimmers. Speedo, sponsor of the Australian Olympic team since the 1956 Games, announced (once again) it would be reviewing the whole deal.

Given the state of play, the category of swimwear sponsorship needs a rethink. It puts a sponsor in an invidious position when high-profile athletes get an exemption because they think, rightly or wrongly, they can do better elsewhere. The more publicity these disputes get, the worse it is for the sponsor. (Ian reckons most people thought adidas sponsored the Olympic team in 2000, since they were the only company with an advertising campaign. If that was the case, it was a highly successful ambush. No wonder Speedo wasn't happy.)

Things were piling up. Through no fault of his own, this latest threat from Speedo could not have endeared Ian to officialdom, who were already annoyed with him for expressing views everybody held about FINA's marketing nous. As well, Ian was always ready to pipe up when he felt the swimmers were getting a raw deal. On top of that, the wound that had opened over the Indianapolis withdrawal was still tender. After the Dorothy Dixer was popped at that Speedo launch, Dave Flaskas was moved to write to Australian Swimming, complaining that even though he fulfilled all his obligations professionally, it seemed his major client was being increasingly isolated from the rest of the team.

All this was capable of being sorted out with some constructive talk. There was plenty of goodwill on both sides. But still, it was not a good time for Ian to fall face-first into the Homebush Olympic pool.

30

TOO PAINFUL FOR WORDS

AT 11.02 ON SATURDAY MORNING, 27 March 2004, on the opening day of the Olympic Trials, Ian lined up on the blocks in the familiar lane four for his heat of the 400 metres. He stood in the feet-together position, as he'd been doing for more than a year, rather than the more stable track stance, where the centre of gravity is shifted further back. He thought he heard a noise. He responded as he was trained to do, then a microsecond later realised it was the wrong noise. As he was falling, he reached back and grabbed the bars on the sides of the block in an attempt to halt his ignominious trajectory. But he couldn't. The video footage would be almost comical if it weren't tragic.

Thorpe tried to rewind the tape. He swam to the side of the pool, walked back to his lane and climbed up on the block again. The crowd sighed audibly. Everyone knew the rules, but no-one wanted to believe what was happening. Referee John Kepple walked over and said: 'Sorry, mate. Can you step down?'

'But I heard a sound in the crowd.'

'I'm sorry, mate. That's the way it is.'

Ian's shoulders slumped. Head bowed, he walked away from the starting area. There were no histrionics – no flinging of poolside chairs or howls of protest to the sporting gods. Somehow, he held it together in that time of grievous injury. His brain's reaction reminded him of the moments that followed his first Olympic victory: while he was animated, everyone else in the picture appeared to be frozen.

The rule that mandated instant disqualification for a false start had been brought in by FINA six years previously. Before that, swimmers naturally tried to manipulate the start, so race and TV schedules were always blowing out. Even the youngest kids now swam under the iron discipline of the one-start rule. Combined with Australian Swimming's strict qualification regime, it meant Ian Thorpe was out of the Olympics in his signature event.

Tracey Menzies went straight into action, determining how she could put in a protest. The first one, directed at the referee, was convened immediately in an anteroom, and just as swiftly dismissed. Then she lodged an appeal to Australian Swimming, arguing that the field was held up longer than usual, and Ian had heard a noise. It was another 45 minutes before three FINA-accredited officials were rounded up to hear the arguments. In the meantime, Margaret called Michelle Flaskas, who was having a late breakfast with Dave and others near his office in Manly. The Flaskases raced across town and arrived to find Tracey, disgruntled at being refused entry to the hearing, and Margaret waiting in the adjoining NSWIS room as Ian went back inside to learn the results of the officials' deliberations. He'd already given his evidence, and there were precedents on his side: both Petria Thomas and Phil Rogers had been granted reprieves over false start rulings.

But Ian's case was stymied by the fact that it was only a heat. Instead of the usual 16 cameras and microphones around the pool, Channel Nine had only two. The adjudicators replayed the video and strained to pick up the sound Thorpe had heard, but they could not. Both Denis Cotterell and photographer Craig Golding were saying they'd heard a sound, but their evidence was inadmissible: it had to be on the official video. Ian came out of the meeting and signalled to Dave that it was no good.

A press conference was quickly convened involving Australian Swimming president John Devitt, CEO Glenn Tasker and Dave Flaskas. The first question, directed at Devitt, asked how he proposed to explain to the public that Australia would be sending its best team to Athens without Ian Thorpe swimming in the 400 freestyle. He replied: 'I don't know how you can convince everyone if they wish to have another opinion, but we'll have the best swim team to go to Athens.' A month-long debate thus began with a totally imponderable statement. Had Devitt become a student of Zen Buddhism, or what?

The tension in that room was phenomenal. There was the sense of a monumental sporting tragedy unfolding, with everyone powerless to halt the direction of the narrative. With the pall of depression hanging heavily in the air, a final question was directed at Flaskas: 'Dave, where do you go from here?'

Dave, of course, was paddling. He had no idea if any avenues would open up. 'The main thing now,' he managed to say, 'is that Ian gets on the team. His and Tracey's meet starts tomorrow.' There was nothing to add. At that moment, John Devitt's phone range so loudly, people almost jumped out of their seats. While Devitt frantically tried to silence the thing, Flaskas quipped: 'And unless that's Perry Mason on the line, I don't know where we go from here.' Everyone in the press conference just cracked up. The same thing happened in the Channel Nine newsroom, where a perspective injection was welcome in the midst of a day of tragic events in Iraq.

Ian and Tracey were, naturally, distressed when Don Talbot approached them at poolside straight after the decision. Tracey wanted to know if there was any way around it. Could they post a time? No. Talbot told Ian he'd made a mistake and he'd have to live with it. He talked of how Kieren Perkins had overcome the disappointment of missing a swim in the 400 at the Atlanta Olympics and produced his famous win in the 1500. This was Ian's time to show the public he could handle such a setback: it was part of what it meant to be a great athlete. At least, that's what Talbot told the press he said. Privately, he also said to the swimmer and his coach: 'Things happen within a team. Don't think this is over yet. Keep your composure, and leave other things for other people to deal with.' Tracey immediately impressed on Ian that he must not live in hope.

Very quickly, Thorpe got himself together. He and Tracey went back into the NSWIS room, where Margaret and Michelle Flaskas were sitting in silence. Ian said simply: 'The decision has been made. We've got to move on. I've still got to get on the team.' His mother asked what was expected of Team Thorpe. 'I want everyone to be here in the stands to watch the final,' he told her.

Then he went back to his room at the Novotel Hotel, alone. Michelle turned up 15 minutes later with some presents she'd bought and hadn't been able to wrap on that hectic morning. 'It's the Greek's wife bearing gifts,' she announced cheerily. There was also a card, she said, but she thought it mightn't be appropriate under the circumstances. Ian insisted on seeing it. Michelle relented and handed it over. 'ENJOY THE MOMENT' it proclaimed. Ian managed a laugh, but of course he was hurting like hell.

An hour later, having got through the press conference, Dave Flaskas bowled in with another rib-tickler: 'I know you wanted the Bulldogs off the front page, but this is ridicuous.' The three of them tried as best they could to lighten things up. It was very hard work. In reality, the only thing that could mollify Ian's pain was his innate sense of destiny. He'd long been a believer in the idea that we each have a predetermined fate, that sensible reasons exist for the things that happen, and our decisions are really made for us by a higher power. In the hours he spent alone in his hotel room, that idea lifted him from the morass of melancholia. It helped him separate himself from his emotions, which he had to do in order to swim well in the 100 and 200. Perhaps the reason for this apparent disaster was that he should now be concentrating on the shorter distances, ushering in a new chapter in his career.

Ian turned up in the evening to cheer on his Sutherland teammates. He watched his mate Grant Hackett win the 400 final, and another good friend, Craig Stevens, swim into second place, also under the qualifying time. Stevens had made it to his first Olympics after failing to get a spot on the Sydney 2000 team. Ian applauded them on the dais, and managed a smile. A photographer captured the moment.

In the meantime, the great debate was up and running. Naturally, officials of all ranks backed the rules. Swimmers and other athletes generally reckoned the rules were too tough and Ian's chances should somehow be resurrected. Shane Gould offered to lead a protest against the disqualification. John Konrads would be right behind her, as would Jane Flemming and Raelene Boyle. Federal Sports Minister Rod Kemp said he wouldn't intervene, but described the situation as 'a tragedy' and hoped Australian Swimming could find a way to resolve it.

Coaches tended to cleave the other way. The new head coach, Leigh Nugent, said the system was fair and there was no recourse. Laurie Lawrence agreed. Don Talbot's unequivocal quote: 'I would violently oppose anyone who would compromise Craig Stevens' place on the team. That would not be justice.' However, the venerable Forbes Carlile was the first to express the notion that it was 'inevitable' Ian would swim the 400 in Athens. He reckoned it was unlikely Stevens would make the Olympic final in that event, and thus if he qualified for an individual swim in his pet event, the 1500, he should consider standing down from the 400 to make way for Ian Thorpe. 'I feel that Stevens would cover himself with glory should he do this,' said Carlile, 'but it is huge pressure to put on him.' Well, yes. It was.

Kieren Perkins weighed in early with the view that the Stevens qualification must stand, and absolutely hammered it at every opportunity over the following weeks. On the other side of the planet, Pieter van den Hoogenband was chased up for his take on things, which was: 'I find that so childish . . . It is laughable that he can't defend his title for something like that.'

It was pretty much a clean fracture down the centre of the sporting universe. At its heart, a system of selection that mimicked the USA's policy for swimming and track and field, both sports where the Americans had incredible depth. The system presumed a great deal more depth in Australia's swimming ranks than actually existed. By contrast,

Aussie track and field athletes were free to wander the planet until the moment arrived when the wind was in the right quarter and all other portents combined to produce a qualifying time, height, distance or whatever.

Did Australian Swimming's rules exist for the benefit of the swimmers or the swimming officials? For those who wanted an exemption for Ian Thorpe, that was the crux of it – because a catastrophe such as this was inevitable. There should have been a limited pre-selection system in place that guaranteed positions for the absolute elite, but still gave every second-tier performer the best possible chance. There'd be the odd dispute, but that's what officials were for. There'd be the odd court case, but that's what courts were for.

The alternative argument also carried weight. In order to shave a few hundredths of a second from his times, Thorpe had adopted a start that was inherently more risky than the track start. Wasn't that what sport was about – the incontrovertible fact that risk may lead to failure? And that rules had to be accepted by all competitors, no matter how misguided they might seem?

The sporting world waited for Ian's thoughts. He'd not been publicly quoted from the moment he walked away from the blocks. The press conference was set down for the evening of day two. Ian had qualified easily for the final of the 200 free, but was not yet in the Olympic team, when he sat down with the nation's media. He was completely in control of his feelings by now.

Was there a chance, he was asked, that he'd still swim the 400 in Athens? 'I've accepted that I'm not swimming it, and that's the way I've got to look at it. I don't see an alternative for how I could swim it.'

What if Craig Stevens were to step aside? 'That's putting a lot of question marks out there on other people, a lot of what ifs. I'm not going to ask Craig to stand down . . . I am not swimming it, and for me . . . continuing to think of all the reasons, all the possibilities – what everyone else is throwing up as an alternative – it's distracting me from what else I have to do here.'

Did his absence mean the best team wouldn't be going to Athens? 'I am the fastest 400 freestyler in the world . . . but now the best in the world is still going to be Australian, going to the Olympics, and that's Grant Hackett.'

Was the disqualification unfair? 'I can understand why people feel that way. But it's pretty clear, and although it doesn't seem fair, in a lot of cases life isn't fair and you just have to deal with it.'

Would he swim the 400 if offered a place? 'I'd have to consider it. It depends under what circumstances . . . It's probably not going to happen . . . It's not the right thing for me to think about it. I dealt with it when it was happening. I've accepted that, and now everyone else has to as well.'

Tracey Menzies later weighed in with this: 'The decision's been made now, so the two contenders for the 400 will be Grant Hackett and Craig Stevens. That's final.' Tracey made her statement, she now says, because 'when you live in hope, your guard is dropped'. She wanted to be sure Ian had his head completely around the situation, so he could concentrate on making the team.

Thorpe was never tacitly assured that Craig Stevens would be making way for him. He remained in the dark for another month, just like everyone else. In his own mind, he *had* accepted that the 400 was gone. He had no choice. People wrote letters to the press extolling his maturity and grace in adversity; the *Telegraph* ran an editorial along the same lines. A few columnists proclaimed him a future political leader.

Ian had no control over the fact that the pressure exerted on Craig Stevens from that press conference onwards was *intense.* It began with the front-page headline in the *Australian* the following day: 'ONLY ONE MAN CAN COME TO THE RESCUE'. After devoting a whole story to how Stevens could step aside if he made the grade in the 1500 – *especially* if he also qualified in the top six in the 200, which would give him a great chance of an Olympic gold as a heat swimmer in the 4 × 200 relay – the piece concluded: 'Cheer for him in Athens even if he does decide to contest the 400.' *Even if?* On the same day, the *Telegraph* ran the front-page headline 'LAST CHANCE' and reported: 'Some of Australia's leading swimming and sporting officials are working behind the scenes to find a compromise that will be acceptable to the man who has qualified to swim, but still allow

Thorpe to compete in the 400m. A spokesman for the AOC said there was a chance "it might play out that way. But it would be totally his [Stevens'] decision. We would not put him under any pressure".'

How does a debate conducted on the front pages of every paper in the land not constitute pressure? Stevens developed a massive headache on day one of the drama, and it didn't go away. He couldn't get to sleep at all that night, and needed sleeping pills for the rest of the week leading up to his 1500 swim. His own Olympic aspirations were in serious jeopardy. Dave Flaskas felt for him, and cringed to think of Craig's extremely shy parents being staked out by the media. So did Tracey. He'd trained with her for years, and been a guest at her 30th birthday party. It was all too damned painful for words.

Stevens and Thorpe fronted up for the final of the 200 on day three. Both accomplished their objectives. Ian won it in 1:45.07 – just a second outside his record and, under the circumstances, a fantastic swim. He was terribly nervous, his start was ridiculously conservative, and he went out much faster than he normally would – just to make sure of it. He'd done everything wrong to post a quick time, yet he was just about on the pace. Was he *happy* with the swim? Well, yes – but he 'expected to swim faster than that'. There was just no let-up with Ian Thorpe. Craig Stevens scraped in sixth.

Immediately afterwards, Ian made a quite unequivocal statement: 'The debate – I had hoped it would be over by now. A lot of people have put a lot of pressure on Craig, and it's undue and undeserved. All of us should support Craig in swimming the 400 freestyle at the Olympics.' He said it because he wanted to relieve himself of the burden of thinking about it any longer; he had to draw a line underneath the whole affair. Ironically, on the very same day as Ian's statement appeared in the *Australian*, a commentary was run on the page opposite – the first of several along these lines – accusing the Thorpe camp of using subtle psychology to pressure Stevens into handing over his spot. According to this line of thinking, when Ian said: 'I'm not going to ask Craig to stand down', what he was really doing was putting the whole idea on the agenda.

Anyway, considering the strength of Ian's latest words, you'd have thought that might be the end of it – especially since Stevens' personal coach, Glenn Beringen, had optimistically stated he was quite capable of shaving three seconds off his best 400 time and getting on the podium in Athens. On top of that, his head coach at the AIS, Pierre La Fontaine, had likewise said everyone should start getting used to the idea that Craig was Australia's second swimmer in the 400.

So now Ian had to get himself up for the 100 metres. He admitted it was not going to be easy, and in the back 50 of the final it looked like Ashley Callus had really stolen the race this time when he led by half a body-length with 25 metres to go. But yet again, the big black shark hauled him in. Along with Klim and Hackett, Callus was well established as the third member of the Aussie triumvirate of perpetual Thorpedo victims. Ian's 48.83 was very close to his PB and, again, under the circumstances, it was a superb effort.

Thorpe would only concede that it was always good to go under 49, but he reckoned he wasn't that tired at the end, which meant he wasn't swimming the race very well, and he was still failing to get through that first 50 fast enough. Twenty-four seconds flat still needed to come down to 23-low, and time was running out. Unfortunately, the idea that dropping the 400 might be a blessing in disguise for Ian, giving him the chance to hone his speed in training for the sprint events, was little more than wishful thinking. Sure there'd be changes to his program, Tracey Menzies said, but with only 14 weeks till the Olympics, it wasn't going to make a substantial difference.

If Craig Stevens was doing it tough, so too was Ian, regardless of his philosophical outlook. As soon as his program was completed, he succumbed to a crippling migraine and its attendant nausea. He'd always steered clear of the conclusion that his migraines were stress-related, but the evidence to the contrary was getting pretty solid. He couldn't make it to the pool on the next-to-last evening.

Then, on the final night of the meet, Craig Stevens lined up to try and fill second place behind Hackett in the 1500, thus picking up another individual swim at the Olympics in his pet event. There was nothing to suggest this would be a shoo-in, particularly with Stevens qualifying fifth-fastest after a week of nerve-racking introspection and nightly sedation. But an extraordinarily courageous effort in the final got him to the wall two seconds faster than his PB, and that was good enough. He was in. And so the door for Ian Thorpe was suddenly, but only slightly, ajar, because the 1500-metre man immediately announced he hadn't decided what he was going to do with his unexpected windfall in the 400. But he did say: 'It would be good to have that event to start off with.'

Stevens headed down the coast to do some fishing and sort out his head. 'I guess I can't delay [the decision] too much,' he said. 'I'll just decide what I'm going to do and I'll come out with it.' Dave Flaskas said he wouldn't rule out the possibility of Ian accepting the swim if it was offered. Stevens' minders – coach Beringen, AIS head coach La Fontaine and AIS consultant psychologist Clark Perry – had tried to wrap him in a media-proof cocoon, but he was still aware that practically every paper in the land was polling readers on the issue, and the general drift was that about 70 percent wanted Ian Thorpe swimming in the Olympic 400 metres, one way or another.

Until this point, give or take the odd inconsequential hiccup, Ian had enjoyed the absolute support of his countrymen, and the swimming world at large. More than that – he'd been lionised, idolised, virtually *canonised* for his personal qualities. He knew that if Stevens were to offer him the swim, and he were to accept it, a sizeable minority of people would strongly disapprove. But still, he didn't really see himself as standing at a personal crossroads, because he was not a politician. His approval rating was not central to his existence, and never had been. Ian was capable of being wounded by public censure, as in the Nicki Voss debacle, but even if he hadn't been vindicated in that case, it would have amounted to a glancing blow. Only the opinions of friends and family really concerned him.

So he didn't spend a lot of time during the week of Trials conferring with others or speculating about how things might pan out. With Dave Flaskas he talked only of his preparations for the 100 and 200. Tracey offered him an ear if he wanted to discuss the issue; Ian was adamant he would handle it himself. As usual, he steered clear of any influence from the media. He'd always been guided by his own moral compass, and so far it had served him well. At one stage during Trials he had the TV in his hotel room on with the sound down, and John Howard's face appeared. He turned up the volume, only to find the Prime Minister was putting in his two bob's worth about the tragedy of Ian Thorpe . . .

Tracey let him take ownership of the conundrum, but she did tell him this: 'You're going to identify things in yourself that you maybe don't want to identify. You're going to find strength you didn't think you possessed. It's going to be a big character-building time for you.' According to Menzies, it boiled down to the simple question: how badly did Ian want to swim in that race? The answer was just as simple: he wanted it *very* badly. He had a powerful emotional attachment, he now realised, to the race that had been his entrée into the Australian team and his signature event ever since.

Thorpe appeared on the Seven network's *Today Tonight* program and reiterated that Stevens had earned the swim and if he decided he wanted it, everyone should get behind him. However, he added: 'If he really doesn't want to swim the event, I will consider it. I don't know if that's even possible, but if he's pressured into it or he's forced not to swim it, I won't be swimming that event.' While Stevens was down the coast cogitating, psychologist Clark Perry decided he needed more clarity. He drove up to Sydney and put the position directly to Ian. 'I don't want Craig to go through all this if you're going to end up not accepting. So I want to hear it from your lips – if you're offered the swim, will it be yes or no?' He got the answer he expected.

The undeniable reality, though, was that the interests of Stevens the swimmer could not be entirely divorced from the interests of Stevens the human being. And Stevens the human being *had* been subjected to massive pressure by the media and the public. Through no fault of his own, he was left to ask himself whether he wanted to be responsible, in the eyes of millions, for denying Ian Thorpe the chance to defend his Olympic title. And for disappointing all those who wanted to see Thorpe do it.

There was only one way Ian could have forever deified himself in the pantheon of Australian sportsmen, and that was to have declared in the very first press conference, before the dust had even settled, that under *no* circumstances would he be swimming the 400 – and if *anyone* suggested Stevens should give up what was rightfully his, he would personally invite them behind the dressing sheds and sort them out. But would it have been even vaguely realistic to expect such a statement? Or to expect Ian to now march over to the slightly ajar door and slam it shut? Having decided that he would swim the race if offered, what more could he possibly have done than state in all sincerity, publicly and privately, that he'd support Craig in whatever decision he came to? 'Thorpe is no sinner in this drama,' concluded the *Australian*'s columnist Patrick Smith after ranging over all the arguments. 'But he is no saint either.' Nor did he claim to be.

Ian went down the coast for a brief surfing holiday, and the two swimmers met for a calamari lunch on Good Friday, at Thorpe's suggestion, at the pub in the town of Huskisson. There was no in-depth discussion of the issue. Ian simply told Stevens that his support was 100 percent genuine: he really wanted Craig to make the decision that suited him best. They shook hands, having reaffirmed their friendship, and moved on.

Meanwhile the heat just kept on coming, with Grant Hackett now declaring he was desperate to swim against Ian Thorpe in the 400 at the Olympics – although he wanted to make it clear that he was not trying to put any pressure on Craig. Since when did one and one not equal two? It was all getting too much for Kieren Perkins, who reckoned he could not understand why one man's Olympic dream should be sacrificed for another's. Perkins permanently crossed himself off Ian's Christmas card list by urging Team Thorpe to 'stop crying' about his misfortune and get on with his preparation. Who was crying?

Anyway, Craig Stevens returned to the AIS after six days in the wilderness to discuss the position with Perry, Beringen and La Fontaine. Just before that crucial meeting, the latter three got together to sort out their own views. The bullishness of the two AIS coaches had faded by now; they'd made some emotional statements early on, but they realised they were kidding themselves if they thought Craig was going to somehow find another three seconds in the 400. And they now figured that under the circumstances, the emotional and physical toll taken on Craig if he swam that race couldn't possibly benefit his preparation for the 1500 – an event where they believed he could win silver and possibly even challenge Hackett for the gold medal. So they fervently hoped Stevens would be telling them he wanted to relinquish the 400 freestyle to Ian Thorpe. However, their plan was to play devil's advocate. Whatever Craig had come up with, they would retaliate with every reason why he was wrong. They knew this was a decision he was bound to reflect upon even on his deathbed – so they had to test the strength of his resolve.

Straight away Craig said: 'I don't want to swim it.' But the reason he gave was one no-one had anticipated: 'When Ian swims well he inspires me to be a better swimmer. He could go under 3:40 in the 400, and that would give me an incredible boost for the 1500. I don't want to deprive myself or the team of that inspiration.' What could the devil's advocates say to that? Still, they played out their roles as planned, and batted every objection around for almost two hours; when Craig was still unmoved, they finally admitted they didn't really believe a word they'd been saying. So the decision was set in stone.

The question of money was not once raised during these deliberations. However, things got a whole lot murkier, in the eyes of the public, when it was mooted that Stevens would be selling his (still undisclosed) decision to the highest media bidder. He'd engaged a manager, Robert Joske, to represent his interests. Since when was a simple announcement a saleable news story? Answer: since somebody was prepared to pay for it.

So it now *appeared* to be the case that there were three factors in the equation: (1) Stevens' swimming interests; (2) Stevens' psychological health; (3) Stevens' bank balance. Most people didn't begrudge an honest toiler on a $30 000-a-year AIS scholarship making a buck out of the ordeal he'd endured, but at the same time, credulity over the sanctity of this decision was being stretched to the limit, and appearances count in these matters. However, the reality was that it was *always* going to be a case of media chequebooks at 20 paces. In fact, unbeknownst to Craig himself, every TV network had been on the blower to Ian Hanson with financial inducements for a Stevens 'exclusive' from the moment he'd qualified for the 400. The weight of offer and counter-offer had gotten too much for the media director to handle at the time, so Hanson had to flick-pass the pile of requests on to a former coach and novice athlete manager, Gary Barclay, who'd offered to help out.

Just to add a little more vibrant colour to the situation, there was a tenacious rumour, flying in the face of all logic, that Ian had deliberately fallen off the blocks because he hadn't done the hard yards at training and was scared of racing Grant Hackett at Trials, or Michael Phelps in Athens, or both. But that was only one of the prevailing mythologies. Adidas had supposedly paid Thorpe to perform his famous flop in order to crank up publicity. Adidas was supposedly paying Stevens $1 million on the sly to pull the pin and hand Thorpe the swim. And so on . . .

Anyway, in defiance of a last-minute plea from both Kieren Perkins and Dawn Fraser that he reconsider, Craig was at last ready to hand the 400 freestyle baton to Ian Thorpe. Swimming's 'worst-kept secret' was finally revealed on Seven's *Today Tonight* program on 26 April, precisely one month after Ian's disqualification. The payment to Stevens was a cash component of 60 grand along with an agreement that would involve media training with the prospect of on-air work in the future, and included a 12-month 'loyalty deal'. The package was variously reckoned to be worth between $100 000 and $130 000.

To some, Stevens was a hero who gave up personal glory for the sake of a mate, or his country, or both. To others he was a victim, pressured into sacrificing a spot he'd rightfully earned. To others he was a mercenary who'd indirectly sold Ian Thorpe an Olympic gold medal. The *Sydney Morning Herald*'s headline was harshest: 'IT'S YOUR RACE, IAN, AT $325 A METRE'. The paper also ran a cartoon with Stevens weighing up a choice between a wad of cash and self-respect. That was a very tough call.

Thorpe's acceptance of the swim, however, was not a fait accompli. He'd said all along that he wanted to be sure Stevens was pulling out for his own benefit and no-one else's. When it boiled right down to it, though, what more could he ask his friend than: 'Are you *certain*?' There seemed little chance that Craig might reply: 'Well actually, no.' But Ian didn't feel it was right for him to go into chapter and verse with Craig. Like Christina's decision to retire, this was a deeply personal issue. It was just a great pity, in Ian's view, that so little of the real story behind Craig's reasoning ever got an airing in any of the media – even though *Today Tonight* had every opportunity. But then, he never really expected it to. He'd seen enough of the way things worked by now.

Would Stevens' decision have been more transparently laudable had it been announced in the absence of any payment? *Of course it would have.* Was it reasonable to suggest that a young man who flogged himself to the limits of endurance on a daily basis for a return of 30 grand a year ought to have contented himself with a slab of beer and a thank-you note from Ian? *Of course it wasn't.* Like Ian Thorpe, Craig Stevens was not a saint. Nor did he claim to be.

Those who followed the story very closely would have been amused to hear the conclusions of Don Talbot. The man who'd tacitly suggested to Ian and Tracey that they leave behind-the-scenes machinations to others, and was then boldly quoted to the effect that he'd 'violently oppose' anyone who'd compromise Craig Stevens' position, was now proclaiming that the outcome of the imbroglio was a 'win-win-win' situation. Stevens was a winner because he got to make a dollar out of it, Thorpe was a winner because he got to defend his Olympic title, and Australia was a winner 'because we cannot be cavalier about giving away gold medals. Believe me, they are going to be hard to come by in Athens.' You could rely on Talbot to see things in black and white.

Only one more act in the drama had to be played out, and that was the ritualistic media blood-letting and moralistic mop-up. The packed press conference was staged on the morning after the *Today Tonight* program out at the Homebush pool, and Ian might have opted to sidestep it in favour of a gracious thank-you note to Craig Stevens dressed up in a press release. Instead, he faced an inquisition unlike any he'd ever experienced. The questions flew thick and fast, unpunctuated by the usual respectful pauses.

It didn't help that Ian had pranged the Audi in a four-car pile-up on the way to the conference and had no opportunity to explain why he was a late arrival. Nor did it take long for things to get fairly uncomfortable. *Has Craig Stevens sold his position to you? Do you feel you've taken the position by default? What makes you confident Craig made the decision on the right basis? What about the* Herald*'s headline – 'Your race at $325 a metre' – did that hurt? Do you think Channel Seven could have handled it better? Kieren Perkins has described this whole affair as 'grubby' – what do you think?* And so on. The hypocrisy of Channel Nine's insinuations was breath-taking, given the network had been waving its own chequebook frantically since day one of the drama, and had lost a bidding war against Seven for the Stevens announcement.

After 45 minutes of thrust and parry, with the target fairly close to losing his cool a couple of times, Ray Martin made the acute observation that Ian didn't look happy. That about summed it up. Ian Hanson told Dave Flaskas he'd never seen a young athlete handle himself so well under such difficult circumstances. Hanson was obviously relieved when he got to announce the end of that conference, but the final word went to Kieren Perkins, who described the whole saga as 'a very, very sad tale for Australian sport'.

Whatever it was, it was over at last. When the Dolphins' orientation camp was convened on 2 May at the Gold Coast, head coach Leigh Nugent made a speech in which he praised both swimmers for their conduct, then declared there'd be no more mention of the subject. Reflecting on Tracey's words about character-building, Ian felt pleased with himself, and proud of the way he'd coped overall with what had been, for him, a monumental disaster. He hadn't really known, deep down, that he was capable of dealing with such a situation. Now he did know, and that could only be a good thing.

≈

On 28 May it was announced by John Mendoza, CEO of ASDA, that the World Anti-Doping Agency (WADA) and the IOC were confident that a test for the previously undetectable human growth hormone would be up and running for the Olympics. Mendoza said: 'Athletes should be aware that an hGH test could be implemented at any time – and this implementation may not be publicly announced by anti-doping authorities until it's too late for athletes illegally using growth hormone.' On top of that, at the IOC's behest samples from the Athens Games would be kept for two years after the event and be subject to any new tests developed in that period. Medals won could be retrospectively stripped following a positive test. Was it possible that at long last, the notoriously recalcitrant IOC had figured out that the world wanted clean sport, and was willing to pay the price to make it happen?

John Mendoza was known to be a straight shooter, and he believed so. There were three different teams working on hGH at the time – blood-based researchers in London and Munich, and another outfit looking at a urine test. The blood tests seemed the most promising for an Athens deadline, and they were a direct test of abuse, not just an indirect 'marker' as with the EPO blood test. The beauty of it was that no-one would know whether the tests had been approved or not before the Athens Games – and even if they weren't, what sort of athlete would want to give an incriminating blood sample and gamble against scientific peer review and legal obstacles being cleared within a couple of years? That's a lot of sleepless nights to get through when you have an ill-gotten Olympic medal under your pillow.

Mendoza was equally enthused about the likely EPO scenario. It wasn't announced exactly who was going to be tested – world record-breakers, medallists, or random athletes – but the boffins weren't going to rely solely on a urine test. They'd be testing blood for markers that would inform them which athletes to chase down until they could get a legally binding urine positive – and those athletes could then kiss their medals goodbye as well. On top of that, it was 99 percent certain that blood tests for direct detection of some of the new haemoglobin-based oxygen carriers (H-BOCs) would be in place. As far as swimming was concerned, the ongoing battle against drugs was looking really promising.

There was, of course, an obvious sense of deja vu about all this. Prior to Sydney 2000, French and Australian teams had worked frantically against the clock to get their testing regimes for EPO in order, but because of legal impediments the upshot was that there was the *appearance* of rigorous pursuit of cheats, while nobody in their right mind was ever going to get busted. Anyone who imagined this was a lot of froth about nothing would have been chastened to read in mid-July the revelation that back at the Sydney Games, seven athletes from a random sample of just 310 had tested positive to the EPO blood 'screen', which the IOC had determined was unlikely to stand up in court without a urine positive. If that sample was representative, *a few hundred* athletes got away with using EPO in the weeks leading up to those Games. As it was, the 'secret seven', whose names, genders and nationalities were protected by a coding system, would never be identified.

Ian Thorpe anticipated the same sort of thing happening at Athens. If all the things Mendoza was envisaging were actually up and running there, 'I'll be more confident than I ever have been that things are cleaning up,' said Ian. 'But I just can't see it. Something will happen before the Games that will stop them from doing it legally – so it will be put off till after the Olympics . . . and by the time we get to Beijing there'll be a new drug out there. That's what I expect – but I hope I'm wrong.'

Ian was entitled to his scepticism. He'd seen so much posturing and so much obfuscation over the years. And some things in sport are as predictable as the sunrise. On 29 July, just two weeks before Olympics lift-off, it was announced that following a breakthrough by the British researchers, a two-stage hGH test involving both blood and urine would be conducted on randomly selected athletes in each event. The first test would be carried out in Athens, with samples also sent back to London for a second test that would show up hGH pumped into an athlete's system up to 84 days before the Games. Only days later, the *Sydney Morning Herald* was quoting Rob Baxter, an expert at Sydney's Royal North Shore Hospital, who reckoned the new tests may not stand up in court: 'Athletes might be able to claim that a positive result for illegal hormone use was caused by natural circumstances such as age.' Mendoza was prepared to accept there was a slim possibility that technicalities would get in the way, but he reckoned the critical factor was the two-year holding period. The drug police mightn't have the satisfaction of throwing cheats out of the Olympic Village, but he believed they were going to nail them in the end.

≈

By the time of the initial hGH announcement in late May, Ian and Tracey were a fortnight into another stint of altitude training in Flagstaff, Arizona. This one would cover three and a half weeks in a program very different from the aerobic base they'd built back in November. There'd be more 'speed endurance' and lactate tolerance work, aimed directly at preparing for the shorter distances. The altitude regime is normally just a case of eat-train-sleep-train-eat-sleep – but this time there were brief trips to the Grand Canyon and Las Vegas, just to relieve the mind-numbing boredom. In Vegas Ian caught up with Amanda Beard, who'd been invited along with a few other American swimmers. After cleaning up on the tables they partied till late, then announced the following day that they'd been married at one of the desert town's famous quickie wedding services – and they had the video to prove it. Which they didn't. But everyone was fooled for a while.

Ian was clearly annoyed when some reporters quizzed him about his rendezvous with Amanda. They'd found out about it via conversations with swim coaches. To come halfway around the world and still not have anything like the privacy he craved was just ridiculous. He was never going to talk about girlfriends to complete strangers.

But anyway, he was loving the discipline of altitude training. In an Olympic year, boredom simply didn't matter. On the second weekend in Arizona, there was a reminder of the tenuous grip athletes hold over their destinies. Ian was doing squats while balancing on a Swiss ball – an exercise to develop core stability – when he slipped off the ball and his sweaty body eluded the grip of his instructor, so that he fell heavily onto a weight bench and came up with an enormous bump on his forearm. There was so much pain he thought it was broken, but Ian figured what he didn't know wouldn't hurt him, so he refused an X-ray and swam on regardless. He could tell he wasn't doing the injury any more damage, so he could only pray there was no break. He watched the lump slowly recede, and thanked God for that.

On 10 June, having come down from the mountain, Ian took the opportunity to tune up with a dozen other Aussies at the Janet Evans Invitational at Long Beach, not far from LA. There were 1100 athletes from 20 countries at this meet, but with everyone in heavy training it was really only about getting race practice and trying to draw some conclusions about how their Olympic preparations were going. Ian wasn't too rapt with his 100 free effort of 49.6, and his 400 victory in 3:46.60 was also solid but unspectacular. He swam inside his comfort zone in that race.

But in his last event, the 200 free, Thorpe exploded, thrashing South Africa's Ryk Neethling by four seconds in the fastest time ever recorded in America. To pull out a 1:45.63 at that stage of his preparation – only half a second slower than he'd swum at Trials – was sensational. Ian wasn't all that surprised with the numbers he'd posted, having expected to go around 1:46 – but his expectations were always way in advance of everyone else's. Tracey Menzies was thrilled. Everything was absolutely on track, and she was acutely aware that if she could get the Thorpedo to Athens in one piece, barring any further illnesses, injuries or bizarre incidents, her efforts as a coach over almost two years could at last be evaluated fairly. That hadn't yet been the case at a major meet. After all she'd been through, Tracey deserved at least that much.

A week after they returned from the US, it was announced that Ian would be rooming with Craig Stevens at the Olympic Village in Athens. People naturally drew all kinds of conclusions, based on the dramas of the previous few months, but the fact was they'd decided before Trials that they'd share a room if they both made the team. It was partly because they'd done it before some years back and got along well, and partly because Craig, at his first Olympics, might benefit from Ian's experience. But mainly, according to Ian, it was because Craig was just as much of a slob as he was. There'd be no way he'd ever want to shack up with Michael Klim again, much as he liked the man: 'The guy is such a neat freak, it's unbelievable. He's so anal

– he even packs my bags for me because he doesn't like the way I fold my pants.' Ian didn't need that kind of pressure on him at these Olympics.

≈

Back in January 2004, with Thorpe's preparation for Trials going so well, the author observed that there seemed to be nothing to stop him from performing at his peak. 'No, there's nothing,' Ian replied. 'Most athletes won't say that. Everyone wants to have an excuse, a trapdoor. I don't have any trapdoors. It's a mechanism that all of us build up. You've got to learn to break it if you ever want to be the best. As long as you fear failing, there's the possibility of failing. If you don't fear it, you can't fail.'

And then, at Trials, he *did* fail. Not by swimming badly. Not by being unable to overcome the effects of an injury or illness. He failed by virtue of being a human being, and thus being capable of making a mistake. There is no doubt that experience affected him. Otherwise he would never have told the press, after his great 200 metres swim at the Janet Evans event, that it was necessary to remind everyone he was human. 'I've had too many injuries and sicknesses [not] to know how mortal I really am,' he said.

It seemed to come out of the blue, and sounded nothing like the 100 percent bulletproof Ian Thorpe. He'd never said anything remotely like it before. And there was a sense that Tracey Menzies would have been relieved to hear it. But she didn't because she was doing a separate interview at the time, discussing the disaster at Trials, and warming to the same theme: 'It just goes to show he is human, and sometimes I think we expect a little bit more from Ian.' What Doug Frost would have made of all this is anyone's guess, but it was not Frost who'd instilled in the young Thorpe the delusion of indestructibility. That was all Ian's own work, and it went with the territory of adolescence anyway. Now that maturity was apparently beginning to encroach on his once immutable self-belief, how might it affect his performances in the water?

Kieren Perkins was one athlete who'd been somewhere near the heights Ian had scaled. From his experience the most important thing for Ian now was to embrace the fact that it was no longer all about excitement and hype and smashing world records. 'It's settling into an older age when it all starts to come down to more intelligence and grit than sheer youthful enthusiasm,' Perkins said. Ian's hormones were going to slow down a bit from around age 22, as they were designed to do. His recovery rate after extreme exertion and sleep deprivation would be slower, and he'd probably become more susceptible to illness. The reality was that he was soon going to have to decide whether to 'manage' himself as an athlete, or remain true to the rigorous ideals he'd always embraced, which would mean he must go full-bore in every important swim and retire as soon as he could no longer improve. From that perspective, if he still refused to compromise at all, Beijing in 2008 would seem a long way away.

But all this was yet to unfold. At 21 Ian Thorpe would be at the absolute peak of his powers for his second Olympics. Had he changed his mind about the treble, or did he still think the 100 metres was marginally out of reach? 'I still do,' he told the author just before leaving for the team's ten-day staging camp in Sindelfingen. 'More and more people are thinking I'm capable of winning it, but I don't see it happening.'

Would he agree that victories in the 100, 200 and 400 in Athens would amount to the greatest feat in the history of swimming? 'No . . . I guess it would be up there with the top three Olympic performances ever, but I wouldn't put it at number one.'

Of course, anyone can win relay medals if they're on the right team. On a purely individual level, would it not beat Spitz's four golds in the 100-200 free and 100-200 fly, given all the difficulties of stretching from 100 to 400 metres? 'It's arguable. I don't think so. I would actually place more importance on winning four individual events.' (That statement contradicts what Ian said way back, when he observed that Doug Frost was criticising Spitz for finding the 'easy way' to seven gold medals.)

'Is that what Ian said?' Don Talbot asked when his opinion was sought. 'He's just saying that to be modest. He needs someone else to spell it out for him, and I'm quite happy to. There's just no question about it – from what we now know about human physiology and the difficulty of training across all the energy systems, it would be *far* more difficult to win the 100-200-400 treble than to do what Spitz did in 1972.'

Talbot remembered that at the Tokyo Games in 1964 the great American Don Schollander had won the 100 and the 400 freestyle, and at the same time held the world record in the 200, although it was not an Olympic event. It might therefore be reasonable to think Schollander could have pulled off the treble. 'But you have to remember,' says Talbot, 'that as good as he was, he was swimming times 40 years ago that can be done these days by 13-year-old girls. To be able to do it at the standard swimming is at today would be a whole other level of achievement.'

But even if Ian were to achieve the fantastic feat, for the first time in Olympic and World Championship history, it would then have to be compared with the individual exploits in Athens of another man who, like Ian Thorpe, may well turn out to be the greatest swimmer of all time: Michael Phelps. With Australia's team still slightly favoured to win the 4 × 200 relay, the American would likely have to win at least *five* individual gold medals to have a chance of matching Spitz's seven and relieving Speedo of $US1 million in cash.

Was there ever a swimming meet more keenly anticipated than the Athens Olympics of 2004?

31

BLOOD IN THE WATER?

Michael Phelps revelled in the unprecedented range of possibilities thrown up by his performance at the US Trials, which ended in mid-July. Phelps qualified for the Olympics in no fewer than *six* individual events – a world record in itself. He was always going to swim the two butterfly races and the two medleys, as well as the three relays, in his attempt to bag The Seven. But nine events all-up would have been totally exhausting, while eight would obviously allow for one defeat, so he was left to make a decision between the 200 back and the 200 free. Phelps milked the suspense before finally opting for the freestyle, declaring his desire to pit himself against the best in the world. He was not scared to line up alongside the greatest 200 swimmer ever in Thorpe, Olympic champion van den Hoogenband, and former world record holder Hackett. Altogether those were the four fastest men in history over 200, and all (with the exception of Phelps himself) Olympic gold medallists. Some experts reckoned no better field had ever been assembled for a swimming race. Michael's best time of

1:45.99 ranked him slowest among that crew, well behind Thorpe's mark of 1:44.06 – but as with Ian in the 200IM the previous year, the American was a wild-card entrant. No-one could predict what he might do.

Immediately the 200 free in Athens was billed as 'the race of the century', the implication being (in some quarters) that it would determine who was the world's best swimmer. That made no more sense than the media beat-up that had surrounded the 200IM in Barcelona, but the headlines looked alluring. The fact was that both Thorpe and Phelps showed real courage by being prepared to step on to each other's turf to test their mettle. The only difference was that Michael actually thought he could win. 'Nothing is impossible and anything can happen,' he said. Maybe.

The Yanks were going to field a powerful men's team, favoured to win nine of the 13 individual events. They'd gotten cocky, too. Klete Keller, their 400 metres Sydney Olympics bronze medallist, was predicting that with the emergence of Phelps, the six-year Australian stranglehold on the 4 × 200 relay was likely to end. On paper the Aussies still looked to have some breathing space, but these American men were pumped. Not so the US women, who looked to be favourites in only two events, while the Australians had unearthed exceptional talents in Jodie Henry, Libby Lenton and Alice Mills to back up the established stars, Leisel Jones and Petria Thomas. After a dozen years of male domination, the Dolphins were heading toward a sea change.

Ian's smooth preparation was in stark contrast to the dramas preceding Sydney 2000. It was business as usual leading up to the departure for Europe. However, there was still a lot of emotion simmering below that calm exterior, both for Ian and his beleaguered coach. In an article in the *Weekend Australian Magazine*, Nicole Jeffrey lifted the veil of discretion to describe the full extent of enmity in coaching circles directed toward Tracey Menzies. 'Thorpe is a national treasure,' wrote Jeffrey, 'which makes Menzies the keeper of a country's dreams. If they don't return from Athens with a fistful of gold, people will be looking for someone to blame, and it won't be "our Thorpey". By [Don]

Talbot's reckoning, Thorpe must win both the 200 and 400 freestyle before Menzies earns even "begrudging credit".'

Jeffrey revealed that Tracey had actually been vilified after Ian's fall from the blocks at Trials: *It's your fault he's not swimming the 400 metres . . . You've cost Australia a gold medal . . . You're the worst mistake he's made . . .* 'People were starting to make personal attacks on both Ian and me,' Menzies confirms. 'Some people were pretty vicious, actually. Directly to my face.' She carried that bundle of vitriol with her to Athens, and so, by association, did Ian. Although it had been a comparatively uneventful period from Trials to Olympics, this was a tough time for Team Thorpe nonetheless. With the media repeatedly referring to Ian's failure to break world records under the new regime, and suspicions lingering after the spate of idiotic rumour-mongering at Trials, there was a palpable weirdness in the air. In the maelstrom of an Olympic Games, that emotional cauldron could easily boil over.

≈

Near the end of July, just before the Dolphins decamped for Sindelfingen, Ian had his customary stoush with FINA over drug testing. This time the trigger was an apparently innocuous comment he made on the Channel Seven news: 'For anyone to think that they're swimming at a clean Olympic Games, they'd be naïve.' The FINA backlash was quick and caustic, 'strongly condemning' Thorpe's attitude and accusing him of bringing the sport into disrepute – even though Ian acknowledged that attempts were being made to improve the situation. Flaskas said the Thorpe camp was deeply offended at FINA's response, while Grant Hackett, Don Talbot, Duncan Armstrong and even Gary Hall Jr clamoured to support the Australian swimmer, with Hall describing FINA's rebuke as 'shocking'. When Ian and Grant arrived in Germany, they were among 12 of Australia's 43-member squad required to give urine samples before they could even unpack at the hotel. The testers never seemed to miss having a shot at the Thorpedo.

And Ian never minded getting under the skin of the FINA suits – in fact, he saw it as his responsibility as a world-class senior swimmer – but he declared at the compulsory press conference at the staging camp that he wasn't going to waste his energy pre-Olympics acting as a quote-for-hire on the subject. It was time to get into total concentration on the task at hand.

Unfortunately, though, that wasn't going to be easy. The media was allowed much more access to the swimmers, both in Germany and later in Athens, than they'd had at the previous Games, where the Dolphins had been expertly sheltered. This time around Ian seemed to be constantly confronted by an aggressor with a microphone. He was hounded, even though he made it clear that he wasn't going to play the media game. He wanted to keep things as low-key as he possibly could, simply because he sensed it was the right approach for him, and that meant refusing the constant round of requests for one-on-one interviews. 'If I'm stepping on people's toes,' he said, '. . . they can live with that, because I have to race at the Olympics and I'm being selfish, because that's what I need to do at this stage.' He hadn't been aware of it at the time, but he recognised that he'd been emotionally exhausted by constant public exposure in the long build-up to the Sydney Games, and it had taken a toll on him. Now he couldn't wait for the event to get underway, so that the protocol strictures of the five-ringed circus could be imposed upon the general madness.

Ian had always been disappointed that after his group's bold debut at 'Rookie Night' back in 1997, the concept was reckoned to be a bit too rich for the officials' blood, so it had been quietly shelved. At last, in Sindelfingen, tentative steps were being taken to reintroduce the tradition (although it still wasn't called 'Rookie Night'), with the new team members being made to do a karaoke performance in Greek. It was a start, and helped ease the monotony of existence in a place where there was, by design, practically nothing to do except swim. And rest.

The Dolphins pulled into Athens on 8 August, five days prior to the Opening Ceremony, and straight away headed to the Aquatic Centre, about half an hour by bus from the Village, to stretch out in the warm-up facility and stare briefly into their pool of dreams. Ian ran into his old mate Hoogie there, and they shared an embrace and a few words of encouragement. Bizarrely, the Dutchman's coach, Jacco Verhaeren, predicted an Ian Thorpe victory in the 200 metres. If it was meant to be a ploy, it had all the subtlety of a Laurie Lawrence harangue. At least van den Hoogenband himself didn't feign total agreement.

Much had been made of the Greeks' failure to provide a roof over the place – it was one of the projects they couldn't squeeze in before the deadline – so hopes were never high. But it turned out to be an impressive swimming complex, its open-air construction providing something of the casual intimacy of a school carnival – albeit with a 10,000-seat capacity. The heat would be on for spectators in the morning, but never really oppressive, and the evenings' dramas were to be heralded by evocative sunsets. But there was always the potential for wind, and wind would naturally mean slower times. That was the one mitigating factor. It wasn't playing on Ian's mind, because he was back into full flight, confidently stating, as usual, that he believed he would swim PBs. Whatever introspection he'd recently undertaken had obviously been put aside. But Ian hadn't reckoned on just how windy it was going to get.

He trained with his team-mates at a pool much closer to the Village, only once venturing back to the competition venue for a full session just a couple of days before showtime. That night was set aside for the one compulsory press conference, deep in the bowels of the main media centre. Ian and team-mates Libby Lenton, Grant Hackett, Petria Thomas and Leisel Jones were escorted there under police protection, and in a room heaving with cameras and tape recorders they faced a fairly benign but quirky inquisition from the pack of international reporters who'd managed to squeeze in before the doors were bolted. These star Dolphins were clearly being viewed as an antipodean Dream Team. The *Sydney Morning Herald* described the encounter as 'part rock concert, part circus, part media scrum, part zoo'.

Ian was cool, parrying questions with patience and good humour. *Would he give his gold medal for the 400 to Craig Stevens?* 'I wouldn't rule it in. There is a small process – swimming the race – to go through first.' *Were the Dutch on drugs?* 'Pass.' *How was he enjoying life in the Village?* 'The Aussies have scammed a really good section. I do get hounded [by other athletes] a bit . . . but most understand there is a job at hand here.' In fact, Ian was constantly harassed in the food hall.

In the wake of the international doping scandal in track and field, which had claimed many of the biggest names in the sport as well as the two darlings of Greek athletics, Kostas Kederis and Katerina Thanou, the Thorpedo was one of a dwindling bunch of uber-athletes at these Games. At least he knew what to expect this time around.

There was a different vibe in many ways from the previous Olympics. Although the Thorpe camp may have felt under pressure, the swim team itself was much more relaxed, supportive and cohesive than in Sydney. Head coach Leigh Nugent was no less passionate about the sport than Don Talbot had been, but his personal style was nowhere near as authoritarian. Still, he expected results, proclaiming Australia's contingent the best-balanced outfit to represent the country in 30 years. The Dolphins comported themselves demurely, with no promises to kick anybody's butt and no references to any abuse of musical instruments . . . but they were obviously brimming with confidence.

And excitement, too – along with the other 439 members of the Australian team. The 2004 Olympians were delighted by the innovative 'induction ceremony' at the Village, where, section by section, they were presented with their prized blazers, sang the national anthem, took a pledge and were welcomed into the exclusive Olympic family. On the way out to the official team reception, held on the Wednesday before Friday's Opening Ceremony on a luxurious estate about 30 clicks out of the Village, Laurie Lawrence in his capacity as 'Athlete Liaison Officer' had an entire busload of athletes singing, clapping, cheering and carrying on like a kids' footy team on its first end-of-season trip. The voice of Delta Goodrem, entertainment for the evening, galvanised the optimistic mood.

The athletes' accommodation turned out to be comfortable, with room-mates Ian and Craig Stevens sharing a three-bedroom apartment with Grant Hackett, Michael Klim, Brett Hawke and Geoff Huegill. It was very congenial, and so too was the training squad Tracey Menzies had been assigned. She felt honoured that the coaches of Travis Nederpelt, Eamon Sullivan, Todd Pearson and Patrick Murphy had requested her to direct their final preparations. Enmity toward Tracey was far from universal; in fact, she would effortlessly endear herself to just about anyone who got to know her. The squad clicked on a personal level, which was a bonus for Ian and Tracey's spirits, and when the boys said they'd like to see her marching in the Opening Ceremony, she took them up on it. It made her very aware of the enormity of what was about to take place over the next eight days.

The irrepressible Lawrence had tried to replicate the Sydney experience by pilfering some turf from somewhere to cover the grassless expanse outside the Aussies' quarters and thus create a rudimentary 'village green', complete with TV screen. Ian and his swimming mates stayed up just long enough to see the much-reduced green and gold contingent wind their way around the stadium. It was already way past their bedtime.

Four years previously, at this point in proceedings, Ian had admitted to being a bit perplexed about the whole Olympic thing. 'Watching the Opening Ceremony excites more emotion when you've already competed in an Olympics,' he says. So he was more stimulated this time, but at the same time better prepared – so it was more of an 'internal' excitement than an overt emotion. 'I knew, as well, what it was going to be like in competition, and I felt that I was ready for it.'

The Thorpe support crew had of course arrived by now, and were staying in an apartment within walking distance of the pool. Margaret would be there tomorrow, and Christina and David Williams, along with Dave and Michelle Flaskas . . . and none other than Ken Thorpe, who had broken a vow – for perhaps the first time in his life – and once again set foot in an aeroplane. But it was a very wobbly foot, because Ken was pumped to the eyeballs with two types of drugs: one the doctor had prescribed to calm his nerves, and the other 'some sort of elephant tranquiliser that knocked him out completely', according to Ian. That was the only way into Athens for Ken Thorpe, and it was going to be the only way out. Ian just hoped he hadn't used up all the gear on the trip over. It would be nice to see the family, just as he had in Sydney a few days into the Olympic meet, but he had no idea how to make it happen.

As he drifted off he was thinking about that, and also about something Tracey had been stressing since long before they'd arrived in

Athens. 'Make sure,' she said, 'that you get everything you want out of these Olympics – not just in the water, but out of it as well.' Ian's thoughts ran parallel with Tracey's: he wanted to make sure that he *got it* this time. That he understood, in his heart, that this was not just about the winning of medals, nor even just about swimming very fast, but more importantly, it was about the sharing of these incomparable experiences with his friends – both his friends on the Australian team, and his friends who swam for other teams. He resolved that for himself, this was to be the essence of the Athens Olympic Games.

≈

Although the Olympic program had been slightly altered, the 400 freestyle final for men remained on the opening night's agenda. A lot of people thought Ian Thorpe was vulnerable in his premier event, and that wasn't surprising. Although he owned the eight fastest times in history, his world record stretched way back to Manchester in 2002; he hadn't even swum a serious 400 since the Barcelona Worlds – and that one was not quick by his standards. The false start fiasco had demonstrated a previously unimagined fallibility. It was noted that Hackett had given Ian a serious run for his money in the 200 at Trials, and even beaten him at a Grand Prix meet in Brisbane in July, although it counted for little because both men were in heavy training at the time. As well, it was widely known that Thorpe had been concentrating on the sprint distances in training. How much would that affect his aerobic capacity? Although Ian repeatedly stated that he'd never trained harder than he did under his new coach, people were sceptical. Some wouldn't swallow the idea that dry-land work was an adequate substitute for laps churned out in the pool, no matter how mature the athlete. They thought it was a cop-out.

'HACKETT CAN SMELL BLOOD IN THE WATER' was the *Australian*'s evocative headline for swimming writer Wayne Smith's analysis. Kieren Perkins was leading the chorus: 'By allowing Grant to see weakness, [Ian] has given him a mental edge he didn't have before.' Talbot agreed that Hackett was in with a real chance, but he had to will himself to grasp it with both hands. 'When he gets up [against

Thorpe], he never really swims his own race,' Talbot observed. 'He opens the door and lets Thorpey lead, and then tries to catch him. No-one's going to catch Ian Thorpe if you let him get away.'

The same observation had been made by any number of experts over the years, including Doug Frost, who'd always been mystified as to why Hackett didn't try burning Ian off in the early stages of a 400, just as he had in his memorable short course triumph in Hong Kong back in 1999. Grant had lost 14 times in succession to Ian over the long course 400 metres, his last victory being at the Fukuoka Pan Pacs in '97. In all that time, one factor had never been taken into account. Grant had always seen himself as a 1500 swimmer who also swam the 400 and the 200. The 400 was always held on the opening day of a major international meet, while the 1500 was always on the final day. No swimmer could possibly hold a taper at peak level over a period of a week; some would swear they could tell not only down to the day when their taper effect had peaked, but even down to the *hour*. Smith reported that in head coach Leigh Nugent's opinion, this was Grant's real problem – not some psychological quirk that prevented him from mounting a serious challenge to the Thorpe supremacy.

But what if Hackett's coach Denis Cotterell reckoned Grant was invincible in the 1500 – reasonable, since he hadn't been beaten in almost eight years – and decided to take a punt by tweaking his taper to deliver him on the blocks for the 400 ready to go at full bore against Ian Thorpe for the first time ever? Apparently Team Hackett *was* thinking along those lines; Cotterell revealed the previous week that they'd given the 400 metres greater priority than ever in their final preparation for Athens. 'If we nail it right, it will be a great race all right,' he'd warned.

Any punter back in Australia wanting to put money on Thorpe to win the 400 would struggle to get better than Sportsbook's return of $1.22 for a dollar – that is, about 5–1 on. All things considered, it looked a somewhat shaky bet – and in fact, it was much shakier than it appeared.

Although he seemed to swim quite comfortably in the morning to qualify second-fastest behind Hackett for the final, Ian knew even then that his head was in a totally different space from where it should have been . . . and that it wasn't going to be any different for the final. Far from being the calculating aquatic predator – nerveless, emotionless, his only thoughts directed toward the technicalities of the process and the execution of the plan – he'd quite suddenly become a bundle of raw emotion, and he knew that if he tried to shut it out it would end up in some sort of scrambled mess, and he couldn't swim through a scrambled mess, so he was going to have to somehow run with it. He'd have to actually swim on emotion – something he'd never even contemplated. All his plans would count for nothing. 'I knew I'd be thinking about things I'd never thought about in a race before . . . all the drama that had gone on at Trials over this event, all that people like Tracey and Craig Stevens had been through, and my family and everyone who'd supported me through these tough times . . . I'd be swimming it not for myself, but for all those people . . . and I kind of felt that was the way I *had* to swim it.'

Tracey Menzies knew the burden he was carrying as he faced up to the final, 'from the look on his face, how he held his body, how he talked to me before the race. It was a tough one.' Kieren Perkins had been the only commentator who'd really flagged this issue – the incredible pressure that would be placed on Ian to succeed, should Stevens decide to relinquish the swim. Flaskas picked it as soon as he saw Ian walk out on pool deck. The Thorpe camp braced themselves for a rough ride.

Bruce McAvaney, anchoring the coverage on Seven, threw to expert commentator Perkins, who intoned repeatedly that Hackett *had* to take it out fast, *had* to establish a lead, *had* to make Thorpey chase him . . . but again, he didn't do that. They went out slowly, with Ian in front from the start. Grant stuck with him all the way, and by the time they got through 100 they were already a second slower than record pace. At 150, the American Klete Keller, way out in lane two, had just snuck into the lead, and with his powerful finish he was a real danger. Ian sensed Keller's presence, picked up the pace, and turned first at 200, now a second and a half outside his record. As they headed into the back end, Hackett looked to be tiring. Perkins: 'I think Grant Hackett's in a bit of trouble right now. He really needs to find something.'

But even at 250, and still at 300, Thorpe's lead was only half a body-length over Hackett and Keller and Massi Rosolino, the three challengers now stalking him all in a row. McAvaney: 'This is normally where Thorpe starts the kick in . . . He starts to move away here . . .' And at that turn, he did begin to surge a little, putting up the biggest margin in the race so far, out by about a body-length as they headed toward the final turn . . . 'but Hackett looks as if he's closed a bit,' observed Bruce. He had. And Ian, his mind crowded by a thousand thoughts, his energy dissipating, the emotional turmoil draining the life from him, was just about spent. He had nothing. They turned, and Hackett came out screaming for the final lap.

McAvaney: 'Thorpe leads. Hackett's close. He's coming at him . . .'

Perkins: 'That was a fantastic turn from Grant Hackett. He's picked up the pace . . .'

McAvaney: 'Thorpe hanging on. Hackett's half a body-length away, then Keller. Thorpe just in front . . . Hackett's closing. Can Thorpe win again? Hasn't lost for six years. Hackett's *very* close . . . *really* close . . . *closing. Thorpe and Hackett – it's going to be a touch. They hit it. Thorpe's got it. What a race!*'

Ian had won by 0.26 of a second. As soon as he stood and looked at the board and comprehended his achievement, he couldn't hold it together. 'No water came out,' he would later say, but in every other respect he was crying for joy and gratitude and relief. He turned toward the wall, indulging in a private moment, and then faced his friend Grant and almost apologetically embraced him, still overcome by the moment. Perkins called it right: 'In all the years we've been watching Ian Thorpe break world records, win gold medals, I don't think we've *ever* seen that kind of emotion before.' Nor anything remotely close to it. The Zen master had shown the world another dimension to his personality, and everyone liked it.

This time there was no triumphal pool deck performance. Ian hauled himself out of the water and turned playful for a time, high-fiving the line of Australian team-mates leaning over the railing, one of whom happened to be Craig Stevens. An alert camera captured the moment. Ian continued to deny he'd actually cried – 'crocodile tears', he called them – and reckoned he'd get a laugh if he saw himself bawling on the front page of the papers. He would have seen exactly that if he'd been at home, because the Aussie media revelled in that image, so unusual and endearing was it. But what would have amused him even more was an editorial in the *Australian* that read: 'His mental game has reached a new level too. By swimming well within his limits in the 400 metres, he left more in the tank, mentally and physically, than in Sydney.' Nothing could have been further from the truth.

Thorpe's time of 3:43.10 wasn't even among his top ten performances, and it was not a windy night. He'd expected to swim that race way faster before coming into this meet, and estimated that perhaps ten percent of the explanation was his concentration in training on the shorter distances, and 90 percent the emotional baggage he'd been carrying. But with the 400 metres gold medal safely in hand, and the warmest of thanks bestowed on an elated Craig Stevens and (once again) a tearful Tracey Menzies, the burden was now lifted and the whole extraordinary episode put to rest. Normal transmission was about to be resumed. 'I think my 200 freestyle will be much better than my 400 indicated,' Ian said. 'It better be, because I'll get really mad if it's not.'

32

VINDICATION

The benefit of the adjusted Olympic program for Ian was that he didn't have to do his Superman quick-change routine on opening night, after swimming the 400 final, to get ready for the 4 × 100 freestyle relay. They'd shifted that event to day two. But this time, after all the usual post-race rigmarole, he was called upon to do a blood test. It was much more of a hassle than a urine test because it had to be done at a Polyclinic back at the Village. Ian requested it be held over for one night because he had the heats of the 200 in the morning, but the testers couldn't accommodate that. Delays of one sort or another were the only blight on the organisation of this meet, and in this case Ian didn't get to give his blood sample until 11.45 pm, and then he had to wait half an hour afterwards (standard procedure), and then it was off to the food hall for dinner, and then finally into bed at . . . *what?* After 1 am?

It didn't get any worse than that, but mostly it didn't get any better. For some reason, following the initial blood test, Ian was urine tested *every* night – he was the only member of the men's 4 × 200 relay team to get the nod – and the doping control room always seemed to be backed up with athletes waiting to be processed. There were nights when Thorpe's schedule finished at 9.30 pm and he still didn't hit the pillow until around 1 am. He was never in bed before midnight, averaging five or six hours' sleep, and he needed much more than that. As the meet wore on, he became more and more fatigued. It was just so frustrating.

Was he being victimised because of his outspoken stance on doping? 'It *felt* that way – but that doesn't mean it was the case. I'm not going to say I was victimised. Sometimes it just gets down to them picking the most recognisable name on a piece of paper.' According to Tracey, this was something that had happened at the Barcelona Worlds, and they were expecting the same deal in Athens. For a man who was taking on a six-event program in the most stressful sporting environment there is, Thorpe was remarkably sanguine about the situation. 'It never ceases to intrigue me,' was all Dave Flaskas would say about the testing routine.

On day two in the morning Ian swam in the heats of the 200 and qualified fastest for the semi-finals. He looked good, and again when he came back in the early evening and slotted in behind van den Hoogenband, just as he had back in 2000, for a final that would be held the following night. Then came the only tight turn-around for him at this meet, as the Australian 4 × 100 freestyle relay team lined up almost an hour later to defend the Olympic title they'd won so dramatically on the back of Michael Klim's world record and Ian Thorpe's extraordinary final leg in Sydney.

So much had changed since the days when the freestyle relay was a two-horse race. The Aussies had been touched out of a medal in Barcelona in 2003. The Russians, the French, the Dutch and even the Italians had lifted themselves into the mix to challenge the heavily favoured Americans, but in the heats at this meet the South African team, led by their sprint sensation Roland Schoeman, had blown everyone away. The same four swimmers were going to back up and mount an assault on Australia's world record in the final. Michael Klim had courageously battled his way back into the Dolphins' team after three years of injury-riddled despair, but although hopes were high, he was not about to set the pool alight with another world record. Ashley Callus, Australia's long-time number two 100-metre man, was completely out of form and couldn't crack it for a spot on the strength of his heat performance, leaving veteran Todd Pearson and the rookie Eamon Sullivan to swim the middle legs before Ian Thorpe anchored the team home. Realistically, the defence of that famously hard-won gold medal was a forlorn hope.

Klim put the Australians into fourth with his lead-off leg, but by the time Ian hit the water the Springboks were untouchable, sailing toward a new world record, with the Aussies just holding fifth spot. Ian's effort of 48.14 didn't make any impression on the field, and he came in sixth. The South Africans naturally went berserk over their first-ever men's swimming gold medal, with Schoeman's lead-off swim of 48.17 making him equal with America's big improver, Jason Lezak, as the second-fastest man in history behind van den Hoogenband. There was nothing for Ian to get enthused about personally, although he'd naturally given it everything he had. It just wasn't a great swim, and he believed he could do better in the 100. But there was a number on the board that spelled trouble for anyone who was swimming the shorter freestyle events in Athens. On a night of howling wind, the Hoogie Man had anchored the Dutch into a miraculous silver medal with a 46.79 split – second only to his mind-blowing 46.70 in Barcelona. He looked to be in fantastic shape.

No Aussie swimmer at this meet was going to find themselves lacking in morale. It started each afternoon in 'the dungeon', a bunker located beneath the boxing team's headquarters that Laurie Lawrence and former great Olympian Michael Wenden had cleared out and roughly carpeted to serve as the psyche-up room for the swim team. There were no tables, no chairs, nothing but a TV set playing inspirational highlight videos. Lawrence ranted his motivational spiels. Head coach Leigh Nugent dispensed sage advice. All 70 members of the team – swimmers, support staff, coaches – had to attend every psyche session, as in the days when Talbot ruled the roost. And then, at the pool, all those who weren't involved in events would stake out their corner and turn it into a riotous pocket of Australian support. The swimmers couldn't help but be affected by the sheer force of it. And nor by the surprisingly vocal encouragement they got from two unexpected parties: the Greeks and the Japanese. The Olympic hosts (most of whom probably had relatives in Melbourne) seemed particularly pleased by the praise the Australians were heaping on them, while the Japanese obviously recognised that their resurgence in the pool had a bit to do with the inspiration of one Australian man. Ian Soap, of course.

And so to the 'the race of the century' on the evening of day three. The sun had dipped behind the stands and the illustrious ones lined up in softening light behind their blocks: Hoogie looking confident in four, Thorpe serene yet steely in five, Phelps engrossed in the thump-thump-thump of his headphones in three, not even hearing his name announced, and Hackett, the ever hopeful one, in two. Having swum in the US 4 × 100 relay team that was surprisingly relegated to bronze, Phelps had to somehow pull this one off to keep The Seven alive. The breeze was not as constant as the previous night, but it was very gusty – far from ideal conditions.

It was a different Ian Thorpe from the man who'd carried such a load on his shoulders two nights previously. Tracey Menzies could see it, and so could Flaskas. 'When he walked out this time,' Tracey recalls, 'it was all business. You just knew he was going to swim well.' He wanted it so badly, and so did Tracey. It was a race that seemed to mean so much, to so many, and for so many different reasons. Regardless of whatever else happened at these Olympics, this was always going to be the defining event.

Hoogie wasn't mucking around at all. By the time he hit the 50 turn he was already 0.37 ahead of Thorpe's world record pace. At 100 metres he turned in a staggering 50.42 – more than a second inside the record. But Ian was only half a body-length behind, with Phelps another half-length back in third, and no doubt wondering what on earth had hit him. Hackett couldn't sustain that sort of pace; it looked like a balls-out 100-metre sprint, only there were two more laps to go. At 150 Thorpe had ranged up alongside van den Hoogenband, with Phelps challenging on his other shoulder. 'It's the sight we wanted to see,' Bruce McAvaney intoned.

As Hoogie turned, still 0.54 seconds in front of the record, Ian was only two-tenths behind. In Sydney the margin had been zero, but to the naked eye it was like watching an action replay. Ian's mind flashed momentarily on that same turn four years ago. He knew exactly where Pieter was. And this time, he also knew he was swimming the race *exactly* as he'd planned – precisely, mathematically, just as he'd trained himself to do – and therefore he knew he had plenty left in the tank. He watched himself sail past the Dutchman on that final lap as the multitude of Australians sitting in their lounge-rooms at 2.45 am heard Bruce McAvaney call it sweetly: 'This is the one Thorpe's been waiting four years for, and he's going to get it, and he's going to do it in magnificent fashion . . . the first Australian in 108 years to win five gold medals in any Olympic sport.'

Hoogie pulled in half a second behind, with Phelps right on his hammer, just 0.09 seconds from the silver medal, but with his dream of The Seven extinguished. It was Ian Thorpe's moment, and again the reaction was something he'd never shown before. He tore off his cap, punched the air in triumph, bellowed and whooped and roared incoherently, providing yet another front-page photo for the ages, but completely different from the previous one. Then, embracing the ever-gracious van den Hoogenband, he said: 'That's one-all. We should do it again in Beijing.'

Reflecting on his reaction now, Ian recalls: 'I'd been told so many times what I wouldn't be able to do – all the reasons Tracey was no good for me, why this whole thing wasn't going to work – and when people are told these things enough times, they start to believe them. I wasn't willing to accept that. For me to swim that race just as I wanted to . . . at that point, my Games had been successful. I'd shown why I'd made my decision, and that I *had* done the hard work, and I guess I was showing everyone how much it meant to me.'

Ian's time of 1:44.71 on that blustery night would undoubtedly have translated to somewhere around his record of 1:44.06, or better, in an indoor pool. The experts were all calling it 'the perfect race'. Although Ian didn't agree – when would he *ever* agree with that proposition? – he thought it was close enough. 'Calculating, ruthless and brilliant' was Nicole Jeffrey's assessment. 'It was marginally slower than the world record, but arguably a better performance.'

In the poolside interview, Perkins congratulated him effusively on being Australia's most prolific Olympic gold-medal winner. Ian was hardly interested, nor in the ongoing debate about who really was 'Australia's greatest-ever Olympian'. Surprisingly, though, he repeated the comment he'd made to Hoogie about doing it all again in Beijing. Perkins let it go through to the 'keeper, then posed a very pointed question: 'You've been through a lot this year. It's been tough on both you and Tracey. Two gold medals in your first two events – is it complete vindication?' Ian's body language changed just slightly and his eyes narrowed, signifying it was time for the doubters out there to listen up, and listen good: 'I think it justifies my decision, and it also means that the success I've had here is greater than I had in Sydney.'

Ian had sometimes referred to an intention to compete in Beijing, but he'd never said he *would* – so this was the closest he'd come to an actual commitment. And what was it that made him blurt out his suggestion to Hoogie? It was all about the resolution he'd made to enjoy these incomparable experiences with his friends. Grant was his friend, swimming the 400 metres. And Pieter was his friend, swimming the 200 and the 100 metres. In the moment of victory, it all crystallised in his mind: the thing that would get him through these next four years would be the opportunity to line up with his friends – not against them, but *with* them – and do it one more time in Beijing.

On the opening night of the program, after the 400, Ian had tried to meet up with his family, but there was no designated area for such a thing – just a gate that you could lean over and barely make contact with another human being. They waited there for so long while Ian was performing his usual duties that the Greek police eventually threatened them with arrest, and they had to give up. Anyway, there was a much better symmetry about it when the rendezvous was finally arranged on the third night, following the 200 metres, because on that same night four years previously Ian had to reassure his mum and dad, during their brief meeting, that he was all right after taking silver in the 200. And this time, of course, it was pure joy – even though the conditions for hugging were lousy, especially with the cops again lurking on the spectators' side and urging them to move on. Christina remembers Ian asking: 'Are you all enjoying yourselves?' They sure were. But once again – how many parallels were there with the Sydney experience? – visiting time was over after less than ten minutes. An athlete's life is so often unlike what it seems.

≈

The strangest race on the men's program in Athens turned out to be the blue riband event: the 100 metres freestyle. Ian swam an effortless 49.17 to come through with the sixth-fastest time in the morning heats. But the two American hopes, Ian Crocker and Jason Lezak, didn't even make the 16-man cut for the semis. That was unprecedented for a US Olympic team. Crocker had blitzed the world short course record only a few months back in March, but was pipped into 17th place. Lezak, who'd so often been tormented by Ian Thorpe in the anchor leg of relays, had made a quantum leap to become the fastest in the world in 2004 and second-fastest in history with his 48.17 at the US Trials – but 20 men swam quicker than he did in the heats in Athens. Both the Americans had taken it easy to conserve energy, miscalculated their pace, and blown it.

Then came the first semi-final, early in the evening on day four, and things got weirder. Ian was feeling ordinary; his increasing fatigue had become a factor. He was easily the slowest into the water, and dead last into the 50-metre turn in a sluggish 23.98. 'He's got lots to do here,' commented McAvaney. 'He's a long, long way back, and I'm not too sure . . .' In the end it was a blanket finish, Thorpe steaming home for third in 49.21, Alex Popov fourth in 49.23. Ian had to pull out all the stops to get there, yet he was marginally slower than in his leisurely heat. What gives? He had no idea: 'I swam slow and everyone else swam slow. I don't know why . . .' he told an equally perplexed Perkins in the post-race interview. He obviously wasn't aware of how tired he really was.

The fastest eight would qualify for the final, so everything naturally rested on the pace of the second semi. It was a nervous wait, but somehow, as Ian padded down to the warm-down pool, he had a powerful feeling he was going to make the cut. But he wasn't too sure about Popov. As it turned out, the premonition was spot on. With the second semi swum at scorching speed, Thorpe qualified eighth, Popov missing out in ninth spot by two-hundredths of a second. The two-time Olympic gold medallist, 'the Czar' of sprint swimming, was a goner.

Maybe, despite his fatigue, it was going to be Ian's lucky night after all. There was plenty of time to warm down and prepare for the second most anticipated event on the men's program, the 4 × 200 freestyle relay. The Americans, so confident before this meet, were just about on their knees. Could the reunited triumvirate of Thorpe, Hackett and Klim, joined by the young Nicholas Sprenger, really put the boot in by denying them the one gold medal they'd coveted longest, the one their anchorman Klete Keller had already pencilled in? The Australians were being cagey by refusing to divulge the time trial Klim had swum to force his way back – but allegedly it was fast. On the other hand, Keller had beaten Hackett for fourth place in the 200 freestyle, while Phelps had swum a big PB for the bronze. Whichever way you did the numbers now, there was simply nothing in it.

Grant Hackett, leading off for Australia against Phelps, needed to be right on his hammer. Phelps had already won the gruelling 200 fly less than an hour earlier that night and some expected him to tire, but he showed his magnificent class by pulling away in the final lap to give the Americans a one-second advantage. Michael Klim chased down his adversary, Ryan Lochte, and quickly drew level, but he'd spent too much early and again the USA surged ahead to lead by 1.11 seconds as Sprenger set out after Peter Vanderkaay. The American looked to be putting the race beyond reach, but Sprenger managed to claw back a metre or so in the last 50, and at the final changeover the margin was 1.48 seconds.

'Let's work it out,' Bruce McAvaney panted. 'In the final of the 200, Thorpe swam 1:44.71 and Keller swam 1:46.13. *This is going to be close . . .* ' No-one had time to work it out, of course, but if they had they'd have come up with a difference of 1.42 seconds – so Ian was going to have to find something, somehow. And he looked to have flown down the first lap, pulling almost level with Keller at the turn.

Surely he'd chased the American too hard, or so it seemed – but Ian was way too experienced for that, and had actually gone out a touch slower than he did in the 200, measuring his swim perfectly. Klete Keller, with his distance background, was a back-end swimmer. It might have looked all over to the lounge-room viewers at home, who'd seen the Thorpedo swim over the top of every opponent in relays, time and time again . . . but it wasn't. Keller dug in, led by 0.4 seconds at the 100, and by 0.6 at the final turn.

McAvaney: 'Keller's tough. Thorpe's one of the all-time greats, if not the greatest . . . Thorpe can't quite get him. *Now* he's coming. Keller's in front. Thorpe's closing. *Really* closing . . . the miracle man . . . draws level to him. *Keller and Thorpe. They touch. It's so close. Keller has won by the narrowest of margins – 0.13 seconds. What a race!'*

Ian Thorpe's 1:44.18 was the second-fastest 200 relay split of all time, but for once it was not enough. The Americans had gone a full three seconds faster than they'd ever done before. It was arguably the greatest 4 × 200 ever staged at an Olympics. 'We put our heart and soul into this,' said Ian in the post-race wash-up. He was absolutely exhausted, very disappointed at relinquishing the supremacy the Aussies had retained for six glorious years, and saddened that he could not deliver a gold medal for Craig Stevens, who'd swum in the morning heat. Ian was seldom more pleased to see the end of a day in his life. His only consolation, as he rode back to the Village in the bus that night, was that he could get plenty of sleep in the morning. So he *knew* he was going to swim fast in the final of the 100 metres.

Oddly enough, Dave Flaskas was thinking the same thing. Out there in lane eight, Ian was obviously going to avoid half the wash that was his great pitfall in the 100 free, because on his outside there'd be no turbulence at all. That's what Ian told himself before the race – but he knew from experience that it was a double-edged sword, because way out there in the boonies he'd feel excluded from the real action, with no-one to really push him to the absolute limit.

As the new wave of 100-metre speedsters filed out for the final, minus any American, minus Popov, and with Croatia, South Africa (twice) and Algeria represented, McAvaney pointed out that Ian

Thorpe was the first man in 100 years to reach the Olympic finals of the 100, 200 and 400 metres. (An American named Charlie Daniels had done it in 1904.) That meant an awful lot, but it would mean even more, of course, if he could grab a medal. A gold one, and hence the Holy Grail of the freestyle treble, looked out of reach – just as Ian had predicted. The evening was windy, but not too bad; maybe it was worth a handicap of three-tenths, at most, over this distance.

The South African Schoeman took off like a rocket, a mile in front of world record pace as he turned in 22.60. Ian got to the wall sixth-fastest in 23.57, which was good enough to put him in with some sort of medal chance, because this was a race stacked with 50-metre men. As Schoeman and Hoogie battled it out in the centre of pool, Thorpe came flying home in the outside lane. Van den Hoogenband got the touch in 48.17, just six-hundredths in front of the South African, and Ian Thorpe grabbed the bronze medal in a personal best time of 48.56. Allowing for the less than perfect conditions, those numbers were just about exactly what Ian had hoped he could achieve: out in 23-low, finishing in 48-low. And although he'd publicly stated that his moment of vindication had arrived after the 200 freestyle, between himself and Tracey Menzies and their small inner circle, it was *this* result that really confirmed it. He'd swum a good PB in the blue riband event, the race he really wanted to make his mark on . . . and although he hadn't pulled off the golden treble, he'd given it a decent shake. It meant that what he and Tracey had been doing in training was working, and it would keep on working, all the way to Beijing.

≈

The US swim team recovered from their early setbacks to finish, as expected, atop the Olympic medal table. What Ian Thorpe had so often done for the Aussies at major international events, Michael Phelps this time achieved for the Yanks, turning their meet around at a critical point on day four with his 200 butterfly and 4 × 200 relay golden double, and going on to win six gold medals and two bronzes. Phelps won four individual events – the medley double and the butterfly double – and took gold in the 4 × 200 and medley relays, along with bronzes in the 4 × 100 relay and the 200 freestyle. An astonishing effort.

Ian's tally of two gold, a silver and a bronze could have been bolstered by a minor medal in the medley relay, but the heat swimmers – Matt Welsh, Jim Piper, Adam Pine and Michael Klim – failed to get the team through to the final, missing out by a single place. Ian had said he'd be happy to swim in the morning, but was told they'd be safe to rest himself and butterfly man Geoff Huegill for the medal race. There were harsh words from the likes of Don Talbot, who accused the medley 'B team' of the heinous crime of selfishness – but the reality was that the Australian men generally were on the wane. Grant Hackett managed to overcome yet another illness to narrowly retain his 1500 metres title, but apart from Ian Thorpe, only Brett Hawke in the 50 free managed a PB. Thankfully for the Aussies, a new era of 'girl power' had arrived, delivering a total for Australia of seven gold and 15 medals overall – easily enough to take second spot after the Americans with their 12 golds and 28 in total, and ranking the 2004 Dolphins as the most successful Australian Olympic swimming team since Melbourne in 1956.

Tracey Menzies could no longer be viewed by anyone as some sort of impostor, although when asked whether there'd be any discernible change in the way she was treated by the coaching clique, she said: 'I don't reckon it's going to be any different.' Even though 'the race of the century' was won by Ian Thorpe, and his popularity and level of recognition in Athens were extraordinary, Michael Phelps was unquestionably the swimmer of the meet and will retain his unofficial position as the world's number one male swimmer. Ian was widely lauded as 'Australia's greatest-ever Olympian' with his record totals of five gold and nine medals overall, but he'd be the first to dismiss the entire notion. There are so many variables over the years of Olympic competition that comparisons can't stand logical scrutiny. Even comparing Phelps' effort with Spitz's is problematic. The relay medals don't count, but how do you stack up the 100-200 freestyle and 100-200 butterfly doubles against the 100-200 butterfly and 200-400 medley doubles? When all arguments are exhausted, only two incontrovertible facts remain: Michael Phelps is the most versatile swimmer of all time, and Ian Thorpe is the greatest middle distance swimmer of all time. As well, most experts are now prepared to say that Ian Thorpe, as the world record holder in the 200, 400 and 800 metres and an Olympic medallist in the 100, is the greatest male freestyler ever.

As far as the sport of swimming is concerned, the story of the 2004 Olympics may not be over yet. WADA and the IOC have confirmed that blood and urine tests for hgH were indeed done in Athens. There could be some surprises when the results of those tests are confirmed by further analysis in laboratories in London and elsewhere – a process that was to take place over the few months following the Games. Tests for haemoglobin-based oxygen carriers (H-BOCS) were also carried out, with final results due within the same time-frame. The strategy of using EPO tests involving both blood and urine was also in place, and the accuracy of the urine test had been upgraded, with the result that three athletes – not swimmers – were actually busted for EPO a few days before the Olympics began. Incredibly, one of them – an Irish distance runner named Cathal Lombard – admitted his guilt. It's hard to recall that ever happening. Maybe they should give him a medal.

Of course, FINA couldn't take any credit for these advances on the drug detection front, but at least they weren't actively burying their heads in the sand any more. The prime movers were firstly the IOC's new president Jacques Rogge, whose administration's determination to clean up sport stands in contrast to the reign of his predecessor, Juan Antonio Samaranch; and secondly the straight-talking (and aptly named) Dick Pound, chairman of WADA, who said the Athens Games were a watershed in the fight against doping. 'It's all over, folks,' Pound pronounced during one of his more manic moods, and while that might have been way over the top, there's no doubt that in terms of determination, and methodology, and willingness to disclose results, the men at the pinnacle of world sport have seriously taken up the challenge. According to ASDA's John Mendoza, 'It's only through the continued efforts of athletes like Ian Thorpe that pressure has built up to the extent that sports administrators have had to respond . . . The leadership now being demonstrated by the IOC is fantastic to see.'

Obviously when it comes to cheating, some sports – particularly track and field – have ingrained attitudes that could take years to break down. The Athens Games, massively affected by an international doping scandal in athletics before they even got underway, were to throw up so many other drug furores that the sport of swimming slipped clean under the radar, without a skerrick of controversy. Swimming doesn't seem to have the same sort of intractable cultural problems as track and field has – at least, not at the moment. Inevitably, though, with companies offering massive incentives for superhuman performances, the wheel will one day turn again.

≈

The big question now for Ian Thorpe is whether or not to continue the pursuit of the golden treble. In one sense the stakes are high, because the reality is that if he drops the 400 to concentrate on the shorter events, he will relinquish the opportunity to be viewed as the greatest swimmer ever. Even if Ian isn't at all interested in that assessment, an awful lot of other people are. When the Olympic partying was over and the welcome home parades all done, he planned to take his customary long break – probably another big trip to Europe and the States – and then begin to sort out, with Tracey, what their strategy would be over the next four years.

Ian realises he has a tremendous emotional attachment to the 400, but the 100 metres is really in his blood now. Looking at the times he posted for his events in Athens, the question obviously remains: is it possible, given the limitations of human physiology, to make incremental improvements across the spectrum from 100 to 400 metres? Can it be done? 'I have believed that up till now,' says Ian, 'and I've continued training for those events with that belief. That's what my decision's going to be based on when I get back from my break – whether or not I still firmly believe I can. At this stage, I'm not sure.' The only thing he says he's certain of is that he won't keep dabbling in the 400 if there's no intention of swimming it in four years' time in Beijing. That would be pointless.

So, Ian, you'll make your decision, and that'll be it then? 'Yeah. I will. *I think . . .*' He laughs.

In reality nothing is certain for Ian Thorpe right now, and that's the way it ought to be for a man who's just turned 22. People have been hassling him for years about what he's going to do with the rest of his life. Immediately in front of him is the opportunity to promote his equity deal with So Natural in Japan and China later in the year. Apparently the interest in the Thorpedo-branded water-based drink – 'advanced hydration ultra-low GI energy water', they're calling it – has exceeded all expectations. According to Ian's accountant, Mark Sheridan, this partnership will build 'extreme wealth', with the Thorpedo brand having long-term value and the genuine potential to outstrip even the mammoth earnings of the Great White Shark brand – presuming that Ian gets involved in the whole thing and drives the business to build his shareholding in So Natural. That sort of incentive, you'd think, would be enough to keep any young man on his toes when he's not otherwise engaged in slogging up and down a swimming pool.

But in the wider sphere, beyond his business pursuits, all sorts of possibilities have been thrown up. He wants to do some further study, but has no idea what it might be. Chances are that whatever profession you can name, Ian has at some stage expressed an interest in it. A couple of years back it was suggested that a special role might be created for him – something like United Nations Ambassador For Youth. 'It's a role I think would be wonderful,' he told *ABC Sport Monthly* at the time, 'but I don't know that it's what I want to do. People sort of work out what path they want to take by actually going out and working at different things – and I haven't been able to do that as yet.'

A valid point. The only thing that's very close to certain is that when he finally does arrive at the end of his career – and it might not even be immediately after Beijing – he will not be taking up a job as a swimming commentator. 'I just hope,' he says, 'that I can find something that will give me as much fulfillment as I've got from swimming.' When he does, you can bet it will be something very challenging, very difficult, but a lot of fun as well. And he'll be giving it everything he's got.

ACKNOWLEDGMENTS

My thanks to Ian Thorpe, foremost, for putting aside great slabs of December 2003, when the bulk of the interviews for this biography were conducted. That concentrated month was pretty taxing for an athlete who'd already been out of bed for four hours by the time I'd roll around just after 8 am for yet another marathon session. He handled it very well. The input of Ian's manager, David Flaskas, has been just as crucial. A great many of the anecdotes in the book are the result of a combination of David's prompting and Ian's subsequent recall of the details. Hence this biography would be nowhere near as colourful without David's long hours of involvement.

Equally, of course, I'm indebted to the Thorpe family: Ken, Margaret, and big sister Christina. Most people, asked to recount details of events that took place many years ago, will develop a headache in no time – but not these three. They each have incredible mental stamina and exceptional recall. I thank them very sincerely for taking me into their trust.

Three coaches each spent hours talking to me about swimming theory in general and Ian Thorpe in particular: Chris Myers, Doug Frost, and Ian's current coach, Tracey Menzies. Others who contributed were Jenni Ashpole, Brian Sutton and Don Talbot.

Four specialist swimming journalists gave up their time to personally help me: Catriona Dixon and Nicole Jeffrey of News Ltd, Michael Cowley of Fairfax, and AAP's Will Swanton. Will is the author of the only existing unauthorised book on Ian Thorpe, a mini-biography called *Early Days* (Melbourne Books). His observations on the Sydney Olympics helped to lift and colour the chapters on that momentous event. The extensive work of News Ltd's Wayne Smith should also be acknowledged here.

Don Talbot's autobiography *Talbot – Nothing but the Best* (Lothian Books) provided invaluable background on the culture of Australian swimming. American scribe P.H. Mullen's brilliant *Gold in the Water* (St Martin's Press) illuminated aspects of the sport that would otherwise have eluded me, and served as an inspirational example of the sporting writer's art. You can order a copy via the website www.goldinthewater.com.

Paul Butler, Ian's favourite primary school teacher, greeted me with a lengthy essay he'd written on his former pupil for my benefit. Ian's high school year adviser and water polo coach, Olga Sovo, was equally keen to help, as was Ryan Barclay, his best mate since he was knee-high. Swimmers who shed light on Ian's character in various ways were Kirsten Thomson, Simon Cowley, Michael Klim, Daniel Kowalski and Duncan Armstrong. Then there were those who provided information on particular aspects of Ian's life: former adidas marketing director Rob Mills; David Flaskas' wife Michelle; managing director of Armani Australia Mary Chiew; Ian's accountant and financial adviser, Mark Sheridan; John Mendoza, CEO of ASDA; journalist Jeff McMullen; and the Japan connection, Miro Mijatovic.

I'd also like to thank Ian Hanson, Dave Mason, Dale Neuberger, David Howman, Chris White, Lisa Stallard, Clark Perry, Ben Thorpe, David Clark, Dr Brian Sando, Peter Sprowles, Steve Thomas, Frank Turner, Kara Barrow, Brett Lovegrove, Helen Wood, John Priestley, Neil Sherring and the friendly folk at Grand Slam International. Staff at Sydney's *Sun-Herald* offered much appreciated research assistance.

My friends Chris and Rose Fydler, both swimming Olympians, provided me with indispensable background knowledge of the sport, and Chris also generously volunteered to read the text for technical (swimming) bloopers. I'm also greatly indebted to manuscript editor Jo Jarrah for correcting several errors before they made it into print. Her attention to detail was extraordinary.

I'm obviously privileged to have begun my time as a biographer with one of the most sought-after subjects in the land. I can only hope to have done him some sort of justice in these pages.

Greg Hunter